U.S.-China Relations, 1784–1992

Ta Jen Liu

University Press of America, Inc.
Lanham • New York • London

Copyright © 1997 by
University Press of America,® Inc.
4720 Boston Way
Lanham, Maryland 20706

3 Henrietta Street
London, WC2E 8LU England

Library of Congress Cataloging-in-Publication Data

Liu, Ta-jen.
U.S.-China relations, 1784-1992 / Ta Jen Liu.
    p.   cm.
Includes bibliographical references.
1. United States--Foreign relations--China. 2. China--Foreign
relations--United States. 3. United States--Foreign relations-
-Taiwan. 4. Taiwan--Foreign relations--United States. I. Title.

E183.C5L4975 1996   327.73051--dc20   96-46100 CIP

ISBN 0-7618-0598-2 (cloth: alk. ppr)
ISBN 0-7618-0599-0 (pbk: alk. ppr.

TABLE OF CONTENTS

PREFACE

America has always felt, among all the countries of Asia, a special kinship with China. An element of sympathetic concern, generated principally by the American missionary enterprise, began to enter into America's foreign policy toward China as early as the Open Door policy, which prevented that country's dismemberment by the Great Powers. This altruism surfaced again after the Boxer Rebellion, when the US set aside its portion of the heavy indemnity that the Manchu regime was forced to pay to the victorious Great Powers, using it to provide scholarships to Chinese students for study at American universities. Then there was the outpouring of U.S. sympathy and support for China following the Japanese invasion.

There are a number of excellent studies of these and other events in Sino-American diplomatic relations written from a Western perspective. But how does the history of these relations look from the Chinese perspective? This is one of the principal questions that Dr. Ta Jen Liu sets out to answer in *Chinese-American Relations: 1784-1992*. This admirably researched and written work begins with the maiden voyage of the *Empress of China* from New York to Canton and ends with the triangular relationship between the Republic of China, the United States, and the People's Republic of China of early 1990's. Along the way, it provides a wealth of detail, especially on the Chinese side (names of key players, internal debates on treaties, etc.), which will be extremely useful to the specialist.

The last chapters of the book cover the diplomatic relations of the Republic of China following the withdrawal of that government to Taiwan, providing a unique—and otherwise unavailable—description of ROC diplomatic initiatives over the last 45 years. To this effort Dr. Liu brings the insights he has gained from his over four decades of experience in the ROC diplomatic corps.

Although the ROC has experienced difficulties in its diplomatic relations with the U.S. over the past 16 years, Dr. Liu points out that its economic development and democratization have left it stronger than ever. It would be a mistake to write Taiwan off. Far from being the wave of the future, the Communist tsunami which swept across China nearly a half century ago has not only crested, it is receding rapidly. History, I believe, will validate Dr. Liu's closing comment: "Taiwan is China's future."

Steven W. Mosher
Director, Asian Studies
The Claremont Institute

ACKNOWLEDGMENTS

I wish to express my heartfelt appreciation to the people who have kindly assisted me in the long course of preparing this book. Prof. Pablo Tangco of the Graduate School of the University of Santo Tomas, Manila, was an inspiring advisor, whose critical review of successive drafts considerably strengthened the manuscript. Prof. Flora O. Go of De La Salle University, Manila, helped to further refine the manuscript, as did Prof. Steven W. Mosher, Director of Asian Studies at The Claremont Institute.

I am equally grateful to my friends, quite a number of whom have generously contributed their time and expertise. Mr. Yi-chun Wang and Mr. Yu-shu Li of the Institute of Modern History, Academia Sinica, Taipei, Mr. Chih-chen Wang of the Foreign Service Institute, Taipei, and Mr. Moon L. Y. Chen, Ministry of Foreign Affairs, Taipei, offered valuable advice on various aspects of the book. Mr. C. L. Pang, Dr. Shee Sung, Mr. George Ricketts, Mr. George Y. C. Ting, Mr. William K. Lee, Mr. Tsong Yao Chen, Mr. Leo Bartzis, and Dr. Anming A. Fu read through several chapters of manuscript and made useful suggestions. Miss Ludivina O. Vinluan, Miss Bilities P. Yuan, Miss Lourdes B. Orellana, and Miss Roxanne Borden offered editorial and secretarial assistance as the book progressed from first draft to final manuscript. Dr.Serafin Quiason of the National Historical Institute, Manila; Prof. Chingtung Liang and Prof. Leonard Allen of St. John's University, New York, offered wise counsel on the final draft.

I would also like to express my profound gratitude to Dr. Fredrick F. Chien for the generous support and guidance in making the publication of this book possible.

Like every author, I am indebted to the authors of the numerous books and scholarly articles I have undertaken to acknowledge in the footnotes and bibliography herein. I alone am responsible for any errors of fact or logic which remain.

I also wish to state categorically that, notwithstanding my present service with the diplomatic field of the Republic of China, the views expressed here are entirely my own. I have made every effort to be objective, bearing always in mind the distinction between the demands of my official duties and those of academic research.

My deep gratitude goes to my wife Eve Yuan-foo, without whose understanding and encouragement this book would never have been written. It is for this reason that I wholeheartedly dedicate this book to her.

Ta Jen Liu
May 4, 1995
Taipei

INTRODUCTION

I. PURPOSE OF THE STUDY

Chinese-American relations began when the United States was still a very young nation and China already a very old one. On February 22, 1784, an American clipper ship, *The Empress of China*, set sail from New York on her first voyage to China, a journey which may serve us as a metaphor for the parlous course of Sino-American relations over the last two hundred-odd years.

Reading the logbook of *The Empress of China*, we discover notations on wind direction and weather changes, the morning and evening compass readings, and estimated location, course, and speed. Sailing, in those days before the advent of navigation satellites and steam power, was an inexact science, and a successful voyage hinged on the captain's vigilant leadership. An error in course, a mechanical failure, an inattentive helmsman, unfavorable weather—any of these could set back the voyage by days or even weeks. If serious enough, they could even lead to the loss of the vessel with its crew and cargo.

The captain of *The Empress of China*, although he had his setbacks, overcame them to lower anchor in the Pearl River off Canton on August 28, six months later. So, too, the course of Sino-American relations has had its successes as well as its setbacks—some the result of natural disasters, others the consequence of human errors or negligence. Studying this two-hundred-year voyage of mutual discovery and diplomatic intercourse should help the diplomats of the future in their efforts to maintain friendly relations with our two countries. What responsible policy maker on either side of the Pacific can afford to disregard the lessons of the past?

"The storm center of the world has gradually shifted to China," observed American Secretary of State John Hay in 1899, "Whoever understands that mighty empire . . . has the key to politics of the next five hundred years." The decades since the Second World War have validated Secretary Hay's prescience, as Greater China—Taiwan, Hong Kong, and the Chinese Mainland—continues to grow in economic and strategic importance. Yet even today our understanding of the Chinese perspective is limited. "There is as yet no historical study of Sino-American relations as seen from the Chinese side," sinologist John King Fairbank once noted. "Our picture of this important subject is still largely a picture of Americans, painted by Americans, and designed for Americans."[1] This study is an effort to rectify this lacuna, adding, as it were, a Chinese background or dimension to the picture painted by others of official relations between the China and the U.S. It is also intended to remedy the inattention paid to the diplomatic relations of the Republic of China following its 1949 move to Taiwan.

II. GENERAL DIPLOMATIC SETTING

The people of China and the United States have distinctive national characteristics and historical traditions. These factors, combined with geographical dissimilarities, have caused their foreign policies toward their Pacific Rim neighbors to vary considerably in conception and implementation.

---

[1]   J. K Fairbank, *The United States and China* (Cambridge, Massachusetts: Harvard University Press, 1961) p. 338.

China

China, the oldest continuous civilization in the world, was for much of her long history content to remain within her own domain. Although capable of conquering and annexing her smaller neighbors, for the most part she chose not to do so. There was no subjugation of conquered peoples, no expropriation of their land and resources. Instead she abided by her Confucian tenets, which not only addressed matters of ethics and morality, but also provided a guide to political action and diplomatic practice. "It is the duty of more fortunate peoples," one such tenet read, "to help revive perished nations and to perpetuate the life of the disenfranchised." It was a philosophy of genuine co-existence and mutual assistance.

In ancient times, the principal thrust of China's foreign policy was to regularize relations with neighboring peoples to the north, west, and south by means of the tributary system, which symbolized the nominal suzerainty of the Emperor of China over the known world. Believing that the reigning dynasty *was* China, and that China *was* the civilized world, there was no place in the Chinese worldview for Western doctrines of state sovereignty and national equality.[2]

The Chinese empire, then under the corrupt misrule of the Manchus, was forced to reconsider its place in the world not by internal demands, but by external pressure. The war of 1839-1842 with Great Britain, commonly known as the "Opium War," resulted in a humiliating defeat. Four more wars followed, all of which likewise ended in defeat.[3] Under the unequal treaties which resulted, China was forced to give up territory, open her ports to foreign trade, and pay heavy indemnities.

Realizing the need for new ways to keep these aggressive foreigners at bay, reformers in Peking opened the Tsungli Yamen (Office for Foreign Affairs) and the Offices of Superintendents for Trade in the Northern and Southern Ports in 1861. The reformers further argued that, while China's Confucian civilization was far superior to that of the West,

---

[2] C. A. Buss, *The Far East* (New York: Macmillan 1955), p.40.

[3] They were the War of 1858-1860 with Britain and France, the War of 1884 with France, the War of 1894 with Japan, and the war following the Boxer Rebellion in 1900. In addition, the Russo-Japanese War of 1904 was fought on Chinese soil in Manchuria.

in such matters as basic science and military technology she lagged behind.[4]   Combine the two, and she would be able to resist further incursions by the European "barbarians."

The reformers' plans to build a modern military never materialized, however, while Chinese diplomacy was conducted in an improvisational, stopgap manner, with no consideration given to long-range planning. The weak Manchu court tried in vain to pursue a policy of appeasement, "playing one barbarian nation against another" in the conduct of foreign affairs.[5]   By the end of the nineteenth century, China faced a real possibility of partition.

The Chinese people revolted against the Manchus on October 10, 1911, and the Republic of China was formally established on January 1, 1912.   The young republic, the first of its kind in Asia, saw its unity threatened as rival warlords competed for power.   It was not until the National government was established, that the ROC was able to regularize the conduct of its diplomatic relations.   The guiding principles of its foreign relations may be summarized as follows:

1.   National Self-Determination and Anti-Imperialism.   The National government was determined to abolish the unequal treaties so that China could achieve complete self-determination and properly benefit from the development of its own natural resources.   While seeking national independence and equality with other nations, the new government also developed concrete policies opposed to foreign armed aggression, economic exploitation, and infiltration.

2.   Spirit of Independence.   Dr. Sun Yat-sen, the founding father of the Republic of China, had hoped to establish a republic based on the Three Principles of the People (San Min Chu I), namely, nationalism, democracy, and people's livelihood, while his ultimate objective was the attainment of China's economic independence from foreign domination and political freedom for Chinese people.   The Min-Tsu Principle, or the

---

[4]   Li Hung-chang, *Li Wen-Chung Kung ch'uan-shu tsou-kao* (Complete Works of Li Hung-chang: Memorials), (Nanking: 1905) 111, pp. 11a-13a.

[5]   To this day many regard the Manchu court's response to the Western challenge in 19th century as irrational. It offered furious resistance on irrelevant, trifling points while conceding major matters without much struggle.

Principle of Nationalism, calls for national independence, and assumes an active role in foreign relations. It does not permit China to be intimidated by aggressive force or to be tempted by undue gains.

Good diplomacy, according to the Confucian tradition, is self-beneficial without being detrimental to others. A nation cannot afford losing good neighbors simply for the sake of capricious selfish interests. International justice cannot be divorced from national interests. Both must be given equal consideration.

3. Pursuit of the Ta-Tung Goal. The idea of Ta-tung, or the Great Commonwealth, is the highest national goal originating in the ancient Book of Rites. It is the perfection of international relations.[6] Moreover, Sun Yat-sen, in his book *The International Development of China*, called for international economic and technical cooperation to eliminate the root causes of war. The ROC's foreign policy was thus to promote international cooperation and justice. Since the Second World War, the ROC has spared no effort in assisting other nations to restore or achieve independence. In recent years, she has contributed much to promote regional cooperation, mutual assistance, and collective security.

Because of these high moral principles, the national government has enjoyed very little freedom of choice or flexibility in its diplomatic maneuvering.

United States

United States' China policy, as well as its policy towards the whole of East Asia, has been a result of three fundamental views of the U.S. role in the Asian Pacific. These three views are expansion into the Pacific, isolationism, and responsibility in world leadership:

1. Expansion into the Pacific. America's goal, in this instance, was to achieve and maintain naval supremacy in the Pacific, which by

---

[6]   In China's external relations since the Han and T'ang dynasties, the just fight for "rescuing the weak and lifting up the fallen" has never ceased in Chinese history. Such diplomatic thinking has been seen in China's leniency toward defeated Japan and her assistance given for the independence of Korea, India, and other Southeast Asian countries in postwar years.

protecting sea routes would open Asia to American trade and commercial interests. This desire to command the Pacific spurred the U.S. to advocate the "Open Door" policy towards China, and to actively attempt to check Japanese expansionism in the Asian Pacific.

2. Isolationism. In its extreme form, isolationism is the view that the U.S. should neither seek influences outside the American continent, nor itself tolerate interference from sources external to that continent. Opposed to any involvement in Asian affairs, it is unwilling to assume any particular responsibilities there. Under the principle of isolationism, only a direct threat to American security or vital interests would justify any involvement in Asia.

3. Responsibility in World Leadership. Developed in the aftermath of World War II, this principle states that the U.S. should take the lead in promoting democracy around the globe, protecting the countries of the world from the perils of Communism. From the 1940s through the 1990s, American might has protected Europe and Asia from Nazi and Communist tyranny. The U.S. has made enormous sacrifices in this cause, for which she has achieved unprecedented national prestige and worldwide acclaim.

III. AN APPROACH

The internal struggles which have torn China over the past century have generated considerable interest in the West. In trying to understand these events, many scholars have turned to the political history of modern China, including her external relations with the Great Powers. Unfortunately, these relations have been inadequately recorded and poorly analyzed. This book represents an effort to clarify the principal events in China's official relations with the United States and evaluate their significance.

The future of Greater China, it is safe to say, will help determine future prospects for peace and prosperity in Asia and the world. A free and democratic China will help to reconcile East and West, in the process creating a sane and happier world order based on law and justice. As long as a major part of China is still fettered by one-party dictatorship, however, it cannot be expected to play a uniformly constructive role in world affairs. It will not be able to resist the natural impulse of tyrannies, which is to resolve their external differences by force, or by the threat of force.

We find ourselves about to set sail into the third millennium, bearing great hopes, yet facing great dangers. True statesmanship is required to navigate the treacherous waters ahead. Working together, we can arrive at the Confucian ideal of the Great Commonwealth, and we shall have made a great contribution to the future of all mankind.

1

FIRST CONTACT WITH THE WEST
1784–1910

For more than three thousand years the Chinese considered themselves the geographical and cultural center of the world. They believed their emperor to be the only legitimate political authority in the world, and viewed themselves as the highest expression of civilized mankind. They spoke of China as *T'ien Hsia*, the "Universe Under Heaven," or as *Chung Kuo*, "The Middle Kingdom." This sinocentric world view survived even foreign invasion and occupation, since the Chinese were invariably able to subdue or assimilate their conquerors within a generation or two.

Toward other states Imperial China behaved as a suzerain, exacting tribute, imposing unequal conditions on relations, and demanding fealty from their rulers. Under the early Ch'ing emperors, for instance, the Chinese empire ruled Mongolia, Tibet, Sinkiang, and Annam directly, while tribute was regularly collected from Nepal, Burma, and other neighboring states.

The first Westerners to reach China by sea were the Portuguese, who by 1557 had established a permanent settlement at Macao. The Spaniards, the Dutch, and the British followed, drawn by the prospect of trade with this huge and prosperous empire. But the Imperial Chinese government, first under the Ming dynasty (1368-1644), then later under the Ch'ing (1644-1911), permitted only limited commercial relations with these seafaring traders. Canton, the capital of Kwangtung province, was designated China's sole entrepôt for the western trade, and even there trading was limited to a clearly defined season.

These inconvenient arrangements were repeatedly protested by the western nations, which demanded free trade and diplomatic representation in Peking, but to no avail. The volume of trade with Europe and America was insignificant to the vast Chinese empire, while direct government-to-government relations were out of the question. Ch'ing emperors and their officials were affronted by the very notion that they should deal with these Western "barbarians" on a basis of equality. Instead, they gave a provincial official, the Viceroy of Kwangtung and Kwangsi, responsibility for political and commercial relations with pesky Westerners. It was an indication of their disdain.

As long as the Ch'ing empire remained strong, these matters remained. But by the end of the eighteenth century the dynasty was clearly in decline, and the over succeeding decades the government became increasingly inefficient, weak, and corrupt. The power of the Western world, on the other hand, was on the rise, fueled by industrialization and scientific advances. Against this backdrop, the Americans arrived upon the scene, drawn by its traders and missionaries into the competition for the China trade.

The Empress of China

The first American ship to visit China was the *Empress of China*, which left New York in February 1784 and returned 15 months later with a cargo of tea and porcelain. Its profit of $37,727 on a total investment of $120,000 created a "China fever" among U.S. businessmen. By 1800 dozens of American vessels were engaged in the China trade, bringing back Chinese products such as spices, silk, cotton fabric, tea, and porcelain, for which there was a good market in the U.S.

The difficulty was finding American products that would sell in a self-sufficient China. Both ginseng root and seal and otter furs brought good prices in Canton, but the income was still insufficient to cover the cost of the return cargo. The balance had to be made up in Spanish silver dollars or, later, in illegal opium.[1]

The growth of the American-Chinese trade was a product of private enterprise supported by the U.S. government, which imposed tonnage and import rates that favored American ships over foreign competitors. For example, the first tariff act of the young United States, enacted on July 4, 1789, gave substantial preferences to goods imported from China and India in American ships. By the mid-1820's, the U.S. was shipping substantial amounts of cotton cloth to China. Although imports from China would continue to exceed exports for many years to come, Americans came to look upon China as a market for manufactured goods. "After 1840," wrote Tyler Dennett, "American policy in Asia was always directed with an eye to the future—to the day when Americans would supply the seemingly limitless markets of the East."[2]

The U.S. first appointed a consul for Canton in 1786, but before the 1844 Sino-American treaty the Chinese government denied this emissary official status. Likewise, when the first American mission to East Asia, led by Edmund Roberts, arrived in Canton in November 1832, the Chinese authorities refused to receive him as a representative of his government and demanded that he leave Canton.

Lacking official status, the American consul could neither effectively protect and promote trade, nor provide protection to the few dozen Americans living within his purview. Americans who violated Chinese laws were tried—and sometimes executed—by the Chinese authorities. The British and French consuls at Canton had more authority and commanded more respect from the Chinese authorities.

The First Sino-American Treaty

Great Britain, dissatisfied with the conditions under which the Chinese permitted trade, determined to coerce the imperial court into granting better terms. A confrontation over the illegal traffic in opium

---

[1] T. Dennett, *Americans in Eastern Asia, A Critical Study of the Policy of the United States with Reference to China, Japan, and Korea in the 19th Century* (New York: Barnes & Noble, 1941), p.7.

[2] *Ibid.*, p. 74.

provided the spark. British merchants had discovered that enormous profits could be made by importing opium secretly into China from India. The opium traffic increased rapidly, growing from 4,000 chests annually in 1800 to 18,000 chests in 1840. Alarmed both at the rapid increase in the number of opium addicts, and the copious silver being drained from the country, Emperor Tao Kwang appointed an Imperial High Commissioner, Lin Tse-su, to stamp out the trade. Arriving in Canton in March 1839, Lin seized and destroyed a total of 20,291 chests of opium from British traders, causing them a loss of some ten million silver dollars, or over two million pounds sterling.

This conflict over opium, added to England's desire to expand its trade with China, flared up into the Opium War of 1840-1842. British naval forces bombarded Chinese ports at will, cut off communications between Peking and the South, and prepared for an assault on Nanking. The Ch'ing government was forced to sue for peace. On August 29, 1842, the Treaty of Nanking was signed.

Under the terms of this treaty, the Chinese agreed to (1) open five ports to the residence and trade of British subjects (Canton, Amoy, Foochow, Ningpo, and Shanghai); (2) cede Hong Kong in perpetuity to Great Britain as a naval and commercial base; (3) permit intercourse between Chinese and British officials on an equal footing; (4) establish and publish a "fair and regular" tariff on exports and imports; (5) abolish the Co-hong system; and (6) pay an indemnity of $21,000,000 (4,500,000 pounds sterling) for British war expenses, Co-hong debts owed British merchants, and the confiscated opium. A supplementary treaty followed in 1843 which fixed a tariff schedule, promised most-favored-nation status to Great Britain, and granted the beginnings of extra-territoriality to its citizens.

With the Treaty of Nanking, the wall of exclusion that imperial China had built around itself tumbled down. The French, Russians, Germans, and Americans clamored for the same special concessions and privileges in China that the British now enjoyed. A series of treaties—later called by the Chinese the "unequal treaties"—were signed, which led to a wholesale opening of China to Western diplomacy, trade, and culture.[3]   In the end the Western powers came to treat China almost as if it were a colony.

Washington moved quickly to take advantage of the new situation. In May 1843 President John Tyler appointed Caleb Cushing as Envoy Extraordinary and Minister Plenipotentiary of the United States to China. Cushing was given a letter from Tyler to Emperor Tao Kwang calling for peace and friendship between their two countries.   The private instructions that Cushing received from Secretary of State Daniel Webster, which constitute the first official statement on the U.S. policy towards China, were considerably more explicit:

> . . . The hostilities which have been carried on between [the Chinese] empire and England have resulted . . . in the opening of four important ports to English commerce. . . . [Y]ou are . . . to secure the entry of American ships and cargoes into these ports on terms as favorable as those which are enjoyed by English merchants. . . . [Y]ou are a messenger of peace, sent from the greatest Power in America to the greatest Empire in Asia, to offer respect and goodwill. . . . [Y]ou will signify . . . that the Government of the United States would find it impossible to remain on terms of friendship and regard with the Emperor, if greater privileges or commercial facilities should be allowed to the subject of any other Government than should be granted to the citizens of the United States.[4]

Cushing arrived in Macao on February 24, 1844, but was not received by Imperial Commissioner Kiying (Tsi-yeng), Viceroy of Kwangtung and Kwangsi, until May. Once under way, the negotiations went smoothly, facilitated by a January 1843 decision of the Chinese government that the treaty ports granted to Great Britain should be open as well to nationals of other powers. Cushing's chief concern—that

---

3   The immediate outcome of the Opium War was the signing by China of four treaties in the years 1842-44. The treaties of Nanking (1842) and the Bogue (1843) were with England; those of Wanghia and Whampoa (1844) were with the United States and France, respectively.

4   Senate Executive Document (457) 28th Congress, 2nd Session, No. 138, pp. 1-5; cited in R. J. Bartlett, *The Record of American Diplomacy* (New York: Alfred A. Knopf, 1948), p. 259.

Americans enjoy equal commercial opportunity with the British—had already been addressed in principle.[5]

A "Treaty of Peace, Amity, and Commerce between the United States of America and the Ta Tsing Empire" was concluded at the village of Wanghia near Macao on July 3, 1844, and ratified at Canton on December 31, 1845. The Treaty of Wanghia, as it came to be called, opened the ports of Canton, Amoy, Foochow, Ningpo and Shanghai to American ships and authorized the U.S. government to station consular officers at these ports. American citizens were permitted to reside in these ports with their families, and to acquire sites for houses, places of business, hospitals, churches, and cemeteries.[6] These Americans were also to enjoy the right of extraterritoriality, that is to say, when accused of a crime or involved in civil dispute, they had the right to be tried before an American official according to American law. The treaty fixed a low-level tariff to be paid by Americans on imports and exports, and stipulated that these rates should not be changed without American consent. Finally, it contained a most-favored-nation clause, assuring the U.S. government that any additional rights or privileges granted in the future to any other power would also be automatically extended to the U.S.

The French, following the British and the Americans, concluded the Treaty of Whampoa on October 24, 1844. Next, Belgium was granted all privileges accorded the other treaty powers by Imperial Commissioner Kiying in a letter dated July 25, 1845. Sweden and Norway were next, signing the Treaty of Canton on March 20, 1847. All of these agreements were virtually identical to Treaty of Wanghia[7] This treaty, the first between China and the United States, thus became the legal

---

5   The Treaty of Bogue (October 8, 1843) between Britain and China already contained a most-favored-nation clause whereby any favors granted by China to another nation would be automatically accorded to Britain.

6   The clauses permitting the building of churches, purchase of books, and employment of Chinese scholars were inserted at the insistence of American missionaries who served Cushing as interpreters.

7   M. C. T. Z. Tyau, *The Legal Obligations Arising Out of Relations Between China and Other States* (Shanghai, 1917, reprinted in Taipei by Cheng Wen Co., 1966), p.6.

matrix in which China's international relations were conducted until the Treaties of Tientsin were signed in 1858.

The Treaties of Tientsin

The Taiping Rebellion, led by Christian convert Hung Siu-tsuen, which broke out in northeast Kwangsi in 1848, reflected the underlying discontent of the Chinese masses with Manchu rule.[8]   The revolt foreshadowed later upsurges of nationalistic feelings directed against both the Manchu and other foreigners. Hung and his band of rebellious peasants fought their way from southern China to the Yangtze River and seized Nanking, proclaiming a new dynasty called the Taiping, or Great Peace, with Hung himself as ruler.

Within a few years the Taipings held much of southern and central China, menaced Shanghai, and attempted to capture Peking. "Any day may bring forth the fruits of successful revolution, in the utter overthrow of the existing dynasty," American Commissioner Humphrey Marshall reported to Secretary of State William L. March on April 28, 1853.[9] Disregarding the excesses of the rebellion and the tyrannical nature of Hung Siu-tsuen's government, many Westerners in China believed that the Taipings were truly Christian in belief and Western in orientation. These optimistic views, crossing the Pacific, were reflected in President Franklin Pierce's annual message to the Congress: "The condition of China at this time renders it probable that some important changes will occur in that vast empire which will lead to a more unrestricted intercourse with it."[10]

The attitude of the Manchu government toward Westerners, especially at Canton, remained arrogant and intransigent.   Neither Commissioner Marshall, nor his successor Robert M. McLane were allowed to present credentials to the High Commissioner for foreign

---

[8]   It is estimated that from the early 18th to mid-19th century China's population grew from 150 million to at least 400 million. This population growth combined with famines led to revolts.

[9]   T. Dennett, *op. cit.*, p. 212.

[10]   Cited in W. A. Williams, *The Shaping of American Diplomacy* (Chicago: Rand McNally Co., 1956), p. 227.

affairs and Viceroy of Kwangtung and Kwangsi, Yeh Ming-chin. No wonder both American diplomats and missionaries alike were sympathetic to the Taipings.

It was not until 1865, seventeen years after the outbreak of the rebellion, that the Taipings were finally defeated. In the meantime, disputes over trade and treaty provisions led England and France to resolve in 1855 to settle these questions by force. The American government spurned overtures from these two powers to join a united front against the Manchu government. It also refused to take advantage of the situation by seeking a protectorate over Taiwan, as its own representative in China, American Commissioner Peter Parker, repeatedly suggested. Secretary of State William B. Marcy directed Parker to "constantly bear in mind" that "[the United States] is not at war with the Government of China, nor does it seek to enter into that empire for any other purposes than those of lawful commerce, and for the protection of the lives and property of its citizens."[11]

In April of 1857, President James Buchanan appointed William B. Reed as Envoy-Extraordinary and Minister Plenipotentiary to China. His instructions from Secretary of State Lewis Case were to press the Chinese government to revise the Treaty of Wanghia to provide for (1) the residence of foreign envoys at Peking, audience with the emperor, and relations with a regularly appointed ministry of foreign affairs; (2) extension of commercial intercourse, with better regulation of the inland dues on foreign imports; (3) religious freedom for all foreigners; and (4) provision for extending the benefits of the proposed treaty to other powers.

While Reed was instructed to cooperate with the envoys of Britain and France, his efforts to open China to foreign trade and intercourse were to rely on moderation, discretion, and the work of time. Lest there be any doubt as to his course, he was pointedly reminded that the authority to declare war was solely vested in Congress, and it was the judgment of President Buchanan that the present relationship between America and China did not justify hostilities.[12]

---

[11] *Ibid.*, pp. 241-242.

[12] Senate Executive Document (1032) 36th Congress, 1st Session, No. 30, pp. 6-9; cited in R. J. Bartlett, ed., The Record of American Diplomacy—*Documents and*

The British occupied Canton on January 5, 1858. Still unable to secure satisfaction from Peking, the British and French plenipotentiaries sailed north. After they captured the forts of Pei Ho, near the mouth of the Pei Ho River, the Manchu government agreed to enter into negotiations. The British and French negotiators were joined by American and Russian representatives who, although remaining neutral, were nevertheless interested in obtaining treaty revisions.

This process culminated in the signing of the Treaties of Tientsin in June 1858, between China and the four powers. This should have put an end to the conflict, but hostilities broke out again a year later when British, French, and American envoys arrived at Pei Ho enroute to Peking to ratify the treaties. The Chinese, understandably reluctant to allow foreign gunboats to sail up the Pei Ho river, requested that the envoys travel overland to Peking. The British refused, and the Anglo-French naval force attempted to force their way up the Pei Ho, attacking the Taku forts that guarded the river's entrance.

The American envoy, John F. Ward, was not prepared to use force to break down this new show of Chinese resistance, and agreed to use the land route suggested. An audience with Emperor Hsien Feng, arranged for the purpose of ratifying the treaty, never took place, however. At the last minute Minister Ward had learned that it would be necessary for him to "kowtow," and had refused. Instead, by imperial decree, ratifications were exchanged between Minister Ward and the Viceroy of Chihli on August 6, 1859.

After capturing the Taku forts, Anglo-French troops marched overland to occupy Peking in October, 1860. Once in the capital, they callously looted the city and, in an act of wanton destruction, burned down the splendid Yuen-ming-yuen Palace. The Manchu authorities now surrendered, acceding to virtually all the conditions set by the victorious powers, including their demand to establish embassies in Peking and have their ambassadors received as representatives of sovereign nations equal in all respects to China.

The Treaties of Tientsin, combined with the supplementary conventions signed at Peking in the winter of 1860, greatly enhanced the

Reading in the History of American Foreign Relation (New York: Alfred A. Knopf, 1964), pp. 262-263.

status of Westerners in China and made it possible for them to penetrate to the far corners of the empire. Ten new treaty ports were designated, including three on the Yangtze River, which Western traders were to be allowed passage on unhindered. Christians, both foreign and native, were guaranteed the right to practice and proselytize their faith. Even more significant, foreigners with proper passports were permitted to travel anywhere in the interior.

Perhaps the most important change involved the strengthening of extraterritoriality, which in the treaty ports now became an absolute guarantee. Not merely the persons of foreign merchants and missionaries, but everything and everyone with whom they came into contact, from their goods and property to their Chinese employees and Christian converts, were exempt from the jurisdiction of local law and magistrates.

The unequal treaties left China wide open to the inroads of Western commerce and culture. Soon foreign concessions, ruled by Western consuls, and protected by Western gunboats, were springing up in one treaty port after another. It seemed only a matter of time until China was carved up into spheres of influence, if not outright colonies.

The Formation of the Tsungli Yamen

In 1860 the Ch'ing dynasty seemed on the verge of collapse, beset by the Taiping rebellion in the lower Yangtze region and by the Anglo-French invasion of the north. Yet, at this critical juncture, a group of principled Confucian officials, chosen by civil examination and loyal to the reigning dynasty, emerged to revitalize the regime. They suppressed the Taiping Rebellion, restored peace and order, reduced the size of the military, remitted taxes, founded schools, and reopened lands for cultivation. Although traditionalists, the leaders of this restoration were quick to adopt Western science and technology. They set up arsenals to manufacture modern weapons, built steamships to ply their waterways, and encouraged the translation of Western textbooks in international law and technology into Chinese.

Perhaps their most important innovation was the creation, under the auspices of the Grand Council, of a foreign office called the Tsungli Yamen. With a growing number of Western emissaries resident in

Peking under the terms of the Treaties of Tientsin, there was a clear necessity to regularize Sino-Western diplomatic contacts. This became the responsibility of the new foreign office, although major foreign policy decisions remained the prerogative of the Grand Council. The Tsungli Yamen was comprised of a secretariat, a records department, and five main sections, one each for the British, French, Russian, and Americans, with a final section responsible for coastal and maritime affairs.[13] An affiliated school, the T'ung Wen Kuan, which was established in 1862 to train badly needed interpreters, gradually evolved into a college for the training of foreign service officers. The Tsungli Yamen would remain the principal organization for dealing with Westerners until 1901, when a regular foreign ministry, the Wai Wu Pu, was established.

The First Chinese Official Mission to America

The first American envoy to reside permanently in Peking was Anson Burlingame, who soon became a staunch advocate of the twin policies which John Hays was later to make famous: full trading rights for the U.S. and the preservation of China's territorial integrity. His aim was to hold China to a strict compliance with all foreign treaty rights, but to follow a course which would in no way interfere in its jurisdiction over its own people or "menace the territorial integrity of the Chinese Empire." Burlingame believed that if the Western powers followed the policy of conciliation and cooperation he advocated, it would be possible to "engraft western upon eastern civilization, without a disruption of the Chinese empire."[14]

His support for the Chinese government won the confidence of the Tsungli Yamen. As he prepared to resign his post as American Minister in Peking in 1867, the Chinese authorities suggested he head a mission on their behalf to America and Europe. When Burlingame agreed, he was promptly elevated to the first civil rank and commissioned as "Our High

---

[13] T. J. Liu, *Wai-chiao-ta-tzu-tien* (*Diplomatic Dictionary*) (Taipei: Wen Hai Publishing Co., 1965), pp. 115-116.

[14] F. R. Dulles, *Prelude to World Power, American Diplomatic History, 1860-1900* (New York: MacMillan Co., 1965), pp. 77-78.

Minister Extraordinary and Plenipotentiary."[15]   The subsequent treaty
concluded between China and the U.S. was unique, in that it was
negotiated by American Secretary of State William H. Seward and the
former American Minister in Peking, now serving as a special envoy of
the Chinese Government.

The "Additional Articles to the Treaty Between the United States of
America and the Ta Tsing Empire of June 18, 1858," was agreed to and
signed on July 28, 1868. Its eight articles provided for the maintenance
of China's territorial integrity, for Chinese control of its own inland
trade, for the appointment of Chinese consuls in American ports, for
reciprocal freedom from religious persecution, for encouraging the
immigration of Chinese laborers to the United States, for reciprocal rights
of residence and travel, for reciprocal access to each nation's schools and
for freedom from foreign interference in the development of China.[16]   Of
these provisions only the last was welcome to the Chinese authorities,
who were nonetheless induced to ratify the treaty on November 23, 1869.
The Burlingame mission proceeded on to London, Paris, and other
European capitals, paving the way for Chinese legations to take up
residence in the capitals of the West in the years following.

The decades between 1860 and 1890 were not entirely without
friction between China and the West. China's ruler, the Empress
Dowager Tzu Hsi (1834-1908), was strongly anti-foreign. Her feelings
reflected the contemptuous attitude that all Manchu officialdom had for
Westerners. She had approved the Burlingame mission not to encourage
trade and friendly relations with the United States and Europe, but merely
to ward off any further Western interference in China's affairs.

Burlingame's successor as American Minister in Peking, J. Ross
Browne (1868-1869), was soon to report that the bright expectations
which the first Chinese official mission had aroused in America were

---

[15]   In the Chinese text of the preamble to the Washington Treaty of 1868, the titles of
the three are identical—"envoys for the regulation of international relations—but
to Burlingame's title is added "senior" and his name is given first place. While
engaged on this mission he received 8,000 pounds sterling a year and all expenses
paid.

[16]   M. C. T. Z. Tyau, *op. cit.*, p. 9.

wholly illusory.[17] Anti-foreign outbreaks and other disturbances, presaging the Boxer Rebellion of 1900, proved that Burlingame had painted a rather fanciful picture of China's attitude towards the West, which was in reality comprised of equal parts of apathy and distrust. While Burlingame was premature in his efforts to build a Chinese-American relationship on a peaceful and friendly foundation, he will be remembered in modern Chinese history as the first goodwill envoy to promote China's cause in America and Europe.

China was in no hurry to establish permanent legations in Western capitals. It was October 28, 1878, before the first Chinese Minister to Washington, Chen Lan-pin, presented his credentials to President Rutherford B. Hayes.[18] Nearly two more decades were to pass before the first ranking Chinese official, Li Hung-chang, commissioned by Emperor Kuang Hsu to attend the coronation of Czar Nicholas II as his Special Envoy and Ambassador Extraordinary, deigned to visit the capitals of Europe and the United States in 1896.

Immigration Issues In America

The Imperial government had never sanctioned outward migration, imposing severe penalties on would-be émigrés, but China was too vast a country for this law to be effectively carried out. By the end of the nineteenth century there were already seven million Chinese living in Southeast Asia.

The discovery of gold in California in 1849 created a heavy demand for imported labor. The first Chinese, 323 in all, disembarked in San Francisco that same year. These early arrivals sent back glowing reports of newfound wealth, and the number of Chinese immigrants skyrocketed, peaking at 18,343 in 1852. All told, 108,741 Chinese entered the United States from 1849 to 1868.[19]

---

[17] Cited in F. R. Dulles, *op. cit.*, p. 81.

[18] Ministry of Foreign Affairs, *List of Heads of Diplomatic Missions in Foreign Countries* (Taipei: Commercial Press, 1969), pp. 50-51.

[19] D. Cleveland to American Ministry in China, J. Ross Browne, San Francisco, July 27, 1968; cited in J. B. Morse, *The International Relations of the Chinese Empire, II*, p. 166.

At first these Chinese laborers received an enthusiastic welcome. They were in demand as farm workers, miners, restaurateurs, and laundrymen. Many worked on the trans-continental railroads then under construction. The Burlingame treaty of 1868, with its proviso for free immigration of Chinese into the United States, was celebrated by California businessmen.

Yet within the space of a few short years this attitude gave way to its opposite, as Chinese immigrants came to be viewed as a threat. The completion of the Central Pacific railroad in 1869 left thousands of workers out of work. The panic of 1873 ushered in a long economic depression. White workers on the Pacific coast, worried about declining wage scales and job security, focused their resentment on the Chinese. The California agitation against the Chinese reached new heights in 1877 with the formation of the Workingman's Party, led by Denis Kearny. Kearny's inflammatory harangues against the Chinese led first to mob violence against them in San Francisco and then to a demand, ultimately supported by most Californians, for a federal exclusion law.[20]

When a congressional commission upheld the popular notion that Chinese immigrants were threatening living standards and endangering public morality in the West, Congress reacted by prohibiting any ship from carrying over fifteen Chinese passengers to America. Although this legislation was vetoed by President Rutherford Hayes as a patent violation of the 1868 treaty, he realized that something had to be done to curb Chinese immigration, and dispatched James B. Angell to Peking to negotiate a new agreement.

The Chinese government, largely because of its own antipathy towards emigration, conceded that the U.S. might "regulate, limit, or suspend, but not absolutely prohibit" the further immigration of Chinese laborers, as long as the limitations imposed were "reasonable." It also insisted that the rights of Chinese already in America be safeguarded. This convention was concluded on November 17, 1880, in Peking.

In 1882 Congress passed the Chinese Restriction Act, which suspended Chinese immigration for ten years and barred Chinese from becoming U.S. citizens. Although this legislation violated the spirit, if

---

[20] M. A. Jones, *American Immigration* (Chicago: University of Chicago Press, 1860), p. 249.

not the letter, of the Angell convention, then-President Chester A. Arthur felt constrained to accept it.[21] Although this new law choked off the flow of new immigrants, it by no means assuaged the agitation against Chinese already living in the U.S. Angry mobs continued to drive Chinese out of their homes and beat them mercilessly. The violence reached a climax in September 1885 when a white mob in Rock Springs, Wyoming, burned the local Chinatown to the ground, killing 28 Chinese, and severely injuring 15 more.

The Chinese government immediately demanded redress for this new outrage. The United States offered to pay an indemnity for the losses the Chinese in America had suffered through mob action in return for China's acceptance of a twenty-year exclusion period for Chinese laborers. While Peking was considering this offer, the Congress, ignoring both the Angell convention and the diplomatic negotiations then in progress, arbitrarily adopted the proposed convention's exclusion provisions. When President Grover Cleveland signed this bill into law, the Chinese government bitterly protested this unilateral action as "a violation of every principle of justice, reason and fair-dealing between two friendly powers." The new legislation, nevertheless, remained law. Moreover, in a further violation of existing treaties, the Chinese Exclusion Act of 1882 was renewed in 1892 for another ten years. After the formal annexation of Hawaii in 1898 the Chinese Restriction Act was applied there as well.

At the urging of the American government, Peking signed a treaty in 1894 agreeing that "the coming of Chinese laborers to the United States" was to be "absolutely prohibited" for a period of ten years.[22] As the end of this term approached nationalism was on the upswing in China, and this treaty was widely denounced. To pressure the U.S. government into permitting renewed immigration, a movement arose in Shanghai in May, 1905, to boycott American goods and quickly spread to other treaty

---

[21] The Statutes at Large of the United States of America, Vol. XXII, pp. 58-61; cited in R. J. Bartlett ed., The Record of American Diplomacy-Documents and Readings in the History of American Foreign Relations (New York: Alfred A. Knopf, 1964), pp. 423-424.

[22] Speech of Senator H. C. Lodge in the U.S. Senate, 1902, cited in J. W. Foster, American Diplomacy in the Orient (New York: Houghton, Mifflin Co, 1903), p. 303.

ports. The boycott collapsed five months later, however, when Chinese traders began to agitate against it.[23]

After 1902, ignoring the objections of the Chinese government, the U.S. Congress prohibited Chinese immigration altogether. This unfortunate aspect of Chinese-American relations was not resolved until sixty years later when on December 27, 1943, the Chinese Exclusion Act was finally repealed.

Evolution of the Open Door Doctrine

The consistent goal of American Far East policy during the 19th century was the continued enjoyment of most-favored nation status with China. Although refusing to be associated with armed intervention or to demand territorial concessions, Washington insisted that Americans should enjoy the same privileges in China as the citizens of other treaty powers, including the right to reside and trade in their colonies and concessions.

As the United States became a manufacturing nation in the closing decades of the nineteenth century, and began seeking markets around the world for its products, it became increasingly concerned to maintain its free and open access to China. In this, the U.S. was following the lead of Great Britain, which for commercial and financial reasons had abandoned further territorial ambitions in the Far East and now opposed the desire of other powers to expand their "spheres of influence" in China in the direction of a formal partition. Washington agreed that dividing China would be bad for business, besides finding its colonial aspect repugnant in principle.

Although the Open Door policy is considered to have originated with U.S. Secretary of State John Hay, there is some evidence that the idea was actually conceived in England. While serving as U.S. Ambassador to the Court of St. James, Hay had been asked by the British government whether the U.S. would cooperate with Great Britain in opposing any action for foreign powers which would "restrict freedom of commerce of all nations in China either by imposing preferential conditions or by

---

23 W. W. Rockhill to State Department, July 6 - Nov. 25, 1905, Department of State, *U.S. Foreign Relations, 1905*, pp. 205-232.

obtaining actual cession of Chinese coast territory."[24]   Hay had been thoroughly in accord with the British idea for a joint declaration, but popular suspicion of "entangling alliances" stopped such a move.

The year 1898 marked the emergence of the United States as a major Pacific power.   Hawaii was annexed, while the Philippines and Guam were wrested from Spain.   Still, President William McKinley was hesitant to make a unilateral American declaration on China.   Then came the news that Russia had publicly promised to make Dalny (Talienwan) an open port.   McKinley then asked Hay, whom he had recently nominated as Secretary of State, to develop an independent American policy.

Hay's Open-Door Notes to the Six Powers

On September 6, 1899, Hay gave instructions to the U.S. Ambassadors to Great Britain, Germany, and Russia to attempt to obtain formal declarations from those governments in favor of an open door policy in the territories held by them in China.   The governments of France, Japan and Italy were to be invited to uphold the proposal only after the three most interested powers had assented to it.

The essence of the American proposal, as stated in the note from Joseph H. Choate, U.S. Ambassador in London, to Lord Salisbury, British Prime Minister and Foreign Secretary was the following:

> . . . [T]he present is a very favorable moment for informing Her Majesty's Government of the desire of the United States to have it make on its own part and to lend its powerful support in the effort to obtain from each of the various Powers claiming 'sphere of interest' in China a declaration to the following effect:
>
> 1.   That it will in nowise interfere with any treaty part or any vested interest within any so-called 'sphere of interest' or leased territory it may have in China.
> 2.   That the Chinese treaty tariff of the time being shall apply to all merchandise landed or shipped to all such ports as are within such 'sphere of interest' (unless they be free ports), no

---

24   John King Fairbank, *The United States and China* (Cambridge: Harvard University Press, 1983 (4th Ed.), p. 251.

matter to what nationality it may belong, and that duties so leviable shall be collected by the Chinese government.

3. That it will levy no higher harbor dues on vessels of another nationality frequenting any port in such 'sphere' than shall be levied on vessels of its own nationality, and no higher railroad charges over lines built, controlled or operated within 'sphere' on merchandise belonging to citizens or subjects of other nationality transported through such 'sphere' than shall be levied on similar merchandise belonging to its own nationals transported over equal distances.

On November 30, 1899, Lord Salisbury replied that ". . . Her Majesty's Government will be prepared to make a declaration in the sense desired by Your Government . . . provided that a similar declaration is made by the other Powers concerned."[25] On December 4, 1899, Count Bernhard von Bullow of Germany advised the American Ambassador in Berlin that "Germany is willing to have the Government of the United States inform these other Cabinets that no difficulty will come from her if the other Cabinets agree."[26] The replies of France, Japan, and Italy were equally unequivocal, accepting the American proposal subject only to its acceptance by the other Powers.

The Russian reply of December 30, 1899, was incomplete and ambiguous, in that it made reference only to the territory which she held by lease and addressed only the question of customs duties. It neither acknowledged a Russian "sphere of interest," nor gave any assurances with regard to navigation dues or preferential railway rates.

The U.S. government nevertheless chose to treat the Russian reply as an acceptance, and informed each of the six powers that all had given their final and definitive assent to the Open Door policy. Copies of each of the acceptances were then circulated to each government.[27] In truth, Russia's vague and incomplete response had automatically released the other powers from their commitments, for each had accepted America's

---

[25] Cited in Philip Joseph, *Foreign Diplomacy in China, 1894-1900* (London: George Allen and Urwin Ltd., 1928), pp. 400-402.

[26] *Ibid.*, pp. 402-403.

[27] *Ibid.*, p. 406.

initial proposal with the proviso that all of the other powers do likewise. Like the United States, however, they all decided to treat the Russian reply as an acceptance, and henceforth held St. Petersburg responsible for the observance of the new policy.

The Open Door policy initiated by the United States and Great Britain did not guarantee full equality of opportunity in China, for it admitted the existence of spheres of influence. It is quite likely, however, that it prevented that country's partition by the continental powers of Europe into colonies.

The Boxer Uprising and the Fall of the Manchu Dynasty

Almost immediately after the diplomatic maneuvering over the Open Door ended, a secret Chinese society known as the Boxers started an uprising against foreigners in North China. This conflagration reached its climax in June 1900, when the Boxers besieged the entire foreign diplomatic corps in Peking's Legation Quarters. An international expeditionary force was assembled, comprised of troops from the United States and seven other nations, and in August fought its way into Peking to break the siege. For the first time the U.S. had participated in a military action in China, a step taken by President William McKinley in order to secure a voice in the settlement talks and prevent the partition of China.

Although the uprising offered a perfect excuse for China's dismemberment, Russia, Great Britain, Germany, France, and Japan could not agree on how to divide the spoils. It was at this juncture that Hay issued a second Circular Note to the eleven powers with interests in China, asking that they support the Open Door not only within their own spheres of influence, but in all parts of the Chinese empire. The note declared that it was the policy of the United States "to seek a solution which may bring about permanent safety and peace to China, preserve Chinese territorial and administrative entity, protect all rights guaranteed to friendly powers by treaty and international law, and safeguard for the world the principle of equal and impartial trade with all parts of the Chinese Empire."[28] This expanded definition of the Open Door meant

---

[28] Mo Shen, *Japan in Manchuria* (Manila: Grace Co., 1961), pp. 26-27.

that every nation would have equal rights to trade with China. By this means, the United States hoped to guarantee the territorial integrity of China.

Hay won over Great Britain and Germany to his views, and then with their support went on to convince the other eight powers to accept a monetary settlement as satisfaction for their losses during the Boxer Uprising. China was required to pay a total indemnity of 40,000,000 taels ($300,000,000) to the powers. The portion allotted to the United States exceeded actual damages and Washington later reduced this obligation, even remitting an unpaid balance. China, in turn, used part of this remission to educate Chinese students in America and to finance higher education in China.

After the Boxer Uprising, Russia took effective control of Manchuria. The first formal protest of this violation of the Open Door policy was made by the U.S. government on February 1, 1902. Hay, in a note to the eleven powers, pointed out that the special privileges obtained by Russia in Manchuria constituted a monopoly in violation of the Open Door. Russia nonetheless pursued its designs, which eventually brought it into open conflict with Japan, another nation with territorial ambitions in the region. The Russo-Japanese War of 1904-05 followed.

President Theodore Roosevelt was sympathetic toward Japanese efforts to check Russian expansionism in Manchuria, warning the French and the Germans against aiding Russia. Neither did he want a clear-cut victory for Japan, fearing that this might lead ultimately to a confrontation between Japan and the United States.

War was declared on February 10, 1904, following a surprise attack by the Japanese upon the Russian fleet at Port Arthur. The U.S. called upon Russia and Japan to respect the neutrality of China and its government during their hostilities, but to little avail. The Russians were soundly defeated, and during the peace negotiation were forced to concede many of their privileges in Manchuria to the Japanese, including the key naval base at Port Arthur and some of the railroads.

President William Howard Taft, who succeeded Theodore Roosevelt, concentrated on promoting American banking and business interests overseas. In Far Eastern relations, William Straight, former Consul General at Mukden and spokesman for American banking interests, argued that dollar diplomacy was the financial expression of the Open

Door policy and would provide "a guaranty for the preservation, rather than the destruction of China's integrity."

In November 1908, Japan and the United States negotiated the comprehensive Root-Takahira Agreement. Both countries publicly agreed to support the Open Door policy in China. The United States tacitly gave Japan a free hand in Manchuria in return for an explicit guarantee of the status quo in the rest of China and the Pacific.

Taft seemed prepared to ignore his predecessor's tacit acceptance of Japan's paramount role in Manchuria. He inclined towards a broad and vigorous interpretation of the Open Door, and supported the right of Americans to invest in Manchuria as well as in other parts of China. The U.S. government even went so far as to propose the commercial neutralization of Manchuria, through the mechanism of an international loan to China, which would be used to repurchase the Russian and Japanese railroads in Manchuria and bring them under international supervision. This proposal was rejected by both Japan and Russia.

Amidst the ongoing diplomatic struggle, China's Empress Dowager, Tzu Hsi, died in 1908, and a mere boy, Pu Yi, was elevated to the imperial throne. On October 10, 1911, the long-smoldering discontent with Manchu rule flared into open rebellion. The boy emperor was forced to abdicate. After 268 years, the Ch'ing dynasty had come to an end.

2

THE ESTABLISHMENT OF THE REPUBLIC OF CHINA 1911–1913

Sun Yat-sen and the October 10, 1911, Revolution

The overthrow of the Manchu dynasty and the founding of the Chinese Republic are inseparably linked with the name of Dr. Sun Yat-sen, the Father of the Republic. Born in 1866 in Hsiangshan (Chungshan), Kwangtung, just north of the Portuguese colony of Maçao, Sun received both a Western and Chinese education. He practiced medicine for a brief period of time, but was convinced by China's disastrous defeat in the Sino-French War of 1884-1885 that the Manchu dynasty must be overthrown. By the early 1890s, he was actively engaged in the anti-Manchu movement. With the Sino-Japanese War of 1894-1895 came another epiphany: It was not enough to found a new and racially pure dynasty, he now realized. China required nothing less than a thoroughgoing political revolution.

Sun was both a man of intellect and a man of action, a rare combination of qualities that made him the most admired leader of the Chinese revolutionary movement. He single-handedly formulated a new political philosophy called San Min Chu I (The Three Principles of the People—nationalism, democracy, and the people's livelihood), which became the movement's guiding ideology. At the same time, he ceaselessly recruited new followers and led uprisings against the failing Manchu regime.

Finding it necessary to flee the country, Sun spent many years abroad raising funds and organizing revolutionary organizations. In 1895, in Honolulu, Hawaii, he founded the Hsing Chung Hui, a patriotic organization whose members were sworn to "revive China and maintain the national unity." By the time he founded the Tung Meng Hui a decade later in Tokyo, Sun's philosophy of the Three Principles of the People San Min Chu I (The Three Principles of the People) had matured. Followers of the Tung Meng Hui swore to "expel the Tartars, revive China, establish a republic and equalize the land."[1] This oath marked the first expression of the idea of a Chinese republic.

A man of iron determination who never gave up hope, Sun instigated no fewer than ten uprisings in various parts of China between the years of 1895 and 1911. The last of these was the famous Canton uprising of March 29, 1911, known in Chinese as the Huang Hua Kang. Although costing the lives of 72 of Sun's followers, it shook the foundations of Manchu rule. Six months later the dynasty fell.

The proximate cause was widespread unrest in the Yangtze Valley over a plan to nationalize the provincial railways, handing over their administration to a central government agency in Peking. On October 10, 1911, three thousand troops in Wuchang rose in revolt, led by their commander, Li Yuan-hung. Over the next month and a half, the revolution spread to fourteen other provinces. A national assembly representing the revolutionaries was hastily convened in Nanking to discuss the formation of a Chinese republic. On December 29, 1911, delegates from seventeen provinces elected Dr. Sun Yat-sen the President of the Provisional Government of the Republic of China. He was sworn into office three days later. He quickly set about reorganizing his revolutionary organization, the Tung Meng Hui, into a political party, the Kuomintang (KMT). Sun, who hoped to establish a parliamentary system of government, was confident that the Kuomintang would emerge as the majority party.

Sun Yat-sen saw his great goal partly realized. The last Manchu Emperor, Hsuan Tung, abdicated on February 12, 1912, ending 268 years of Manchu rule. But Yuan Shih-k'ai, Hsuan Tung's prime minister

---

[1] Central Committee of Kuomintang, *Kuomintang, A Brief Record of Achievements* (Taipei: Chinese Cultural Service, 1969).

and commander-in-chief, proved to have ambitions of his own. And Yuan's power base, the ultra-conservative Pei Yang Army and the loyalty of provincial warlords, was far greater than Sun's own revolutionary forces. To save the country from further strife, Sun resigned as president.

Upon Sun's advice the National Assembly in Nanking elected Yuan Shih-k'ai as president. Li Yuan-hung, the hero of the Wuchang Uprising, was elected vice president. Yuan moved the central government back to Peking, and then set about strangling the infant republic in its cradle. In 1914 he introduced a new constitution giving enlarged powers to the president, that is, to himself. At about the same time, a number of warlords began demanding the restoration of imperial rule and calling for Yuan's installation as emperor. Yuan, who seems to have orchestrated the whole thing, was only too happy to comply.

Yuan Shih-k'ai, however, had made many enemies. Protests poured into the capital. In the provinces, one general after another announced that he would not support the Peking government. Yuan was forced to yield, canceling the edict by which he had elevated himself to the throne. By the time Yuan died in June 1916, China was badly divided. Provincial military governors had become the dominant force and would remain so for the next ten years.

Diplomacy and Recognition of the Republic

Although the Wuchang uprising took place suddenly, the revolutionaries maintained a high degree of military discipline and conducted their diplomacy well. The British Minster, Sir John Jordan, initially instructed his consuls to have no dealings with the revolutionaries to avoid misunderstandings with the Manchu government. However, the revolutionary government quickly assured the consular corps in Hankow that it would respect foreign treaty rights, leading the consuls in turn to publicly adopt a position of neutrality. Their joint declaration of October 14, 1911, gave the revolutionary army international status, and encouraged other provinces to break away from

Peking.[2]   While there was fighting in Nanking, Sian, Foochow, and Kunming, all the other provinces declared their independence peacefully between late October and early November, 1911.

The Manchu government, confused and disorganized, found itself confronted with a nationwide revolution. While it tried unsuccessfully to mend the situation, the revolutionaries, confident of ultimate victory, began an appeal for international recognition. On November 15, 1911, the revolutionaries announced that the Republic of China was already a fact and should be recognized as such. They pointed to the fact that fourteen of China's eighteen provinces had declared independence from Manchu rule and pledged allegiance to the new government. On November 18 Thomas Cheng-t'ing Wang, then vice president of the revolutionary Board of Foreign Affairs in Wuchang, called upon the American Consul General in Hankow, Roger S. Greene, to discuss prospects for recognition. Wang hoped that the U.S. would be the first power to grant recognition to the republican organization of the revolutionaries as the government of China. Greene responded that his government could only recognize facts. Until the leaders of the revolutionary movement formed a responsible and authoritative control organization, there could be no basis for the consideration of Wang's request.[3]

After a provisional government was established in Nanking in January 1912, the newly appointed foreign minister, Wang Chung-hui, sent an identical note to Washington, Tokyo, London, Paris, Berlin and St. Petersburg, requesting recognition. The powers, who were awaiting the outcome of the revolution, took no immediate action in response.

President William H. Taft's administration did not show any special favor to the revolutionary party, maintaining an attitude of strict neutrality in the negotiations between the Manchu government and the revolutionaries. Instead, Washington was intent upon bringing the armed conflict to a speedy end, so that Russia, Japan, and Britain would not be

---

[2]   C. T. Liang, *The Chinese Revolution of 1911* (New York: St. John's University Press, 1962), pp. 19-20.

[3]   Roger S. Greene to American Minister in Peking, W. J. Calhoun, November 22, 1911, Department of State Archives in the National Archives, file 893.00/894; cited in T.Y. Li, *Woodrow Wilson's China Policy* (New York: University of Kansas City Press, 1952), p. 58.

tempted to intervene. The United States strongly advised the other powers that, unless their interests in China were seriously threatened, they should follow a policy of neutrality rather than intervention.[4]

Taft's International Concert Policy

As the revolutionaries gathered wider support from the Chinese people, American public opinion gradually shifted in favor of the republican government. William Sulzer, a congressman from New York, introduced a resolution in January 1912, expressing sympathy with the efforts of the Chinese people towards republicanism and favoring recognition of the new government at the earliest possible date. Sulzer's resolution easily passed the House of Representatives, as did a joint resolution the following month, which congratulated China upon establishing a sister republic.[5]

Following the abdication of the Manchu emperor on February 12, the Taft administration was ready to establish closer ties with the republican government. The opportunity came when it was officially announced that the Chinese Minister in Washington, Chang Ying-tang, would continue to discharge his functions under the designation of "Provisional Diplomatic Agent."[6] This was agreeable to Washington, according to acting Secretary of State Huntington Wilson, for it was the policy of the United States to enter into only informal relations with a new government which had yet to win the consent of the governed and discharge its international obligations. President Taft, therefore, granted the Chinese request and ordered W. J. Calhoun to continue as representative in Peking. The U.S., therefore, had de facto relations with the ROC throughout its formative period.

---

4 On December 19, 1911, the Japanese Chargé d'affaires in Washington, D.C. proposed in a note to the State Department the establishment of a nominal Manchu regime under the joint guarantee of the powers. The United States and Germany turned down the proposal. Britain was also opposed to the idea. C. T. Liang, *op. cit.*, p. 54.

5 W. H. Ma, *American Policy Toward China, as Revealed in the Debates of Congress* (Shanghai: Kelly and Walsh, 1934), p. 239.

6 The Chinese Minister to the Secretary of State, February 14, 1912, Department of State, *U.S. Foreign Relations, 1912*, p. 66.

Although the Taft administration preferred as a matter of principle to act in concert with other powers on the issue of formal diplomatic recognition, it did not wish to become too deeply involved in international complications in China. When Japan and Great Britain inquired about the U.S. attitude toward the principle of concert and the guarantees to be secured from China at the time of formal recognition, Washington agreed to cooperate only insofar as this would entail no undue delay.[7]

Despite the American warning, the other powers refused to extend recognition to China's new government without specific conditions which went beyond those covered in previous treaties and conventions. The Taft administration resisted these new conditions, and bargaining among the powers went on for months with no agreement in sight.

At this juncture the newly appointed President of the Council of Ministers of the ROC, Lu Cheng-hsiang, on July 7, 1912, appealed again to the United States for recognition. Secretary of State Philander C. Knox reacted by circularizing the governments of France, Germany, Great Britain, Italy, Japan, Russia, and Austria on July 20:

> The powers are in full accord . . . that a stable central government is the first desideratum in China and that formal recognition by the powers, when granted, would go far to confirm the stability of the established government.
>
> The Provisional Government appears now to be generally in possession of the administrative machinery, to be maintaining order and to be exercising its functions with the acquiescence of the people. The situation accordingly seems to resolve itself to the question whether there are any substantial reasons why recognition should any longer be withheld.
>
> Would the Government of [name of country] now be disposed to consider whether the present Chinese Government may not be regarded as so far substantially conforming to the accepted standards of international law as to merit formal recognition. . .[8]

---

[7] Department of State, *U.S. Foreign Relations, 1912*, p. 69-70.

[8] *Ibid.*, p. 81

Knox went on to intimate that, in response to public opinion in the United States, Congress would probably make a strong demand for early recognition if the executive branch did not take action before long. The powers unanimously rejected the American proposal. They held that, until such time as a permanent constitution was adopted by a national assembly and the provisional government was succeeded by a permanent one expressive of the popular will, conditions in China did not warrant formal recognition.

The powers' refusal placed the American government in an awkward position. If the U.S. took unilateral action and recognized the Chinese republic, it would mean the end of the principle of concert, the cornerstone of Taft's China policy. It would also mean the collapse of an international consortium of bankers in which Taft had strongly advised American bankers to participate. At the same time, the public abandonment of the idea of unilateral recognition would alienate the Chinese people and would anger the American public. The safe course was to cling to the principle of concert, accept the new formula for recognition offered by the other powers, yet hold open the possibility of independent recognition if concerted action proved unattainable.

Over the last half of 1912 the political situation in China gradually improved. Civil war was avoided, despite the increasing power of Yuan Shih-k'ai, dispelling doubts as to the ability of the Chinese to establish a stable government. Elections were held for the representatives to a new National Assembly scheduled to convene the following January.

Given these auspicious signs, the movement for the immediate recognition of the Chinese Republic steadily gained support in America. Yet President Taft continued to delay and equivocate, a posture which aroused much dissatisfaction on both sides of the Pacific.[9] Taft attempted to defuse criticism by focusing on the de facto relations already in existence. In his annual State of the Union address to Congress of 1912, for instance, he stated that "During the formative constitutional stage and pending definitive action by the assembly, as expressive of the popular will, and the hoped-for establishment of a stable republican form of government, capable of fulfilling its international obligations, the

---

[9]   T. Y. Li, *op. cit.*, pp. 66-67.

United States is, according to precedent, maintaining full and friendly de facto relations with the provisional Government."[10]

The newly elected National Assembly of China did not, in any event, meet on schedule, and the Taft administration came to its constitutionally mandated end. The problem of recognition was left to Woodrow Wilson, who was inaugurated in January, 1913.

Wilson's Independent Action

The recognition movement continued to gain strength, with the U.S. Chamber of Commerce, American missionaries, newspapers, and various clubs and societies urging the new administration to take speedy action. In answering these petitions the Wilson administration did not mention the principle of concerted action, but simply replied that it was giving the question full and careful consideration and would dispose of it soon.

The American legation in Peking now strongly favored immediate recognition. Chargé d'affaires E. T. Williams reported that conditions in China were improving, with localism and provincialism giving way to the new central government under the leadership of Yuan Shih-k'ai. He felt prompt recognition would keep China from returning to monarchism, deepen China's friendly feelings toward the United States and, above all, check aggressive actions by other powers.[11]

The Chinese provisional government sensed the changing attitude of the new American administration. Minister of Foreign Affairs Lu Cheng-hsiang requested that Williams communicate to William J. Bryan, the new Secretary of State, Yuan Shih-k'ai's desire for immediate diplomatic recognition. Bryan responded that the issue was receiving careful and sympathetic attention in Washington.

At a cabinet meeting on April 1, 1913, it was noted that the Chinese National Assembly was slated to convene in a week's time, and that this would afford an appropriate occasion for recognition. Wilson decided to move ahead, afraid that certain powers were trying to prevent China from

---

[10] Department of State, *U.S. Foreign Relations, 1912*, the annual message of the President, XXI-XXII.

[11] E. T. Williams to Secretary of State, William J. Bryan, March 18, 1913, *U.S. Foreign Relations, 1913*, pp. 96-98.

establishing a stable government. In weighing the Chinese situation he placed internal stability and freedom from foreign aggression above a republican form of government.[12] The following day Secretary of State Bryan sent the following note to the eighteen Washington-based ambassadors of countries having relations with China:

> The President wishes me to announce to you . . .that it is his proposal to recognize the Government of China on the 8th of April upon the meeting of its Constituent Assembly. He wishes me to say that he very earnestly desires and invites the cooperation of your Government and its action to the same effect at the same time.[13]

On April 3, Williams again urged prompt recognition. The assassination of Kuomintang leader Sung Chiao-jen had aggravated partisan sentiments in China, and threatened to delay the opening session of the National Assembly. Even if the session were delayed, Williams argued, U.S. recognition on April 8 would serve to check separatist tendencies and quiet civil unrest. Williams was in effect siding with Yuan Shih-k'ai against Sun Yat-sen's nationalists.

Rejecting Williams's advice, Wilson reversed course and decided at an April 4 cabinet meeting to await further developments in China before extending recognition. The threat of the collapse of the National Assembly and renewed civil war was too high. On the chance that the session might open on schedule, however, it was decided that the U.S. must be fully prepared to act.

The other powers had been taken aback by Wilson's note announcing his intention to recognize the Chinese Republic on April 8. They unanimously rejected his invitation to do the same, arguing that they had not yet procured a guarantee of their rights and interests from the new Chinese government. The British government replied in the negative, attaching renewed importance to a formal reconfirmation of the rights, privileges, and immunities enjoyed by its citizens in China. Germany joined Great Britain in reminding the U.S. Department of State of the importance of maintaining the principle of concerted action. Japan, too,

---

[12] T. Y. Li, *op. cit.*, pp. 71-72.
[13] Department of State, *U.S. Foreign Relations, 1913*, p. 108.

declined Wilson's offer, expressing concern that premature recognition would constitute interference in favor of Yuan Shih-k'ai against Sun's nationalists. Among the nations with treaty relations with China, only four—Brazil, Mexico, Peru, and Cuba—gave their full consent to Wilson's proposal.[14]

The National Assembly opened as scheduled on April 8, but the Wilson administration itself, discouraged by events in China and the negative reaction of the powers, took a wait-and-see attitude. If the National Assembly could make progress in the direction of the ultimate establishment of a republican government and the adoption of a permanent constitution, then Wilson would reconsider recognition. At a minimum, the U.S. would wait until the National Assembly had proven itself capable of organizing itself and addressing China's basic problems.

These new conditions were soon met. The Chinese Senate completed its organization on April 25. The Lower House elected a speaker on April 30, and a deputy speaker the following day. Williams was immediately instructed to deliver to President Yuan a message of recognition from the President of the United States. Williams was received by Yuan on May 2, and presented the following message from Woodrow Wilson:

> The Government and people of the United States of America, having abundantly testified their sympathy with the people of China upon their assumption of the attributes and powers of self-government, deem it opportune at this time, when the representative National Assembly has met to discharge the high duty of setting the seal of full accomplishment upon the aspirations of the Chinese people, that I extend, in the name of my Government and of my countrymen, a greeting of welcome to the new China thus entering into the family of nations. In taking this step, I entertain the confident hope and expectation that in perfecting a republican form of government the Chinese nation will attain to the highest degree of development and well being, and that under the new rule all the obligations of China which passed to the Provisional Government will in turn pass to and be observed by the Government established by the Assembly.[15]

---

[14] *Ibid.*, pp. 109-110, 114-115.

[15] Department of State, *U.S. Foreign Relations, 1913*, p. 110.

In reply, Yuan expressed his gratitude and stressed the common faith of the Chinese and American peoples in the soundness of democratic government.[16]

Brazil, Mexico, Peru and Cuba followed the lead of the United States, but the powers, particularly Japan, were displeased that the United States had violated the principle of international concert. With a view to gaining more satisfactory terms from China, the Japanese government attempted to continue to delay international recognition of the Chinese republic. Britain, France, and Russia were ready to cooperate with Japan, but Germany became impatient, and recognized the republic as soon as the election of Yuan Shih-k'ai as President was approved by the National Assembly. It was October, 1913 before Japan, Great Britain, France, Russia, Italy, and other nations followed.

After the Republic was recognized, Professor Paul S. Reinsch of the University of Wisconsin, a political scientist, was appointed by Wilson as the first U.S. Minister to the Republic of China. Like President Wilson, Reinsch was an opponent of imperialism and a champion of underdeveloped countries. China appointed Shah Kai-fu (1910-1915) and later V. K. Wellington Koo (1915-1920) as Ministers to the United States and, concurrently, Cuba.

America and the International Consortium

Since the 1850's American diplomats with experience in Asia had been predicting that U.S. trade with that region would ultimately eclipse trade with Europe. Such speculation was especially rife among the expansionists of 1898. Alfred T. Mahan promised American businessmen millions of Chinese customers. American bankers entertained visions of great opportunities for capital investment in China and mining interests—a second El Dorado of mineral wealth awaiting American exploitation.[17] Such were the economic motivations behind the Open Door policy.

---

[16] *Ibid.*, p. 118.

[17] Captain Alfred T. Mahan of the United States Navy, author of "The Influence of Sea Power upon History," and other books, was a foremost naval strategist in the

William McKinley and Theodore Roosevelt based their Far Eastern policy on the anticipated economic benefits of a China open to U.S. goods and investments. The harsh realities of power politics, however, combined with the existence in the Chinese market of long-entrenched foreign competitors, kept American gains modest. Presidents Taft and Wilson were equally committed to the Open Door policy, though their methods of maintaining equal commercial opportunity in China often differed in practice.

President Taft, who had served in the Philippines and personally visited China, found it a prudent policy to actively participate in international financial assistance to China. By acting in concert with other leading powers, Taft reasoned, the U.S. could counterbalance their unscrupulous actions in China, restraining them from the kinds of political, economic, and military interventionism towards which they were constantly tending. This policy, known as "Dollar Diplomacy," was nowhere more apparent than in the ongoing diplomatic struggle over railroad concessions and bank loans.

At the time, the Chinese government was negotiating with international banking groups of the great powers for loans to assist in Chinese currency reform, and to accelerate railroad construction. The powers were eager to oblige, for although they had temporarily abandoned their immediate territorial ambitions in China, they were engaged in a heated rivalry for economic concessions. It was to temper this rivalry, as well as benefit American banks, that Taft gave sanction to American participation in an international consortium of private bankers.

The Hukuang railway loan, which gave rise to the international consortium, was intended for the construction of the Hupeh and Hunan railways in the Yangtze River valley. The negotiations were initiated by Britain and France, later joined by Germany, for a railway loan in the amount of 6,000,000 taels. It was to this group that President Taft in July 1909 demanded that American banks be admitted.[18] This being

---

1890s. He had advocated the annexation of Hawaii, the construction of the Nicaraguan Canal, and the acquisition of Caribbean bases. Political leaders of that new imperialist era, such as Theodore Roosevelt, Henry Cabot Lodge, and Albert J. Beveridge, acknowledged their indebtedness to Mahan's thoughts.

[18] The American banking group came into existence in June 1909 at the initiation of the State Department for the purpose of negotiating the Hukuang loan. It consisted

accomplished, the group became known as the Four Power Consortium, and a loan agreement was signed in 1911.[19]

While the authorized loan was actually issued in 1911, the outbreak of the Chinese Revolution made railway construction impossible. The actual construction of the projected railroad did not begin until two years later and was never completed. The Four Power Consortium never fulfilled the terms of the loan agreement.

In 1910 the Chinese government had informed the Taft administration that it would give American bankers preference if they were willing to undertake a loan of 50,000,000 taels. The U.S. government agreed immediately, and the two sides signed a preliminary agreement on October 27, 1910, for a proposed loan "to facilitate certain changes in the administration of Imperial and Manchurian Finance and to undertake certain Industrial Enterprises in Manchuria."[20] The Taft administration, with the consent of the Chinese government, extended an invitation to other powers to share the loan equally. Thus the American banking group and its consortium partners, the British, French, and German groups, entered into negotiations with China. An agreement was signed on April 15, 1911, under the terms of which a loan of 10,000,000 taels was to be made available to the Chinese government for the reform of Chinese currency and for land reclamation, grazing, forestry, agriculture, and mining. This loan was postponed when the October 10 Revolution broke out and the Manchu Dynasty was overthrown.

The new government of China was confronted with many difficulties. Its treasury was empty, and it had to resort to foreign loans to fund its nascent administration. The Four Power Consortium responded to loan

---

of four banking institutions: J. P. Morgan and Company, Kuhn Loeb and Company, the First National Bank of the City of New York, and the National City Bank of New York.

[19] The main financial interests in the consortium, besides the United States, were for Britain, the Hong Kong and Shanghai Bank; for France, the Banque de l'Indo-Chine; for Germany, the Deutsch-Asiatische Bank; for Russia, Banque Russo-Chinoise; and for Japan, Yokohama Specie Bank.

[20] John V. A. MacMurray, *Treaties and Agreements with and Concerning China, 1894–1919* (Washington: Carnegie Endowment for International Peace, 1921), p. 851.

requests from the Peking government by making several advances totaling some 12,100,000 taels on a projected "Reorganization Loan."

In 1912 the international banking group was further expanded to a Six Power Consortium with the admission of Russia and Japan, which had earlier blocked American plans for international investment in Manchuria. The Taft administration welcomed this development as a way of winning over two powers whose cooperation was essential if the Dollar Diplomacy was to succeed. At Paris the banking groups of the six powers concluded the Inter-Bank Conference Agreement with China on June 18, 1912, allowing for equal participation in the Reorganization Loan under discussion.[21] The Six Power Consortium, it was announced, would henceforth be the sole source of all foreign loans to China.

The negotiations over the Reorganization Loan focused on the degree of supervision or control the six banking groups would have over the new government. This loan, in the amount of 60,000,000 taels, was qualitatively different from previous loans, as it was to be used for general administrative purposes rather than for a specific program. Too much control by foreign banking groups over the reorganization work of the Chinese government could lead to infringement on China's sovereignty. Strong domestic opposition made the Peking authorities shrink from accepting the strict terms of the Six Power Consortium, and the negotiations were deadlocked.[22]

During the winter of 1912-1913, as the negotiations dragged on, a dispute arose among the members of the consortium over whether to relax the supervisory requirements of the loan. The powers disagreed among themselves whether it was really necessary to appoint auditors and financial supervisors within the Peking government to control the use to which the loan funds were put. This was, of course, as much a political question as an economic one.

The American banking group kept politics out of the loan negotiations as much as possible, although it had joined the consortium at the request of the State Department and kept in touch with Washington. The U.S. government, of course, wanted to avoid compromising China's

---

21 R. J. Bartlett, *The Record of American Diplomacy* (New York: Alfred A. Knopf, 1964), p. 417.

22 T. Y. Li, *op. cit.*, pp. 28-29.

administrative integrity by relaxing the loan requirements. The U.S. bankers, impatient at the delay in concluding the loan agreement, were soon expressing a desire to withdraw from negotiations. Their attitude is revealed in a letter of February 21, 1913:

> The outlook [on the negotiations] is such that there can be no hope of early signature. To my mind it is no longer a question of friendly international cooperation to help China but a combination of big powers with common interests to accomplish their own selfish political aims.[23]

Learning of the intention of the U.S. bankers to withdraw, Secretary of State Knox let it be known that the bankers should not decide on any important change in the consortium until the next administration had declared its policy on the matter. Such was the situation when the Taft administration gave way to that of Woodrow Wilson.[24]

President Wilson lacked personal experience in Asia, and had no practical knowledge of the interplay of international politics and business. Motivated solely by a benevolent sympathy for weak nations, he sought to keep himself and his administration aloof from all collective endeavors which might interfere with the autonomous development of China as a sovereign nation. In this way, Wilson imagined, the U.S. would be free to use its moral influence to China's advantage.[25]

At a cabinet meeting on March 18, 1913, President Wilson read a statement which not only condemned the loan but severely criticized several nations belonging to the consortium. Several cabinet members suggested that this unnecessary castigation be deleted and this was done, but a leak compelled the White House to release the entire statement to the press on the same day. There was no time for the U.S. State Department to officially notify the governments concerned, and the Japanese government—one of those criticized—expressed resentment that it had learned of Wilson's decision from the newspapers.

---

[23] Department of State, *U.S. Foreign Relations, 1913*, p. 164.
[24] J. Daniels, *The Wilson Era, Years of Peace, 1910-1917* (Chapel Hill, NC: University of North Carolina Press, 1946), p. 157.
[25] T. Y. Li, *op. cit.*, pp. 23-24.

Wilson's statement opened by summarizing the Taft administration's purpose in seeking American participation in the loan, namely, that American capital play a role in the development of China, and that the United States share in the responsibility for the conduct of the foreign relations involved in administering the loan. However, Wilson noted, the American banking group had already declared that it would continue in the consortium only if expressly requested by the government to do so.

The conditions of the loan, Wilson went on, touched on the administrative independence of China itself, and he did not feel that the U.S. should be a party. The several guarantees demanded by the bankers would make interference in the financial and political affairs of China mandatory. The pledge of particular taxes to the loan's repayment, and the provision that the Chinese revenue agencies concerned be administered by foreign nationals, were contrary to American principles. Wilson concluded by stating that:

> The Government of the United States is not only willing, but earnestly desirous, of aiding the great Chinese people in every way that is consistent with their untrammeled development and its own immemorial principles. The awakening of the people of China to a consciousness of their responsibilities under free government is the most significant, if not the most momentous, event of our generation. With this movement and aspiration the American people are in profound sympathy. They certainly wish to participate, and participate very generously, in the opening to the Chinese and to the use of the world the almost untouched and perhaps unrivaled resources of China. . . . This is the main interest of its citizens in the development of China. Our interests are those of the open door--the door of friendship and mutual advantage. This is the only door we care to enter.[26]

This statement marked a dramatic change in American foreign policy and occupies a significant place in the annals of Sino-American relations. President Wilson's critics called it "amateurish and sentimental," but these were few in number. The American press praised Wilson, and

---

[26] Department of State, *U.S. Foreign Relations, 1913*, pp. 170-171.

hopefully speculated that he had delivered a coup de grâce to Dollar Diplomacy. The reaction of the general public was favorable as well, for they read in Wilson's statement a return to America's traditional wariness of entangling alliances, a vigorous encouragement of American industrial and commercial activities in China, and a deep respect for the rights of the Chinese people. Secretary of State Bryan, for one, believed that his president had won "the lasting gratitude of China."

On March 19, 1913, the day after Wilson's statement became public, the American banking group met in New York and decided to withdraw from the loan. After the Reorganization Loan in the amount of 25,000,000 taels was concluded between Yuan Shih-k'ai's government and the five remaining consortium members on April 26, 1913, the American advances were repaid.

Sincerity and disinterest characterized Wilson's approach to the thorny problems of China. He combined lofty moral principles with a suspicion of international power politics. But China, faced with the tremendous task of building and modernizing, needed something more than high idealism and goodwill. The U.S. hands-off policy left an open field for an aggressive Japan to aggrandize its power, wealth, and position in China.

3

WORLD WAR I AND POSTWAR SETTLEMENTS
1914–1920

I. AMERICA'S INVOLVEMENT IN SINO-JAPANESE NEGOTIATIONS

Hostilities in China, 1914

The reorganization loan made to Yuan Shih-k'ai by the international consortium increased the grip of foreign financiers on China. So insecure was Yuan's government that it could not withstand pressure from abroad, much less command order within China. In setting himself up as a virtual dictator, Yuan had alienated the revolutionary leaders with whose support he had become president. The civil conflict this precipitated, between the northern military groups and the champions of democratic government in the south, continued even after Yuan's death in June 1916.

The young Chinese republic, its diplomacy hampered by internal division, could not hope to remain unaffected by the outbreak of war in Europe. With Great Britain, France, Germany, and Russia now embroiled in conflict, Japan seized the moment to advance its interests in China. With China's foreign trade disrupted by the hostilities, and the customs receipts that were the central government's main source of revenue in free fall, Yuan was forced to seek more foreign loans, further weakening his ability to resist Japanese aggression.

As soon as war was declared in Europe, China announced that it would remain neutral in the conflict. On August 3, 1914, the United States was asked to "endeavor to obtain the consent of the belligerent European nations to an undertaking not to engage in hostilities either in Chinese territory or marginal waters in adjacent leased territories."[1] This was the first serious Chinese attempt to convert long-standing American sympathies for China into instruments of her national policy.

Three days later, on August 6, Peking formally proclaimed a Neutrality Act. Among other things, this Act guaranteed the neutrality of leased territories, which would have left the German territory in Shantung province, Kiaochow Bay, in German hands until the termination of hostilities. By this means Peking hoped to forestall Japanese expansion.

On August 7 Secretary of State Bryan authorized American participation in the scheme, but only insofar as foreign settlements, not leased territories, were concerned. The State Department immediately began sounding out the powers on their willingness to observe the neutrality of the Pacific Ocean and the status quo of the entire Far East.[2] Nothing came of the American proposal which Germany, alone of all the powers, accepted on August 13.

On August 14 the Japanese government delivered an ultimatum to Germany demanding that its naval vessels be withdrawn from Japanese and Chinese waters and that the leased territory of Kiaochow be turned over to Japan with a view to its eventual restoration to China. No reply was given by the German government, and on August 23 Japan declared war against Germany and commanded its "army and navy [to] carry on hostilities against that Empire with all their strength. . . ." Few were surprised by this action, given the Anglo-Japanese Alliance of 1911, a Franco-Japanese entente dating from 1907, and the entente and treaties with Russia. But it was not merely to keep treaty commitments that Japan entered the war, however. Japan's designs on China proper were rapidly growing. Tokyo saw unrestricted access to China's markets as vital to the development of Japan's industry and trade. With the

---

[1]   MacMurray to Bryan, August 3, 1914, Department of State, *U.S. Foreign Relations, 1914*, Supplement, 162, cited in A. W. Griswold, *The Far Eastern Policy of the United States* (New Haven: Yale University Press, 1964), p. 178.

[2]   Department of State, *U.S. Foreign Relations, 1914*, Supplement, pp. 163-170.

European powers distracted by the war, Japan was presented with a perfect opportunity to secure more concessions and territory from China for itself.

As soon as Japan declared war, Bryan reminded the Japanese government of its pledge to support "the independence and integrity of China and the principle of equal opportunities for the commerce and industry of all nations in China," as contained in the Root-Takahira Agreement of November 30, 1908. He noted with satisfaction that Japan had publicly declared that, in demanding the surrender by Germany of the entire leased territory of Kiaochow, it did so with the purpose of restoring that territory to China, and was seeking no territorial aggrandizement in China. Bryan rejected the suggestion of the Chinese government that the American government seek the Kiaochow leasehold for itself, with the idea of promptly restoring it to China. "The Department feels sure that such a course would do more to provoke than to avert war," Bryan replied.[3]

Ignoring China's protests, Japan invaded Shantung province on September 3, 1914. The Japanese force came ashore at Lungkow, a town far to the north of Tsingtao, their primary objective. Three weeks later, they were joined by a token force of 910 British troops. China attempted to define a war zone but Japan paid little attention to its limits. Ignoring an understanding that the Shantung Railway be policed by Chinese troops, the Japanese took over the railroad as far as Tsinan, the provincial capital, located two hundred miles away. The Japanese claimed that this action, although obliged by military necessity, did not extend the belligerent zone. On November 6, two months after the Japanese landing, the German governor, Admiral Meyer Waldeck, surrendered his force of 4,500 men at Tsingtao. The victory cost the Japanese 1,968 casualties, and one destroyer and one torpedo boat were lost.[4]

The American Minister to China, Paul S. Reinsch, reported that the Chinese government was more disturbed over the Japanese occupation of

---

[3] *Ibid.*, pp. 173-174.
[4] *The North China Herald*, November 14, 1914, cited in R. W. Curry, *Woodrow Wilson and Far Eastern Policy, 1913-21* (New York: Bookman Associates, 1957), p. 109.

the Shantung Railway than over the original invasion. The Japanese intended to dominate Shantung province, Peking asserted, and perhaps one day to annex it as Korea had been annexed. In fact, after capturing Tsingtao, the Japanese laid claim to all former German concessions and leaseholds in Shantung, and effectively occupied most of the province.

Prior to the German surrender at Tsingtao, Acting Secretary of State Robert Lansing informed Reinsch that the U.S. would keep its troops in China at maximum strength and would increase the number of naval vessels stationed in Chinese waters. As was made clear to the Chinese government, however, this was done solely to protect American rights and interests in China from possible internal disorders, not to guarantee China's territorial integrity. America's attention was focused almost exclusively on the cataclysm under way in Europe. America's interests in China were limited, and were certainly not worth a war with Japan. Herein lay much of the weakness of U.S.-China policy.

Opposition to the Twenty-One Demands of Japan

Japan's ambitions far exceeded China's fears, for it soon became clear that Tokyo intended to use Shantung province as a springboard to hegemony over all China. While Peking continued vainly to protest Japan's trespasses on neutral Chinese territory, the Japanese government was quietly preparing the most ambitious démarche in the history of its diplomatic relations with China, the Twenty-One Demands. Bypassing the Chinese foreign office, the Japanese Minister in Peking, Eki Hioki presented the texts of the demands directly to President Yuan Shih-k'ai on January 18, 1915.

The demands were divided into five groups. The first group referred to Shantung province, and required China to automatically assent to any agreement which Japan might make with Germany for the disposition of the latter's concessions and leaseholds, to promise not to alienate any part of the coast to any third power, to open additional cities to foreign trade, and to grant Japan certain railway privileges. The second group stipulated that, in South Manchuria, the Japanese leaseholds—on Port Arthur and Dairen and the railways—were to be extended to ninety-nine years, that anywhere in South Manchuria and Eastern Inner Mongolia Japanese might reside, travel, engage in business, lease or own land, and open mines, and that in these regions no official advisers were to be employed without the consent of Japan. The third group provided that the Han-Yeh-Ping Company, an iron mining and smelting concern in Central China, was to become a joint enterprise and that it could not be sold without Japan's consent. The fourth group wished to bind China not to cede or lease to a third power any harbor, bay, or island along its coast. The fifth group demanded that China employ Japanese as advisers, share with Japanese the administration of police departments, purchase a Sino-Japanese arsenal, grant railway concessions in the Yangtze Valley, grant rights for religious propaganda and the purchase of land in the interior for schools, hospitals, and churches, and consult Japan before foreign loans were contracted for mines, railways, and harbor works in Fukien province.[5] If China acceded to these demands, she would become in effect a Japanese protectorate.

Although the Japanese government warned China that its demands must not be made public until after an agreement had been reached, the Chinese government leaked them through secret diplomatic channels. V. K. Wellington Koo, a counselor of the Ministry of Foreign Affairs, visited Minister Reinsch and told him in confidence that Japan had presented a set of "categorical demands" which, if accepted, would reduce China to a state of vassalage. He further remarked that the demands meant Japanese control of China's natural resources, finances, and army.[6]

Reinsch, who was highly sympathetic to the Chinese people and suspicious of Japanese designs on China, immediately grasped the seriousness of the situation. On January 23 he reported to the State Department that not only the Open Door but China's independence were being threatened by the new Japanese move. The American Minister expressed the fear that, if China failed to comply with the demands,

---

[5] K. S. Latourette, *The Chinese, Their History and Culture* (New York: MacMillan Co., 1954), pp. 416-417.

[6] P. S. Reinsch, *An American Diplomat in China* (Garden City, New York: Doubleday, Page Co., 1922), p. 131.

Japan would instigate revolutionary uprisings which, in turn "would offer a pretext for military occupation."[7]

President Wilson, though apprised of the situation by Bryan, reacted with his customary caution. He informed Reinsch in a letter dated February 2, 1915, that he did not want to directly intervene in the negotiations for fear that it would "excite the hostility of Japan, which would be first manifest against China herself."[8]

It was not until the Chinese Minister in Washington, Shah Kai-fu, provided the complete text of the Twenty-One Demands to Secretary of State Bryan that the Wilson administration took action. On March 13 Bryan notified the Japanese Minister in Washington that Japan's demands were inconsistent with its past assurances regarding the sovereignty of China, and expressed the hope that it would take "no steps" which would be "contrary to the spirit of those assurances." Bryan pointed out that, under the terms of its past treaties with China, the U.S. had grounds on which to object to the Japanese demands concerning Shantung, South Manchuria, and East Mongolia, but conceded that territorial contiguity had created special relations between Japan and these districts. What the U.S. could not be indifferent to, he asserted, was the attempted political, military or economic domination of China by a foreign power. Nor could it accept proposals which would exclude America from equal participation in the economic and industrial development of China and limit the political independence of that country. In short, Bryan seemed to imply that the U.S. found only group five of the Japanese demands truly objectionable.[9]

On April 26, 1915, the Japanese Minister in Peking presented a revised list of demands to the Chinese government. The Chinese reply on May 1 proved unacceptable to Japan, which drafted an ultimatum and began to make preparations for war. In a last-ditch effort to avert open conflict, Bryan sent a personal message to the Japanese Premier, Shingenobu Okuma, urging that negotiations be continued until a

---

7   Reinsch to Bryan, February 1, 1915, *U.S. Foreign Relations,* 1915, pp. 81-82; cited in T. Y. Li, *Woodrow Wilson's China Policy, 1913-1917* (New York: University of Kansas City Press-Twayne Press, 1952), p. 105.

8   P. S. Reinsch, *op. cit.,* p. 137.

9   Department of State, *U.S. Foreign Relations, 1915,* pp. 105-111.

peaceful settlement could be reached. A similar appeal was sent to the Chinese government through Reinsch. Bryan also requested that Britain, France, and Russia join the U.S. appeal to Japan and China to continue negotiations until a satisfactory conclusion was reached.

Little came of these efforts. Bryan's appeal to Premier Okuma did not reach Tokyo until May 7, after the Japanese government had already decided to deliver its ultimatum. Bryan's appeal to the Chinese government was delayed in transmission, so that Reinsch did not act on it. His invitation to Britain, France, and Russia for a joint representation to Japan was rejected by the Entente. Only Britain, although unwilling to issue a joint admonition to an ally, independently opposed the Japanese action in China. The British especially disapproved of group five of the demands, and their repeated and strong warnings to Japan in this regard helped to secure their withdrawal.[10]

On May 9 the Chinese government reluctantly informed the Japanese Minister in Peking that it unconditionally accepted the Japanese ultimatum, thus bringing more than three months of strenuous negotiations to a close. Two days later Bryan sent a note to both the Japanese and the Chinese governments stating that the U.S. would not recognize any agreement between Japan and China which "impair[s] the treaty rights of the United States and its citizens in China, the political or territorial integrity of the Republic of China, or the international policy relative to China commonly known as the open door policy."[11]

The effect of this warning was to cast doubt on Bryan's statement of March 13, 1915, concerning Shantung, South Manchuria, and East Mongolia. The Japanese government, unaffected by either foreign or domestic criticism of its policy toward China, on May 25 imposed two treaties and thirteen exchanges of notes upon Yuan Shih-k'ai's government. Japan received far-reaching concessions regarding Shangtung, South Manchuria, Eastern Inner Mongolia, and a controlling interest in the Han-Yeh-Ping company. The fifth group of demands was left for future consideration, although Japan did have its way with

---

[10] T. Y. Li, *op. cit.*, pp. 123-125.
[11] Department of State, *U.S. Foreign Relations, 1915*, p. 146.

Fukien.[12]   The Sino-Japanese treaties of May 25, 1915, were never ratified by the Chinese parliament as required by the constitution, and on these grounds were later claimed to be invalid.

Wilson's thoughts were far from Asia. On May 7 the Lusitania had been sunk by a German submarine, sending 128 Americans to their death. Although Reinsch continued to urge that the U.S. play a more active role in China, Wilson would have none of it. In his view, China's internal weakness had invited foreign aggression. Before other nations would respect her rights as a sovereign nation, she would have to set her house in order.

The greatest opposition to the Twenty-One Demands did not come from Japan's western competitors but from the Chinese people themselves. The demands aroused the people against Japan, and greatly accelerated China's unsteady progress toward national unity.

II. PARTICIPATION IN THE FIRST WORLD WAR

China Severs Diplomatic Relations with the Central Powers

At the outbreak of World War I, China declared its neutrality, although its sympathies lay increasingly with the Allies. The new national consciousness which followed the Twenty-One Demands brought a clearer realization of what was at stake for China in the war. If China was to have a place at the peace conference which would follow the war, and at which the thorny questions of the disposition of German interests in Shantung and perhaps even the Twenty-One Demands as a whole would be revisited, then it must enter the war. Peking did not want a *reprise* of the negotiations leading up to the 1905 Portsmouth Treaty concerning Manchuria, in which Japan and Russia had excluded Chinese representatives until the terms of the treaty were already set. Twice,

---

12 In mid-April, 1915, Wilson assumed control of the correspondence and injected a more resolute tone. The May 7 Note flatly stated that America had no idea of surrendering any treaty rights or asking China to do so. Britain's simultaneous objection to the fifth group enabled Japanese elder statesmen to persuade them to omit the fifth group from its May 9 ultimatum.

since 1915, Peking had been disposed to join the Allies, only to be checked by Japanese opposition.

A final consideration of the Chinese government was the reaction of the United States, whose eventual participation in the hostilities seemed increasingly likely. The Chinese government desired to keep its foreign policy closely aligned with that of its great and good friend. So it was, that, when President Wilson sent out his peace inquiry of December 19, 1916, Peking readily expressed its willingness to join in an international effort to eradicate wars of aggression. Chinese Minister of Foreign Affairs, Wu T'ing-fang declared that China was "ready, and even eager" to join with the U.S. "to assure the respect of the principle of the equality of nations, whatever their power may be, and to relieve them of the peril of wrong and violence."[13]

On January 31, 1917, the German government declared that it would wage unlimited submarine warfare on all vessels bound for Allied ports. The United States responded two days later by severing diplomatic ties with Germany, and urging all neutral states, including China, to do likewise.

The Chinese government was divided on the wisdom of this course of action. Premier Tuan and elder statesman Liang Chi-chao were among those who were eager to follow America's lead. President Li, Feng Kuo-chang, and others counseled caution and continued neutrality. Following a marathon cabinet meeting on February 9, caution carried the day, and the Chinese government limited itself to sending a strongly-worded note of protest to Berlin. In a note sent to the American Minister that same day, Foreign Minister Wu explained that "The Chinese government, like the President of the United States, is reluctant to believe that the German government will actually carry into execution those measures which imperil the lives and property of citizens of neutral states."[14]

This viewed proved mistaken. In early March the French ship Atlas, among whose passengers were five hundred Chinese laborers, was torpedoed. On March 14 the Chinese government, with the acquiescence of both houses of parliament, severed diplomatic relations with both

---

[13] Cited in W. R. Wheeler, *China and the World War* (New York: MacMillan Co., 1919), pp. 65-66.
[14] *Ibid.*, p. 70.

Germany and Austria-Hungary and expelled their ministers. China had taken its first step toward participation in the cause of the Allies.

China Declares War Against the Central Powers

The United States declared war against Germany and Austria-Hungary on April 6, 1917. The question of whether China ought to follow suit became so enmeshed with domestic politics that it brought down the government. Supporters of Premier Tuan and the northern military governors advocated entering the war while southerners, from whose ranks came most of the Kuomintang members, argued for continued neutrality. After several weeks of rancorous dissension, President Li on May 23 dismissed Tuan from the premiership. The military governors then forced Li to dissolve parliament on June 11. An abortive coup d'état took place on June 30 in which the Manchu boy emperor Hsuen Tung (Pu-Yi) was placed on the throne by the old militarist Chang Hsun. Then, on July 14, Tuan attacked Peking with his own army and recaptured the city. President Li was forced to resign and Tuan resumed the premiership. Most of the progressive Kuomintang members of the dissolved parliament had by then decamped to Canton, where they set up a military establishment and nominated Sun Yat-sen as generalissimo.[15]

President Wilson viewed this civil strife with dismay, reminding Foreign Minister Wu on June 7 that the question of China's entry into the war with Germany was secondary to "the maintenance by China of one central united and alone responsible government." All parties and persons in China should "work for the re-establishment of a coordinated government and the assumption of that place among the powers of the world to which China is so justly entitled; but the full attainment of which is impossible in the midst of internal discord."[16]

This note was welcomed by Peking, which somewhat disingenuously interpreted it as a pledge to support the central government. Sun also expressed his gratitude to President Wilson for his "foresight and timely

---

[15] M. E. Cameron, T. H. D. Mahoney, and G. E. McReynolds, *China, Japan and the Powers* (New York: Ronald Press, 1952), pp. 369-370.

[16] Lansing to Reinsch, June 4, 1917, *U.S. Foreign Relations, 1917*, pp. 48-49.

warning." The various political factions did not take the American advice, however, and China remained divided into a conservative north, with Peking as its capital, a progressive south, with its headquarters at Canton, and a more or less neutral center situated along the Yangtze River valley, which had Nanking as its principal city. On August 1 Vice President Feng Kuo-chang succeeded Li Yuan-hung as Acting President in Peking. When Premier Tuan again brought up the question of entering the war, there was little opposition. China formally declared war on the German and Austro-Hungarian Empires on August 14, 1917.

Once at war, China seized German and Austrian ships in its waters and confiscated various properties belonging to enemy citizens, who were deprived of their extraterritorial rights. Control over the German concessions at Hankow and Tientsin, as well as over the Austro-Hungarian concession in Tientsin, was resumed by the Chinese government.

In recognition of China's entrance into the war, the Allies made several concessions to China in a collective note dated September 8. First, they agreed to postpone for five years payment of the Boxer Indemnities, and that Germany and Austria-Hungary should permanently forfeit any payments remaining due. Second, they allowed an increase of five per cent in Chinese custom duties. Third, Chinese troops were granted entry to Tientsin, a city from which they had long been barred.

China's military contribution to the Allied cause was limited by the ongoing civil war between Peking and the South, which absorbed every available resource.[17] A special military commission was sent to France, although a planned Chinese expeditionary force never materialized.[18] A detachment of Chinese troops did join the Allied forces in the Siberian expedition in December 1917.

China's main contribution to the war effort was the dispatch of labor battalions, totaling more than 175,000 men, to France and Mesopotamia to dig and repair trenches and earthworks, thus freeing soldiers for the

---

[17] The Military operations against the South by the Peking government were financed largely by Japanese loans known as "Nishihara loans" 1917-1919, amounting to 200 million Chinese dollars.

[18] C. F. Chang, *Chung-hua min-kuo Wai-chiao shih* (Taipei: Cheng Chung Book Co., 1943), pp. 228-229

front.[19]   These battalions performed their work well under difficult conditions, and their casualties numbered in the thousands.   China also supplied large quantities of rice, eggs, and other staples to the Allies in Europe.[20]

The Lansing-Ishii Agreement, 1917

America's entry into the war disturbed Tokyo, which was apprehensive lest American military might be used to check its designs on China. Japanese suspicions were further heightened by the activities of Minister Reinsch on behalf of Chinese unity. As Secretary of State Lansing later wrote, "Japanese psychology could not understand America's altruistic purpose of fighting for liberty and democracy in Europe."[21]   In return for much-needed naval assistance to the Allies in the Mediterranean, Japan sought and obtained assurances from Britain, France, Italy, and Russia that these countries would support its claim to the German leasehold and concessions in Shantung.

As 1917 progressed, the Allied powers each sent war missions to the United States to arrange for military cooperation and financial support. The Japanese government also decided to send a mission, appointing former Foreign Minister Kikujiro Ishii as its head. President Wilson received Ishii upon his arrival, telling him that America regretted the spheres of influence carved out by the powers in China and desired, above all, the preservation of the Open Door policy. Ishii agreed with Wilson, saying that Japan never failed to uphold this principle. Wilson asked Ishii to speak with Lansing on this question, and the Lansing-Ishii talks began in secret on September 6, 1917. Over the next eight weeks the two men held thirteen conferences, the result of which was the cautiously phrased Lansing-Ishii Agreement.   Ishii made nominal concessions to the American position on the territorial sovereignty of

---

[19] The distribution of these labor battalions, according to a report received at the Chinese Legation in Washington, in October 1918, was as follows: With the British forces, 125,000; with the French; 40,000, with the Americans, 6,000; in Mesopotamia and North Africa, about 4,000. Total: 175,000.

[20] W. R. Wheeler, *op. cit.*, p. 151.

[21] Robert Lansing, *War Memoirs*, p. 286, cited in R. W. Curry, *op. cit.*, p. 176.

China and the Open Door policy, while extracting from Lansing a cover for Japan's aggressive policy in China in studiously worded language:

> The Governments of the United States and Japan recognize that territorial propinquity creates special relations between countries, and consequently the Government of the United States recognizes that Japan has special interests in China, particularly in the part to which her possessions are contiguous. . . . The territorial sovereignty of China, nevertheless, remains unimpaired, and the Government of the United States has every confidence in the repeated assurances of the Imperial Japanese Government that, while geographical position gives Japan such special interests, they have no desire to discriminate against the trade of other nations or to disregard the commercial rights heretofore granted by China in treaties with other powers. . .[22]

Tokyo was content with this wording, and believed that the agreement could be interpreted to its own satisfaction. Indeed, in translating this agreement into Chinese, the Japanese government substituted characters that meant "paramount interest" for the original term "special interest." In view of this interpretation, the Chinese government immediately declared that it was not bound by this agreement, and a note to this effect was delivered by the Chinese Minister to the U.S., V. K. Wellington Koo, to Secretary Lansing on November 9, 1917.[23]

Lansing assured Koo that he had earlier refrained from discussing the negotiations with him only to avoid any suspicion that China had somehow assented to the agreement. He insisted that it was a temporary measure, an effort to maintain the status quo in China while getting on with the war in Europe. Indeed, one positive result of the face-saving ambiguities of Lansing-Ishii Agreement was the temporary lessening of tensions between the U.S. and Japan. However, the apparent recognition by the U.S. of the Japanese claim that "territorial propinquity" had given it "special interests in China" was to have long-term repercussions.

---

[22] Department of State, *U.S. Foreign Relations, 1917*, p. 264.
[23] J. V. A. MacMurray, ed., *op. cit.*, II, pp. 1396-1397.

III. THE PARIS PEACE CONFERENCE AND OTHER ISSUES

Revival of the Consortium

Between 1913 and 1916 Japan tightened her grip on Shantung, South Manchuria and Inner Mongolia, while at the same time, through a multitude of loans, demands, and investments, gaining control of China's financial structure. With German and Russian banks no longer able to participate in the International Banking Consortium, Japan had come to dominate it for its own purposes. Concerned British and French bankers sought to convince their American colleagues to rejoin the international banking consortium to overthrow Japan's near-monopoly of Chinese finances. With the Allies eager for China to increase its war effort, and willing to provide loans for this purpose, the time was ripe for the Americans to take the initiative.

American private loans to China had been notably unsuccessful, and both Wilson and Lansing gradually came to accept the impracticability of the independent approach they had earlier championed.[24] On June 20, 1918, with the support of the Treasury Department, Lansing proposed that Washington sponsor the organization of a new consortium. Wilson consented to the idea, albeit with reservations.[25]

The American banking group accepted Lansing's proposal on two conditions. First, its interests must be pooled with the French. Second, the U.S. government must announce that the loans were being made at its behest, in order that they could be successfully floated on the American market. These conditions were accepted by the American government, which thus assumed heavy and public responsibilities toward the American banking group and its investors.[26]

The basic principles for the new consortium, as outlined by the Wilson administration, were that each national group should receive the active and exclusive support of its government, that all preferences and options in China held by member banks should be pooled, and that the

---

24 Lansing to Wilson, June 20, 1918, Department of State, *U.S. Foreign Relations, 1918*, pp. 170-171.
25 Wilson to Lansing, June 21, 1918, *Ibid.*, p. 171.
26 Cited W. A. Williams, *op. cit.*, p. 650.

administrative integrity and independence of China should be respected. As in 1909, with the Knox neutralization loan in Manchuria, the U.S. was again attempting to challenge Japanese efforts to establish a financial monopoly, this time over all of China.

Prolonged American-Japanese negotiations ensued, in which Japan sought to exclude Manchuria and Mongolia from the activities of the proposed consortium. To Japan, the pooling of options and internationalization of loans in these two areas would mean the end of its domination there. Moreover, between 1917 and 1918 Japan had extended more than thirteen separate loans to the Tuan Ch'i-jui administration. These loans were powerful political instruments, and Japan was not prepared to give them up at an American injunction.

A compromise was eventually reached. The U.S. assured Japan that it and the other two consortium powers, France and Britain, would refuse to undertake any operation inimical to the vital interests of Japan. Even so, Japan refused to join until the U.S. had agreed to place a number of specified railway projects, and related mining and industrial rights in Manchuria and Mongolia, outside the scope of the consortium.[27]

The new consortium came into being October 15, 1920, although it found no immediate scope for its activities. The Chinese government was hostile to the consortium, fearing that, under the guise of aiding China, its real motive was to establish international financial domination. This fear was gradually allayed, however, and loans were eventually concluded.

President Wilson's economic policy toward China was as impractical as it was morally laudable. America sat idly by as Japan embarked upon a great economic expansion in China, advancing rapidly towards hegemony. When Wilson eventually decided to act, the American position in many parts of China was already becoming untenable. Wilson reverted to the old policy of concerted action chiefly for the sake of restraining Japan, but in so doing virtually ratified that country's economic gains in China.

---

[27] A. W. Griswold, *op. cit.*, pp. 224-225.

The Shantung Question and The Treaty of Versailles

On January 8, 1918, President Wilson set forth his famous Fourteen Points. Contrived in part to break down German resistance and keep Russia, then in the throes of the Bolshevik revolution, in the war, they also contained a sincere declaration of Wilson's own views on world peace. The Fourteen Points provided for freedom of the seas, the removal of economic barriers, the reduction of armaments, the evacuation of all conquered territory, the impartial adjustment of colonial claims, autonomy for the peoples of Austria-Hungary, and the creation of an independent Poland. Finally, Wilson called for the creation of "a general association of nations . . . for the purpose of affording mutual guarantees of political independence and territorial integrity to great and small nations alike."[28]

The Fourteen Points, particularly those relating to self-determination and the rights of weak nations, made a deep impression within Chinese intellectual circles. Such was the instant popularity of Wilson's collected war addresses that bookstores in Shanghai found it impossible to meet the demand for copies.[29] The Allies accepted the Fourteen Points with reservations, but the Chinese people took Wilson's pledges at face value.

With Austria-Hungary's surrender on September 14, 1918, the end of the war was in sight. The Peking government was aware that a continuance of civil strife might react to its disadvantage at the peace conference. The election of a new President of China, Hsu Shih-ch'ang, who was inaugurated on October 10, 1918, and the retirement of Premier Tuan the following day, seemed to offer an opportunity for a policy of conciliation to succeed. On November 17, 1918, President Hsu ordered the cessation of domestic hostilities, and began to prepare for peace negotiations with a view toward the reunification of China.

Wilson took the occasion of Hsu's inauguration to urge that an end be made of domestic dissension so that China may "assume its rightful place in the council of nations." In reply, Hsu pledged his best efforts to

---

[28] Wilson's Address to the U.S. Congress, January 8, 1918, *Congressional Record*, 65th Congress, 2nd Session, pp. 680-681.

[29] R. T. Pollard, *China's Foreign Relations, 1917-1931* (New York: MacMillan Co., 1931), p. 50.

bring about a restoration of internal unity and to "meet the wishes of the people of the whole country that in coming councils of the family of nations our country may assume its rightful place and work with your country hand in hand toward realization of the highest ideals."[30]

After the armistice of 1918, the delegates of the Allied powers met in Paris to formulate peace treaties. Disappointed when no invitation came to participate, the Chinese government determined to send a delegation anyway, certain that the Allies would not refuse to seat it once it reached Paris. China was eventually permitted "limited representation," placing it on a level with Greece, Poland, Portugal, and other small nations.

The Peking and Canton governments agreed to send five delegates, three from the north and two from the south. The members of the delegation were Peking's Minister of Foreign Affairs, Lu Chen-hsiang; the Chinese Minister to Washington, Wellington Koo; the Representative of Canton Military Government in the U.S., Thomas Cheng-t'ing Wang; the Minister to Great Britain, Alfred S. K. Sze; and the Minister to Belgium, Sheng-tsu Wei. The fact that the Chinese delegation represented a divided country did not prevent the delegates from agreeing on their aims, though it did weaken their overall position at the conference.

The Fourteen Points seemed to hold special promise for China, especially Wilson's proposal that in the adjustment of colonial claims "the interests of the population concerned must have equal weight with the equitable claims of the government whose title is determined." The Chinese delegation therefore operated under the assumption that it would be possible to obtain satisfaction for all of China's past grievances. In addition to requesting the return to China of all Shantung concessions and leaseholds, the liquidation of all German and Austro-Hungarian economic interests in China, and the abrogation of all treaties and notes originating from Japan's Twenty-One Demands, the Chinese delegation also planned to submit the so-called Questions for Readjustment, which concerned the unequal treaties. Passing through the United States in early January 1919 they declared that they would stand for the principles enunciated by President Wilson. The Chinese and American delegations

---

[30] Department of State, *U.S. Foreign Relations, 1918*, p. 111.

were on very friendly terms in Paris from the beginning, and together planned how China's case was to be presented at the conference.[31]

Shortly after the Peace Conference formally opened on January 18, 1919, the Council of Ten was created.[32] It was as a member of this Council, in which China had no representation, that Japan asserted her claim to the German rights in Shantung and insisted, on the basis of its wartime treaties with China, as being recognized as the dominant power in East Asia.

The Chinese delegates were allowed to appear before the Council of Ten on January 28, 1919. Koo was brilliant in presenting the Chinese case for Shantung, even though he had just been informed that the Japanese had secretly paid twenty million yen to Peking the previous September to secure their position in Shantung. Koo painted the province as China's holy land--the cradle of Chinese civilization, the birthplace of Confucius and Mencius, and so on. Its enormous population of thirty-six million in an area of 35,000 square miles made it unfit for colonization, he argued, while its strategic location made it the gateway to North China. China felt indebted to Japan and Britain for having freed the territory from Germany, but now China looked to the Peace Conference to see that justice was done and the province returned forthwith to her possession.[33]

The Japanese delegate, Foreign Minister Nobuaki Makino, responded by pointing out that Japan had been in possession of the area since the victory of Tsingtao, and had entered into a friendly understanding with China under the Twenty-One Demands and the 1918 treaties and notes, which governed the question. At this point President Wilson interrupted, asking that the treaties and notes governing this understanding be laid before the Council of Ten. This was the last thing Japan wanted, since did not want these wartime arrangements to come under public scrutiny, merely recognized as governing the disposition of German rights in Shantung. Makino therefore answered that he could not submit the

---

[31] R. W. Curry, *op. cit.*, p. 252.

[32] The Council of Ten composed of two leading delegates of each of the Big Five, including France, Great Britain, Italy, Japan and the United States. The Council of Four composed of Clemenceau, Lloyd George, Orlando, and Wilson.

[33] R. W. Curry, *op. cit.*, p. 263.

agreements in question without his government's permission.   Koo, however, readily agreed to submit them to the Council.   George Clemenceau at this point revealed to Wilson that the Allies had entered into certain secret treaties with Japan concerning its claims in the Orient, further complicating the issue.[34]

Makino continued to insist that Japan would honor its agreement to return Shantung to China, but that its rights to the German leaseholds and concessions there must first be recognized by the Peace Conference. Koo maintained that China's declaration of war against Germany had ipso facto abrogated all German claims in China and superseded the Sino-Japanese agreements of 1915 and 1918.   Germany therefore had no interests in Shantung, or anywhere else in China, which could be transferred to Japan.   Koo was counting on the establishment of a new Wilsonian order in the world, for he maintained that these earlier arrangements with Japan had been merely provisional and were now subject to revision by the Peace Conference in the light of the new era of justice which was now dawning.[35]

Koo had given an eloquent defense of China's position, and was roundly congratulated by the other delegates.   Lansing, for one, thought that Koo "simply overwhelmed the Japanese with his argument."   In China there was general rejoicing.   Tokyo attempted to pressure the Chinese government into adopting a more conciliatory attitude at the conference.   This machination became known, however, and only succeeded in rousing the Chinese public to a general hatred of the Japanese and their puppet in Peking.   The delegation, encouraged by the support from home, took an increasingly tough stand in Paris, expanding its demands against Japan to include Manchuria and Mongolia.[36]

The situation initially looked hopeful.   The Japanese were embarrassed into producing a number of the secret treaties they had forced upon China, and the American delegation was most sympathetic to the Chinese cause.   But the sympathy and friendship of one of the members of the all-important Council of Four was not enough to

---

[34] Department of State, *U.S. Foreign Relations*, Paris Conference III, pp. 520-525.

[35] *Ibid.*, Paris Conference, III, pp. 755-757.

[36] W. Levi, *Modern China's Foreign Policy* (Minneapolis: University of Minnesota Press, 1953), p. 154.

guarantee victory. In fact, the secret agreements of 1917, which Japan had entered into with Britain and France, virtually guaranteed the support of these powers for the Japanese position. As a consequence, the Chinese delegation was given only a few minutes to present its case to the Council, and had to limit itself to the Shantung question.

President Wilson stood firmly with China, proposing that German interests in Shantung be restored directly to China. He based his proposal on both moral and legal grounds, as the Chinese had done earlier before the Council of Ten. The Japanese, supported by the British and French delegates, claimed that Germany's rights in Shantung were legally theirs. China's case could be won only by political maneuvering, but Wilson's standing had been so weakened by the time the Shantung question was discussed in April 1919 that his defeat on this question was certain. The American delegation suggested, as a compromise, that Shantung be placed under the joint protection of the powers with a view toward their eventual restoration to China. Japan rejected this proposal, and was no less adamantly opposed to Lloyd George's subsequent idea of making Shantung a League of Nations mandate. The Japanese delegation angrily threatened to refuse to sign the peace treaty at all if its demands were not granted.

Wilson, who was unwilling to risk losing Japan not only as a participant in the Peace Conference, but in the League of Nations he hoped would follow, decided to accept the Japanese demands. Articles 156, 157, and 158 of the Treaty of Versailles awarded Japan all former German rights in Shantung. Japan then announced that its policy would be "to hand back the Shantung Peninsula in full sovereignty to China, retaining only the economic privileges granted to Germany and the right to establish a settlement under the usual conditions in Tsingtao."[37]

Wilson tried to console the Chinese delegation with the theory that, by sacrificing Chinese interests now, he had saved the League of Nations, by means of which China's grievances might eventually be settled. The Chinese delegates replied, however, that they found Articles 156, 157, and 158 unacceptable. When the Treaty of Versailles was signed at 3 p.m. on June 28, 1919, the Chinese delegates were not present.

---

[37] M. E. Cameron, etc., *op. cit.*, p. 377.

The May Fourth Movement, 1919

News of the Shantung decision was greeted in China with anti-Japanese rioting and boycotts, followed within days by a resumption of the civil war. "Indignation, discouragement and despair are expressed throughout China," cabled Reinsch from Peking. "Anti-Japanese boycotts are being started in many places. . . . Japanese, triumphant, assert predominance in China recognized, Great Britain and France submissive, United States must admit opposition futile."[38]

The Chinese people, who felt betrayed by the Treaty of Versailles, focused their indignation on the Japanese and their collaborators in Peking. Despite the growing power of the Kuomintang in the south, the north remained under the thumb of military men, who had little concern for democracy and the niceties of parliamentary procedure. Some of these officials, such as Tsao Ju-li, Minister of Communications, Chang Chung-hsiang, Minister to Japan, and Lu Tsung-yu, who helped negotiate the 1918 treaties with Japan, were notoriously pro-Japanese.

On May 4, 1919, students from the National Peking University and other schools demonstrated against the Treaty of Versailles. After a rally, some three thousand students marched in protest to Minister Tsao's house, where secret meetings of the pro-Japanese faction were supposed to have been in progress. Tsao and Lu escaped from the mob but Chang was caught and badly beaten. The episode ended Tsao's political career.[39]

This event terrorized the pro-Japanese faction and encouraged patriots all over China. Following Peking's lead, students in many cities began to organize demonstrations and speak out against the Japanese and their puppets. The press sided with the students, newly organized labor unions struck in sympathy, and merchants joined in the boycott against Japanese goods. The student movement stirred nationalist sentiments to new heights.

The May Fourth Movement, as it came to be called, not only helped the Chinese people become conscious of their existence as a nation, it

---

[38] Reinsch to Acting Secretary of State, May 16, 1919, *U.S. Foreign Relations, 1919*, I, p. 691.

[39] Mon-lin Chiang, *Tides from the West* (Taipei: World Book Co., 1963), p. 120.

broke the back of the Confucian traditionalists who were opposed to any change. The classical style of writing was abandoned in favor of the vernacular, and the ideas and customs of traditional Confucian society were attacked.[40] American pragmatism and liberalism were everywhere admired, and democracy, science, and modern education were seen as China's salvation. There were those, it is true, who argued that Marxism, not democracy, was the proper remedy for China, but these were still a tiny minority. The May Fourth Movement laid the groundwork for the success of the Nationalist revolution.

---

[40] Among others, Chancellor Tsai Yuan-pei and Dean Hu Shih of National Peking University played a prominent role in the intellectual May Fourth Movement. The Chinese Literacy Movement, the aim of which was to bring about a thorough-going modernization of all aspects of Chinese literature, was touched off in 1916 by Hu Shih, who was then studying in the United States. He had come to advocate the urgent need for a new national literature for China, to be written in the living language of the people.

4

THE WASHINGTON CONFERENCE AND AFTER
1921–1924

The atmosphere at the end of World War I was conducive to setting up a new international order. The Central European Powers were defeated, ambitious Japan needed time to consolidate the spoils of victory, revolutionary Russia was still too weak to be a factor in international affairs, and the victorious Allies desired peace and were apparently capable of enforcing it. For a war-weary world it seemed that no moment in recent history was more opportune for establishing international peace and order on firm foundations.

On the negative side, however, the League of Nations had come into existence minus the United States. Discord and friction were festering over rights in the Pacific islands and East Asia. Japan continued to make advances in China. Rising political tensions and economic necessity demanded an end to the naval arms race that Japan and other powers had embarked upon. The Anglo-Japanese Alliance, of concern to both China and the U.S., needed to be checked. Relations between China and the Allied powers needed clarification. It was with these problems in mind that President Warren G. Harding, who succeeded Wilson in the White House, took the initiative in convening what came to be known as the Washington Conference.[1]

---

[1] For details, see Westel W. Willoughby, *China at the Conference, A Report* (Baltimore: Johns Hopkins Press, 1922).

Nine nations were invited to participate in the conference. The five principal Allied powers, Great Britain, France, Italy, Japan, and the United States, would try to reach agreement on a proposed limitation on naval armaments. Four more nations—China, Belgium, the Netherlands, and Portugal—would join the deliberations over the situation in the Pacific and Far East.

The Peking government welcomed the opportunity to present China's accumulated grievances to the world. The Chinese press presented the upcoming forum as a kind of international court at which Japan would be forced to stand trial for the misdeeds of her militarists in China. Not only would the Shantung settlements be overturned in China's favor, but sympathetic attention would be given to numerous other grievances such as the tariffs, extraterritoriality, and foreign concessions.[2]

The reactionary government in Peking was hardly in a position to take advantage of the opportunity presented by the conference, however. In the words of the new American Minister, Jacob Gould Schurman, this government had "virtually ceased to function," and faced the real possibility of financial collapse. By October 1921 it owed an estimated $376,000,000 in unsecured loans, in addition to $50,000,000 in short-term notes held by Chinese banks. Moreover, it had failed to meet payments on a $5,500,000 loan held by the Continental and Commercial Bank of Chicago, which had damaged its international credit.[3]

Even more serious than the financial chaos in Peking was the disunity that continued to rack the country. On May 5, 1921, Sun Yat-sen was sworn into office as President of the Republic of China, having been elected by parliament in an extraordinary session. The new government in Canton recognized neither the legality nor the authority of the Peking regime.

---

[2] R. T. Pollard, *China's Foreign Relations, 1917-1931* (New York: MacMillan Co., 1933), pp. 205-206.

[3] This default led to a protest by the U.S. Department of State. Subsequently the representative of Dr. Sun Yat-sen in Washington, Ma Soo, notified State Department that with a view of protecting the credit of the Chinese nation, the Canton Government was willing to assume responsibility for the refunding and ultimate payment of this loan. *China Review* I, November 1921, p. 314 and December 1921, p. 346; cited in R. T. Pollard, *Ibid.*, p. 206.

Instead, Sun's government sought separate recognition from the U.S. and other countries, along with an invitation to send its own delegation to the Washington Conference. Secretary of State Charles Evans Hughes was notified that the Minister of Foreign Affairs in Canton, Wu T'ing-fang, had declared that the Canton government would insist on separate representation. Despite enthusiastic reports by the local American consul of the achievements of the Canton government, however, Washington rejected these overtures, continuing to treat the rump Peking regime as the sole legitimate authority in China.

Reservations of China and Other States

When the U.S. Government failed to support the Canton government's bid to send a second Chinese delegation to the conference, President Sun announced that none of the decisions of the conference relating to China would "be recognized as having any validity or force."[4] He also rejected suggestions that his government send an unofficial delegation.

On October 6, 1921, the president of the Peking government, Hsu Shih-ch'ang, appointed four delegates to the Conference: Sao-ke Alfred Sze, Minister to the U.S.; V. K. Wellington Koo, Minister to Great Britain; Wang Chung-hui, Chief Justice of the Supreme Court; and Wu Chao-shu, Vice President of the Board of Foreign Affairs in Canton. Wu was included over his objections to represent the government in Canton, but immediately telegraphed Peking to decline the appointment.

Japan, although it had much at stake, was originally reluctant to attend the Washington Conference. The feeling in Tokyo was that the U.S. intended to compensate for its nonparticipation in the League of Nations by adopting an extremely firm policy in the Far East. The Japanese chose nonetheless to send a delegation, which consisted of Prince Tokugawa, President of the House of Peers; Tomosaburo Kato, Minister of the Navy; Kijuro Shidehara, Ambassador in Washington; and M. Hanihara, Vice Minister for Foreign Affairs. This was the beginning of the so-called "liberal decade" in Japan (1921-1931), when Tokyo was

---

4   Letter signed by Sun Yat-sen and Wu T'ing-fang, transmitted by Ma Soo to Secretary Hughes, *China Review* I, October 1921, p. 232.

generally cooperative with the Western powers and pursued a less aggressive policy in China than previously.[5]

Great Britain, which at the time included England, Canada, and Australia, took an active interest in the solution of Far Eastern questions. The British government was under particular pressure from Canada not to renew the Anglo-Japanese Alliance, which was due to expire in July 1921, and had itself gradually come round to this view. France, which like Russia and Japan, claimed a sphere of interest in China, had leased territories and an economic stake in the republic. Italy was invited because of its status as one of the five naval powers, though it had few interests in the Far East. Among the other states, the Netherlands was invited by reason of its large colonial possessions in the East, Portugal for its possession of Macao, and Belgium because of its financial interests in Chinese railways. Russia was not invited because the U.S was unwilling to have any relations with the Soviet authorities.[6]

The Progress of the Conference

The Washington Conference opened in Washington, D.C., on November 12, 1921. The U.S. Secretary of State, Charles Evans Hughes, was elected chairman and, to the astonishment of the delegates, immediately proposed that "preparations for offensive war stop now." He offered a plan to reduce naval strength according to an agreed-upon ratio, which was finally fixed at 5-5-3-1.7-1.7.[7] This involved the sinking or scrapping of some ships by the three naval powers, along with a holiday in the construction of new capital ships for ten years. The American proposal carried the day, although the Japanese managed to have included in the final treaty a limit on the fortification of certain Pacific islands, including the Philippines and the Aleutians. The effect of

---

[5] M. C. Cameron, T. H. D. Mahoney & G. E. McReynolds, *China, Japan and the Powers* (New York: Ronald Press, 1952), p. 442.

[6] H. M. Vinacke, *A History of the Far East in Modern Times* (New York: Appleton-Century-Crofts, 1959), pp. 420-421.

[7] Great Britain, 5; United States, 5; Japan, 3; France, 1.7; Italy, 1.7.

the agreement was to make it impossible for any one naval power to fight an offensive war in the Pacific alone.[8]

The "Limitation of Armaments" was the first order of business of the conference. The second was "Pacific and Far Eastern Question," the agenda for which read like a summary of U.S. foreign policy in the Far East. China was the primary focus, and topics here included China's territorial and administrative integrity; the "Open Door" and equality of commercial and industrial opportunity; concessions, monopolies or preferential economic privileges of the powers; and preferential railway rates, tariffs, and loans.

From November 12, 1921, to February 6, 1922, the five-power committee on disarmament and the nine-power committee on the Pacific and Far Eastern questions held parallel sessions. The business of the twin committees was sifted through by groups of experts and numerous subcommittees before being acted upon in plenary sessions of the conference as a whole. However, real control of the conference was in the hands of Hughes, Balfour, and Kato of Japan, who became the "big three" at Washington much in the same way that Wilson, Lloyd George, and Clemenceau had been at Paris. Their secret negotiations underlay the public debates and largely governed their outcome.[9]

The Washington Conference resulted in seven treaties and agreements and twelve resolutions. While it was in progress, a new Sino-Japanese agreement and Japanese-American treaty were also concluded.

Committee On The Pacific And Far Eastern Question

One important goal of the Washington Conference, as far as the U.S. was concerned, was to halt Japan's advances in China and to help stabilize chaotic political and financial conditions by concerted international action. For its part, China hoped that some of the existing infringements on its sovereign rights would be removed, yet feared at the same time further encroachments. The U.S. and Britain saw that the

---

[8] S. F. Bemis, *A Short History of American Foreign Policy and Diplomacy* (New York: Henry Holt Co., 1959), pp. 458-459.

[9] A. W. Griswold, *The Far Eastern Policy of the United States* (New York: McGraw Hill, 1968), pp. 305-306.

relations of the powers with China needed to be governed by certain guiding principles, although their purpose was primarily to preserve the status quo. The principles they sought to codify were by no means new, although this was the first time they would be pledged in a multilateral context.

With the exception of items relating to the Pacific islands and Eastern Siberia, the Committee on the Pacific and Far Eastern Questions devoted itself entirely to China. Thirty of the thirty-one sessions of the Committee concerned her problems and claims. These ranged from relatively simple topics, such as the abolition of foreign postal agencies and radio stations, to far more complex problems such as the restoration of tariff autonomy and the abolition of extraterritorial rights. There was also the thorny question of Shantung. Indeed, it appeared as though the entire corpus of the unequal treaties and ancillary agreements had been brought to the Conference for a thorough review.

A number of these issues were addressed in a series of resolutions which were adopted by the Conference at its various plenary sessions. These resolutions concerned the following items: 1) Establishment of a Board of Reference for Far Eastern questions; 2) Relinquishment of extraterritoriality (with China concurring by virtue of an additional resolution); 3) Abolition of foreign postal agencies (agreed to by the four powers having post offices in China, namely, Japan, France, Great Britain, and the United States); 4) Withdrawal of foreign armed forces (China not voting); 5) Elimination of foreign radio stations; 6) Unification of Chinese railways; 7) Reduction of Chinese armed forces; 8) Review of the commitments of China or with respect to China; and 9) Possession and control of the Chinese Eastern Railway.[10]

With the exception of the two concerning the foreign postal agencies and radio stations, these resolutions offered no definite solution to the problems with which they were concerned. At best they provided a procedure for taking future action; at worst they merely expressed a desire to that end.

---

[10] W. King, *China at the Washington Conference 1921-1922* (New York: St. John's University Press, 1963), pp. 4-5.

The Nine Power Treaty Relating to Principles and Policies to be Followed in Matters Concerning China

At the first meeting of the Pacific and Far Eastern Committee, held on November 16, 1921, the head of the Chinese delegation, Alfred Sze, presented a list of ten general principles for the consideration of the Conference. The powers were asked to respect China's territorial integrity and administrative independence, to remove limitations on her political jurisdiction and administrative freedom, to review treaty privileges already in existence and set a definite time for their expiration, and to nullify any concessions made without public knowledge. The powers were also asked not to conclude, among themselves, any agreement affecting China without her prior knowledge. In return, China undertook not to alienate or lease any portion of her territory or littoral region to any power and to apply the principle of the Open Door to all countries with which she has treaty relations. Sze concluded by proposing that periodic conferences be convened to discuss international questions relative to the Pacific and Far East.[11]

The Chinese delegation hoped that the Conference would first adopt its Ten Point Program, and then go on to apply the general principles it embodied to specific issues concerning China. If the Conference first committed itself to general principles, these might even be given a certain retroactive force. The other delegations rejected this approach, however, preferring to discuss concrete issues. The one exception was the Open Door policy, which the Americans desired to have restated in treaty form.

Elihu Root drafted a resolution on this question, consisting of the four clauses which bear his name. This resolution was submitted to the Committee on its third meeting, on November 21, and was approved after only two hours of discussion. It had not been shown to the members of the Chinese delegation prior to its presentation, although they did not ask

---

[11] One evening, four days after the opening of the Conference, the Chinese delegation was given only ten hours notice to present its case. These four days had been sufficient to indicate that the mood of the conference was not favorable to an elaborate discussion of China's problems. So all through the night the delegates worked to reduce their programs to ten points. Cited in W. Levi, *Modern China's Foreign Policy* (Minneapolis: University of Minnesota Press, 1953), p. 161.

for an extended discussion.[12]   The four clauses, as finally adopted by the
Conference, were as follows:

> The contracting Powers, other than China, agree:
> 1. To respect the sovereignty, the independence and the
>   territorial and administrative integrity of China;
> 2. To provide the fullest and most unembarrassed opportunity
>   to China to develop and maintain for herself an effective and
>   stable government;
> 3. To use their influence for the purpose of effectually
>   establishing and maintaining the principle of equal
>   opportunity for the commerce and industry of all nations
>   throughout the territory of China;
> 4. To refrain from taking advantage of conditions in China in
>   order to seek the rights of subjects or citizens of friendly
>   States and from countenancing action inimical to the
>   security of such States.[13]

Elihu Root stated that these principles were not intended to be
retroactive or to modify existing treaties and agreements.   Rather, they
merely summed up views previously expressed by the powers during
sessions of the Conference or in past exchanges of notes and declarations.
This interpretation was generally accepted, although not without
questions from the Chinese delegation.

Concerned about the purpose and implications of the fourth principle,
Chinese delegate V. K. Wellington Koo sought clarification.   He
suggested that, while the draft resolution clearly took the status quo as a
point of departure, it could not be intended to maintain and still less to
perpetuate such conditions, which impaired China's sovereign rights.
Chairman Hughes merely replied that these would be particular
questions. Curious about the use of the word "security" in the latter part
of the fourth clause, British delegate Balfour also queried how the
security of any state would be affected, although he did not press the
point.[14]

---

[12] W. King, *op. cit.*, pp. 31-32.
[13] *Conference on the Limitation of Armaments*, Washington, 1922, pp. 890-900.
[14] W. King, *op. cit.*, pp. 32-33.

A careful examination of the record reveals the origins of the fourth clause. The first part of the fourth clause—that is, that the rights of other states not be abridged—was actually a reaffirmation of the secret promise made by Japan as part of the Lansing-Ishii Agreement of 1917. As for the second part, when the Four-Power Consortium was formed, Japan had urged the exclusion of certain regions of Manchuria and Mongolia from the pooling arrangements on the grounds that Japan's national and economic security would be adversely affected. Japan eventually withdrew this demand, having obtained formal assurances from the United States, Great Britain, and France that the Consortium would not undertake any operations prejudicial to the economic life or national defense of Japan. As W. W. Willoughby has correctly observed, "one sees in this language a possible source of some of the words of the fourth Resolution adopted by the Conference." Willoughby also points out that this clause was unlike the other three in that it was not based "upon statements previously made in the Committee by the several Delegations." In fact Elihu Root "had received no specific instruction from the Committee to frame and introduce [this clause]," which "was initiated by the American delegation upon its own responsibility."[15] The two parts of the fourth clause complement one another, confirming the Japanese position in Manchuria in return for safeguarding the rights of other powers in China proper.

The four Root principles were incorporated into the Nine Power Treaty as Article I. In addition, in Article II, the signatories agreed "not to enter into any treaty, agreement, arrangement, or understanding either with one another, or, individually or collectively, with any Power or Powers, which would infringe or impair the principles stated in Article I."

Article III of the treaty even more explicitly reaffirmed the Open Door policy, pledging the powers not to seek "any superiority of rights with respect to commercial or economic development in any designated region of China," nor "any such monopoly or preference as would deprive the nationals of any other Power of the right of undertaking any legitimate trade or industry in China."

The remaining articles bound the signatories not to support their nationals in seeking spheres of influence or "mutually exclusive

---

15 W. W. Willoughby, *op. cit.*, p. 197, p. 43.

opportunities in designated parts of Chinese territory," to respect China's neutrality in case of war to which she was not a party, and to communicate fully and frankly among themselves whenever circumstances required. China agreed not to countenance any form for railway rate discrimination, which was one of the principal points of the original Hay notes. Finally, all nonsignatories having relations with China were invited to adhere to the treaty.[16]

The powers also noted in a separate declaration that "China upon her part is prepared to give an understanding not to alienate or lease any portion of her territory or littoral to any power."[17]

These commitments remained the basis for foreign activities in China until the Japanese offensive of 1931. However, those in China who opposed the Nine Power Treaty felt it was demeaning for a sovereign nation to seek a guarantee of independence from other nations. The Open Door principle, they argued, was merely a cover for the joint aggression of all the foreign powers against China.[18]

The Nine Power Treaty and the Chinese Customs Tariff

Constantly in financial embarrassment and jealous of her sovereign rights, China attached great importance to including the question of customs tariffs on the Conference agenda, with a view to an early restoration of tariff autonomy. When China submitted a tentative agenda for the Conference on October 19, 1921, the conspicuous omission of the Shantung question, as such, was matched by the equally conspicuous presence of the question of tariff autonomy. In a conversation with Hughes on November 5 Sze again expressed the desire of the Chinese government to bring up the question of tariffs, suggesting that this could

---

16 The Nine Power Treaty was signed in Washington, February 6, 1922, by Belgium, the British Empire, France, Italy, Japan, the Netherlands, and Portugal; adhered to by Bolivia, Denmark, Mexico, Norway, and Sweden; in force from August 5, 1925, United States Treaty Series No. 723, Washington, 1925.

17 *Conference on the Limitation of Armaments*, Washington, 1922, pp. 894, 898.

18 Sharp internal differences had also arisen within the Chinese delegation. A few members felt uneasy because of alleged pressure from the English speaking delegates upon the Chinese delegation for compromise. Cited in W. King, *op. cit.*, pp. 34-35.

be done under the heading of the administrative integrity of China.[19] When presenting China's Ten Point Program a few days later, Sze was emphatic in demanding that China be freed from various constraints which deprived her of the ability to act autonomously in administrative matters and prevented her from securing adequate public revenues. The question of customs tariffs was therefore included in the proposals concerning China's administrative integrity.

The Subcommittee on Chinese Revenue, chaired by Oscar W. Underwood, minority leader of the U.S. Senate, held six meetings from November 29, 1921, to January 4, 1922. China proposed the immediate increase of the tariff schedule to 12 1/2 percent, the abolition of likin, and the levy of certain surtaxes, to be followed within a short period of time with the establishment of a new treaty regime with a definite cut-off date.[20] Ten years from the date that the new treaty was signed, all treaties and agreements relating to the customs tariff and its administration would be abrogated.

The Chinese delegation did not mention the upward revision of the tariff schedule from the actual rate of 3 1/2 percent to the treaty rate of 5 per cent, taking for granted that this would occur.[21] In fact, this was the only point on which agreement could be obtained. A further increase in the tariff schedule was opposed by the powers. Even China's willingness to impose surtaxes in return for the abolition of likin met with objections, namely, that it would take too long to put these changes into execution. Many of the powers did not want an increase in China's customs revenue for fear that the additional revenue, instead of going to the central government, might be absorbed by the provisional military governors and cause further internal division. The restoration of China's tariff autonomy, at least in the foreseeable future, was virtually ruled out.[22]

---

[19] Department of State, *U.S. Foreign Relations, 1921*, Vol. I, pp. 70-82.

[20] Likin–A provincial transit duty in China on commodities which was originally levied to meet the expenditures of the military campaigns against the Taiping rebels in the middle of the 19th century. It was finally abolished in 1929. Department of State, *U.S. Foreign Relations, 1921*, Vol. I, pp. 70-82.

[21] Treaties of 1843 and 1844 between China and Great Britain, and America, and France, and subsequently with other countries.

[22] W. King, *op. cit.*, pp. 40-41.

The Nine Power Treaty relating to the Chinese Custom Tariff was signed at Washington on February 6, 1922, to take effect on the date all contracting powers deposited ratifications. The upward revision of the tariff schedule to 5 percent, which was not conditioned on ratification, was completed immediately. In due time, all the powers except France ratified the treaty.[23]

Disappointed by this result, China unilaterally declared on January 5, 1922, that it enjoyed the right to exercise full tariff autonomy. Over the next few years, it continued to urge the powers in this direction. On July 25, 1928, this effort bore its first fruit. An agreement was signed in Peking between the U.S. and China annulling all treaty provisions relating to tariff matters and restoring tariff autonomy to China, subject to the restrictions of the most-favored-nation clause. The American lead was followed by other powers and lastly, by a reluctant Japan. The first Chinese national tariff was established in February 1929. The structure of the unequal treaties, imposed on China nearly a century before, had finally begun to crack.

The Shantung Question at Washington

Between the Paris Conference of 1919 and the Washington Conference of 1921, the United States and, to a lesser extent, Great Britain, had exerted more or less continuous pressure on Japan to honor her promise to restore her rights and concessions in Shantung to China. This effort proved futile, as did a series of notes exchanged between China and Japan on this subject. Both sides were firmly entrenched in their respective positions. Japan repeatedly proposed opening direct negotiations, but on her own terms, which China found unacceptable. On the eve of the Washington Conference, Hughes was informally approached by Japan with the request that he try and bring the Chinese to the negotiating table, but he met with no more success than had Japan. Mindful of public opinion at home, China steadfastly refused to enter into

---

[23] France delayed her ratification until 1925 when a dispute between her and China, known as the Gold Franc controversy, was settled to the satisfaction of France so that the Boxer Indemnity payments would be made in gold francs.

direct negotiations with Japan.   The stalemate continued until the Washington Conference was convened.

Now China had the international forum she had long sought in which to discuss Shantung, but the U.S. dissuaded the Chinese delegation from bringing up the question, pointing out that most of the participating countries considered themselves bound by the relevant clauses in the Versailles Treaty.   Japan, too, firmly opposed U.S. efforts to mediate a solution, accepting Washington's invitation to attend the Conference only on condition that such matters "as are sole concerns to certain particular Powers or such matters that may be regarded accomplished facts should be scrupulously avoided."[24]   Japan obviously desired to exclude the Shantung problem from the agenda.

It was due to the good offices of Hughes and Balfour that negotiations on the Shantung question were held at all during the time of the Washington Conference, though technically detached from it.   Hughes and Balfour brought Chinese and Japanese representatives together for the first time on December 1, 1921, indicated their readiness to render service should circumstances call for their friendly intervention, and then withdrew.   The two sides then carried on their negotiations in the presence of observers, including John Van Antwerp MacMurray, chief of the Far Eastern Division of the U.S. State Department.

Eleven items were discussed in thirty-six separate meetings held over the course of two months.   These were the restoration of Kiaochow, the transfer of public properties, the withdrawal of Japanese troops, the maritime customs at Tsingtao, the Tsingtao-Tsinanfu Railway, the extensions of the Tsingtao-Tsinanfu Railway, the mining industry, the opening of Kiaochow, the salt industry, submarine cables, and wireless status.[25]

The most difficult question proved to be the Tsingtao-Tsinanfu Railway, which had been constructed by Germany at the turn of the century.   The railroad ran through the heart of Shangtung province, and

---

24   Telegram from Hughes to American Legation in Peking and American Embassy in Tokyo, September 19, 1921, *U.S. Foreign Relations*, 1921, Vol. I, p. 621. Hughes stated, "it is necessary, constantly to bear in mind, however, that the United States cannot place itself, in any phase of the negotiations, in the position of either acting or appearing to act as an attorney for either China or Japan."

25   W. King, *op. cit.*, p. 11.

its control by Japan created de facto a sphere of influence in her favor. Foreign control of a railroad carried with it the threat of economic exploitation, political penetration, and military intervention, as could be seen along the Japanese-controlled South Manchurian Railway, where this particular kind of imperialism was full-blown.

The Japanese initially proposed that the railroad be operated as a joint enterprise, but this proved unacceptable to the Chinese delegation. Next, the Japanese suggested that China purchase the railroad, using funds borrowed from Japan, and that, during the term of this loan, a number of Japanese managers and engineers be employed. This proposal, too, was rejected. While the negotiations turned to other issues, Hughes and Balfour sought to mediate a compromise on the matter of the railroad, arranging informal discussions with the two delegations. During one such meeting on January 18, 1922, the Japanese made what they considered to be their maximum concession. The Chinese were to purchase the railroad, using Chinese treasury notes redeemable after five years. The director-general of the railroad was to be Chinese, but the traffic manager and one of two chief accountants were to be Japanese.[26]

Hughes and Balfour promised to encourage the Chinese side to accept this compromise, realizing that the entire matter of Shantung would go unresolved if agreement could not be reached on this key issue. In discussions with the Chinese delegates on January 19 and 22, Hughes reminded them that the situation was serious. The Japanese, having actual possession of the railroad, could not be compelled to withdraw except by force if an agreement were not reached. Moreover, the Japanese delegation, in retreating from its original position of operating the railroad as a joint enterprise, had in fact made large concessions to China. Either accept Japan's offer, Hughes told the Chinese side, or face the irretrievable loss of Shangtung. Balfour expressed similar views.

Hughes cabled the American Minister in Peking, Jacob G. Schurman, with instructions to press Peking to accept the terms offered. "I have the President's authority for stating this," Hughes wrote on January 22, "The Chinese should realize that if they choose to break off negotiations they cannot count on any support either from public sentiment in the United States or from this government." When Peking still hesitated, President

---

[26] Department of State, *U.S. Foreign Relations, 1922*, Vol. I, p. 942.

Harding himself met with Sze on January 25, 1922, telling him that "it would be a colossal blunder in statecraft if China were not to take advantage of the opportunity now offered her for the settlement of the Shangtung question as the alternative might involve a risk of losing the province."[27]

The Peking government, under the leadership of President Hsu Shih-ch'ang and his acting Premier and Foreign Minister, W. W. Yen, decided to accept the terms, notwithstanding some strong opposition within the cabinet. Yen felt that the terms were better than could have been expected under the circumstances, although others were of the opinion that heavy pressure from Americans and British had pushed Peking into accepting a settlement unfavorable to China.[28]

Once the railroad question had been resolved, other differences were overcome with comparative ease, and the talks came to a successful close. The two delegations then separately communicated to the U.S. Secretary of State the substance of the terms agreed upon. On February 1, 1922, Hughes read the Sino-Japanese Treaty Relative to Shantung into the record of the Washington Conference at the Fifth Plenary Session. Four days later, with Hughes and Balfour serving as witnesses, the Treaty was signed by the Chinese and Japanese chief delegates.

As provided for in the Treaty, the complete withdrawal of Japanese troops stationed along the Tsingtao-Tsinanfu Railway was accomplished before the June 1922 date on which the Treaty was to come into effect. The Kiaochow Leased Territory was transferred from Japan to China in October of that same year, while the port of Tsingtao was handed back the following month. The formal transfer of the railroad to China took place on January 1, 1923, the Japanese receiving 40,000,000 Japanese yen, roughly $19,000,000 in treasury notes in exchange.[29] So it was that Japan finally carried out the promises made to President Wilson and the world at the Paris Conference.

---

[27] *Ibid.*, p. 945.
[28] W. King, *op. cit.*, pp. 23-24.
[29] H. H. Ling, *Chung Kuo Tieh-Lu Chih (A Comprehensive Survey of Railway Development in China, 1963)*, (Taipei: World Book Co., 1963), p. 106.

Related Issues at the Washington Conference

If the Shantung question was resolved largely to China's satisfaction, the Washington Conference failed to find solutions to many of that country's other concerns. Only the Anglo-Japanese Alliance and the Lansing-Ishii Agreement were disposed of at the Conference. Other issues—the Twenty-One Demands, the leased territories, and extraterritoriality—were settled only partially or not at all.

The Anglo-Japanese Alliance was a source of concern not only for China, but for the United States and other countries as well. Indeed, even Britain was occasionally embarrassed by her commitments to Japan. At the Washington Conference the Alliance was replaced with the Four Power Treaty of December 13, 1921, whose signatories were the United States, Great Britain, France, and Japan. These powers agreed to respect one another's insular possessions in the Pacific and to consider, in the event of a threatening situation, common measures for collective security. Still more unpopular, at least in China, was the Lansing-Ishii Agreement of 1917, which asserted that "territorial propinquity" created special relations between neighboring countries. This Agreement was superseded by the reinvigorated Open Door policy adopted at the Conference, and was formally terminated by an exchange of notes between Hughes and Japanese Ambassador Hanihara in Washington on April 14, 1923.

The Twenty-One Demands were to prove more intractable, despite the hostility and indignation they continued to arouse in China and the U.S. The Chinese delegation raised the issue, the resulting treaties and notes at the Washington Conference and asked for their abrogation on the grounds that they had been obtained by force. The Japanese delegate, Kijuro Shidehara, at the February 2, 1923, meeting of the Committee of the Whole, made clear his government's position:

> If it should once be recognized that rights solemnly granted by treaty may be revoked at any time on the ground that they were conceded against the will of the grantor, an exceedingly dangerous precedent will be established, with far-reaching consequences upon the

establishment of the existing international relations in Asia, in Europe and everywhere.[30]

To which the Chinese delegate, Wang Chung-hui, replied the following day:

> A still more dangerous precedent will be established . . . if, without rebuke or protest from other Powers, one nation can obtain from a friendly, but in a military sense, weaker neighbor, and under circumstances such as attended the negotiation and signing of the treaties of 1915, valuable concessions which were not in satisfaction of pending controversies and for which no quid pro quo was offered.[31]

In Secretary of State Hughes, the Chinese delegation had a staunch ally in its attack on the Twenty-One Demands. Great Britain and France, however, were no less committed to the Japanese position, for they knew that to accept the Chinese position would undermine the Treaty of Versailles, to whose defense both were firmly committed. Moreover, these two powers were no more willing to relinquish their Chinese spheres and leaseholds than Japan. Without the active support of London and Paris, Hughes's chances of ousting Japan from Manchuria were no better than Knox's or Lansing's.

The result of the debate was most unsatisfactory for China. The Japanese delegation made only a few predictable concessions, agreeing to withdraw the Group V demands, for example, which had already met with insuperable obstacles in practice. They also agreed to relinquish certain preferential rights which would have violated the principle of the Open Door. For its part, China reserved the right to continue to seek a solution to the Twenty-One Demands during future negotiations.

The Washington Conference did little to improve China's situation vis-à-vis Japan. Indeed, Japan's position in Manchuria may have actually been strengthened by the obvious unwillingness of the powers to support China's request that the treaties in question, in particular the South Manchurian Treaty, be abrogated. Japan's position was so

---

[30] *Conference on the Limitation of Armaments*, Washington, 1922, p. 1580.
[31] *Ibid.*, pp. 1556-1560.

impregnable, Elihu Root remarked, that "it would be impossible to expel her unless by force."[32]

As far as the Leased Territories were concerned, China was able to improve its position slightly. There were originally five such Territories in China: two in Shantung province, Kiaochow leased to Germany and Weihaiwei to Britain; two in Kwangtung province, Kwangchow-wan leased to France and Kowloon to Britain; and Port Arthur and Dairen on the Liaotung peninsula, both of which were first leased to Russia and subsequently to Japan.

At the December 3 meeting of the Committee, Wellington Koo asked "for the annulment or early termination of these leases." Leased Territories, he argued, "greatly prejudiced China's territorial and administrative integrity, constituted virtually an 'imperio,' hampered its national defense, and constituted 'points d'appui' for developing spheres of interest to the detriment of the principle of all nations in China." Pending the termination of such leases, Koo went on, the territories concerned should be demilitarized. Following the return of these areas, the Chinese government would respect and safeguard the legitimate vested interests of the different powers there.[33]

Koo's proposal came up against the combined opposition of France, Britain, and Japan, although some gains were made in Shantung, with Kiaochow and Weihaiwei restored to China. Japan would not return her Manchurian leaseholds, nor would Britain return Kowloon. France, for her part, stated she would only join in a collective restoration.

Concerning the issue of extraterritoriality, Chinese delegate Wang Chung-hui argued that it had become superfluous, as China had recently make much progress in the reform of her judiciary and the codification of her laws. He asked that the powers set a definite date by which to abolish their systems of consular jurisdiction. Hughes responded by suggesting that, before this step was taken, an inquiry should be conducted into the actual conditions then existing in China.

The Washington Conference thereupon adopted a resolution calling for the establishment of a commission to inquire into the actual practice

---

[32] V. K. Wellington Koo's interview with Elihu Root, December 15, 1921 at the Navy Building, Washington, D.C. cited in W. King, *op. cit.*, p. 51.

[33] *Conference on the Limitation of Armaments*, Washington, 1922, pp. 1060-1062.

of consular jurisdiction as well as into the laws and judicial system of China. The mandated commission of inquiry was created in Peking in January 1926, and spent almost a year on its investigations. The report it issued, which recommended the gradual abolition of extraterritoriality, was shelved, however.[34] Neither did the separate negotiation conducted by China with several powers in the late 1920's produce any result, although they did make it clear that the powers were only prepared to surrender their rights collectively.

The Conference adopted several other important resolutions concerning China. Foreign post offices and foreign radio stations were to be withdrawn from Chinese territory, except for the leased areas and, in the case of the radio stations, the Manchurian railway zone. Foreign troops were to be withdrawn from the territory of China whenever the representatives in Peking should find it expedient.

Evaluating the Conference

The Washington Conference came to a close on February 6, 1922. In the withdrawal of the Japanese from Shantung, and the laying of a foundation for tariff autonomy, China had scored two major successes. Expectations had been so high going into the Conference, however, that these limited results failed to excite the public. The tone of the official Peking communiqué announcing them even indicated disappointment. The press was even less complimentary. One newspaper pointed out that not a single concession in favor of China had been made with even a semblance of good grace or without some condition attached to it—even though all the concessions referred to privileges which China had never been willing to grant in the first place.[35]

The Chinese delegation was not entirely blameless for the generality of the Nine Power Treaty which resulted. They had decided at the outset to discuss abstract principles rather than concrete issues, thus allowing the powers to avoid making specific commitments. "The Ten Point Program," later commented an American adviser to the Chinese

---

[34] W. King, *op. cit.*, p. 52. Text of the Report published by Department of State, Washington, 1927.
[35] W. Levi, *op. cit.*, p. 164.

delegation, "defined China's position in language so mystifying to the general public and so consolatory to the bureaucracy, as only general principles were involved, that there was an almost audible sigh of relief from the U.S. delegation which had greatly feared that China at one blow would mobilize the immense force of American public opinion and sweep the field."[36]

In the United States, the Washington Conference was hailed as a brilliant diplomatic achievement, for it had resolved the Shantung question and a number of other issues left unsettled at the Paris Peace Conference. Evaluations of the Nine Power Treaties ranged from a deprecatory characterization of them as "a face-saving retreat of the United States from active diplomacy in the Far East"[37] to enthusiastic praise as "the apotheosis of the traditional Far Eastern Policy of the United States."[38]

The essential U.S. impetus, apart from an interest in naval disarmament, was a desire to put an end to imperialistic diplomacy in China. In fact, "the treaties went as far as pen and ink could go to preserve a peace founded on such antithetical elements as those inherent in the status quo in the Far East."[39]

The Nine Power Treaties of 1922 represented a reasonably clear and fairly unequivocal acceptance by other powers of American views on China, namely, respect for its independence and territorial integrity, renunciation of spheres of influence, and deference to the Open Door policy of equal commercial opportunity for all nations.

---

[36] *North China Herald* (Lennox B. Simpson), January 28, 1922.
[37] S. F. Bemis, *op. cit.*, p. 460.
[38] A. W. Griswold, *op. cit.*, p. 331.
[39] *Ibid.*, p. 331.

5

THE FORMATIVE PERIOD OF THE NATIONAL GOVERNMENT 1925–1930

I. UNIFICATION OF CHINA UNDER THE KUOMINTANG

The Rise of New Nationalism

The special rights and privileges enjoyed by foreigners in China survived the Washington Conference intact. Despite pressure from the Chinese delegation, whose views reflected the growing nationalist fervor of the Chinese public, the nine powers conceded only that the unequal treaties might be revised after China achieved an "effective and stable government." The Tariff Conference and the Commission on Extraterritoriality were both delayed for several years by almost continuous civil strife.

The only concession made to Chinese nationalistic feeling was the remission of the balance of the Boxer Indemnity payments. On May 21, 1924, the U.S. Congress authorized that the balance of the indemnity due ($6,127,552.90), be remitted to the Chinese government "in order to further develop the educational and other cultural activities of China."[1] Other European powers followed the U.S. example, strengthening the Chinese system of higher education as well as making it possible for many Chinese students to pursue studies in America and Europe.

---

[1] H. F. MacNair, and D. F. Lach, *Modern Far Eastern International Relations* (New York: D. Van Nostrand, 1955), p. 219.

Though this was to create much goodwill over the years, it had little immediate impact on the intense anti-foreign sentiments of Chinese students.

Following his election as President of the Military Government of the Republic of China in 1917, Dr. Sun Yat-sen set about organizing a modern democratic government in South China. The plan for the political and economic reconstruction of China which Sun gradually devised was elaborated in its fullest form in a series of lectures he delivered in Canton in the early months of 1924.[2]   In these lectures, which soon became the holy writ of Chinese nationalism, Sun advocated three principles which, if adopted, would not only guarantee China's survival as a nation but ensure that she regained her ancient greatness. These principles were nationalism, democracy, and the people's livelihood. Nationalism meant the overthrow of imperialism and the achievement of equality with other nations. Democracy meant the replacement of militarism and despotism with a system of constitutional form of government based on separation of powers. The people's livelihood referred to a far-reaching program of social welfare which would improve the economic well-being of the masses.

Sun realized that such an ambitious program for the reconstruction of China could only be achieved in stages. First, reactionary militarists must be overthrown by military force. Then, the people must be educated to accept their political responsibilities during a period of tutelage by an intelligent and purposeful minority. Thus would Sun's third and final stage be achieved: a constitutional government in which the people would rule themselves through popularly elected representatives.

When the U.S., Japan, and Britain refused to aid his program of nation-building, Sun decided to accept an offer of support from Soviet Russia. ' Though not himself a communist, he agreed to collaborate with the Soviets on a limited basis to further his revolutionary cause. The new arrangement was announced in January 1923 in a joint statement by Sun

---

2   *San Min Chu I*, or *The Three Principles of the People*, edited by L. T. Chen and translated into English by Frank W. Price, Shanghai, 1927. It has also been translated into English with abridgment and adaptation by Baen Lee, and published by The Commercial Press, Shanghai, 1929.

and the Soviet representative, Adolph Joffe. The statement made clear that Sun believed that communism was inappropriate for China, that Joffe agreed that China needed unity and independence, and that Soviet aid was intended to further the Chinese nationalist revolution.[3]

Convinced that the nationalist revolution could only succeed if radical measures were taken, Sun imposed rigid party discipline on KMT members and strengthened the party's organizational structure. He also permitted members of the tiny Chinese Communist Party, which had been founded in Shanghai only two years before, to be admitted into the KMT on an individual basis. With the advice of Comintern organizer Michael Borodin, a revolutionary strategy based on winning popular support through the establishment of labor unions, peasant unions, and other mass organizations was adopted. Finally, a revolutionary army was created. These measures immediately injected new life into the revolutionary government in Canton.

Sun did not live to see his ideal of a united, free, and prosperous Chinese republic fulfilled. He was struck down by cancer on March 12, 1925. The day before his death he signed his last will and testament, enjoining his followers not to abandon the revolutionary cause to which he had devoted forty years of his life.[4]

The revolutionary movement was enormously strengthened by the outburst of popular indignation which followed a series of clashes between Chinese and foreigners in 1925. On May 30 striking workers from a Japanese textile mill in Shanghai were fired upon by police under the command of a British officer. A number of demonstrators were killed or wounded in what became known as the Shanghai Incident. Violent anti-foreign riots in Shanghai, Peking, and other cities followed in the ensuing weeks. In Canton, on June 23, students and workers demonstrating outside the foreign concession of Shameen were fired upon by British soldiers and suffered many casualties. The wave of hostility against Great Britain that followed led to a widespread and effective boycott of British goods for the next fifteen months. The strength of

---

[3] Fu Ch'i-hsueh, *Chung-kuo Wai-chaio-shih (A Diplomatic History of China)* (Taipei: San Min Book Co., 1957), pp. 335-336.

[4] Dr. Sun Yat-sen's will, consisting of two brief paragraphs, was read regularly at all formal gatherings in China up to the 1950's.

these anti-foreign protests made such an impression on public opinion in the United States that it eventually led to a change in American policy towards the nationalist revolution.

The Northern Expedition, 1926-28

The leading general of the KMT was a long-time follower of Sun Yat-sen named Chiang Chung-cheng, known to the West as Chiang Kai-shek. Chiang, who had long been prominent in the revolutionary struggle, was in 1924 appointed commandant of the Whampoa Military Academy. Within a few years, Chiang's newly trained Nationalist troops were ready to deliver a blow to the northern warlords.

In July 1926 Chiang launched the Northern Expedition. The new army under his command swept northward from Canton to Hankow, while another wing of his forces moved up the coast to Hangchow. In a pincer movement, the two then converged on Nanking, which was made capital of the national government following the entry of the victorious army into the city in March 1927.[5]   It was widely predicted that the Nationalist army would be in Peking by fall.

This further campaign, however, was delayed by a serious rift which developed within the ranks of the Nationalist party over the question of continued cooperation with the Chinese Communists and Soviet advisors. The right wing of the KMT, fearing that Communists were trying to dominate the party, wanted to end the collaboration between the two parties and oust all Communists, while the left wing of the KMT, led by Wang Ching-wei, was opposed to this step. The right wing and moderates organized a new government in Nanking on April 18, 1927, in open defiance of the left and Communists, who had moved the Canton government to Hankow. Before the end of 1927, public opinion had turned overwhelmingly against communism. The left KMT broke with the Communists and the Hankow government came to an abrupt end. The KMT was reunited with the moderate faction led by Chiang in full

---

5   Chiang Mon-lin, *Tides from the West* (Taipei: World Book Co., 1963), p. 145. After 1928 the Nationalist Government was called the National Government of China.

control. Soviet consulates were closed and Comintern advisers were sent back to Russia.

In the spring of 1928 the Nationalist army continued its northward advance, entering Shantung en route to Peking. The Japanese government, on the pretext of protecting its nationals in Tsinan, dispatched a force of 5,000 soldiers to that city. Instead of escorting the small colony of Japanese residents out of the war zone, the Japanese forces took up a position in Tsinan, fired upon crowds of Chinese civilians, and subjected parts of the city to an artillery bombardment on May 3, 1928.[6] These troops were not withdrawn from Shantung until after a wave of vigorous protests by the Chinese people. Despite the Japanese intervention, Chiang's forces continued to march northward, entering Peking in June 1928. As their troops marched to Mukden, the Nationalists learned that the formidable Manchurian warlord, Chang Tso-lin, had been assassinated. His son and successor, Chang Hsueh-liang, made peace with the Nationalists and accepted a place in the new government in December 1928.

In theory at least, the country was now united. A new administration, headed by Chiang, was in place in Nanking. It was based on the five-part separation of powers proposed by Sun, who had sought to combine the Occidental political ideas with the best of traditional Chinese governance, such as regular civil service examinations and an independent body of government watchdogs called censors. Modern and progressive leaders, many of whom had studied abroad, were coming to the fore.[7]

The National government's first decade in Nanking, 1927-1937, saw marked economic progress under an administration whose authority and efficiency continued to grow. Most of the Pei-yang warlords disappeared from the national scene. The National Economic Council promoted development, especially in the areas of modern communications, industrialization, and the use of natural resources. Education made remarkable progress as substantial government support enabled many

---

[6] M. C. T. Z. Tyau, *Two Years of Nationalist China* (Shanghai: Kelly & Walsh, 1930), pp. 94-95.

[7] K. S. Latourette, *The Chinese, Their History and Culture* (New Haven: Yale University Press, 1963), p. 410.

new schools and universities to be established. Foreign trade, mainly with Japan and the U.S., multiplied in volume. China faced a greater promise of peace and prosperity than she had at any time since the founding of the Republic in 1912.

American Attitudes Towards the Nationalist Revolution

Both London and Washington had been reconsidering their respective China policies even before the Shanghai Incident of May 25, 1925. British policy during the first phase of the Northern Expedition was guided by the realization of growing Nationalist strength, and London gradually shifted its attention from the Peking government to the new regime. Great Britain had major economic interests in China, and was willing to relinquish considerable treaty rights in order to keep them. This new China policy was published on Christmas Day, 1926, and stated that the powers should abandon the idea that the economic and political development of China can only be secured under foreign tutelage. The so-called "Christmas message" proposed that the powers jointly declare their willingness to revise the treaties of the Washington Conference "as soon as the Chinese themselves have constituted a Government with authority to negotiate."[8]

U.S. Secretary of State Frank B. Kellogg was equally determined to put an end to this period of uncertainty in Sino-American relations. As the former U.S. Ambassador to Great Britain, his past efforts at joint action in the Far East had proved futile, however, and he was loath to continue them. In his own view, Sino-American friendship was the cornerstone of peace in Asia. The U.S. should adopt a conciliatory policy in China regardless of the attitude of other powers, for this would encourage the impression that America was a true friend of China and exempt it from much of the anti-foreign feeling.[9]

During this period American public opinion, led by the press and the Board of China Missions, was increasingly sympathetic to the Chinese desire to abolish the unequal treaties and extraterritoriality. The

---

[8]   A. Iriye, *After Imperialism, The Search for a New Order in the Far East (1921-1931)* (Cambridge: Harvard University Press, 1965), pp. 99-100.

[9]   *Ibid.*, p. 64.

American Chamber of Commerce in Shanghai, comprised of traders and businessmen in China, did not share these views. It took the position that Chinese nationalism was a creation of radicals under the influence of Soviet Russia, and continued to recommend a tough and uncompromising policy toward China.

A similar schism of opinion divided America's senior diplomats. Kellogg, supported by the Chief of the Far Eastern Division in the State Department, Nelson T. Johnson, took a generally sympathetic view of China's nationalist aspirations and worked cautiously on their behalf. The U.S. Minister to China, John Van A. MacMurray, disagreed, arguing that existing treaty rights should be vigorously defended, if necessary by the use of force, against any encroachments by the Chinese authorities.[10]   The American Consul General in Shanghai, Edwin S. Cunningham, defended the action of the police in the May 30, 1925, riot, and requested the dispatch of additional U.S. naval vessels to protect American nationals.   Washington remained committed to a moderate approach, however.

China policy was further complicated by the activities of the U.S. Congress, where sentiment in favor of adopting an independent approach in order to bring about a generous readjustment of the unequal treaties was growing. Republican Representative Stephen G. Porter, Chairman of the House Committee on Foreign Affairs, introduced a resolution in the House of Representatives on January 4, 1927, requesting that President Calvin Coolidge "enter into negotiations with the duly accredited agents of the Republic of China, with a view to the negotiation and the drafting of a treaty . . . to replace the existing unequal treaties."[11]

On January 27, 1927, Kellogg issued one of his few public declarations on America's policy toward China.   He emphasized American sympathies for China's nationalist aspirations, and underlined

---

[10] F. H. Michael and G. E. Taylor, *The Far East in the Modern World* (New York: Henry Holt & Co., 1956), pp. 621-622.

[11] House Concurrent Resolution 46, 69th Congress.   The Porter Resolution was passed by the House of Representatives on February 21, 1927, by a vote of 262 to 43.   The session closed before it could come to a vote in the Senate.   For details of the Porter Resolution and related Congressional debates see D. Borg, *American Policy and Chinese Revolution, 1925-1928* (New York: The Macmillan Co., 1947), pp. 242-256.

the U.S. government's commitment to the principle of noninterference in the internal affairs of China. Kellogg stated that the U.S. "desire[s] that tariff control and extraterritoriality provided for by our treaties with China should as early as possible be released. . . The United States is…prepared to enter into negotiations with any Government of China or delegates who can represent or speak for China . . . [for the purpose of] entirely releasing tariff control and restoring complete tariff autonomy."[12]

The Kellogg Statement was welcomed by the American Congress and public as a manifestation of the historical friendship between the U.S. and China. But, in asking for delegates who could represent the whole country, Kellogg had avoided making reference to either the Peking government or the Nationalists, whose armies were even then approaching Nanking. For this reason the reaction of both sides was rather cool. The Chinese Minister to the U.S., Alfred Sao-ke Sze, remarked that is was not clear from the Statement precisely what the U.S. was prepared to do. In China, the Statement was regarded as a mere reiteration of long-standing American policy.[13]

The Kellogg Statement did help reemphasize America's interest in forming amicable ties with China once there was an organized representative body in the country. Soon after, Kellogg instructed the U.S. Legation in Peking "to study the question of the provisions which should be written into a new treaty to take the place of existing treaties between the United States and China."[14] The Far Eastern Division of the State Department in Washington also began a similar study. While actual talks on treaty revision would not open for some time because of continued instability in China, these studies would lay a foundation for future talks.

---

[12] Department of State, *U.S. Foreign Relations, 1927*, Vol. II, p. 350.
[13] *Ibid.*, pp. 353-354; pp. 360-362.
[14] Nelson T. Johnson Papers, The U.S. Library of Congress. Cited in A. Iriye, *op. cit.*, pp. 108-109.

II. THE NANKING INCIDENT AND ITS SETTLEMENT

The Nanking Incident of 1927 and Major Power Demands

The Nanking Incident marked a critical phase in the relations of the nascent Nationalist government with the major powers. On March 23, 1927, a stream of defeated Northern soldiers under Chang Tsung-ch'ang and Sun Ch'ua-fang retreating through Nanking became disorderly and began firing indiscriminately into crowds. Nationalist troops soon entered Nanking and restored order, but not before radical elements under the command of Lin Tsu-han, the Director of the Political Department of the Sixth Army and a Communist, had instigated the rioting troops to attack foreigners.[15] It was later shown that this attack was a deliberate attempt by Communist agents to discredit the KMT with the powers and prevent Chiang from securing international recognition and support for the new government.

Several American, British, Italian, French and Japanese nationals were killed or wounded in the attack. American, British, and Japanese consulates were ransacked and a number of homes and institutions owned or operated by foreigners were set on fire. Many of the Americans and other foreign nationals took refuge in buildings belonging to the Standard Oil Company on Socony Hill, while others assembled at the University of Nanking. The U.S.S. Noa and H.M.S. Emerald stationed in the Yangtze River began to drop shells on the city.[16] Order was gradually restored after stern action was taken by the commander of the Nationalist army, Cheng Ch'ien, who entered Nanking on the evening of March 24. In the meantime, American and British naval officers and the American Consul had negotiated with representatives of the Nationalist forces for the safe conduct of all foreigners out of the city, and on March 26 most foreigners, except for those few who insisted upon remaining in Nanking, sailed for Shanghai without further casualties.

On April 11, 1927, the U.S., Great Britain, Japan, France, and Italy united in making the following written demands on the Hankow

---

[15] A detailed report of the American Consul in Nanking, John K. David, was recorded in *U.S. Foreign Relations, 1927*, pp. 151-163.

[16] *China Yearbook, 1928*, pp. 723-729.

government with regard to the Incident:[17]   1) Adequate punishment of the commanders of the troops responsible for the murders, personal injuries, and indignities and material damage, as well as of all persons found to be implicated; 2) A written apology from the commander-in-chief of the Nationalist army, expressing an intention to refrain from all forms of violence and agitation against foreign lives and property; 3) Complete reparation for all personal injuries and material damage.   Unless the Nationalist authorities complied with these terms, the note concluded, the signatories would be compelled to take certain unspecified measures.

Although the five powers had acted jointly in presenting their demands, the Nationalist government decided to respond separately. On April 14 Eugene Yu-jen Chen, Minister of Foreign Affairs in Hankow, sent individual replies to each of the governments concerned. The note to the U.S. government stated that the Nationalist government was prepared to make good the damages suffered by Americans at Nanking, except in cases where it could definitely be proven that the damages had been caused by the British-American naval bombardment or by Northern troops and provocateurs.   As far as the punishment of specified individuals and a written apology from the commander-in-chief were concerned, these questions should be set aside until the question of guilt concerning the Nanking Incident had been properly determined, either by a government inquiry already underway or by an international commission.   A commission of inquiry should also investigate the circumstances of the bombardment of Nanking by American and British warships. In the future, Chen pledged, effective measures would be taken for the protection of foreign lives and property.

Chen declared that the best guarantee against the recurrence of such incidents would be the abolition of "the unequal treaties," pointing out that "these inequitable treaties . . . constitute the chief danger to foreign lives and property in China and [that] this danger will persist as long as effective government is rendered difficult by foreign insistence on conditions which are at once a humiliation and a menace to a nation that has known greatness and is today conscious of renewed strength."   He

---

[17]   Department of State, *U.S. Foreign Relations, 1927*, pp. 186-187.

proposed that the U.S. and the Nationalist government should enter into negotiations to revise the existing treaty system.[18]

None of the five governments were satisfied by the Chinese reply. Britain, France, and Italy sought strong measures to enforce compliance with their demands, and Japan showed an inclination to follow their lead. The U.S. government, however, declined to associate itself with coercive measures, stating on May 3 that President Calvin Coolidge was unable to see where the U.S. would gain by acting with the other powers and presenting a second note—an ultimatum, really—to the Nationalist government.[19]

The powers decided to abandon plans for joint action. Their decision was influenced in part by a desire not to embarrass the newly established Nationalist government in Nanking. The new government, unlike its Hankow rival, took a more conciliatory attitude toward the Western powers. Prompt steps were taken to suppress the Communists responsible for the Nanking Incident. The powers refused to have any further contact with the radicals in Hankow, and negotiations were undertaken separately between the Nanking government and individual foreign powers.

Sino-American Negotiations on The Nanking Incident

The Nationalist government, eager to put the Nanking Incident behind it, in May 1927 sent a representative to the American Consul in Shanghai to discuss a settlement of the issue. Secretary of State Kellogg, equally anxious to dispose of the incident, indicated his willingness to accept more moderate terms than those originally demanded by the five powers. Informal negotiations between the two sides twice led to definite proposals by the Chinese in May and in July.[20] However, the continuing political upheaval in China convinced the U.S. Minister John Van A.

---

[18] For full text of the Chinese Note of April 11, 1927, see *U.S. Foreign Relations, 1927*, pp. 192-194.

[19] R. T. Pollard, *China's Foreign Relations, 1917-1931* (New York: Macmillan, 1933), p. 307.

[20] D. Borg, *op. cit.*, pp. 378-379.

MacMurray that there was little point in rushing into formal negotiations to conclude an agreement.

Early in 1928 MacMurray visited Shanghai, where he conferred informally with Minister of Foreign Affairs Huang Fu on February 26 on the matter of a settlement. MacMurray then directed the U.S. Consul General in Shanghai, Edwin S. Cunningham, to explore the possibilities of a settlement with a representative from the foreign ministry.[21] Meanwhile, similar negotiations were underway between Minister Huang and British Minister Miles Lampson.

Both the American and British representatives asked that foreigners who had suffered losses in Nanking be compensated, that an official apology be made, and that those responsible for the assaults be punished. As a gesture of good faith, the Nationalist government announced that nineteen soldiers and thirty-two locals involved in the Nanking disorders had been executed, and that orders had been given for the arrest of Lin Tsu-han, the Communist chiefly responsible for the Incident. A directive issued at the same time ordered that full protection be given to foreigners and their property. Minister Huang, for his part, asked that the American and British governments express regret that their warships had fired upon Nanking, and announce their intention to deal immediately with the issue of treaty revision. The British minister declined to admit that his government had been responsible for the naval bombardment, and it was on this point that negotiations between the British and the Chinese were abandoned.[22]

The Sino-American negotiations proceeded more smoothly, however. On March 30, 1928, three notes concerning the Nanking Incident were exchanged between Huang and MacMurray resolving the matter to the satisfaction of both sides.[23] In the first, the Nationalist government expressed its regret over the indignities to the American flag and to official representatives of the American government, the loss of property sustained by the American consulate, and the personal injuries and

---

[21] *North China Herald*, CLXVII, April 7, 1928, p. 2; *Ibid.*, CLXVI, March 10, 1928, p. 377; cited in R. T. Pollard, *op. cit.*, pp. 388-389.

[22] R. T. Pollard, *op. cit.*, p. 339.

[23] The text of the notes can be found in *Treaties and Agreements With and Concerning China, 1919-1929* (Washington: Carnegie Endowment for International Peace, 1929), pp. 223-226.

material damage done to American residents in Nanking. Although the investigation of the incident demonstrated that it was entirely instigated by the Communists prior to the establishment of the National government in Nanking, the government was nevertheless prepared to accept responsibility. Effective steps had already been taken to punish those implicated in the incident. Compensation would be made for all personal injuries and material damages done to the American Consulate, its officials, American residents, and their property in Nanking. For this purpose, a Sino-American commission would be set up to verify the actual injuries and damages suffered by Americans.

In his reply, MacMurray accepted the terms laid out in the note "in definite settlement of the questions arising out [the Nanking] incident," and expressed hope in the "the loyal fulfillment of the said terms of settlement."

In his second note, Huang referred to the fact that American warships had opened fire on Socony Hill in Nanking on the afternoon of March 24, 1927. In his reply, MacMurray pointed out that the act in question had constituted a "protective barrage," confined to the immediate neighborhood of the house in which the American Consul, together with many others, was seeking refuge, and had provided the "only conceivable means" by which the lives of this party and other Americans in Nanking had been saved. "The American Government, therefore, feels that its naval vessels had no alternative to the action taken," he wrote in conclusion, "however deeply it deplores that circumstances beyond its control should have necessitated the adoption of such measures for the protection of the lives of its citizens at Nanking."

In his third and final note, Huang proposed a revision of the unequal treaties. In reply, MacMurray stated that the American government looked for the remedying of the conditions which had "necessitated the incorporation of exceptional provisions in the earlier treaties" to "afford opportunities for the revision, in due form and by mutual consent, of such treaty stipulations as may have become unnecessary or inappropriate." The American government hoped that there would develop "an administration so far representative of the Chinese people, and so far exercising real authority, as to be capable of assuring the actual fulfillment in good faith of any obligations such as China would of necessity have for its part to undertake incidentally to the desired readjustment of treaty relations."[24]

A similar agreement was signed with the British government in August 1928. An agreement with the Japanese was eventually signed as well, though it was delayed until May 1929 by the Tsinan Incident of May 3, 1928, and the serious friction that ensued.

After the exchange of notes, MacMurray had planned to reopen the American Consulate in Nanking at once, in joint ceremonies with General Chiang Kai-shek, believing that such a gesture of goodwill and reconciliation might furnish at least some guarantee of improved relations. Chiang, however, had already departed for the front. MacMurray temporarily set aside the issue, believing that it might be dangerous to reestablish the consulate and permit the return of American citizens to Nanking without such public ceremonies.[25] He raised the matter again in September 1928, and plans were made to reopen the consulate in the third week of September. Chinese authorities would not agree to take part in a program honoring the American flag, however. MacMurray felt that the U.S. should take no further action, but was overruled by the State Department, which directed that the consulate be reopened without any ceremony whatever.[26] On December 15, 1928, the American Consul quietly resumed his work in Nanking.[27]

III. RIGHTS RECOVERY AND PROGRESSIVE DIPLOMACY

Formal Steps for Treaty Revision

The step-by-step effort to abrogate the unequal treaties by the Nationalist government was known as the Rights Recovery Movement. It gained momentum after it became apparent that the signatories of the 1922 Washington Treaty were unwilling to fulfill their modest obligations, and that demands by the increasingly irrelevant Peking

---

[24] Department of State, *U.S. Foreign Relations, 1928*, pp. 332-333.
[25] *Ibid.*, pp. 335-336, 338.
[26] *Ibid.*, pp. 363-365.
[27] D. Borg., *op. cit.*, p. 385.

government had little effect. A series of incidents involving foreigners intensified xenophobic feelings almost beyond belief, and the Chinese people demanded a fundamental change in the way relations with foreign states were conducted. Various political groups competed in their proposals to abolish the unequal treaties.

The First National Congress of the KMT in Canton on January 30, 1924, laid down guidelines for the conduct of China's foreign policy.[28] All unequal treaties were to be abolished, and new treaties concluded on the basis of absolute equality and mutual respect for sovereign rights. All other treaties which were in any way prejudicial to the interests of China were to be reviewed according to the principle of mutual non-infringement of sovereignty. All countries that were willing to abandon their special privileges in China were to be accorded most-favored-nation treatment.

The first concrete expression of this manifesto was the recovery of the British concessions in Hankow and Kiukiang. Eugene Yu-jen Chen entered into negotiations with Owen O'Malley, Counselor of the British Legation, on this question in early January. Agreement was reached late that month, but the dispatch of British forces to Shanghai delayed exchange of notes until February 19 for Hankow, and March 2 for Kiukiang. The two British concessions were unconditionally transferred to the Nationalist government.[29]

After the Nationalist government was formally established in Nanking, the Ministry of Foreign Affairs issued declarations on August 13 and November 2 underlining the new government's determination to change the way China conducted her foreign policy. The latter declaration, signed by Foreign Minister Wu Ch'ao-ch'u, read in part:[30]

As there is no reason for the existence of the unequal treaties and agreements concluded between former Chinese Governments and the Governments, corporations and individuals of foreign States, they shall be abrogated by the Nationalist Government within the shortest possible period. . . . Any treaty or agreement purporting to be made

---

[28] M. C. T. Z. Tyau, *Two Years of Nationalist China* (Shanghai: Kelly & Walsh, 1930), pp. 29-30.

[29] *Ibid.*, pp. 472-477.

[30] *Ibid.*, p. 94.

by any Chinese authority with any foreign Government, corporation or individual without the participation of sanction of the Nationalist Government is of no validity whatsoever. . . . No treaty or agreement relating to China to which the Nationalist Government is not a party, shall be deemed binding on China.

Communicated to representatives of all foreign powers still in Peking, this statement prepared the way for subsequent diplomatic negotiations. The Nationalist government had a definite program in mind, which derived from KMT ideology. First, unequal treaties and other arrangements which impaired the integrity of China as a sovereign state were to be eliminated. Second, new treaties were to be concluded upon the principles of equality and reciprocity. Finally, the principles of equality and reciprocity should be extended to all international negotiations and become the foundation of lasting peace.

Of the inequalities which held China in political and economic subordination to the powers, only the question of tariff autonomy was on the way to being resolved. Some small steps had also been taken in the direction of eliminating extraterritoriality and the privilege of coastal navigation by foreign ships. Foreign settlements, concessions, and military bases, however, would continue to exist on Chinese territory for some time.

In 1928 there were 23 countries enjoying treaty relations with China.[31] These were Austria, Belgium, Bolivia, Brazil, Chile, Denmark, Finland, France, Germany, Great Britain, Italy, Japan, Mexico, Netherlands, Norway, Persia, Peru, Portugal, Spain, Sweden, Switzerland, Union of Soviet Socialist Republics,[32] and the United States.

The treaties with Belgium, Denmark, Italy, Japan, Portugal, and Spain had expired. The new Minister of Foreign Affairs in Nanking, Wang Cheng-t'ing, made it known that he was prepared to enter into

---

[31] For details, see *Chinese Maritime Customs Treaties, Conventions between China and Foreign States* (Shanghai: Kelly and Walsh Co., 1927) and Ministry of Foreign Affairs: Chung-wai t'iao-yueh Ch'ien (*Treaties between the Republic of China and Foreign States, 1927-1957*) (Taipei: Commercial Press Ltd., 1958).

[32] The first treaty with Russia was the Treaty of Nipchu Nerchinsk signed on August 27, 1689.

prompt negotiations with these countries for preliminary treaties on the basis of the principle that China should enjoy full and complete tariff autonomy and exercise full and qualified jurisdiction over all nationals within her territory. Countries whose treaties with China were still in force needed only to recognize the first of these two principles.[33]

Pending the conclusion of preliminary treaties, provisional regulations governing relations between Chinese nationals and foreigners was promulgated by the Nationalist government on July 7, 1928. Of the seven articles, the four most important were as follows:

Article 3: The persons and property of foreigners in China shall receive protection according to Chinese law.

Article 4: Foreigners in China shall be amenable to Chinese law and subject to the jurisdiction of Chinese law courts.

Article 5: All goods imported into China from foreign countries or by foreigners, as well as all goods exported from China to foreign countries shall, until the Chinese national tariff comes into operation, be subject to the customs tariff in force.

Article 6: Foreigners in China, shall, in accordance with the regulations now in force, pay all taxes which should be paid by the Chinese.[34]

These regulations were intended to apply to the six countries whose treaties with China had expired. Their governments were notified that it was the desire of the Nationalist government to enter into negotiations at the earliest opportunity for the conclusion of preliminary treaties. Identical notes were dispatched to six other countries whose treaties were still in force for the negotiation of new treaties recognizing China's right to exercise complete tariff autonomy. The Western powers were in general more ready to terminate the customs arrangements than they were to end extraterritoriality.

---

[33] M. C. T. Z. Tyau, *op. cit.*, pp. 100-101.
[34] T. S. Chang, *Chung-wai t'iao-yueh tsung-luen* (Treaty Relations between China and Foreign Powers) (Taipei: Wu Chia Press, 1969), p. 134.

Sino-American Tariff Treaty, 1928 and Tariff Autonomy

The capture of Peking, now renamed Peiping by the Nationalist government, raised two important questions in Washington. Should the U.S. accord recognition to the Nationalist Government? Should an attempt be made to effect some form of treaty revision? Secretary of State Kellogg became increasingly determined to effect a basic readjustment in treaty relations with China. He regarded his statement of January 27, 1927, offering to enter into negotiations as soon as the Chinese were able to agree on the composition of a delegation that could speak for the Chinese people as a whole, as a definite commitment.[35]

In the autumn of 1927 MacMurray returned to Washington to discuss the Chinese situation with Kellogg. In a memorandum dated October 21 of that year, he stated that the Chinese looked upon Kellogg's position as a tactical maneuver to delay the issue. What was needed, he suggested, was a good faith gesture, a proposal for immediate revision of part of the existing treaty system.[36] He suggested that the State Department negotiate a simple treaty with China which would recognize tariff autonomy on condition that American trade would not be discriminated against.

On July 11, 1928, after a congenial meeting with Chinese special envoy Wu Ch'ao-ch'u, Kellogg cabled MacMurray with instructions to seize the first opportunity to open discussions on the tariff question.[37] He followed up with a note to the Nationalist government, dated July 25, informing it that ". . . the American Government is ready to begin at once, through the American Minister in China, negotiations with properly accredited representatives whom the Nationalist Government may appoint, . . . with a view to concluding a new treaty in which it may be expected that full expression will be given . . . to the principle of national tariff autonomy and to the principle that the commerce of each of the contracting parties shall enjoy in the ports and the territories" of the other most favored nation status.[38]

---

[35] D. Borg, *op. cit.*, pp. 386-387.
[36] Text of MacMurray memorandum in *U.S. Foreign Relations, 1928*, p. 363-365.
[37] *Ibid.*, p. 454.
[38] *Ibid.*, p. 466.

The Treaty between the U.S. and China Regulating Tariff Relations, 1928, was signed in Peking on July 25 by MacMurray and the Chinese Minister of Finance, Soong Tse-ven. The treaty consisted of the following two brief articles:

All provisions which appear in treaties hitherto concluded and in force between the United States of America and China relating to rates of duty on imports and exports of merchandise, drawbacks, transit dues and tonnage dues in China shall be annulled and become inoperative, and the principle of complete national tariff autonomy shall apply subject, however, to the condition that each of the High Contracting Parties shall enjoy in the territories of the other with respect to the above specified and any related matters treatment in no way discriminatory as compared with the treatment accorded to any other country.

The nationals of neither of the High Contracting Parties shall be compelled under any pretext whatever to pay within the territories of the other Party any duties, internal charges or taxes upon their importation's and exportations other or higher than those paid by nationals of the country or by nationals of the country or by nationals of any other country.[39]

The success of this Sino-American tariff treaty simplified matters for other countries.[40] Similar, albeit preliminary, treaties were signed with Norway, the Netherlands, Sweden, Great Britain, and France that same year. These new treaties recognized China's right to determine her own tariff rates, and on February 1, 1929, a new schedule was put into effect raising the rates of import duty from 7 1/2 percent to 27 1/2 percent. This schedule was to be applied for one year to see how it would react upon the country's trade and commerce, after which revisions would be made and the treaties finalized. The revised national tariff was held in abeyance until 1931, however, by delays in the conclusion of a tariff

---

[39] Department of State, Treaty Series, No. 773; *Treaties and Agreements With and Concerning China, 1919-1929*, pp. 230-231.
[40] Ratifications were exchanged in Washington, February 29, 1929.

treaty with Japan. In that year the decades-long struggle to realize complete tariff autonomy was finally concluded.[41]

Recognition of the Nationalist Government

As the 1928 Sino-American Tariff Treaty was being concluded, the question arose in Washington as to whether it constituted de jure recognition by the United States of the Nationalist government in Nanking. It was MacMurray's opinion the U.S. government already had de facto relations with the administration in Nanking and that the question of de jure recognition "did not arise under present circumstances." Kellogg sounded out a number of foreign diplomats in Washington on these questions. While they were divided on the question of whether their governments had de facto relations with the Nanking government, it was clear that de jure recognition was under consideration in many capitals. The main issue which remained to be settled was whether the new Chinese government could be considered sufficiently stable.[42]

In August 1928 Kellogg addressed a letter to President Calvin Coolidge, stating that there was no doubt that the signing of the tariff treaty constituted a technical recognition of the Nationalist government, and that ratification by the Senate was not necessary to give effect to recognition. Because there was some confusion on this question, Kellogg indicated that he would like to make a public announcement to this effect. "The more influence we can give to the Nationalist Government," he wrote, "the better just now." Coolidge agreed immediately.[43]

Kellogg thus informed Minister Albert Sao-ke Sze in mid-August that, in the view of the Department of State, the U.S. already enjoyed diplomatic relations with the Republic of China and offered to announce this fact.[44] After consulting with Nanking, Sze replied that no further

---

[41] The Sino-Japanese Tariff was signed on May 6, 1930, and came into effect on May 16, 1930.

[42] Department of State, U.S. Foreign Relations, 1928, pp. 182, 184, 188, 190-191.

[43] Ibid., pp. 192-194.

[44] Ibid, pp.196.

attention need be paid to the question as it had been taken care of by the tariff treaty. Though the U.S. was eager to lend support to the new government, it did not immediately move its embassy to Nanking. The new American Minister to China, Nelson T. Johnson, who reached China at the end of 1929, remarked that for the present the Legation of the United States would be his suitcase. Johnson divided his time between Shanghai, Nanking, and Hankow, using the American Consulate in Shanghai as his principle base of operations. On June 14, 1930, Johnson recommended to Washington that the Legations be immediately removed from Peking. The Department of State did not approve this recommendation, rather continuing to follow Great Britain and the other powers whose legations remained in the former capital.[45]

During 1930-31 Cuba, Norway, Finland, Turkey, and Italy transferred their diplomatic representatives from Peking to Shanghai. All other foreign legations remained in Peking's Legation Quarter, however, loath to give up the special rights and privileges diplomatic representatives had long enjoyed there. Foreign governments recognized the government in Nanking as China's sole legitimate authority, but chose to keep their ministers in a city hundreds of miles distant.

The Abolition of Extraterritoriality

The elimination of German, Austrian and Hungarian extraterritorial rights in China after World War I, followed by the Soviet renunciation of these same rights in 1924, gave impetus to China's campaign for the complete abolition of extraterritoriality. At that time the privilege of consular jurisdiction in China was still enjoyed by sixteen foreign powers. Then in 1928 five nations—Belgium, Italy, Denmark, Portugal, and Spain—concluded treaties with the Nationalist government in which they abandoned extraterritorial rights. These treaties provided, among other things, that "nationals of each of the two High Contracting Parties be subject, in the territory of the other Party, to the laws and jurisdiction

---

[45] L. Curtis, *The Capital Question of China* (London: The Macmillan Co., 1932), pp. 174-179.

of the law courts of that Party, to which they shall have free and easy access for the enforcement and defense of their rights."[46]

On April 27, 1929, Foreign Minister Wang Cheng-t'ing addressed notes to six of the powers with major interests in China, namely, the United States, Great Britain, France, Netherlands, Norway and Brazil. With the exception of Brazil, all had concluded tariff treaties with China the preceding winter. Wang expressed "the desire of China to have the restrictions on her jurisdictional sovereignty removed at the earliest possible date and [the] hope that Your Excellency's Government will take this desire of China into immediate and sympathetic consideration and favor me with an early reply so that steps may be taken to enable China, now unified and with a strong Central Government, to rightfully assume jurisdiction over all nationals within her domain."[47]

With the exception of the Brazilian government, all those who received the note eventually replied. None of these expressed a willingness to transfer their nationals to the jurisdiction of the Chinese courts, stating that conditions in China did not yet correspond to those laid down for the abolition of extraterritoriality by the international commission of 1926. Several did express their willingness to enter into negotiations to that end, however.

The American response, dated August 10, 1929, was typical. Although the U.S. government appreciated the effort being made in China to assimilate Western judicial principles, there did not yet exist "a system of independent Chinese courts free from extraneous influence which was capable of adequately doing justice between Chinese and foreign litigants." Only when the recommendations made by the Commission on Extraterritoriality had been fulfilled in greater measure would it be possible "for American citizens safely to live and do business in China and for their property adequately to be protected without the intervention of the consular courts." Nevertheless, the U.S. government was ready "to participate in negotiations which would have as their object the

---

[46] M. C. T. Z. Tyau, *op. cit.*, p. 104. See the preliminary treaties of amity and commerce between China and, respectively Belgium, Italy, Denmark, Portugal and Spain.

[47] The Notes to the American, British and French Ministers were identical. The text is to be found in the *China Yearbook, 1929-1930*, pp. 904-905.

devising of a method for the gradual relinquishment of extraterritorial rights," provided that this was paralleled by actual improvements in the Chinese legal system.[48] The Nationalist government replied in September, observing that conditions in China had materially changed since the commission had made its recommendations and that a number of countries had already consented to relinquish their extraterritorial privileges on January 1, 1930. The former system "has outlived its usefulness and should be replaced by one in harmony with the actual state of things."[49]

Intent upon forcing the issue with the principal powers, the Central Political Council of the KMT passed a resolution on December 26, 1929, requesting the State Council of the Nationalist government to terminate extraterritoriality for all foreigners on January 1, 1930. Great Britain, supported by the United States and Japan, replied it was not unwilling in principle to *commence* on that date the process of bringing the existing system to an end. Under considerable domestic pressure to act because of the looming National People's Convention, at which a constitution would be adopted, the Nationalist government promulgated regulations governing foreigners. The regulations, which would end extraterritoriality by bringing all foreigners under the jurisdiction of Chinese courts, were slated to take effect on January 1, 1932.[50] It was hoped that the unequal treaties could be revised before that date.

In order to expedite this process, the negotiations were transferred to London and Washington, as well as other European capitals. Through prolonged discussions, in which Great Britain took the lead, treaty drafts were gradually hammered into shape. By the summer of 1931 agreement had been reached on a wide range of questions, with only a few important issues remaining to be resolved.

Then the Manchurian Crisis erupted, and the treaty negotiations were suspended. On December 29, 1931, two days before the regulations governing foreigners were to come into effect, they, too, were suspended.

---

[48] MacMurray to Wang, *China Yearbook, 1929-1930*, pp. 905-907, J. V. A. MacMurray, *op. cit.*, pp. 279-283.

[49] M. C. T. Z. Tyau, *op. cit.*, p. 106.

[50] H. M. Vinacke, *A History of the Far East in Modern Times* (New York: Appleton-Century-Crofts, 1959), p. 459.

Fifteen years were to pass before the U.S. finally concluded a treaty relinquishing its extraterritorial rights in China in January 1943.[51] Even so, as early as 1929 over half of the 130,000 foreigners (excluding Koreans) living in China—some 75,000 in all—were without extraterritorial status.[52]

The Nationalist government steadily regained control of the areas of its cities administered by foreigners. World War I and public agitation brought an end to some concessions, while pressure from the Nanking government increased Chinese participation in the administration of others. At the insistence of Foreign Minister Wang Cheng-t'ing, for example, the Sino-Foreign Mixed Court and prisons in the International Settlement of Shanghai were restored to Chinese control. Irredentist territory within China, however, was not completely recovered until World War II.

The 1929 Chinese Eastern Railway Dispute

Relations between China and Soviet Russia during the 1920's were primarily regulated by the Sino-Soviet Agreement of May 31, 1924, in which the governments mutually pledged that they would neither engage in propaganda directed against the political and social systems of the other, nor permit organizations to exist within their country whose aim was the violent overthrow of the other.[53] The Soviet authorities observed none of the pledges they had made.

The tide of nationalism that swept the Nationalists northward in the late twenties brought it into direct conflict with the Soviets in Manchuria. By mid-1929 an acrimonious dispute over the Chinese Eastern Railway had developed between China and the Soviet Union, leading to armed clashes along the Sino-Soviet border. On July 8, 1929, U.S. Secretary of State Stimson attempted to intervene, reminding both parties of their obligations under the Kellogg-Briand Pact for the renunciation of war, which had been signed in Paris on August 27 of the preceding year. The

---

[51] D. Borg, *op. cit.*, pp. 416-417.

[52] K. S. Latourette, *A Short History of the Far East* (New York: MacMillan, 1958), p. 429.

[53] M. C. T. Z. Tyau, *op. cit.*, p. 113.

fighting continued to escalate, however, and in November 1929 Soviet troops invaded Manchuria in force.

On November 25 Stimson tried to induce Great Britain, France, Germany, Italy, and Japan to join with the U.S. in an effort to restore peace between China and the U.S.S.R. Germany and Japan declined, but Britain, France, and Italy joined the U.S. in making identical appeals to both nations on December 2, 1929. The U.S. note expressed the hope that the two nations would abide by their past agreements and settle this controversy by peaceful means.[54]

This pressure brought the U.S.S.R. and China to the negotiating table. On December 22, 1929, the two nations signed a Protocol in Khabarovsk which restored the status quo ante, allowing the Soviet Union to retain its special privileges in the Chinese Eastern Railway zone.[55]

Achievements and Challenge

Four years after the establishment of the National government, tariff autonomy had been regained, ten countries had lost extraterritorial rights, and another group of countries had agreed to their eventual abrogation. One leased territory had been returned to China, a number of residential concessions had been brought under Chinese administration, and judicial sovereignty had been recovered in the International Settlement of Shanghai. These advances were made in spite of a constant struggle for internal unity against Communists and other divisive elements.

It may be argued that these achievements, substantial though they were, were made possible by the conciliatory policies of the Western powers. But these policies were in large part reactive, adopted to assuage the demands of the Nationalists, who possessed the confidence and assertiveness that their immediate predecessors had sorely lacked. Credit for the improvement in China's foreign relations is largely due to the skillful Nationalist diplomats who, with tact and perseverance,

---

54 Department of State, Press Release, December 7, 1929, pp. 83-84, cited in A. W. Griswold, *op. cit.*, pp. 396-397.

55 The text may be found in the *China Yearbook, 1931*, pp. 497-498.

initiated and conducted negotiations with their Western and Japanese counterparts in the years after 1926.

By 1931 China under the Nationalists seemed well on the road to achieving unity and stability. The warlords were gone, the Communist bid for control had failed, and the unequal treaties were being phased out. Sun's farsighted program of nationalism, democracy, and economic well-being seemed to be working. Then, without warning, Japan struck in Manchuria. China's evolution into a modern state was halted as the government concentrated on mobilizing its resources to resist this new aggression.

6

THE SINO-JAPANESE CONFLICTS
1931–1936

I. THE MANCHURIAN CRISIS

Japan's Closure of the Open Door

From 1931 onward the Japanese threat became the main preoccupation of the Nationalist government. Despite almost constant provocations from Japanese militarists, war did not yet appear to be inevitable. The Japanese threat to China had been just as grave at the time of the Twenty-One Demands, but war had been averted. The Japanese occupation of Shantung had been rolled back by U.S. pressure without the use of force. The Chinese met a new Japanese crisis in the hope of a solution short of war.

Since the Russo-Japanese War of 1904-5, Japan had been trying to wrest Manchuria, with its great natural wealth and relatively sparse population, away from China.[1] Chang Tso-lin, Manchuria's long-time ruler, had allowed himself to be used by the Japanese to further their ambitions. His son and successor, Chang Hsueh-liang, had not only drawn back from the Japanese embrace, he had joined forces with Chiang and begun to resist Japan's encroachments.

---

[1] H. F. MacNair & D. F. Lach, *Modern Far Eastern International Relations* (New York: D. Van Nostrand Co., 1955), p. 297.

The key to Japanese influence was the South Manchurian Railway, which ran from Port Arthur up the Liaoning Peninsula into Manchuria proper. Japan treated a broad zone bordering the railway as a virtual colony, controlling taxation, public utilities, and even education. It enforced its dictates with the powerful, 20,000-man Kwantung Army.

When Chang Hsueh-liang started construction of a grid of competing railway lines, Tokyo accused him of attempting to strangle Japanese economic interests. By the summer of 1931 feelings were running high between the Chinese and Japanese forces stationed in the neighborhood of Mukden (Shenyang) the capital of Liaoning province. Japanese reinforcements were secretly sent from Port Arthur and cannons were prepositioned for an attack on Chinese North Barracks. The War Ministry in Tokyo awaited a pretext to drive Chang out of Manchuria.[2]

Mukden Incident, September 18, 1931

On September 18, 1931, an explosion on the South Manchurian Railway line north of Liutiaokou station in Mukden tore out thirty-one inches of rail. Within six hours the Kwantung Army, under the command of General Shigeru Hojo, had occupied the entire city of Mukden.[3] Most observers realized that the attack was part of a larger Japanese plan for the conquest of Manchuria, if not all of China. "The forceful occupation of all strategic points in South Manchuria," wrote U.S. Minister Nelson T. Johnson, "is an aggressive act by Japan apparently long planned and decided upon most carefully and systematically put into effect. I find no evidence that these events were the act of minor and irresponsible officials."[4]

Japan had shrewdly timed her Manchurian adventure, for at the time China faced serious difficulties. The Yangtze River provinces had been

---

[2] H. K. Tong, *Chiang Kai-shek* (Taipei: China Publishing Co., 1953), pp. 187-188.

[3] For details see C. T. Liang, *The Sinister Face of the Mukden Incident* (New York: St. John's University Press, 1969). The Tanaka Memorial supposed to have been addressed by Japanese Premier Giichi Tanaka to the Emperor on July 25, 1927, sketched a design for Japanese foreign policy.

[4] Johnson to Secretary of State Stimson, September 22, 1931. In *Peiping, Peace and War, United States Foreign Policy, 1931-1941* (Washington: U.S. Government Printing Office, 1943), Doc. I (793-94/1838), pp. 155-156.

ravaged by disastrous floods, while parts of Kiangsi province had fallen under the control of Mao Tse-tung's guerrillas. Within the KMT Central Committee, a Cantonese bloc broke away from the Nanking government and set up a separate administration in Canton. So faction-ridden had Chinese politics become that on December 15, 1931, three months after the Manchurian coup, Chiang was compelled to resign as president.

The international situation was also favorable to Japan. The West was in the throes of the Great Depression. The U.S.S.R. was absorbed by its first five year plan. While British and American naval construction had fallen off after 1922, Japan had built up its navy to the limit allowed by the treaty, and now dominated the western Pacific. "If anyone had planned the Manchurian outbreak with a view to freedom from interference from the rest of the world," wrote Secretary of State Henry L. Stimson, "his time was well chosen."[5]

II. REACTIONS TO JAPAN'S MANCHURIAN INVASION

China's Appeal to the League of Nations

Following the Mukden Incident, the National government decided against an immediate resort to military force. Instead, it would try to temporize with Tokyo in the hope that foreign pressure would eventually induce the Japanese to withdraw. This tactic, which had worked well in resolving the earlier impasse over Shantung, seemed appropriate here, since the Japanese Army had virtually blackmailed Prime Minister Osachi Hamaguchi and the Cabinet into resolving the Manchurian problem by force.

So it was that the seizure of Mukden was referred to the as-yet-untested League of Nations. On September 21, 1931, Minister to Great Britain Alfred Sao-ke Sze formally requested that the League take immediate steps "to prevent the further development of a situation endangering the peace of the nations; to reestablish the status quo ante and to determine the amounts and character of such reparations as may

---

5   H. L. Stimson, *The Far Eastern Crisis: Recollections and Observations* (New York: Harper and Row, 1936), pp. 5-6.

be found due the Republic of China."[6] China also called on the U.S. for assistance under the Kellogg-Briand Pact.

Within the State Department, however, there were pro-Japanese as well as pro-Chinese experts, and Secretary of State Stimson was perplexed by the conflicting opinions he received. Initially inclined to be sympathetic to Japan, he was moreover anxious not to appear more pro-Chinese than the League of Nations. He therefore informed Eric Drummond, Secretary General of the League of Nations, that the U.S. was following developments closely, mindful of the obligations of the Kellogg-Briand Pact and the 1922 Nine Power Treaty. He assured Drummond of "co-operation and frankness," and passed on to him the Chinese appeal for aid as well as other information that the State Department had received on the situation in China. He ventured that it would be wise to avoid exciting nationalistic feeling in Japan in support of the military and against Foreign Minister Kijuro Shidehara.[7]

On September 22 the Council of the League met to discuss the Chinese appeal.   The Japanese representative proposed direct negotiations between the two countries, which idea Minister Sze rejected. Since the days of the Twenty-One Demands, public opinion in China had been strongly against direct negotiations with Japan.   Most of the members of the League, along with Stimson himself, appeared to favor this approach, however.[8]   Finally, the President of the Council, Alejandro Lerroux of Spain, addressed an urgent appeal to both China and Japan to withdraw their troops and to refrain from aggravating the situation.

The Council, anxious to involve the Americans in its deliberations, forwarded the minutes of each meeting to the State Department. When the Chinese proposed sending a commission of inquiry to Manchuria for

---

6   Official Journal of the League of Nations, December, 1931; cited in W. King, *China and the League of Nations, the Sino-Japanese Controversy* (New York: St. John's University Press, 1965), p. 12.

7   H. L. Stimson, *op. cit.*, pp. 41-42.

8   Under Article XI, the Council was called upon to take such action as it deemed wise and effectual for the safeguarding of the peace of nations. Its sole purpose was to bring about a peaceful solution. Any resolution to be adopted by virtue of this Article required unanimity including the affirmative votes of the parties to the disputes. One could easily imagine the difficulty of reaching decisions.

investigation, Stimson was quick to register his disapproval, cabling that "There would be serious danger that, if the League sought to approve such investigation upon Japan against her opposition, it would be popularly resented and would throw at once additional difficulties in the path of Shidehara's efforts at solution."[9] When the Japanese representative to the Council learned of Stimson's position he also came out against the Chinese proposal.

American Cooperation with the League of Nations

While the League was debating the Manchurian crisis, Stimson on September 22 transmitted an "earnest memorandum" to Japanese Foreign Minister Shidehara stating that the situation was "not exclusively a matter of concern to Japan and China. It brings into question at once the meaning of certain provisions of agreements, such as the Nine Power Treaty of February 6, 1922, and the Kellogg-Briand Pact. . . . It would seem that the responsibility for determining the course of events with regard to the liquidation of this situation rests largely upon Japan, for the simple reason that Japanese armed forces have seized and are exercising de facto control in south Manchuria." Settle your differences with China without further hostilities, Stimson urged Shidehara.

The League's appeal to the disputants, backed by U.S. diplomatic support, was fruitless. Its only practical effect was to cause Japanese diplomats to redouble their efforts to convince the world that Japan had been acting in self-defense and had no territorial designs in Manchuria. A September 30, 1931, resolution of the Council was a product of these efforts, for it noted with approval that the Japanese representative had pledged that "his government will continue, as rapidly as possible, the withdrawal of its troops . . . into the railway zone . . . and that it hopes to carry out this intention in full as speedily as may be."[10]

In fact, the Kwantung Army, under the command of Shigeru Hojo, was continuing its campaign, bringing more and more of Manchuria under its control. Buoyed by these successes, militarists in Tokyo rapidly

---

[9] H. L. Stimson, *op. cit.*, pp. 42–44.
[10] *U.S. Senate Document, No. 55*, 72nd Congress, 1st Session, "Conditions in Manchuria," p. 405.

gained followers. Liberal elements in the Japanese government were helpless to check the rising ultranationalism of the population.

On October 8, 1931, the Japanese further widened the scope of the war by bombing Chinchow, the city to which the government of Liaoning province had evacuated following the fall of Mukden. The Kwantung Army attempted to justify this attack by saying that the last vestige of the Chang Hsueh-liang's authority in Manchuria must be destroyed. This aerial bombardment of a civilian population center opened the eyes of many Western statesmen, including Stimson, to the gravity of the situation and destroyed their confidence in the bland reassurances of Japanese diplomats.

On October 3 China urged the U.S. government to cooperate with the League to investigate the situation. The U.S. Minister, Nelson T. Johnson, replied on October 5 that the U.S. had already sent Legation personnel to Manchuria.[11] That same day, in a further effort to check Japanese aggression, Stimson sent a telegram to Drummond which read in part:

> Both the Chinese and Japanese have presented and argued their cases before the Council . . . The Council has formulated the conclusions and outlined the course of action to be followed by the disputants; and as the said disputants have made commitments to the Council, it is most desirable that the League in no way relax its vigilance and in no way fail to assert all the pressure and authority within its competence toward regulating the action of China and Japan in the premises. . . . On its part the American government . . . will endeavor to reinforce what the League does and will make clear that it has a keen interest in the matter.[12]

At the Chinese government's request the Council reconvened early on October 14, 1931. The first item of business was to determine whether to invite the U.S. government to send an observer. The Japanese representative strenuously objected, but was overruled by a majority of the Council. The arrival of the American representative, Prestiss Gilbert, two days later was greeted with great excitement, which subsided when

---

[11] *Ibid.*, pp. 12-14.
[12] Stimson to Drummond, October 5, 1931, *Ibid.*, p. 14.

he announced that the U.S. government would not "participate with the members of the Council in the formulation of any action envisaged under [the Covenant of the League of Nations]."[13]

At this Council session Briand introduced a resolution which, for the first time, called upon "the Japanese Government to begin immediately and to proceed progressively with the withdrawal of its troops into the railway zone, so that the total withdrawal may be effected before the date fixed for the next meeting of the Council," scheduled for November 16. Once the withdrawal was completed, the resolution continued, direct negotiations should be opened. While Sao-ke Sze accepted Briand's proposal as a bare minimum, the Japanese representative was vociferously opposed. When Japan's negative vote effectively scuttled the measure, Briand nonetheless declared that his resolution retained its full moral force.

On November 5 Stimson sent a memorandum to Foreign Minister Shidehara underlining U.S. support for the Council's efforts to speed the withdrawal of Japanese troops, adding that Japan should not insist upon entering into negotiations prior to their evacuation of occupied territory. Stimson doubted the wisdom of fixing a date for the withdrawal however, and did not associate the U.S. with that effort.[14]

The Commission of Inquiry

While diplomats debated in Paris, the Kwantung Army was launching a two-pronged attack for control of Manchuria. One force moved southwestward across the Liao River, although it stopped short of Chinchow and Shanhaikwan, the eastern terminus of the Great Wall. A second force moved northward across the Nonni River toward Tsitsihar, the capital of Heilungkiang province.[15] Despite fierce resistance by the Chinese Frontier Defense Army under the command of General Ma Chan-shan, Tsitsihar fell to the Japanese on November 19, 1931.

---

13 *Ibid.*, pp. 18-19.
14 For text see *Ibid.*, pp.30-32.
15 The Nonni River, a tributary of the Sungari River in North Manchuria, flows northerly through the railway center of Angangki at the junctions of the Chinese Eastern Railway and Taonanfu-Angangki-Tsitsihar line. Tsitsihar, capital of Heilungkiang province, is eighteen miles to the north of Angangki.

On November 21, its conquest of southern Manchuria largely completed, Japan now agreed to China's proposal that the League set up a commission to investigate the situation there. A resolution to this effect was adopted on December 10, and the Commission of Inquiry thus established reached the Far East at the end of February 1932. The Commission was headed by Lord Lytton of Great Britain, and included a Chinese assessor, Wellington Koo, and a Japanese assessor, Isaburo Yoshida. The League, a largely European institution, was to face its first and greatest test of strength, in Simpson's words, "in an issue between other races on the opposite side of the world."[16]

III. THE U.S. NON-RECOGNITION DOCTRINE

The Stimson Doctrine and the League of Nations

After the close of the December 1931 Council session, both China and Japan resigned from the League of Nations. In Nanking, in the more radical elements of the KMT formed a new coalition government under President Lin Sen, and Eugene Yu-jen Chen was appointed Minister of Foreign Affairs. Chiang resigned, but was soon called back to head the Military Affairs Commission after the Japanese assault upon Shanghai in March, 1932. In Tokyo, the Seiyukai party, which was more amenable to the military clique, came into power. General Sadao Araki, a leader of the ultranationalist group of young military officers, became war minister.

No sooner had the new Japanese government been formed than an offensive was launched against Chinchow. The U.S., Great Britain, France, and the League of Nations all protested this new aggression, only to be told by Japanese Foreign Minister Kenkichi Yoshizawa that the Japanese army was only engaged in a police action against bandits. By early January 1932 both Chinchow and Shanhaikwan had been captured, and both North China and Inner Mongolia lay exposed to Japanese designs. There were also indications that the Kwantung army was preparing to continue its march northward, towards the city of Harbin.

---

[16] H. L. Stimson, *op. cit.*, p. 201.

Anti-Japanese boycotts and demonstrations in China were seized upon by Japan as a pretext to discredit the Chinese government and to justify further aggression.

Alarmed by the deteriorating situation in China, Stimson sought some means to arouse U.S. public opinion and warn Japan without putting the U.S. at risk of war. He decided to invoke the Bryan-Lansing non-recognition doctrine earlier applied to the Twenty-One Demands. On January 4, 1932, he obtained President Herbert C. Hoover's consent to step out of his role of collaborator with the League of Nations, enlist the support of Britain and France, and apply the non-recognition doctrine as a sanction against Japan's Manchuria aggression. He revealed his plan to the British and French ambassadors the following day and invited their governments to take similar steps. Without waiting for replies from London or Paris, on January 7, he delivered identical notes to the Japanese Ambassador, Katsuji Debuchi, and to Chinese Minister William W. Yen. The key section read:

The American Government continues [to be] confident that the work of the neutral commission recently authorized by the Council of the League of Nations will facilitate an ultimate solution of the difficulties now existing between China and Japan. But in view of the present situation and of its own rights and obligations therein, the American Government deems it to be its duty to notify both the Governments of the Chinese Republic and the Imperial Japanese Government that it can not admit the legality of any situation de facto nor does it intend to recognize any treaty or agreement entered into between these governments, or agents thereof, which may impair the treaty rights of the United States or its citizens in China . . and that it does not intend to recognize any situation, treaty, or agreement which may be brought about by means contrary to the covenants and obligations of the pact of Paris of August 27, 1928. [17]

---

[17] "Conditions in Manchuria," *op. cit.*, pp. 53-54. Department of State, *Foreign Relations of the United States, Japan, 1931-1941*, Vol. I, p. 76. The ultimate intent of non-recognition in this instance is not entirely clear. Richard Current has suggested that there were in fact two non-recognition doctrines. The first was suggested by President Hoover as an alternative to sanctions or military action. The enunciation of non-recognition was envisaged by the President as a final measure. Stimson, on the other hand, saw the doctrine not as an alternative to

In invoking the Nine Power Treaty of 1922 against Japan, Stimson expected British and French support. However, the British Foreign Office, in a private reply dated January 9, took the position that Great Britain's membership in the League of Nations precluded it from sending a similar note. An official communiqué followed, stating that, because Japan had declared her adherence to the Open Door policy in Manchuria, the British government considered it unnecessary to follow the U.S. lead. This was interpreted in both Washington and Tokyo as a rebuff to the United States. Other nations were approached with similar results.

Encouraged by the lack of international support for the American initiative, Yoshizawa on January 16 sent the State Department a sarcastic reply "conceived in a vein of elegant irony which came within an ace of insolence." "At the present juncture," he wrote, "when the very existence of our national policy is involved, it is agreeable to be assured that the American Government is devoting, in a friendly spirit, its sedulous care to a correct appreciation of the situation." He also explicitly denied the applicability of the Nine Power Treaty, asserting that "the present distracted and unsettled state of China is not what was in the contemplation of the high contracting parties at the time of the treaty of Washington."[18]

Even as the Lytton Commission was carrying out its inquiry, Japan was moving rapidly to consolidate her military and political position in Manchuria. As each new area was occupied by Japanese troops, local government administrations were reorganized and Japanese nationals installed in key positions. The culmination of this process was the creation of the puppet state of "Manchukuo" on February 18, 1932. The last Manchu emperor, Henry Pu Yi, was installed as Manchukuo's "regent," but his government was totally dominated by Japanese, with nearly two hundred serving in the central government alone.

---

further action but as a preliminary step to economic and military sanctions, a way of sharpening the issue between the United States and Japan. "The Hoover Doctrine and the Stimson Doctrine," *The American Historical Review*, XLVIII (1954), pp. 512- 542.

18 "Conditions in Manchuria," *op. cit.*, pp. 54-56.

Earlier, on January 28, 1932, Japan had launched an attack upon Shanghai using naval forces. This expansion of the Sino-Japanese conflict alarmed the League of Nations, which began to align itself with the U.S. non-recognition doctrine. On March 11, 1932, the Assembly of the League formally adopted the Stimson Doctrine in a resolution which declared "that it is incumbent upon the members of the League of Nations not to recognize any situation, treaty or agreement which may be brought about by any means contrary to the Covenant of the League of Nations or to the Pact of Paris."[19] This resolution did not deter Japan from extending formal diplomatic recognition to Manchukuo on September 15, thus presenting the League with a fait accompli.

The Lytton Commission Report, submitted the following year, found Japan guilty of aggression. This was accepted by the Assembly of the League, which went on to adopt a resolution obligating League members not to recognize Manchukuo. Only a few states, chief among them Nazi Germany and Fascist Italy, ever recognized the Japanese puppet state.

Stimson's Letter to Senator Borah, February 23, 1932

After the Japanese attack on Shanghai and the creation of Manchukuo, Stimson issued another public warning to the Japanese, this time in the form of an open letter to Senator William E. Borah, Chairman of the Senate Committee on Foreign Relations. This letter, dated February 23, 1932, reaffirmed American sympathy for Chinese nationalism and the principle of noninterference in China's internal affairs. Commenting on the Nine Power Treaty and other agreements signed at the Washington Conference, Stimson stated that the American government had surrendered its then commanding lead in battleship construction in return for assurances "against the military aggrandizement of any other power at the expense of China." He also suggested that other nations join the U.S. in applying the non-recognition principle to "any situation, treaty or agreement entered into" by Japan

---

[19] Cited by M. Shen, *op. cit.*, pp. 311-312.

and China "in violation of the covenants of these treaties, which affect the rights of our Government or its citizens in China."[20]

Stimson's declaration caused a stir in diplomatic and naval circles in Japan, primarily because the threatened resumption of naval competition in the Pacific would challenge the effective supremacy that Japan now enjoyed in those waters. Stimson's warning was not followed up by action, however, and did not have a decisive effect upon the Manchurian situation. His non-recognition doctrine, on the other hand, was an event of historical importance in Sino-American relations, for it defined the American position on Japanese aggression in China for the entire period from 1931 to 1945. It placed the U.S. government, as well as American public opinion, firmly on the side of China.

IV. THE BATTLE OF SHANGHAI

Shanghai Episode, January 28, 1932

Nationalist feelings were running high in China after the Manchurian aggression, especially in Shanghai, which had become a center of anti-Japanese agitation. In an unfortunate incident, a group of Japanese was mobbed by a Chinese crowd at Chapei, near the International Settlement. One Japanese was killed and another seriously wounded in the melee. Further deaths occurred when a crowd of Japanese residents took it upon themselves to secure revenge. Tension mounted. The Japanese Consul General in Shanghai issued an ultimatum to Mayor Wu Te-chen demanding, among other things, the immediate dissolution of all anti-Japanese organizations. Although Wu accepted these terms, the local commander of the Japanese fleet, Rear Admiral Koichi Shiozawa, nonetheless decided "to teach the Chinese a lesson."[21] The Japanese navy, chafing at the army's victories in Manchuria, hoped to score a few of its own. On January 28 Shiozawa ordered Japanese marines to attack Chinese emplacements north of the Settlement. Chapei was bombed, and

---

[20] Department of State, *Foreign Relations of the United States, Japan, 1931- 41*, Vol. I, p. 83.
[21] W. King, *op. cit.*, p. 31.

a nearby railway station bombarded. The battle of Shanghai lasted for six weeks.

International Intervention

Unlike Manchuria, where Westerners had few interests, Shanghai was the very center of foreign commercial activity in China. Stimson wrote that the fighting in Shanghai shocked "the merchants of Great Britain into a realization of what Japanese aggression toward China ultimately meant to them,"[22] The British, as a consequence, vigorously protested the Japanese bombings at Shanghai, and immediately sent naval and marine reinforcements to the International Settlement in Shanghai. Washington ordered the 31st Infantry Division transferred from Manila to Shanghai and concentrated the entire American Asiatic Squadron offshore.[23]

The U.S. and Great Britain, along with France, Italy, and other countries, joined forces in an effort to halt hostilities, using the League of Nations machinery to coordinate their efforts at mediation. Neither the American position (that the U.S. must act independently of the League) nor the British position (that Britain could not act independently of the League) was allowed to hinder their collaboration.

The Chinese government invoked Articles X and XV of the Covenant, which obliged the League to adjudicate responsibility for the conflict and opened the possibility of sanctions. Drummond immediately created a committee of inquiry consisting of consular representatives from France, Italy, Great Britain, Germany, Norway, and Spain to report directly to the Council on conditions in Shanghai. Stimson ordered the American Consul General in Shanghai to cooperate with the committee, and further directed the American Ambassador to Switzerland to serve as a liaison officer between the U.S. and the League on the Shanghai situation.[24]

---

22 H. L. Stimson, *op. cit.*, p.134.
23 H. L. Stimson, *op. cit.*, p. 140. Stimson attributed the Japanese accommodation to international pressure in Shanghai in part to the presence of the United States battleship fleet in the Pacific, where it had come for previously scheduled maneuvers centered at Hawaii.
24 H. L. Stimson, op., cit., p. 141.

On February 16, 1932, the Council appealed to Japan to "recognize the very special responsibilities for forbearance and restraint which develop upon it in the present conflict, in virtue of the position of Japan as a member of the League of Nations and as a permanent member of the Council." The appeal went on to state that League members would not recognize as valid territorial gains obtained by military force, thus adopting, as its formal policy towards Japan's encroachments in China, the Stimson doctrine of non-recognition.

Japan, much annoyed by this demarché, replied on February 23 that the appeal should have targeted the "the aggressive Chinese forces." Tokyo then proceeded to deny that China was a nation: "The Japanese Government does not and cannot consider that China is an organized people within the meaning of the Covenant of the League of Nations. We must face the facts: and the fundamental fact is that there is no unified control in China and no authority which is entitled to claim entire control in China."[25]

The Ceasefire Agreement

Efforts to arrange a truce and establish neutral zones in Shanghai were fruitless, and the battle continued to rage. To the surprise of the Japanese, the Chinese 19th Route Army put up a stiff resistance. It took the Japanese forces, heavily reinforced, three weeks to capture the Woosung Fort, which commanded the entrance to Shanghai's port.[26] The military stalemate was broken and the Chinese army executed an orderly retreat westward. Japan's losses totaled 634 killed and 791 wounded, against Chinese military losses of 4,274 killed and 1,770 wounded.[27] By March 1932, when the Special Assembly of the League convened in Geneva, fighting was limited to sporadic skirmishes.

---

[25] Cited in W. King, *op. cit.*, p. 33.

[26] The original invading force of 3,000 Japanese marines had to be supplanted by three divisions and a mixed brigade of the Japanese Army before the Chinese forces were finally driven back creating a profound impression upon the overall Chinese morale. Cf. *The Report of the Commission of Enquiry*, League of Nations Publications No. C. 663 M. 320., 1932, pp. 86-87. This document was hereafter referred to as the Lytton Report.

[27] Cited in H. K. Tong, *op. cit.*, p. 193.

With the unofficial assistance of neutral diplomats, China and Japan eventually agreed upon terms for a cease-fire, which was signed on May 5, 1932. The status quo ante in Shanghai was fully restored. In signing the agreement, the Chinese made two reservations, one of which was that nothing in the agreement imply a permanent restriction on the movement of Chinese troops in Chinese territory. The Japanese did not take exception at the time but, when fighting broke out in Shanghai again in August 1937, falsely claimed that the presence of Chinese troops in the Chinese administered suburbs of Shanghai constituted a breach of the ceasefire agreement.

Ten days after the signing of the Sino-Japanese cease-fire agreement, Japanese Premier Tsuyoshi Inukai was assassinated. Admiral Minoru Sato became the new Premier and Yasuya Uchida the new Minister for Foreign Affairs. The new Japanese government proposed to the U.S., Great Britain, and other powers that a conference be held in Tokyo to review the question of Western interests in China, presumably for the purpose of ratifying the gains that Japan had made at China's expense. The U.S. and Great Britain carefully avoided this pitfall, maintaining that any international conference dealing with China must take place in that country and include the Chinese government as a party.[28]

V. THE LEAGUE AND THE LYTTON REPORT

The report of the Lytton Commission, which was published by the League on October 2, 1932, was heavily critical of Japan. Among its principal conclusions were that "The military operations of the Japanese troops [in regard to the original attack on Mukden] . . . cannot be regarded as measures of legitimate self-defense." The Japanese were in actual control of Manchukuo, a regime that "cannot be considered to have been called into existence by a genuine and spontaneous independence movement." The maintenance of the present regime in Manchuria would be unsatisfactory, while a mere restoration of the status quo ante would be no solution. The report recommended the creation of an autonomous Manchuria within the Chinese Republic, the

---

[28] W. King, *op. cit.*, pp. 36-37.

negotiation of a new Sino-Japanese commercial treaty and, finally, temporary international cooperation in the internal reconstruction of China, as earlier suggested by the late Dr. Sun Yat-sen.[29]

Although the Lytton Report incensed Japan, it fell short of satisfying China. Its elaborate plan for the stabilization of peace in Asia failed to include any concrete measures for the expulsion of Japan from Manchuria. When Japan failed to accept the Report's recommendations, however, the Assembly unanimously passed a resolution on February 24, 1933, stating that any future "plan of agreement should observe the principles of the League Covenant, the Pact of Paris, and the Nine Power Treaty of Washington . . . [and] conform to the principles and conditions laid down in the Lytton Report.[30] In addition, an advisory committee on Manchuria was formed to examine the question of non-recognition as well as the question of a possible arms embargo.

The reaction of the American government to the February 24 resolution was very favorable, and the League's offer of observer status on the new committee was accepted by Washington. The Japanese representative, however, walked out in protest when the resolution was adopted. The following month Japan gave notice of its intention to withdraw from the League in two years. On March 27, 1935, Japan ceased being a member of the League of Nations.

The League had pronounced its judgment on the Japanese aggression in Manchuria, and had agreed not to recognize her gains there, but to no effect. The only action which might have been forced a withdrawal—the imposition of economic sanctions—was carefully avoided. The rise of Nazism in Germany, combined with the continuing worldwide depression, forced the Manchurian crisis into the background. No European power was willing to risk a confrontation with Japan over an issue so far removed from its everyday concerns. Neither was the United States, which had just embarked upon the domestic revolution known as

---

[29] S. F. Bemis, *op. cit.*, pp. 469-470.

[30] Forty-four states were present out of a total membership of fifty-seven in the Assembly. Forty-two, including China, voted for the report. Siam abstained, Japan voted in the negative. The report was adopted unanimously, since it had, as required by the Covenant, obtained the affirmative votes of a majority of the member states including all the members of the Council other than the parties to the disputes.

the New Deal, eager to embroil itself in the Far East. Manchuria, and increasingly China herself, was left to the mercy of an ever more rapacious Japan.

VI. THE JAPANESE MOVE SOUTH

China's Dilemma

Japanese militarists, now firmly in power in Tokyo and emboldened by the League's lack of resolution, continued their advance in China. Shanhaikwan, the gateway into China proper, was occupied in early January 1933. Jehol province was brought within "Manchukuo" in February, while the following month Chahar was taken. By May Japanese troops had moved inside the Great Wall in eastern Hopei province, directly menacing Peking.

Chiang, knowing that the Nationalist army could not yet face the Japanese onslaught alone, and that no aid would be forthcoming from abroad, decided to buy time by asking for a truce. He recognized that such a decision would not be popular, and that it would give political capital to his domestic enemies, including the Kiangsi Communists. Nevertheless, he took the course which he believed best for China.

The result was the Tangku Truce Agreement, signed on May 31, 1933, by the local military representatives of both countries. Realizing Chiang's dilemma, the militarists in Tokyo drove a hard bargain. The Chinese were forced to withdraw their troops to a line just north of Peking, leaving the Kwantung Army in effective control of northern Hopei. The Japanese were soon making new demands, and in May 1935 a new truce, the so-called Ho-Umetsu agreement, was signed. China was forced to consent to the complete withdrawal of its troops from Hopei province, the dismissal of many officials not acceptable to Japan, and the discontinuance of anti-Japanese agitation in China. Chiang paid a high price in territory and prestige for the time he needed to strengthen and reunify China.[31] Following the withdrawal of Chinese troops from Hopei, the Japanese established a second puppet regime in the border

---

[31] H. K. Tong, *op. cit.*, pp. 194-195.

provinces, and ran smuggling operations from the occupied north into free China.

The Japanese "Monroe Doctrine" for East Asia

The full magnitude of Japanese ambitions in East Asia were first revealed in early 1934 by Koki Hirota, the Japanese Foreign Minister. In a speech to the Diet, Hirota declared that Japan arrogated to itself the "entire burden of responsibility" for the preservation of peace in East Asia and would henceforth exercise veto power over China's international relations.[32]   In the Amau Statement of April 17 Japan revealed more fully the parameters of its "divine mission" in East Asia. All foreign assistance to China which would, in the judgment of the Japanese government, imperil "peace" was to stop. Other nations were to refrain from supplying not only munitions and military equipment to China, but also technical and financial assistance.[33]

The Chinese government rejected the Amau Statement, declaring on April 26, 1934, that China would permit no single nation, or even the League of Nations, to infringe upon her sovereignty. The maintenance of peace in the Far East was, as China reaffirmed, the responsibility of the world collective-security system represented by the League, and neither Japan alone, nor Japan in combination with China, could assume this role.[34]

The Chinese government attempted to invoke the Nine Power Treaty, but the League did not respond. The U.S. and Great Britain, whom Nanking had expected to vigorously oppose Japan, were instead satisfied

---

[32] There was a fundamental difference between the original American Monroe Doctrine and what the Japanese described as their "Asiatic Monroe Doctrine." While the American policy under the Monroe Doctrine has been to give South American republics the fullest opportunity for self-development without interference by European nations, the Japanese Doctrine, as indicated by her activities since 1931, had an exactly opposite effect. The Japanese conception of the Monroe Doctrine was to exclude competitors while providing for her own self-aggrandizement in contradiction to the Open Door doctrine.

[33] For the full text of the Amau Statement, see the *New York Times*, April 21, 1934, M. Shen, *op. cit.*, pp. 409-410.

[34] Cited in W. Levi, *Modern China's Foreign Policy* (Minneapolis: University of Minnesota Press, 1953), p. 208.

to send notes of protest. The American note, which was signed by the new American Secretary of State, Cordell Hull, and delivered in Tokyo on April 29, 1934, merely reiterated American policy toward China and reaffirmed U.S. treaty rights. This weak reaction so encouraged the Japanese that they immediately attempted to obtain an agreement from the U.S. dividing the Pacific into spheres of influence. The proposed agreement, which was presented by Japanese Ambassador Hiroshi Saito to Hull in May, would have given Japan a free hand in China with no compensation or gain to the U.S. Hull had the good sense to reject it.[35]

Undeterred, the Japanese continued in their efforts to make China a protectorate. All foreign assistance to China's reconstruction, such as the technical aid program drawn up by the League experts, Anglo-American financial assistance, the Frederick Leith-Ross economic mission sent by the British government to China, and the currency reforms introduced by the Chinese government, met with opposition from Tokyo.

Hull Statement of December 5, 1935

In early 1935 the Japan army began to advance again in Chahar province and along the Great Wall, penetrating into China proper. By summer Tokyo's intentions were clear: five provinces in North China— Hopei, Chagar, Suiyuan, Shansi, and Shantung—were to be detached from the jurisdiction of the Nanking government and another puppet state established. Chiang again authorized truce negotiations with the object of checking Japanese designs and salvaging as much territory as possible.

Although Washington coursed concern over the deteriorating situation in North China, there was no basic change in the American position. In a press statement on December 5, 1935, Hull simply reiterated the long-standing U.S. position:

Political disturbance and pressures give rise to uncertainty and misgiving and tend to produce economic and social dislocations. They make difficult the enjoyment of treaty rights and the fulfillment

---

[35] J. C. Grew, *Turbulent Era, A Diplomatic Record of Forty Years, 1904-1945* (Boston: Houghton-Mifflin Co. 1952), Vol. II, p. 997.

of treaty obligations. . . . The views of the American Government with regard to such matters, not alone in relations to China but in relation to the whole world, are well known. . . . This Government adheres to the provisions of the treaties to which it is a party and continues to bespeak respect by all nations for the provisions of treaties solemnly entered into for the purpose of facilitating and regulating, to reciprocal and common advantage, the contacts between and among the countries signatory.[36]

The only concrete demonstration of U.S. concern for China was a mutual agreement with the Nanking government to raise their legations to embassy status. Both the Chinese Minister to America, Alfred Sao-ke Sze, and the American Minister to China, Nelson T. Johnson, two veteran diplomats, were promoted to ambassador in June 1935.

The Collapse of Collective Security—Overture to War

Overall, the Manchurian crisis constituted a disheartening test of the principle of collective security. A powerful permanent member of the Council attacked a weaker member of the League of Nations, bringing it into direct confrontation with other powers both inside and outside the League.[37] Although the League was able to investigate and publish the Lytton Report, neither Great Britain nor France, the two powers which dominated the League, was prepared to apply sanctions against Japan without the positive support of the United States. Caught in the grip of the Great Depression, the U.S. was even more isolationist in the thirties than it had been the decade before. The only sanction that Washington was willing to apply, however, was the non-recognition doctrine, which had no deterrent effect on Japan. Japanese aggression continued unabated.

---

[36] Department of State, *Foreign Relations of the United States, Japan, 1931- 1941*, Vol. I, p. 240.

[37] The period 1919-1931 was not one of unbroken peace. There were armed conflicts between Poland and Russia, Poland and Lithuania, Greece and Turkey, as well as armed intervention by the western powers and Japan in the Soviet Russia. But all these were of short duration and were settled without endangering the peace of the great powers.

The Sian Coup d'État

In its negotiations with China in 1936 Japan's basic demands were (1) cessation of anti-Japanese activity in China, (2) tacit de facto recognition of Manchukuo by China, and (3) cooperation between China and Japan for the suppression of communism.[38] The Japanese Army, which continued to insist on "autonomy" for China's five northern provinces, succeeded in prolonging the negotiations by invading Suiyuan province, but in December Tokyo moderated its demands. For its part, the Nationalist government was being advised by the British to ignore the nearly continuous Japanese provocations and make reasonable concessions.

Chiang's policy during this period was internal unification—that is, the eradication of the Chinese Communist Party—before resistance to external aggression. Chang Hsueh-liang had been appointed deputy commander-in-chief of the anti-Communist campaign to accomplish this end, but for some time had been conspiring with the communists to oppose Chiang's policy. Although aware of this plot, Chiang flew to Sian on December 12, 1936, hoping to win back the rebellious general to the anti-Communist cause. Instead, he found himself put under house arrest and detained for a fortnight. He finally convinced Chang to release him "without having to sign any terms," to quote the late Dr. Hu Shih, and the two left Sian together on Christmas day.[39] Further negotiations with Japan were soon called off, however, and the following July full-scale hostilities broke out.

This attempted coup d'état was a master stroke by the Chinese Communists, who realized the benefits that a united anti-Japanese front with the Nationalist government would bring them. Stalin also favored the idea, hoping that strenuous Chinese resistance to Japan under Chiang's leadership would absorb Tokyo's energies. Thus began an

---

[38] These demands were contained Hirota's so-called "Three Points Program" presented to the Chinese Ambassador in Tokyo, Chiang Tso-ping, by Japanese Foreign Minister, Koki Hirota, on October 28, 1935.

[39] S. Hu, "China in Stalin's Grand Strategy," *Foreign Affairs*, October 1950, pp. 27-33.

eight-year period of collaboration between the Nationalist government
and the Chinese Communists in the war of resistance against Japan.

7

THE SINO-JAPANESE WAR
1937–1941

I. START OF JAPAN'S UNDECLARED WAR ON CHINA

International Situation and Causes of Japan's Attack

By 1937 the coming lines of conflict in the world were already drawn in sharp relief. The Seventh Congress of the Comintern, assembled in August 1935, held that Fascism must be combated wherever it appeared, and adopted "United Front" tactics for this purpose. Germany and Japan responded on November 16, 1936, by concluding the Anti-Comintern Pact.[1] Russo-Japanese hostility steadily increased in intensity, as each power tried to prevent the other from penetrating further into China.

Meanwhile, the Western powers did nothing. The isolationist attitude of the U.S. was matched by the appeasement sentiments of Britain and France. Although the Fascists and Communists were fighting openly in neighboring Spain, the democratic nations adopted A policy of non-intervention. In China, too, the Western powers stood idly by. The Western powers even permitted the Washington (1922) and London (1930) naval treaties to expire at the end of 1936, allowing Japan to embark upon a rapid expansion of its naval strength.

---

[1] Italy joined the Anti-Comintern Pact on November 6, 1937. H. F. MacNair & D. F. Lach, *Modern Far Eastern International Relations* (New York: Van Nostrand Co., 1955), p. 474.

When Japan launched a full-scale attack on China in 1937, it did so virtually certain that no foreign power would intervene. Great Britain, France, and the Soviet Union were preoccupied with the growing strength of the Fascist states under Hitler and Mussolini. As far as America was concerned, her repeated protests of Japanese actions in Manchuria and North China had come to be regarded as just so much talk. Isolationist America could not even bring itself to make threats, much less take action.[2]

Within Japan, the military was in firm control by 1937, and was eager to undertake a large-scale military operation in China proper and push southward into Indochina. There was also concern that China, under the leadership of Chiang, was making such substantial political and economic progress that in a few years time she might prove impossible to completely conquer. Another factor was the coming confrontation with the Soviet Union, since Japanese strategists were convinced that it was only a matter of time before the U.S.S.R. would be strong enough militarily to resume Czarist Russia's traditional role as the principal challenger of Japan's aims on the Asian continent. They favored a quick consolidation of the Japanese hold on China while Moscow was still militarily weak.

The Japanese militarists had repeatedly tried to win Chiang's cooperation with their plans, but he had steadfastly refused to allow China to be drawn into Japan's "co-prosperity sphere." In the end they decided that since Chiang and the Nationalist government would not yield, they must be eliminated. Wildly overconfident after their uncontested advance into North China, they assumed that Nanking's resistance would be brief and ineffectual.

By early 1937 Chiang was in the midst of vigorous military preparations for the impending showdown with Japan. He refused to consider further compromises, even though his army was poorly equipped, and his navy and air force only a fraction of Japan's.[3]

---

[2] H. Feis, *The Road to Pearl Harbor, The Coming of War Between the United States and Japan* (Princeton: Princeton University Press, 1950), p. 7.

[3] For details see Chang Chi-yung (ed.), K'ang-jih Chan-shih (*A History of China's War of Resistance against Japanese Aggression*), (Taipei: United Publishing Center, 1966), pp. 17-18.

The Lu-kuo-chiao Incident

The Sino-Japanese war began with a minor skirmish between Chinese and Japanese troops on the night of July 7, 1937, at Lu-kuo-chiao (Marco Polo Bridge), nine miles southeast of Peking. Tokyo later claimed that its soldiers had been fired upon by Chinese troops while engaged in "night maneuvers" near the village of Wanping. What is beyond dispute is that the Japanese commander the following day launched a major attack on the 29th Army, under the command of General Sung Cheh-yuan, which was based in the vicinity. Within six days the Japanese had assembled 20,000 troops in the Peking region, and reinforcements were en route from Japan. The militarists were on the march, and the conflagration spread rapidly.

China made one last effort to seek a peaceful, yet honorable, solution to the conflict. "We seek peace," Chiang declared on July 17, "but we do not seek peace at any cost. We do not want war, but we may be forced to defend ourselves."[4] He still hoped for peace, he said, but this hope depended upon the Japanese Army.

Chiang also tried to enlist foreign assistance. On July 16, 1937, the Nationalist government delivered a circular note to Germany, the U.S.S.R., and all the signatories of the Nine Power Treaty except Japan. The invasion of North China by Japanese military forces constituted a clear violation of China's sovereignty, the note stated, and was contrary to the letter and spirit of the Nine Power Treaty, the Pact of Paris, and the Covenant of the League of Nations. China "holds herself in readiness to settle her differences with Japan by any of the pacific means known in international law and treaties."[5] This was a clear signal that China would welcome an international peace conference in which the U.S. would be expected to play a leading role.

That same day Secretary of State Hull issued a statement on the principles of international relations which, although it did not mention the Sino-Japanese conflict, was clearly applicable to it. Hull's principles

---

[4] H. K. Tong, *Chiang Kai-shek* (Taipei: China Publishing Co., 1953), p. 239.
[5] W. King, *China and the League of Nations: The Sino-Japanese Controversy* (New York: St. John's University Press, 1965), p. 71.

included the maintenance of peace, noninterference in the internal affairs of other nations, and the resolution of international problems by processes carried out in a spirit of mutual helpfulness and accommodation. "We avoid entering into alliances or entangling commitments," he concluded, "but we believe in cooperative efforts by peaceful means in support of the principle herein above stated."[6] A later statement, issued on August 23, reaffirmed these principles and made somewhat more explicit reference to Asia.

The U.S. did not respond to Nanking's idea for an international conference, merely urging China and Japan to seek peace. Privately, the U.S. on August 10, 1937, offered its good offices to Japan to help mediate the dispute. Not surprisingly, the Japanese failed to respond. No parallel approach was made to the Nationalist government, since the U.S. felt that this would serve no useful purpose.

At first Washington took a neutral stance toward the two belligerents, following the advice of the U.S. Ambassador to Japan, Joseph C. Grew. Grew had suggested that America should not get involved in the conflict. Instead, American lives, property, and rights should be protected in China, and friendship maintained with both governments. Additional U.S. Marines were sent to Shanghai for the protection of the International Settlement, but U.S. citizens in China who could leave were advised to do so. The governments of both Japan and China were notified that the United States reserved all its treaty rights in China, and the right to compensation for damages inflicted.[7]

After a short lull in the fighting, Japanese troops attacked Peking, Tientsin, and Tungchow. On August 9, 1937, the ancient capital of China fell, and Tientsin soon followed. General Chiang issued a statement to the nation, declaring that the Nationalist government was prepared to "struggle to the bitter end." Chiang's strategy was to "trade space for time," making the enemy pay dearly for each advance. Retreating Chinese armies would practice a scorched earth policy, so that the pursuing invaders would have no food or shelter. Chiang hoped to

---

6   Department of State, *Foreign Relations of the United States, Japan, 1931- 41*, Vol. 1, p. 396.

7   J. W. Pratt, *A History of United States Foreign Policy* (New York: Prentice-Hall, 1955), p. 624.

draw the Japanese deep into the vast interior of China where, with front lines spread thin and supply lines exposed, they would be vulnerable to counterattack. It was a strategy of war by attrition, and Chiang was confident that the Japanese would eventually crack under the strain.[8]

The Second Battle of Shanghai, August 13, 1937

The Japanese government was determined to extend the war into the lower Yangtze, and a large fleet of thirty warships from Japan was soon anchored off Shanghai. Japanese forces in the city made feverish preparations for an attack upon Chinese defenses. By August the city was in a state of extreme tension.

Two days before the outbreak of hostilities on August 13, the ambassadors of the five Western powers in Nanking, Britain, the United States, France, Germany and Italy, made a last-ditch effort to persuade China and Japan to spare Shanghai from hostilities. The American government also independently appealed to both combatants to avoid making Shanghai a base of military operations or a theater of war.[9]

Once the fighting began, Great Britain proposed that both sides should withdraw their troops and warships from the vicinity of Shanghai, and that the U.S., France, and Britain would undertake to protect Japanese lives and interests in the International Settlement. The Chinese government eagerly accepted this proposal, but Japan refused to give way. Instead, Japan demanded that all Chinese troops be withdrawn from the Chinese-administered territory of Shanghai and all defense works there demolished, falsely claiming that these violated the terms of the 1932 Cease-fire Agreement. These demands were rejected by the Nanking government, which declared on August 16 that China would exercise her right of self-defense against foreign aggression.

On August 13 Japanese marines attacked the Chinese Civic Center in Shanghai. The Nationalist government, which had decided that the Japanese must be resisted to the full extent of the nation's strength, ordered the 87th and 88th Divisions to counterattack. The Chinese army's best divisions and the entirety of her small air force were thrown

---

[8] H. K. Tong, *op. cit.*, pp. 240–241.
[9] W. King, *op. cit.*, p. 73.

into the defense of Shanghai. Although the Chinese military had little in the way of modern equipment, the indomitable spirit of her fighting men helped to make up for material deficiencies. The Second Battle of Shanghai was one of China's ablest military operations when, for three months, outgunned Chinese troops withstood a Japanese force numbering 150,000 men, inflicting heavy losses upon them.

The Shanghai stand-off was finally broken in early November 1937, when a Japanese force landed at Chapoo, fifty miles southwest of Shanghai. The outflanked Chinese army was compelled to abandon the defense of Shanghai, and the Japanese advanced quickly upon Nanking. The nationalist capital fell on December 13, 1937, and the resulting slaughter of hundreds of thousands of helpless men, women, and children by rampaging Japanese soldiers shocked the civilized world.

On December 12, 1937, the U.S.S. Panay was sunk at anchor by Japanese aircraft, and two American sailors were killed. Three Standard Oil tankers were also attacked and destroyed. After an American protest, the incident was brought to a close on December 24 by a Japanese note "admitting responsibility, expressing regret, and offering amends." The Japanese agreed to pay an indemnity amounting to U.S. $2,214,007.36 to the U.S. government.[10]

President Roosevelt's "Quarantine" Speech

As Japanese military operations in China increased in intensity, the Roosevelt administration grappled with the question of whether to apply the Neutrality Act of 1937 to the conflict.[11] It decided against doing so because neither Japan nor China had actually declared war, and also because it was thought that China would suffer more from an embargo than would Japan. There was also the concern that war with Japan might result. Roosevelt did forbid the use of government-owned ships to carry

---

[10] For details see H. F. MacNair & D. F. Lach, *op. cit.*, pp. 478-479.
[11] Specifically, the Third Neutrality Act of May 1, 1937. See Department of State, *Peace and War, United States Foreign Policy, 1931-1941* (Washington: 1943), pp. 355-365. By a joint resolution of January 8, 1937, U.S. Congress had prohibited the exportation of arms, armaments, ammunition, and implements of war from the United States to Spain. Cf. R. J. Bartlett, *op. cit.*, pp. 572-577.

arms, ammunition, or implements of war to either party, and warned private shipowners that they engaged in such trade at their own risk.[12]

On October 5, 1937, President Roosevelt gave his famous "quarantine" speech in Chicago. He spoke of the "spread of an epidemic of world lawlessness," declaring that if "an epidemic of physical disease starts to spread, the community approves of and joins in a quarantine of patients in order to protect the health of the community against the spread of the disease." He asserted that "war is a contagion, whether it be declared or undeclared. It can engulf states and peoples remote from the original scene of hostilities." While no nations were specifically mentioned, clearly implicit in his speech was a condemnation of Japan. Roosevelt recommended no concrete course of action, however, merely concluding that "America hates war. America hopes for peace. Therefore, America actively engages in the search for peace."[13]

The following day the Department of State issued an official protest against Japanese actions in China: "In the light of the unfolding developments in the Far East the Government of the United States has been forced to the conclusion that the action of Japan in China is inconsistent with the principles which should govern the relationships between nations and is contrary to the provisions of the Nine Power Treaty of February 6, 1922, regarding principles and policies to be followed in matters concerning China, and to those of the Kellogg-Briand Pact of August 27, 1928."[14] A Nine Power Treaty conference was proposed to discuss Japan's actions in China and measures to deal with them.

So strong was isolationist feeling in the U.S. Congress that Roosevelt hastened to explain that he had proposed a Nine Power Treaty conference

---

12 On September 16, 1937, the USS Wichita, operated by the U.S. Maritime Commission, was required to offload at San Diego a cargo of airplanes that it was transporting from Baltimore to China.

13 Roosevelt Address at Chicago, October 5, 1937. Department of State, *Peace and War, U.S. Foreign Policy, 1931-1941*, pp. 383-387.

14 Department of State, *Foreign Relations of the United States, Japan, 1931- 41*, Vol. 1, p. 396.

only for the purpose of mediating the Sino-Japanese conflict.[15] The only tangible result of the "quarantine" speech was that many Americans began boycotting Japanese goods. As always, America's words had not been followed by any concrete action, and hence had no effect on Tokyo's behavior.

As a whole, America was inclined to speak more sternly to Japan in official pronouncements than the European powers, but it was equally reluctant to consider military or economic sanctions. King George VI on October 26 indicated that the British Government would "persist in its policy of attempting, in cooperation with other governments, whether members of the League of Nations or not, to mitigate the suffering caused by the conflict and to bring it to a conclusion." Foreign Secretary Eden, in an address to the House of Commons on November 1, made it clear that action by the American Congress was the sine qua non for British action in regards to Asia.[16] "Great Britain would go as far as the United States," he stated, "not rushing ahead and not being left behind."

Throughout the 1930's the U.S. was inclined to maintain a separate peace if war should come in Asia or Europe. President Roosevelt's only reference to foreign affairs in his first inaugural address in 1933 was a brief reference to the Good Neighbor policy. His second inaugural address in 1937 made no reference to international relations at all.

II. THE BRUSSELS CONFERENCE IN 1937

China Appeals Again to the League

On September 12, 1937, the Chinese government, invoking Articles 10, 11, and 17 of the Covenant, appealed to the League of Nations to "take such action as may be appropriate and necessary" in the face of Japanese aggression. The first two articles had been invoked previously.

---

[15] In fact, the "quarantine" passage was inserted in the speech without the knowledge of the State Department and was deplored by Cordell Hull, who foresaw the adverse public reaction.

[16] I. S. Friedman, *British Relations with China*, 1931-1939 (New York: Institute of Pacific Relations, 1940), pp. 104-105.

Article 17 provided for the League to invite Japan, no longer a member, to assume the obligations of membership on an ad hoc basis. The Assembly of the League turned the matter over to its Far Eastern Advisory Committee.[17] The U.S. sent an observer, American Minister to Switzerland Leland Harrison, to follow the deliberations of this Committee, but he was instructed not to take the initiative in any action the League might decide upon.

The Advisory Committee, on October 5, denounced Japan for violating the Nine Power Treaty, and called for the League to invite this Treaty's signatories to initiate a discussion of Japan's actions in China. These suggestions were ratified by the full Assembly the following day, with the U.S. signifying her general accord.[18]

Although both Great Britain and the U.S. wanted to see a Nine Power Treaty Conference convened, neither wanted to be the inviting power. London and Washington feared embarrassment in case of failure. France and Holland also declined, for fear of offending Japan. The British and the Americans finally prevailed upon the Belgian government to issue invitations for a conference to be held in Brussels on October 30.[19]

All the signatories of the Nine Power Treaty, with the exception of Japan, accepted the Belgian invitation. Japan declined on the grounds that her actions in China were taken in self-defense and thus did not violate the Treaty. She also pointed out that the conference had

---

[17] The Far Eastern Advisory Committee was created in 1932, and had remained in being after a few years of inactivity. It became a committee of twenty-three states including China, the Soviet Union and the United States in its non-voting capacity. Munters, Foreign Minister of Latvia, was the chairman. The Committee declined to form a sub-committee to study the matter.

[18] The complete account of deliberations is in the League of Nations Official Journal, Special Supplement, No. 177, *Sino-Japanese Conflict* (Geneva: League of Nations, 1937), pp. 8-26.

[19] Be it noted, however, in connection with the convening of the Brussels Conference, that while the Four-Power Pacific Treaty contained the provision for calling under specified conditions, a conference of its signatories, no such stipulation was incorporated in the Nine-Power Treaty. The provision for "full and frank communication" did not render it mandatory upon any of the states to use an international conference as the channel for "communication."

originally been proposed by the League, whose resolutions had been unfriendly to Japan.[20]

Of the other countries which had been invited because of their "special interest in the Far East," only Germany declined. Berlin had signed the Anti-Comintern Agreement with Tokyo some time before, and did not wish to offend its ally. Nineteen countries participated in the conference: Australia, Belgium, Bolivia, Canada, China, Denmark, France, Great Britain, India, Italy, Mexico, Norway, New Zealand, the Netherlands, Portugal, Sweden, the Union of South Africa, the United States and the Soviet Union.

III. THE DELIBERATIONS OF THE CONFERENCE

The Opening of the Conference

The Brussels Conference was opened on November 3, 1937, by the Belgian Foreign Minister, Henri Spaak, who regretted the absence of Japan. The U.S., British, and French delegates all expressed devotion to the sanctity of treaties and hoped that the conference would succeed in bringing about a fair settlement of the conflict between China and Japan.[21] The aim of the Conference, they insisted, was to expedite the end of the fighting by friendly means. If conciliation failed, they had no other plans.[22]

Another group, consisting of the Soviet Union, Mexico, and New Zealand, believed that if conciliation failed, positive steps should be taken

---

[20] Department of State, *U.S. Foreign Relations with Japan, 1931-1941*, Vol. 1, pp. 402-403.

[21] For details see T. Tsien, *China and the Nine Power Conference at Brussels in 1937* (New York: St. Johns University Press, 1964).

[22] The American delegates, led by Norman H. Davies, went to Brussels, as President Roosevelt was at pains to point out, "without any commitments on the part of this government to other governments." Roosevelt also emphasized the fact that the purpose of the conference was "to seek by agreement a solution of the present situation in China" rather than to coerce or bring pressure on either of the belligerents. Press Release, October 23, 1937, p. 313. As quoted in A. W. Griswold, *The Far Eastern Policy of the United States.* (New Haven: Yale University Press, 1964), p. 460.

to aid China. After Soviet delegate Maxim Litvinov left Brussels on November 9, nothing more was heard about positive steps. A third group consisted of the Scandinavian countries, Denmark, Norway, and Sweden, which were afraid of offending neighboring Germany and therefore abstained from voting.

The only openly pro-Japanese power was Italy. The Italian delegate tried to obstruct the work of the Conference by advocating direct negotiations between China and Japan. After Japan refused a second invitation, he stated that the Conference had nothing further to do. He voted against the Declaration of November 15, as well as the Conference report of November 24.

The remaining powers, weak and with fewer interests in Asia, followed the lead of the big powers, professing devotion to the sanctity of treaties and supporting China's just cause. Their spokesmen included Foreign Minister Spaak of Belgium and Foreign Minister de Graeff of the Netherlands.

The Chinese delegation, led by V. K. Wellington Koo, did not object to mediation. In the event that mediation failed, however, the powers should commit themselves to increase their aid to China and impose economic sanctions on Japan. War material and war credits should be withheld, and a boycott of Japanese exports and shipping carried out. To that end the Chinese delegation circulated a memorandum on November 13, pointing out the vulnerability of Japan's financial institutions and economy to sanctions.[23]

The aim of the conferees was mediation, however, and that required the presence of both parties. It was decided to send a second communication to Japan. The tone of the communication was deliberately neutral to avoid offending Japan, and refrained from mentioning Japan's military actions in China and her violation of the Nine Power Treaty. Still, the Japanese government again refused to join the Conference, repeating its previously expressed view that its actions in China were undertaken in self-defense and did not come within the scope

---

[23] Chinese Diplomatic Problems Research Association, *Lu-kuo-chiao shih-pei chien-hou ti chung-jih kuan-hsi* (Taipei: China Diplomatic Problems Research Association 1966) (*Sino-Japanese Diplomatic Relations Before and After Lu-kuo-chiao Incident*), pp. 399–402.

of the Nine Power Treaty. Japan could not agree to participate in a meeting based on the provisions of this Treaty which it was simultaneously being accused of violating.

IV. DECLARATION OF THE CONFERENCE AND ITS EVALUATION

Adoption of the First Declaration

The participating powers felt somewhat slighted when Japan again refused to attend the Conference. On November 13, French delegate Yvon Delbos noted that the Japanese reply added another problem for the Conference to consider, namely, that country's refusal to abide by Article 7. He added, however, that no solution by force could either in law or in fact provide a lasting adjustment of relations between two countries. British delegate Anthony Eden said that it would be impossible for the Conference to assent to the doctrine that the settlement of the conflict in East Asia was a matter for China and Japan alone. The U.S. delegate, Norman H. Davies, opined that the question before the Conference was whether international relations were to be determined by arbitrary force or by law and respect for international treaties. But he still hoped Japan might see her way clear to participate.

A declaration was drafted by the U.S. delegation stating that the Conference could not accept the view that the conflict concerned only the two countries directly involved; it was a concern in law to all parties to the Nine Power Treaty and the Pact of Paris.[24] After expressing the hope that Japan would not persist in its refusal, the declaration concluded that the Conference "must consider what is to be their common attitude in a situation where one party to an international treaty maintains, against the views of all other parties, that the action which it has taken does not come within the scope of the treaty and sets aside provisions of the treaty which the other parties hold to be operative in the circumstances."[25]

---

[24] I. S. Friedman, *op. cit.*, p. 106.
[25] Department of State, *Foreign Relations of the United States, Japan, 1931- 41*, Vol. 1, pp. 410–412.

On November 15 this Declaration was adopted with a vote of fifteen to one, with the Scandinavian delegates abstaining. Italy's negative vote was anticipated but the joint Scandinavian abstention greatly jeopardized further collective action by demonstrating that the Western camp was split on the issue.

Adoption of the Report and the Final Declaration

After a week-long adjournment, the Conference reconvened on November 22, 1937, to consider a draft declaration submitted by the delegations. At its final session on November 24 the Conference adjourned *sine die*, after having adopted a report and a second declaration. Only the Italian delegation voted against it.

After summarizing the work of the Conference, the declaration reaffirmed ". . . the principles of the Nine Power Treaty . . . . [and] strongly urges that hostilities be suspended and resort be made to peaceful processes. . . . In order to allow time for participating governments to exchange views and further explore all peaceful methods by which a just settlement of the dispute may be attained consistently with the principles of the Nine Power Treaty and in conformity with the objectives of the Treaty, the Conference deems it advisable temporarily to suspend its sittings. The conflict in the Far East remains, however, a matter of concern to all the powers assembled at Brussels and especially to those immediately and directly affected by conditions and events in the Far East."[26]

Under the guise of a temporary adjournment, the Conference was closed. A disappointed Chinese delegation accepted the declaration in the spirit of "solidarity." China's efforts to restrain Japan through international action had come to naught. Still, the Chinese delegation had held fast in the position: (1) Refusal of direct negotiation; (2) Acceptance of legitimate mediation; (3) Determination to continue the resistance; and (4) Extension of aid to China, and imposition of some

---

[26] Department of State, *The Conference of Brussels*, November 3-24, 1937 (Washington: Government Printing Office), pp. 75-77.

financial and economic restriction on Japan in case of failure of mediation.[27]

The Brussels Conference failed to have any effect on the Sino-Japanese conflict. Neither Great Britain, preoccupied with Europe, nor the U.S., the original sponsor of the Nine Power Treaty, was willing to lead the firm collective action against Japan that the situation demanded. As Herbert Feis wrote in The Road to Pearl Harbor: "The failure of the Brussels Conference could not be made up. The last good chance to work out a stable settlement between China and Japan was lost in 1937."[28]

V. THE UNITED STATES' EFFORTS PRIOR TO PEARL HARBOR

The Puppet Regime in Nanking

By the end of 1937 the Japanese were in command of most of the railroads, the lower reaches of the chief navigable rivers, and the main coastal ports. Yet China's heroic resistance, based upon the tactic of "trading space for time," continued. After the fall of Nanking, the Nationalist government moved westward to Hankow. A victory of Chinese forces in March 1938 at Taerchuang on the border of the Shantung and Kiangsu provinces delayed for a considerable time the Japanese plan of converging assaults on Hankow. After its eventual fall in October 1938 the Nationalist government moved further westward to Chungking, 1400 miles from the coast and relatively secure from attack, except by air. The Japanese forces bogged down in the vast interior of China, and the Nationalists continued their dogged resistance until the Allied victory in 1945.

On November 3, 1938, the Japanese government announced the establishment of a new order in East Asia, founded on the "tripartite relationship of mutual aid and coordination between Japan, Manchukuo and China in political, economic, cultural and other fields." Its object

---

[27] Chinese Diplomatic Problems Research Association op. cit., pp. 408-416.
[28] H. Feis, op. cit., p. 16.

was "to secure international justice, to perfect the joint defense against Communism, and to create a new culture and realize a close economic cohesion throughout East Asia." Other powers were called upon to adapt their attitude to the new conditions in East Asia.

A new Japanese peace offer was categorically rejected by Chiang. Speaking at the Kuomintang headquarters in Chungking on December 6, 1938, he described it as an attempt to create a "vassal China with which to dominate the Pacific and to dismember the other states of the world."[29] The new Japanese move also evoked strong rejoinders from the U.S., Britain, and France, which alike repudiated Japan's pretensions to establish a Pax Japonica, reasserting that international relations in the Far East must continue to be governed by the terms of existing treaties.[30] These protests had little, if any, effect.

Meanwhile, Japan was using other means besides the military to break down China's resistance, including demoralizing "peace" offers and schemes to instigate division within the Chinese people.[31] To accomplish this latter purpose, they needed an influential and popular Chinese leader who was willing to throw in his lot with the Japanese "East Asia Co-Prosperity Zone" program. Their past experiments with various puppet leaders had been unsatisfactory. In Manchuria, they had resurrected the last Manchu emperor. In Peking their "provisional government" was headed by Wang Keh-min, a former Minister of Finance who had no support among the Chinese people. Finally, in late 1938, Japanese military schemers found Wang Ch'ing-wei, an important Nationalist politician who favored peace negotiations. Moreover, Wang was ambitious and resentful of Chiang's leadership of the Kuomintang. In December 1938 he traveled to Hanoi from Chungking to enter into negotiations with the Japanese about the setting up of a "government of China."

---

29 W. King *op. cit.*, p. 93.
30 For the texts of the American notes to Japan, October 6 and December 30, 1938, see Department of State, *Foreign Relations of the United States, Japan, 1931- 41,* Vol. 1, pp. 785-820.
31 The Germans, who were closer to both the Japanese and the Chinese governments than other neutrals, were often asked by Japan either to initiate or to act as intermediaries, in the transmission of "peace" proposals to the Chinese government.

In February 1940 it was reported that Wang had signed eight "agreements" with Japan, providing for the Japanese exploitation of China. He established his "capital" in Nanking on March 30, 1940, but this did little to lessen the people's support for the Nationalist government. Japan recognized the Wang regime on November 30 of that year, and Manchukuo soon followed suit. On July 1, 1941, Germany and Italy, followed by their Axis satellites Romania, Bulgaria, Slovakia, Croatia, and others, also recognized the Wang regime, which led the Nationalist government in Chungking to sever diplomatic relations with the Axis Powers.[32] Wang never possessed real power, and died in 1944.

Secretary of State Cordell Hull denounced this new Japanese puppet regime the day it was founded, reconfirming that, "The Government of the United States has ample reason for believing that the Government with its capital now at Chungking, has had and still has the allegiance and support of the great majority of the Chinese people. The Government of the United States, of course, continues to recognize that Government as the Government of China."[33]

On September 1, 1939, German troops invaded Poland, and two days later Britain and France declared war on Germany. World War II had officially begun. The Tripartite Alliance among the Axis powers was formally signed in Berlin on September 27, 1940. Under the terms of the Pact, Japan recognized German and Italian leadership in Europe, while Germany and Italy recognized Japan's leadership in the establishment of a "new order" in Greater East Asia. If one of the three were attacked by a power at present not involved in the European War or in the Chinese-Japanese conflict, the three agreed to cooperate militarily.

By November 1940 Chiang was convinced that a clash between Japan and America was inevitable and publicly aligned China with the U.S. and Great Britain in opposition to Axis aggression. "The democracies must stand or fall together," was the new watchword. Any peace offers from Tokyo that aimed at a separate arrangement with China would be spurned.

---

[32] H. K. Tong, *op. cit.*, p. 280.

[33] Department of State, *Foreign Relations of the United States, Japan, 1931- 41*, Vol. II, p. 59.

American Support of the Chinese Resistance

From the beginning of the Sino-Japanese war the sympathies of the American people were with China. Nevertheless, in accordance with its principles of neutrality and freedom of the seas, the U.S. continued to sell war supplies to Japan for two and half years. As Japanese bombings on Chinese cities brought heavy civilian casualties, Americans began to question the policy of selling scrap iron to Japan for use in armament factories.

The U.S. government gave notice to Japan on July 26, 1939, of its desire to terminate the 1911 Treaty of Commerce and Navigation between the United States and Japan. Once this Treaty lapsed on January 26, 1940, Washington was in a position to apply economic sanctions against Japan. Roosevelt, now reelected to a third term, reversed the open export policy by requiring export licenses for all iron ore, plate iron, iron alloys, and a number of manufactured products bound for Japan. This was followed by the imposition of a complete embargo on steel, oil, and other war materials for Japan in the summer of 1941. On July 26, 1941, in response to the Japanese advance into Indochina, Roosevelt issued an Executive Order freezing all Japanese assets in the United States, which had the effect of cutting off all trade with Japan.

The U.S. government supported China in its resistance against Japan in an increasingly active way. American aviators on active duty were permitted to enter the U.S. Air Force Reserve and join the Chinese armed forces. The "Flying Tigers" were launched on August 1, 1941, under the command of retired American Colonel Claire Lee Chennault, who had been chief instructor of the Chinese Air Force Cadet School.[34] Two months before the Japanese attack on Pearl Harbor the U.S. Government sent a military mission of forty officers, led by Brigadier-General John Magruder, to Chungking.

---

[34] On April 15, 1941, President Roosevelt had signed an unpublished executive order permitting United States Army, Navy and Marine Corps fliers and ground crews to resign from the Service for the specific purpose of joining the American Volunteer Group as civilian employees of the Chinese Government. The American Volunteer Group became the U.S. 14th Air Force after the United States entered the war.

On March 15, 1941, Roosevelt declared that "China . . . expresses the magnificent will of millions of plain people to resist the dismemberment of their Nation. China, through the Generalissimo, Chiang Kai-shek, asks our help. America has said that China shall have our help." On May 6, 1941, he made China eligible for Lend-Lease assistance by declaring the defense of China to be vital to the defense of the United States. Lend-Lease aid to China began in 1941, and was aimed at improving the 700-mile Burma Road, but the Japanese invasion of Burma in early 1942 put an end to the project. A formal Lend-Lease Agreement was signed between Cordell Hull and Chinese Foreign Minister T. V. Soong on June 2, 1942.[35]

In the meantime, China was encouraged to continue her resistance by substantial loans. The first American loan of $25 million was made on February 8, 1939, for the purchase of non-military supplies and was secured by Tung oil exports. Other loans followed in 1940 and early 1941 for similar amounts secured by tin and tungsten exports. There is no gainsaying that these loans, plus the $26 million in Lend-Lease that was extended in the latter half of 1941, helped to sustain China during this period of deep adversity.[36] But this help was too little and too late to make a decisive difference in the desperate defensive struggle China was waging against great odds. It was like *pei shui ch'e hsin*, "using a cup of water to put out a burning cartload of wood," sums up the aid received by China.

The American-Japanese Negotiations of 1941

Passage of the Lend-Lease Act in March 1941 made it the national policy of the U.S. to serve as the "arsenal of democracy" for the anti-

---

[35] Department of State, *Relations with China, 1944-1949*, p. 27.

[36] Total foreign credits to China authorized before the Pacific War amounted to $513.5 million, excluding Lend-Lease aid. Most of this was for purchases; $93 million was for currency support. Russia granted $250 million to pay for supplies and services. United States provided $170 million, of which $120 million was for purchases and $50 million, of which $35.5 million was for purchases and $43 million for currency support. France provided $15 million for railway construction. Cf. A. N. Young, *China and the Helping Hand, 1937-1945* (Cambridge: Harvard University Press, 1963), pp. 207; 439-440.

Axis powers.[37]   The Japanese economy was soon feeling the pinch of restrictions on exports from the U.S. and other countries. By early 1941 shipments of iron, steel, other metals, machinery, high quality gasoline, and petroleum technology from America to Japan had practically ceased. Petroleum shipments continued, however, for fear that an embargo would prompt a Japanese attack on the oil-rich Netherlands East Indies.

As Japan extended its reach beyond China into Southeast Asia, tension between the U.S. and Japan increased, although neither was yet prepared to face war in the Pacific. American public opinion, especially in regard to Europe, had moved from away from insistence on "neutrality" to acceptance of a policy of non-belligerence involving all but direct military participation in war. The U.S. government recognized that America was unprepared for war, and when Tokyo suggested that it might alter its political alignments and modify its attitude toward China, Washington agreed to enter into informal, exploratory conversations for a peaceful settlement of political and economic problems in the Far East.[38]

In conversations with Japanese Ambassador Kichisaburo Nomura, beginning in April 1941, Cordell Hull proposed four principles as a basis for negotiation with Japan: (1) Respect for the territorial integrity and the sovereignty of each and all nations; (2) Support of the principle of non-interference in the internal affairs of other countries; (3) Support of the principle of equality, including equality of economic opportunity; and (4) Non-disturbance of the status quo in the Pacific except as the status quo may be altered by peaceful means.[39]   These principles were virtually a reiteration of the underlying premises of the 1922 Nine Power Treaty, and their proper application would require a radical modification of Japan's aggressive policy.

The negotiations focused on the China question. The U.S. proposed that all Japanese forces in China be withdrawn, and that the Nationalist

---

[37] In a "fireside chat" on December 29, 1940, President Roosevelt declared that Britain and the British fleet stood between the New World and Nazi aggression. Britain asked for war materials, not for men. "We must be the great arsenal of democracy, Roosevelt" concluded. ". . . I call upon our people with absolute confidence that our common course will greatly succeed."

[38] Department of State, *Foreign Relations of the United States, Japan, 1931- 41*, Vol. II, pp. 328-329.

[39] *Ibid.*, Vol. II, p.332.

government be supported against any other regime in China. In return, the U.S. was willing to reestablish normal trade relations with Japan and improve economic relations. Japan, on the other hand, sought to obtain formal recognition from the U.S. of Japanese hegemony in East Asia, to discontinue aid to the Nationalist government in Chungking, and to pressure it into peace negotiations with Japan. Neither power would accede to the other's demands, and both continued war preparations.

In November, the Konoye cabinet fell and General Hideki Tojo came to power. Although Tojo's rise was seen as a sign that military action was imminent, Tokyo nonetheless sent Sabuko Kurusu, former Japanese Ambassador to Germany, to Washington to assist Nomura in continuing the negotiations. On November 20 the final Japanese proposals, defining the conditions of a temporary agreement, were presented to Hull. The U.S. responded with an "Outline of Proposed Basis for Agreement Between The United States and Japan."[40]   To Hull's original prescription for peace in the Pacific had been added several additional demands. Japan was asked to enter into a multilateral nonaggression pact with Great Britain, China, Netherlands, Soviet Union, Thailand, and the U.S. Moreover, Japan was to withdraw its military forces from China and Indochina, and enter into an international agreement to respect the territorial integrity of Indochina. Japan was to recognize the Nationalist government and relinquish, along with the U.S., extraterritorial privileges and other rights it enjoyed in China. Finally, the two governments were to resume normal trade relations and conclude a new commerce treaty.

The U.S. viewed its proposal as a reasonable way to reestablish peace and stability in the Far East. The Japanese saw it as an ultimatum, the acceptance of which would require Japan to abandon all her territorial gains in East Asia along with the policies that had led to them. When the American reply was received by the Tojo cabinet, the "final, the definitive, the irrevocable decision" on war was taken.[41]   The Japanese fleet steamed toward Pearl Harbor, headquarters of the U.S. Pacific Fleet.   Diplomatic conversations were continued in Washington,

---

[40]   *Ibid.*, Vol. II, pp. 768.
[41]   H. M. Vinacke, *A History of the Far East in Modern Times* (New York: Appleton-Century Crofts, 1959), pp. 622-623.

becoming daily more hopeless. On December 6 Roosevelt telegraphed a personal appeal to Emperor Hirohito of Japan. On December 7, 1941, while bombs were already raining on Pearl Harbor, Japanese emissaries notified the U.S. government that further negotiations were useless. The U.S. declared war on Japan on December 8, 1941. The next day China declared war against Japan, Germany, and Italy.

8

THE ALLIANCE IN WORLD WAR II
1942–1945

I. THE PACIFIC WAR

Pearl Harbor combined the separate wars in Asia and Europe into one global conflict. The hard pressed powers of China and Great Britain and the European nations under the Nazi boot saw in the suicidal action of Japanese militarists the dawn of their own salvation. The day after Pearl Harbor, Britain and the Netherlands committed themselves to the war against Japan. A few days later Germany and Italy declared war against the United States.

Round one in the Pacific War went to Japan. In six months' time, Japan gained control of 1,500,000 square miles of territory and 140 million people.[1] Hong Kong and Sarawak fell on Christmas Day, 1941. Japanese forces overran the Malay Peninsula, capturing Singapore on February 15, 1942. The Philippines, after a last, courageous defense at Corregidor, fell on May 6, 1942. Thailand capitulated within few days, and by June 1942, Burma was in Japan's possession. In a series of victories, Japan had driven the British, Americans, and Dutch from East Asia.

The Japanese attacks in the Pacific ended China's long period of isolation. Her long struggle against the Japanese now appeared as an

---

[1] C. A. Buss, *The Far East: A History of Recent and Contemporary International Relations in East Asia* (New York: MacMillan Co., 1955), p. 412.

important holding operation buying America precious time to mobilize for a future offensive. The immediate consequence of Pearl Harbor, however, was to increase the strain upon China. The U.S. and Great Britain, hard-pressed to defend their own territories, closed down their trickle of help to China.

On December 9, 1941, China officially declared itself at war with Japan, Germany, and Italy. In a brief message to President Roosevelt, General Chiang Kai-shek summarized China's position: "To our new common battle we offer all we are and all we have to stand with you until the Pacific and the world are freed from the curse of brute force and endless perfidy."[2] The "China incident" had at last broadened into a world war.

When the news of Pearl Harbor reached Chungking, Chiang was first among the Allied leaders to propose concerted action. In two conferences on December 8 with the American and British military representatives who stationed in China, Chiang outlined his idea for a great coalition to defend the Pacific region. All enemies of the Axis powers—China, Britain, Canada, New Zealand, Australia, the Soviet Union—would join a military alliance under U.S. leadership and establish a joint military war council to coordinate strategy. Chiang suggested further that they should all sign an agreement not to conclude a separate peace.

Roosevelt replied on December 14, suggesting that a joint military conference be held in Chungking no later than December 17 for the purpose of exchanging information and formulating a definite plan for joint action to defeat Japan.[3] The resulting Joint Military Conference for East Asia met in Chungking on December 23, under Chiang's chairmanship. Major General George H. Brett was the U.S. representative. Britain was represented by General Archibald Wavell, head of the British command in India. Wavell was preoccupied with a Japanese attack on Burma, which was thought to be imminent. Chiang, however, stressed the importance of formulating a long-range, comprehensive plan. He agreed to Wavell's request for Chinese forces to assist in the defense of Burma, and agreed to release American lend-lease

---

[2] H. K. Tong, *Chiang Kai-shek* (Taipei: China Publishing Co., 1953), p. 290.
[3] H. Feis, *The China Tangle, The American Effort in China from Pearl Harbor to the Marshall Mission* (Princeton: Princeton University Press, 1953), pp. 4-6.

materials for this campaign.

The first Allied conference paved the way for Chiang's appointment as Supreme Commander for the Allied Powers in the China theater as suggested by Roosevelt on July 1, 1942.[4] Lieutenant General Joseph W. Stilwell was appointed to be the American representative on the joint planning staff to command American armed forces in China, and to supervise and control the handling of all lend-lease materials consigned to China. Chiang responded by appointing Stilwell as the Chief of Staff to the Supreme Commander of the Allied Powers forces in the China theater. Stilwell's authority was vaguely defined, and unfortunate misunderstandings were later to arise between the two men.[5]

In March 1942 a China-Burma-India (CBI) theater of operations was set up with headquarters in Chungking and a branch office headquarters in New Delhi. Besides the India-China Ferry Command, a training command was established in Karachi and Lahore to prepare air crews for air combat and transport duty. In April 1942 a training center at Ramgarh in Bihar province was created for Chinese soldiers who had retreated from the Burma front. Some 45,000 Chinese troops received further training in Ramgarh, and went on to fight well and bravely in the Burma campaign beginning in 1943. The U.S. Army also began to operate artillery and infantry centers for Chinese troops in China proper. American officers also served as advisers in the Chinese Army, and also worked in the fields of medicine, engineering, and communications.

In July 1942 the legendary Flying Tigers were incorporated into the U.S. Tenth Air Force, which had been organized in the China-Burma-India theater earlier that year. In March of the following year, as the air war over China intensified and operations against the Japanese home islands were begun, it became the U.S. Fourteenth Air Force. A program begun for training Chinese aviation personnel in America resulted in the formation of a Chinese-American Composite Wing of the Chinese Air Force in November 1943. This wing, composed of Chinese and American airmen and ground units and equipped with fighter and

---

[4] H. K. Tong, *op. cit.*, pp. 292-293.
[5] They do even before Stilwell's arrival in China, as the Soong-Stimson notes of January 29-30, 1942, indicate. Cf. Department of State, *U.S. Relations with China, 1944-1949*, pp. 468-469.

bombing planes, formed the nucleus of a strong Chinese Air Force.[6] In June 1943 Chinese naval personnel also began receiving training in the United States, although the Chinese Navy did not begin to utilize American-built ships until August 1945. A Sino-American Cooperative Organization composed of 25,000 Americans and 50,000 Chinese was also set up to train and operate guerrilla and intelligence forces in Japanese-occupied territories.

American Lend-Lease and Financial Aid

The amount of military aid that China received from its allies during this time was small, partly because of the extreme difficulty of transport. The closure of the Burma Road by the Japanese in early 1942 meant that nearly all supplies had to be flown from Assam, India by cargo planes over the towering "hump" of the Himalayas to the Yunnan plateau. This was the most difficult supply operation of the entire war.[7] The key factor, however, was Washington's adherence to a Europe-first policy, which relegated the Asiatic front to secondary importance. Up to October 2, 1944, China had received only five percent of the total lend-lease exports, then totaling over $21 billion, which the U.S. had sent to its Allies. To make matters worse, even these meager supplies were frequently snatched away en route to meet critical Allied needs elsewhere.

The situation did not improve until after the Japanese were expelled from Burma at the end of 1944, and the Ledo Road from Assam across Upper Burma to Yunnan province was opened. An important pipeline was also completed in early 1945 to import petroleum from India at the rate of 54,000 tons per month. At the same time, the monthly tonnage carried by air transports over the "Hump" was increased to 46,000 tons.[8]

---

[6] Department of State, *United States Relations with China, with Special Reference to the Period 1944-1949* (Washington, D.C.: Government Printing Office, 1949), pp. 28-29.

[7] It should also be pointed out that the supplies flown into China were, for the most part, destined for the use of American military forces operating there, Cf., *Ibid.*, p. 27.

[8] C. Y. Chang (ed.), *History of China's War of Resistance Against Japanese Aggression* (Taipei: United Publishing Co., 1966), p. 371.

Despite such meager military aid, China was able to sustain her resistance for four years after Pearl Harbor, holding down seventy-two Japanese divisions, twenty-two in Manchuria and fifty in other parts of China. If Japanese manpower had not been immobilized on such a vast scale in China, the outcome of battles for various Pacific islands and Okinawa might have been different.[9] China also provided, under the terms of a "counter lend-lease agreement"—signed with the U.S. in December 1943—tungsten, tin, pig bristles, tung oil, silk, antimony, mercury, and tea for the Allied war effort.

After Pearl Harbor, the U.S. also extended financial support to the struggling Chinese government. By the end of 1941 Chungking faced grave difficulties. Japan had taken over a large part of the revenue and resources of China. Acute inflation was ravaging an economy already strained by four years of war. Prices had risen about twenty-fold since 1937.

Learning of China's difficulties, Roosevelt sent Congress a draft of a joint resolution authorizing the Secretary of Treasury, with the approval of the President, "to loan or extend credit or give other financial aid to China in an amount not to exceed in the aggregate $500,000,000." This resolution was promptly passed by Congress and was signed by Roosevelt on February 7, 1942, as Public Law 422.[10]

That same day, Roosevelt sent Chiang a telegram expressing his satisfaction that the aid resolution had been passed so quickly. "The unusual speed and unanimity with which this measure was acted upon by Congress," Roosevelt wrote, "testifies to the enthusiastic respect and admiration which the Government and people of this country have for China. . . . The gallant resistance of the Chinese armies against the ruthless invaders of your country has called forth the highest praise from the American and all other freedom loving peoples. The tenacity of the Chinese people, both armed and unarmed, in the face of tremendous odds in carrying on for almost five years a resolute defense against an enemy far superior in equipment is an inspiration to the fighting men and all the peoples of the other United Nations." He closed with the hope that the funds would help "the Chinese government and people to meet the

---

[9] H. K. Tong, *op. cit.*, pp. 295-296.
[10] Department of State, *op. cit.*, p. 32.

economic and financial burdens which have been thrust upon them by armed invasion and towards solution of problems of production and procurement."[11]

The U.S. and China signed an agreement on March 21, 1942, establishing a credit in the amount of $500 million in the name of the government of the Republic of China. Article II of the loan agreement provided that final settlement would be deferred "until the progress of events after the war makes clearer the final terms and benefits which will be in the mutual interest of the United States and China and which will permit the establishment of lasting world peace and security."[12]   This credit, the financial counterpart of lend-leased war materials, partly compensated for absence of effective material aid.

In early February 1942 while visiting Mahatma Ghandi in India to persuade him to align himself with the Allied cause, Chiang acknowledged the American loan in a message of thanks to Roosevelt. "Apart from military needs," Chiang wrote, "the money will be used principally for strengthening our economic structure, for redemption of legal tender notes, for control of currency notes, for stabilization of the commodities, for maintenance of wartime standard of living and for an increase of production."[13]

The U.S. loan was followed immediately by a British loan of $50,000,000.   A Joint Stabilization Board was set up, with the participation of both American and British representatives, with the result that Chinese currency was placed on a sound basis for the remaining war years.   The U.S. credit was used to secure dollar obligations issued in China ($200 million), to acquire gold for sale in China ($220 million), to pay for bank notes ($55 million), and to pay for imported textiles ($25 million).[14]

---

[11] Department of State, *Bulletin*, February 7, 1942, p. 142.
[12] Joint Statement of U.S. Secretary of the Treasury Henry Morgenthau, and Chinese Minister of Foreign Affairs T. V. Soong, March 21, 1942, Cf. *Ibid.*, pp. 510-512.
[13] H. K. Tong, *op. cit.*, pp. 294-295.
[14] A. N. Young, *China and the Helping Hand*, 1937-1945 (Cambridge, Mass: Harvard University Press, 1963); pp. 233-234.

II. ACHIEVING EQUAL STATUS

The End of Extraterritoriality

The century-old system of extraterritorial rights for foreigners in China and the system of foreign treaty port control came to an end during World War II. On several occasions prior to America's entry into the war, the U.S. government publicly expressed its willingness to act when "circumstances permit." As Acting Secretary of State Summer Welles put it on July 19, 1940, the U.S. "desires to move rapidly by process of orderly negotiation and agreement with the Chinese Government, whenever conditions warrant, toward the relinquishment of extraterritorial rights and of all other so-called 'special rights' possessed by this country as by other countries in China by virtue of international agreements."[15] Similar sentiments were expressed by Secretary of State Hull on May 31, 1941, who promised an end to extraterritoriality "when conditions of peace again prevail."[16]

It was not until October 9, 1942, that the U.S. government informed Chinese Ambassador Wei Tao-ming that it was prepared to enter into negotiations for the "immediate relinquishment" of extraterritorial rights and would shortly submit a draft treaty toward that end.[17] The actual negotiations went quickly, since the U.S. side had already conceded that American nationals in China would henceforth be subject to Chinese jurisdiction and that other special rights, such as those granted in the Boxer Protocol of 1901 and relating to the international settlements in Shanghai and Amoy, should be terminated. The Chinese government, for its part, agreed to protect existing rights and titles to real property in China held by American nationals or by the U.S. Government. Americans would be accorded the same right to travel, reside, and carry on trade throughout China which Chinese nationals enjoyed in the U.S.[18]

---

[15] Department of State, *Foreign Relations of the United States, Japan, 1931-1941,* Vol. I, p. 927.

[16] *Ibid.,* p. 929.

[17] For details of these preliminary moves, see Department of State, *Bulletin,* October 10, 1942, pp. 805-808.

[18] For the text of treaty and notes, see *Treaty Between the Republic of China and the United States for the Relinquishment of Extraterritorial Rights in China and the*

The Sino-American Treaty for the Relinquishment of Extraterritoriality in China was signed on January 11, 1943, and became effective with the exchange of ratifications on May 20, 1943. A Sino-British treaty was negotiated at the same time, and both were warmly received by the Chinese people. On January 12 the day after the signing, Chiang broadcast a message to the nation pointing out that "After fifty years of bloody revolution and five-and-a-half years of war resistance, we have transformed the painful history of one hundred years of the unequal treaties into the glorious record of their abolition. . . . By doing so, the United Nations, who are our comrades-in-arms, have to fight for humanity and justice. . . . With our past humiliations wiped out and our independence and freedom regained, we can have the chance to make our country strong."[19]

After these first two treaties were concluded, other countries followed suit: Brazil on August 20, 1943; Belgium on October 20, 1943; Norway on November 10, 1943; Canada on April 5, 1945; and the Netherlands on May 29, 1945. France surrendered the leased territory of Kwangchow-wan in an agreement signed in Chungking on August 18, 1945[20], and the rest of her concessions in China on February 28, 1946.[21] Japan and Italy, of course, had already lost their treaty status on account of the war.

Regulation of Related Matters, signed at Washington, January 11, 1943, with Accompanying Exchange of Notes, Ministry of Foreign Affairs, *Treaties between the Republic of China and Foreign States*, 1927-1961 (Taipei: Commercial Press, 1958), Vol. I, pp. 659-669. Also, Department of State, *U.S. Relations with China, 1944-1949*, pp. 514-519.

[19] H. K. Tong, *op. cit.*, p. 299.

[20] The text of the Sino-British treaty of 1943 will be found in the Ministry of Foreign Affairs, *Treaties between China and Foreign States*, 1927-1961, pp. 589-603; Cmd 6456, H.M.S.O. London, July, 1943. The text of the Sino-French Treaty of 1946 will be found in the Ministry of Foreign Affairs, *Treaties between China and Foreign States*, 1927-1961, pp. 152-160; Journal Official de la Republique Francaise, May 19, 1946.

[21] Certain issues with regard to foreign leaseholds still remain to be adjusted, such as the retrocession of Hong Kong itself.

Repeal of the Chinese Exclusion Acts

Since the passage of the Chinese Exclusion Act there had been a virtual ban on Chinese immigration to the United States. Roosevelt proposed that this legislation be repealed in order to "correct an historic mistake" and give "additional proof that we regard China not only as a partner in waging war but that we shall regard her as a partner in days of peace."[22]   In response to Roosevelt's urgings, hearings to rectify this situation began on May 19, 1943, before the House Committee on Immigration and Naturalization.

There was some opposition in Congress to the admission of Orientals, even though the proposed quota was so small as to be negligible.   Popular opinion in the U.S. was, however, generally favorable.   The measure was barely reported out of committee on October 7, but strong administration support produced large majorities in the House of Representatives on October 21, and in the Senate on November 26.[23]

The new law, entitled "An Act to Repeal the Chinese Exclusion Acts, to Establish Quotas, and for Other Purposes," repealed some fifteen acts, or parts of acts, regarding the exclusion or deportation of persons of Chinese race.   It provided for the admission of a quota of Chinese immigrants under provisions of the Immigration Act of 1924, and made them eligible for citizenship.[24]   On December 17, 1943, this legislation was signed into law by Roosevelt, who, in accordance with its provisions, set an annual quota for Chinese of 105 on February 10, 1944.[25]   An unjust stigma was therefore removed from the Chinese people.

The goodwill generated by the visit of Madame Chiang Kai-shek to the U.S. early in 1943 helped to carry these two measures through Congress.   She spoke before the Senate and the House on February 18,

---

[22] Department of State, *U.S. Relations with China, 1944-1949*, p. 37.
[23] T. A. Bission, America's Far Eastern Policy (New York: MacMillan Co., 1945), pp. 140-141.
[24] U.S. Public Law No. 199, 78th Congress. "An Act to Repeal The Chinese Exclusion Acts, to Establish Quotas, and for Other Purposes," Chapter 344 1st Session, H.R. 3070.
[25] U.S. Federal Register, Vol. 9, No. 29, p. 1587.

and later addressed a capacity crowd in Madison Square Garden.[26] She impressed the American public with her grace and oratory, and quickly became a symbol of China's will to resist the common enemy. Her forceful speeches convinced the American people that the U.S. should do more for China. Relations between the two countries had never been better.

III. DECISIONS OF THE CONFERENCES

Wartime Diplomacy

Between the years 1941 and 1945 China was confronted with a number of important diplomatic decisions, as a series of crucial conferences were held to determine the structure of the postwar world.[27] Unfortunately, the U.S. from the early days of the war made a distinction between the Asiatic and European theaters, and excluded China from discussions of European strategy. This was unfair to China, and ultimately resulted in the Yalta debacle of 1945, in which Chinese territory was secretly awarded to the Soviet Union without the foreknowledge or consent of the Nationalist government.

Before the U.S. joined the war, President Roosevelt and British Prime Minister Winston Churchill roughly outlined their war aims in the Atlantic Charter in August 1941. When they met again in Casablanca in January 1943 it was to adopt a policy of "unconditional surrender." This policy changed the whole character of the war, prolonging German resistance, and giving the U.S.S.R. an opportunity to enter the Asian war and occupy Chinese territory. Chiang, who was not invited to participate, was concerned that it would have grave consequences for China, but American and British policymakers took little notice. Also adopted at Casablanca was a "Europe First, Pacific Second" policy in the

---

26 M. E. Cameron, T. H. D. Mahoney & G. E. McReynolds, *China, Japan and the Powers* (New York: Ronald Press, 1952), p. 549.

27 For details of the Atlantic Conference and the Atlantic Charter, 1943, see W.L. Langer & S. E. Gleason, *The Undeclared War, 1940-1941* (New York: Harper Bros., 1953), pp. 663-692.

allocation of war supplies. It might have been called the "China Last" policy, for the scant attention that was paid to the China-Burma-India theater.[28]

During spring and summer of 1943 Churchill pressed for more American action in the European theater, while Stalin demanded the opening of a second front. Little attention was paid to the China-Burma-India theater at the Trident Conference held in Washington in May, 1943. All China received was a promise that more tonnage would be flown over the "Hump."

Roosevelt and Churchill met again in Quebec in August 1943 for the Quadrant Conference. Although Churchill was against the idea of a Burma campaign, he reluctantly agreed to plans calling for an attack against Upper Burma and a small amphibious landing in Lower Burma in 1944, and an increase in the tonnage airlifted from India to China. The Chinese were not invited to participate, and were only informed to the extent the principal Allies deemed advisable.[29]

In October 1943 Lord Louis Mountbatten, Chief of the Southeast Asiatic Command, came to Chungking to confer on the upcoming campaign in Burma, as well as overall strategy vis-à-vis Japan. Chiang emphasized the need to achieve naval superiority in the Bay of Bengal, preliminary to undertaking the Burma campaign, but his advice was apparently not taken to heart by the British.[30]

Other Chinese requests were refused by the American-British military authorities for various reasons. The Combined Chiefs of Staff rejected the idea of a Chinese representative who would participate in strategic decisions affecting the China theater. Chinese were refused seats on other existing joint and combined agencies such as the important Munitions Assignment Board. This unfair treatment caused a certain amount of resentment among Chinese leaders.

Roosevelt decided to personally reassure Chiang that China was a leading ally of the U.S. He also hoped to bring the Chinese and Soviet governments into some kind of accord to prevent the ongoing civil strife from exploding into a dangerous international crisis. A joint meeting

---

[28] H. K. Tong, *op. cit.*, pp. 306-307.
[29] C. A. Buss, *op. cit.*, pp. 422-424.
[30] H. K. Tong, *op. cit.*, pp. 307.

with Chiang and Stalin was out of the question because Russia was still neutral in the Asiatic war. Roosevelt and Churchill therefore arranged for a joint declaration to be issued from Moscow, after which they would meet Chiang in Cairo and Stalin in Teheran.[31]

On October 30, 1943, the U.S., U.K., the U.S.S.R., and China declared the need for an international organization of peace-loving states and for the maintenance of peace and security, and pledged that after the termination of hostilities they would not employ their military forces within the territory of other states.[32]

The Cairo Conference: Political Matters

Chiang came to Cairo on November 22 as the President of China, having assumed that office on August 11, following the death of the former president, Lin Sen. After four days of meetings, Roosevelt, Churchill, and Chiang issued a joint communiqué "agree[ing] upon future military operations against Japan. . . [and] resolv[ing] to bring unrelenting pressure against their brutal enemies by sea, land, and air."

From China's point of view, the most important part of the communiqué was the solemn pledge by China's allies that "all the territories Japan has stolen from the Chinese, such as Manchuria, Formosa, and the Pescadores, shall be restored to the Republic of China."[33] Later, at the Yalta conference in 1945, this pledge was to be violated.

Roosevelt and Chiang had parted with mutual sentiments of friendship, despite earlier disagreements over Roosevelt's demand that Chiang form a coalition government with the Communists.[34] Chiang later wrote the American president that the effect of the Cairo Declaration on "the morale of our army and our people has been electric. In fact the whole nation is articulate to a degree that has never been

---

[31] H. Feis, *op. cit.*, pp. 103-104.

[32] Subsequently China participated as a great power in the Dumbarton Oaks Conference in the summer and fall of 1944.

[33] The joint statement was issued simultaneously in Washington, London, and Chungking on December 1, 1943. Department of State, "In Quest of Peace and Security," *Selected Documents on American Foreign Policy 1941-1951*, p. 10.

[34] H. K. Tong, *op. cit.*, p. 308.

known before in unanimously hailing the Cairo Declaration as a sure signpost leading the Far East toward post-war peace"[35]

On December 24, 1943, Roosevelt spoke to his nation about the conferences in Cairo and Teheran, remarking of Chiang that, "I met in the Generalissimo a man of great vision, great courage, and a remarkably keen understanding of the problems of today and tomorrow. We discussed all the manifold military plans for striking at Japan with decisive force from many directions, and I believe I can say that he returned to Chungking with the positive assurance of total victory over our common enemy. . . . Today we and the Republic of China are closer together than ever before in deep friendship and in unity of purpose."[36]

The Cairo Conference: Military Plans

At Cairo an offensive was planned which was to break the Japanese encirclement of China. The leading American strategists were convinced that the surest way to victory over Japan was to reopen the Burma Road, equip China's vast manpower with American arms, and then, in concert with American air and naval forces, defeat the Japanese army.[37] For the Burma campaign they had at their disposal two Chinese armies, trained by Stilwell and equipped with American weapons, which were eager to take the offensive against the Japanese. The so-called "X" Force consisted of two Chinese Army divisions, later expanded to five, which had been trained in Ramgarh, India. The "Y" Force was a Chinese Expeditionary Force consisting of thirty divisions based in Yunnan.

Under the "Anakim" plan, Chinese-American forces were to launch a two-pronged offensive against the Japanese in Upper Burma. At the same time, the British would make an amphibious landing with 50,000 troops in Lower Burma aimed at the recapture of Rangoon. A sizable allotment of American Lend-Lease equipment was allocated for the

---

[35] H. Feis, *op. cit.*, p. 109.
[36] *Ibid.*, pp. 109-110.
[37] *Ibid.*, p. 115.

Burma assault.[38]   Roosevelt also gave a preliminary commitment to Chiang's proposal to equip ninety divisions of the Chinese Army.[39]

The "Anakim" plan formulated at Cairo was mutilated in the Teheran Conference, which was held from November 28 to December 1. Stalin pledged that Russia would enter the war against Japan as soon as Germany was defeated, but was against diversion of equipment to Asiatic ventures.   Churchill, who had agreed to a Burma campaign only at Roosevelt's urging, seconded Stalin's request that all available resources be poured into the invasion of Normandy.   Chiang was not present in Teheran, and could do nothing to prevent the cooling of his allies toward their Chinese commitments.

After Teheran, Churchill and Roosevelt conferred again, and the promises made to Chiang ten days before were broken.   The British amphibious landing in lower Burma would be called off, they agreed, and Chiang's request that the U.S. arm ninety divisions of the Chinese Army refused.   China and the U.S. were to wage the Burma campaign alone. Chiang was deeply disappointed by this breach of trust, but made the decision to strike in Burma forthwith, with or without the British. Stilwell was given command of the Chinese troops in India, with full authority to initiate an offensive.

The objective in upper Burma was the construction of a highway connecting India and China, thus breaking the Japanese blockade of China.   The "X" Force began its advance from the Indian border, crossing 200 miles of jungle and mountains before capturing the Japanese-held cities of Myitkyina and Mogaung.   Engineering troops followed, constructing the Ledo Road and its parallel pipe line.   The "Y" Force struck at the Japanese from Yunnan.   The campaign took a terrific toll on men and supplies, but was successfully completed in January 1945.   The long blockade of China was broken.

Stilwell became so caught up in the Burma campaign, however, that he diverted desperately needed American Lend-Lease aid from the China

---

[38] H. K. Tong, *op. cit.*, pp. 316-317.

[39] General George C. Marshall informed the U.S. Joint Chiefs of Staff on November 25, 1943, that General Chiang had made the request; that President Roosevelt had postponed any definite commitment but made it clear that the United States had planned eventually to equip ninety divisions. Cf. H. Feis, *op. cit.*, p. 122.

theater. In April 1944 the Japanese launched Operation "Ichi-Go," a vast sweep by sixteen divisions southward through the Central and East China. Chinese troops in Honan and Hunan provinces were confronted with six times as many Japanese troops as Stilwell faced in upper Burma, and were soon critically short of munitions. Stilwell, who had stockpiled Lend-Lease munitions in Yunnan for the Burma campaign, refused to release them for use on the East China front as crucial battles raged. As a result, important cities such as Changsha, Hengyang, Kwellin, Liuchow, and others were lost in rapid succession and seven joint Sino-American air bases had to be abandoned. Stilwell's errors of judgment were directly responsible for this disaster.

IV. THE DETERIORATION OF ALLIED COOPERATION

The Stilwell Episode

Before Stilwell left Washington in early 1942 to take up his duties in China, he made it clear, in conferences with Secretary of War Henry L. Stimson and General George C. Marshall, that when he reached Chungking he would pressure Chiang to turn over command of the Chinese Army to him.[40]   As supreme commander of the China theater, Chiang was willing to appoint Stilwell as his chief of staff, for he hoped to benefit from the American general's knowledge of modern warfare. But it was unthinkable that he would yield his own post to a foreign subordinate.

The question of authority became a problem as soon as Stilwell reached Chungking on March 6, 1942. In his initial interview with Chiang, Stilwell stated that he was empowered to command all the American forces in China, Burma and India, to act as representative for the U.S. government on all international war councils in China, to supervise and control all American defense aid to China, including Lend-Lease, to serve as the liaison officer between Chiang and the commander

---

[40] H. L. Stimson and M. Bundy, *On Active Service in Peace and War* (New York: Harper Brothers, 1948), p. 340.

of the British forces in Burma and India, and to be Chiang's chief of staff.[41]

Stilwell's multifarious roles, not to mention his apparent lack of tact and self-restraint, made him extremely difficult to deal with. Stilwell himself sought to clarify his status by explaining that in international war councils he would present and maintain the policy of the U.S. rather than China, while in the allocation of Lend-Lease equipment he would carry out the wishes of the U.S. president. As the U.S. military representative in China he could call into question any military decision by Chiang that he thought was not in the U.S. interest. As the Lend-Lease administrator he could withhold at will any consignment from Chiang.[42]   Friction between the two men was inevitable.

The Nationalist government was particularly unhappy that the U.S., while giving all other heads of state the authority to allocate American Lend-Lease within their respective countries, denied this to the Chinese president. Only Chiang was required to submit requests to an American administrator on a project-by-project basis. Perhaps Washington was fearful that, if Chiang were given full authority, he would withhold Lend-Lease from the Chinese Communists. Whatever the reason, Stilwell proved to be high-handed in his role as Lend-Lease administrator, which not only poisoned relations between himself and his Chinese commander-in-chief, but brought him into conflict with the Commander of the U.S. Fourteenth Air Force, Major General Claire Chennault.

Stilwell, influenced by pro-Communist advisers such as John Paton Davies, Jr., and John S. Service, angrily demanded that Chiang withdraw the Chinese divisions which were deployed in the Northwest to contain the Chinese Communists. Stilwell apparently envisaged reequipping the

---

[41] According to the original Stimson-Soong notes exchanged on January 29-30, 1942, "the functions of the United States Army representative are to be generally as follows: To supervise and control all United States defense-aid affairs for China. Under the Generalissimo to command all United States forces in China and such Chinese forces as may be assigned to him. To represent the United States Government on any international war council in China and act as the Chief of Staff for the Generalissimo. To improve, maintain and control the Burma Road in China." Cf. Department of State, *U.S. Relations with China, 1944-1949*, pp. 468-469.

[42] H. K. Tong, *op. cit.*, pp. 340-341.

Red Army with American Lend-Lease and deploying them in other parts of China. He also demanded a complete reorganization of the Chinese Army and other drastic reforms which would have cut deeply into the existing system of command and administration. Chiang made every effort to compromise, and Stilwell was granted a number of his demands. He was not permitted to carry out his more unrealistic schemes, however, which Chiang regarded as improper interference in China's internal affairs.

At the time, Roosevelt had come round to Stilwell's idea of an American commander for the Chinese Army, and even to his notion of arming and deploying Chinese Communist troops. To sell these bitter ideas to Chiang, Roosevelt sent Major General Patrick J. Hurley, a former Secretary of War, as his personal representative to China. Hurley arrived in Chungking on September 6, 1944, and had soon carried his task almost to success.[43] Chiang tentatively agreed to make Stilwell Commander-in-Chief of the Chinese Army and to incorporate Communist troops into the General War program. In return, he asked for control over Lend-Lease, and insisted that the Communists must accept the authority of the Nationalist government.

Then Roosevelt sent Chiang a strongly worded note, drafted by the War Department, criticizing the delay in giving Stilwell "unrestricted command of all your forces."[44] The message, delivered in person by Stilwell on September 19, read to Chiang like an ultimatum: Accede to Stilwell's demands or face the withdrawal of American aid. He was especially offended that Stilwell, his chief of staff and subordinate, had been chosen as Roosevelt's messenger.

Chiang replied on September 24 with a blunt request for Stilwell's recall. He made it clear that this was a problem of personalities. "[O]n

---

[43] U.S. Vice President Henry A. Wallace, in connection with his visit to China in June, 1944, recommended that Roosevelt recall Stilwell and replace him with a high officer who could gain Chiang's confidence. Cf. C.F. Romanus, Y R. Sunderland, *Stilwell's Command Problems* (Washington, D. C.: Department of Army, 1956), pp. 374-379.

[44] For the text see *Ibid.*, pp. 445-446. On September 15, Stilwell telegraphed a pessimistic report to Marshall, saying that South China was lost and that this was largely due to a lack of proper command.

policy America and China are in complete agreement," he wrote, "but it is equally essential to find the right man to implement the policy."[45]

Roosevelt did as requested, advising Chiang on October 18 that the authority Stilwell had enjoyed as commander of the China-Burma-India theater would be divided between two successors. Major General Albert C. Wedemeyer would be the commander of American forces in the China theater, while Lt. General Daniel L. Sultan would be the commander of the Burma-India theater.[46] Chennault would remain in command of the U.S. Fourteenth Air Force and Hurley would continue as his personal representative to Chiang to deal with military affairs. When Ambassador Clarence E. Gauss subsequently resigned, Hurley was chosen to replace him, presenting his credentials on January 8, 1945.

All of this, especially Wedemeyer's appointment, was highly pleasing to Chiang. He promptly appointed Wedemeyer Chief of Staff of the Chinese National Army, and the two men worked together in harmony for the remainder of the war. His success as Stilwell's successor belied the propaganda that Chiang alone was at fault in the controversy. The episode cost China considerable capital in Washington, however, which became more accommodating toward the Chinese Communists, while pressing the Nationalist government ever harder to accept a coalition.[47]

The Yalta Agreement, February 11, 1945

Another bitter blow to China's post-war prospects was the secret Yalta Agreement of February 11, 1945. On August 21, 1937, the U.S.S.R., worried about Japanese aims in East Asia, had signed a nonaggression treaty with the Nationalist government.[48] This treaty became a dead letter after the Hitler-Stalin Pact of August 21, 1939, when the Soviet Union began wooing Japan. The Russo-Japanese

---

[45] H. K. Tong, *op. cit.*, p. 350.
[46] The China war theater included the mainland of China, Manchuria, and Indochina, as well as the islands immediately offshore. Cf. A. C. Wedemeyer, *Wedemeyer Report* (New York: Henry Holt Co., 1958), p. 271.
[47] A. N. Young, *op. cit.*, p. 316. Hurley saw clearly that the two strong personalities were incompatible. Cf. Romnaus & R. Sundreland, *op. cit.*, pp. 462-465.
[48] In 1938-1939, Russian credits of $250 million were extended to China; in 1940, $50 million were added.

neutrality treaty of April 13, 1941, provided that the U.S.S.R. would respect the territorial integrity of "Manchukuo" while Japan would respect the territorial integrity of the "Mongolian Peoples' Republic."[49]

When the tide of war began to turn against the Axis powers in 1943, Stalin saw in the approaching Japanese defeat an opportunity to inherit Japan's interests in Manchuria and North China. Communist Chinese armies already held strategic positions throughout North and Northwest China, and the Chungking government, weakened by seven years of war, would not be able to put up much resistance. Only the U.S. was in a position to block a Soviet advance, but by 1944 he was convinced that it would not intervene. Fanned by the activities of American leftists and further inflamed by the Stilwell controversy, American opinion was turning against Chiang's Nationalist Government.

There was no doubt that Stalin would eventually enter the war against Japan in order to share in the spoils of victory. Yet Roosevelt and Churchill arrived at Yalta with the strange notion that Stalin would have to be bribed into taking action. On the eve of certain victory, concessions were made to Stalin at China's expense that would forever change the face of Asia. Why was this? Was it because of the atmosphere of Soviet idolatry which gripped America during the closing months of war? Was Roosevelt, in the grip of a fatal illness, unable to resist the force of Stalin's personality? Or did he think to wean Stalin away from his revolutionary goals of world communism into accepting the United Nations and world peace?

The Yalta Conference of February 4-11, 1945, was one of the most dramatic displays of personal diplomacy in modern history. Yet it was marred by the practice of secret diplomacy, a relatively unknown phenomenon in American history, practiced by the Commander-in-Chief of the Armed Forces of the United States during World War II under his authority to make "military agreements."[50] The joint public announcement at the end of the Yalta Conference masked this fact, of

---

[49] Outer Mongolia, under its name of "People's Republic," had been a Soviet satellite state in East Asia since the late 1920's.

[50] S. F. Bemis, *A Diplomatic History of the United States* (New York: Henry Holt, 1957), p. 598. This does not mean confidential discussions or negotiations, but rather secret international agreements not even known to the U.S. Congress.

course. It said that the three heads of state had agreed on the timing, scope, and coordination of military plans for the defeat, unconditional surrender, and occupation of Germany. Nazism and Facism would be destroyed, and democratic governments established. A conference of nations would meet in San Francisco on April 25, 1945, to establish world organization on the basis of the Dumbarton Oaks proposals. Tacit acceptance was given to the Soviet advance in the Baltics and Eastern Europe, and Poland, by way of compensation, was to be enlarged at Germany's expense.[51]

The text of the secret agreement with the Soviet Union, which was not revealed until much later, was as follows:

> The leaders of the three Great Powers–the Soviet Union, the United States of America and Great Britain–have agreed that in two or three months after Germany has surrendered and the war in Europe has terminated the Soviet Union shall enter into the war against Japan on the side of the Allies on condition that:

> 1. The Status quo in Outer Mongolia (The Mongolian People's Republic) shall be preserved;
> 2. The former rights of Russia violated by the treacherous attack of Japan in 1904 shall be restored, viz;
>   (a) the southern part of Sakhalin as well as all the islands adjacent to it shall be returned to the Soviet Union,
>   (b) the commercial port of Dairen shall be internationalized, the preeminent interests of the Soviet Union in this port being safeguarded and the lease of Port Arthur as a naval base of the U.S.S.R. restored.
>   (c) the Chinese-Eastern Railroad and the South-Manchurian Railroad which provides an outlet to Dairen shall be jointly operated by the establishment of a joint Soviet-Chinese Company it being understood that the preeminent interests of the Soviet Union shall be safeguarded and that China shall retain full sovereignty in Manchuria.
> 3. The Kurile Islands shall be handed over to the Soviet Union.

---

[51] For the text of Agreements of Yalta Conference, see W. A. Williams, *The Shaping of American Diplomacy* (Chicago: Rand McNally, 1956), pp. 930-935.

It is understood that the agreement concerning Outer Mongolia and the ports and railroads referred to above will require concurrence of Generalissimo Chiang Kai-shek. The President will take measures to obtain this concurrence on advice from Marshal Stalin.

The heads of the three Great Powers have agreed that these claims of the Soviet Union shall be unquestionably fulfilled after Japan has been defeated.

For its part the Soviet Union expresses its readiness to conclude with the National Government of China a pact of friendship and alliance between the U.S.S.R. and China in order to render assistance to China with its armed forces for the purpose of liberating China from the Japanese yoke.[52]

Neither Chiang nor any Chinese representative had been invited to the Yalta Conference. Roosevelt and Churchill compromised vital Chinese interests without China's knowledge or consent, despite pledging at Cairo two short years before not to alienate one square inch of Chinese territory in the final war settlement. Here was a reversion to the old practice of the big powers—which China had fought for decades—of making deals at China's expense without consultation. All the great Powers were once again united in conspiring against China.

The Chinese government was not officially informed of the secret agreement by the U.S. government until June, 1945. It was a fait accompli of the worst kind: a secret agreement that provided for Soviet claims to be "unquestionably fulfilled" by the U.S. and Great Britain. Short of jeopardizing her relationship with her two most important allies, China had no choice but to go along. The blow was felt all the harder because the Chinese were convinced that their contribution to the war effort had definitely raised them to the status of a great power.[53]

Chinese representatives embarked upon a humiliating journey to Moscow to draft a new Sino-Soviet pact. Negotiating from a position of weakness, Premier T. V. Soong and Foreign Minister Wang Shih-chieh

---

[52] The secret agreement, signed by Roosevelt, Churchill and Stalin on February 11, 1945, was made public on February 11, 1946. Bulletin of the Department of State. February 24, 1946. Department of State, *U.S. Relations with China, 1944-1949*, pp. 113-114.

[53] W. Levi, *Modern China's Foreign Policy* (Minneapolis: University of Minnesota Press, 1953), p. 241.

made the best deal they could under the circumstances, and a thirty-year Sino-Soviet Treaty of Friendship and Alliance was signed on August 14, 1945.[54]　China agreed to the joint use of Port Arthur as a naval base, to the constitution of Dairen as a free port, to the determination of the status of Outer Mongolia by a plebiscite, and to joint ownership of the Chinese Changchun Railroad in Manchuria.　In return, China's "full sovereignty" over Manchuria was recognized.　The U.S.S.R. also promised to begin withdrawal of its troops from Manchuria within three weeks after the capitulation of Japan and to complete the withdrawal within three months.　These and other stipulations were cynically repudiated by Moscow as soon as it was expedient to do so.　The secret Yalta Agreement concerning China was a disaster of the first magnitude, and played a major role in the decline of the Nationalist government's fortunes after World War II.

The Surrender of Japan

By the end of 1942 the American forces in the Pacific had regained the initiative against the Japanese.　U.S. Naval forces under the command of Admiral Chester W. Nimitz retook the Gilberts, the Marshalls, the Carolines, and the Marianas from 1943 to 1944.　Landings were made on Leyte in October 1944, and General Douglas MacArthur returned to the Philippines.　Manila was liberated by March 1945, and Okinawa and the whole Ryukyu Islands the following month.　From these land bases the U.S. Air Force could attack the Japanese home islands, destroying Japanese cities and production facilities.　What was left of Japan's navy was destroyed in the Battle of Leyte Gulf.[55]

China had been exhausted by her battle losses of 1944, and the months after Wedemeyer's arrival in China were devoted to reorganization and recruitment.　After the reopening of the Burma Road, it was thought that Japan's position in China could only be attacked by

---

[54]　For the text, see Ministry of Foreign Affairs, *Treaties between the Republic of China and Foreign States, 1927-1957*, pp. 505-523, The treaty and other related documents were formally declared null and void by the Chinese government on February 25, 1953.

[55]　H. M. Vinacke, *A History of the Far East in Modern Times* (New York: Appleton-Century Crafts, 1959), pp. 635-637.

the landing of a powerful American expeditionary force in the south. To cooperate with the landing, half a million new soldiers were recruited in the Chinese Army, given training, and equipped with American arms. Both Chinese and American military staffs were engaged in this task early in 1945.[56]

Chinese troops moved from the defensive to the offensive. In June 1945 they recaptured Liuchow and Kweilin. In Kwangtung, preparations were made for an assault on Kwanchow Wan. The naval war continued to go well, and the U.S. Air Force was now pounding Japanese cities at will.[57] The landing of the American expeditionary force was now scheduled for mid-August.

On July 26 the Allies sent Japan an ultimatum calling for its unconditional surrender, promising its "prompt and utter destruction" if it failed to comply.[58] When no reply was received by August 6, an atomic bomb was dropped on Hiroshima; three days later a second bomb was exploded over Nagasaki.[59]

On August 8 Stalin declared war on Japan. By the next day, Soviet troops were already pouring into Manchuria. The Sino-Soviet Treaty of Friendship and Alliance was signed on August 14, and a few hours later Emperor Hirohito announced that Japan had surrendered. The Soviet Union, by virtue of brief participation in the war, became the occupying power in Manchuria and northern Korea.

The day after Japan's surrender, General Douglas MacArthur, now Supreme Commander of the Allied Powers in the Pacific, issued his

---

[56] The projected "Carbonado" plan was to take the offensive against Japan in South China. For details of the plan and related operations, see A. C. Wedemeyer, *op. cit.*, pp. 321-343.

[57] The second Cairo Conference (December 4-6, 1943) allowed discussions between military leaders and staff of the U.S. and Britain on preparations for the Normandy invasion.

[58] The Potsdam Proclamation, defining the terms of Japan's surrender, was signed in Potsdam on July 26, 1945 by President Harry Truman and Churchill. Chiang concurred by dispatch. For the full text, see U.S. Department of State, *Bulletin*, July 29, 1945, Vol. XII, pp. 137-138.

[59] Regarding the Atomic Bomb dropped on Hiroshima on August 6, 1945, President Truman declared: "If [Japan's leaders] do not now accept our terms they may expect a rain of ruin from the air, the like of which has never been seen on this earth."

General Order Number One. Among other things, this designated General Chiang as the agency for accepting the Japanese surrender in China (excluding Manchuria), Formosa, and Indochina north of the 16th parallel. The order gave prima facie support to the Nationalist government's claims to be the sole legitimate authority in China. On behalf of Chiang, General Ho Ying-chin, Commander-in-Chief of the Chinese Army, accepted the surrender of two million Japanese troops in the China theater in Nanking on September 9, 1945.[60]

The long and terrible struggle with Japan had ended in total victory.[61] Never in history were a people more eager for the return of peace and normality than the Chinese were at this moment. But the interlude of peace was to be brief, for within months the nation would descend into a cataclysmic civil war.

China's joy over the close of the war was heightened by the realization that she had taken part in the launching of the United Nations. China, along with the U.S., Great Britain, and the Soviet Union, had helped to draft the Dumbarton Oaks proposals. When the U.N. Charter was signed on June 26, 1945, in San Francisco, China was there as one of the four sponsoring powers. The Chinese delegation, led by Premier and Foreign Minister T. V. Soong, played a prominent part in this meeting.[62] At its close, in recognition of the major role that China had played in the world arena, she was chosen as one of the four permanent members of the Security Council.

---

[60] C. Y. Chang, *op. cit.*, pp. 404-405.

[61] Japan conditionally accepted the Potsdam ultimatum on August 10, 1945.

[62] The Chinese delegation to the San Francisco meeting was a strong one, composed of T. V. Soong, V. K. Wellington Koo, Wang Chung-hui, Wei Tao-ming, Hu Shih, Miss Wu Yi-fang, Carsun Chang, Li Huang, and Hu Lin. Tung Pi-wu, a Communist representative, was included at the insistence of the U.S. State Department.

9

THE FALL OF THE MAINLAND
1946–1949

I. THE MARSHALL MISSION

Internal Developments in China: Economic and Military Crisis

The end of the war did not mean the end of China's problems. There were two million Japanese soldiers and civilians to be repatriated, and 600,000 puppet government soldiers to be demobilized. There was raging inflation, and a pressing need for rural economic reform.[1] There was the need to draft and adopt a new constitution, and bring one-party rule to its promised end. Most seriously, there was the continued armed rebellion of the Communist Party.

T. V. Soong, who had become premier in December 1944, sought to come to grips with China's urgent economic difficulties. Several important programs were launched during the two years after the war, including the reduction of military expenditures in the national budget, the restoration of the railroads and other means of transportation, and the rehabilitation of the rural economy. These efforts were badly delayed and eventually wrecked by Communist hostilities.

Among the few favorable aspects of the postwar economy was the return of Japanese-owned industrial plants and enterprises to the Chinese

---

[1] On V-J Day, the official rate of exchange in American dollars was 20 to 1, by early 1946, it was 2,020 to 1, and by February 1947, 12,000 to 1.

government. The most important of these national assets were placed in the hands of either the National Resources Commission or government-managed corporations.

Another lift to China's economy was foreign aid. Lend-Lease was continued after the end of the war until June 30, 1946, during which time China received allocations totaling $513,700,000. However, this figure included a huge sum for the transportation of Chinese troops to the north to accept the Japanese surrender.[2]   The United Nations Relief and Rehabilitation Administration (UNRRA) also provided significant aid, including not only much-needed food and medicine, but also fertilizer, railway equipment, and machinery.   In all, China received through UNRRA some 2.5 million tons of supplies worth $518 million.   The agency also sent over 1,000 foreign experts to China to help with reconstruction.[3]

The great hope of the Chinese government was for an American loan to help stabilize its depreciating currency. Application was made to the Import-Export Bank in Washington, D.C., for a loan in the amount of $500 million. The Bank approved the loan, but required detailed project-by-project approval as one of its conditions. There were also political conditions, as President Harry S. Truman revealed on December 18, 1946, when he said that credits would not be extended until China implemented the Marshall program for a coalition government. When this did not happen, the loan was allowed to lapse.[4]

The failure to secure a substantial loan from the U.S., at a time when Great Britain had been awarded an American credit of $3,750,000,000 caused considerable frustration in Chinese governmental circles. China did receive five separate loans totaling $62,550,000 from the Import-Export Bank in 1946 for reconstruction purposes, but this amount was too small to have much effect on inflation. To be sure, the ultimate cause of the sickening drop in the value of Chinese currency was the ongoing civil war. Until this was resolved, no amount of foreign aid could put

---

[2]   H. K. Tong, *Chiang Kai-shek* (Rev. ed. Taipei: China Publishing Co., 1953), pp. 379-380.

[3]   For details see Harry B. Price, *UNRRA in China, 1945-1947* (Washington, D.C., UNRRA, 1948). The figure above is cited by A. N. Young, *China and the Helping Hand, 1937-1945* (Cambridge: Harvard University Press, 1963), p. 371.

[4]   H. K. Tong, *op. cit.*, pp. 380-381.

China's currency on a sound footing. T. V. Soong, unable to cope with the problem, resigned on April 18, 1947, and General Chang Chun was appointed premier in his place.

Then there was the ongoing civil war with the Communists, which threatened to split the whole country. When the war began the Chinese Communists controlled only 30,000 square miles of Shensi province and had no more than 70,000 men under arms. By the time the war ended they had an army of 910,000 backed by a huge number of militiamen, and held territories throughout northern China. In Manchuria, their position was reinforced by the Soviet Far East Army.

On the eve of V-J Day, Chiang sent a message to all Japanese and puppet army commanders to surrender to the Chinese National Army only. He also ordered the Communists to hold their present positions and await further instructions. "We consider that you have sent us an erroneous order," Chu Teh, Commander of the Communist 18th Group Army, replied. "[W]e refuse to carry out this order."[5] From September 11 to October 11, 1945, Communist forces seized two hundred Japanese-occupied cities and towns. Nationalist and Communist forces were soon in open conflict in the newly liberated areas. Before 1945 was over, civil war raged in eleven provinces south of the Great Wall.

The U.S. government, as it had since 1943, sought to broker a political solution to this conflict. Ambassador Patrick J. Hurley, following Roosevelt's instructions, tried for a year to bring the Nationalists and the Communists together in a unity program. He gradually became convinced of the hopelessness of this efforts, the only practical result of which was to undermine the authority of the Nationalist government, America's recognized wartime ally. He returned to Washington in November 1945, determined to bring about a change in U.S. China policy.

Secretary of State James F. Byrnes largely agreed with Hurley's analysis, and in his presence dictated a new set of instructions for the ambassador to take back to China. When Hurley returned to the State Department the following day to pick up his typed instructions, however, he discovered that they had been altered. He was directed to continue to

---

5   Lionel MacChassin; *The Communist Conquest of China, A History of the Civil War, 1945-1949* (Cambridge: Harvard University Press, 1965), pp. 56-57.

work for a coalition government in China. Hurley resigned his ambassadorship in protest against what he considered persistence in error.[6]

Truman then intervened, announcing that he was sending General George Marshall as his special representative to China. Marshall's instructions, unfortunately, were virtually identical to those Hurley rejected. He was to mediate between the Nationalists and the Communists, bringing about the unification of China by peaceful, democratic methods, "and the cessation of Nationalist-Communist hostilities as quickly as possible."[7] Marshall accepted the appointment, and left for China on December 15, 1945.

American Attempts at Mediation

The day Marshall left, Truman made a public statement of U.S. China policy. The goal of the U.S. government was "a strong, united, and democratic China" achieved by "peaceful negotiation." He proposed "a cessation of hostilities," followed by "a national conference of representatives of major political elements . . . to develop an early solution to the present internal strife . . . [and] agree upon arrangements which would give those elements a fair and effective representation in the Chinese National Government. . . . With the institution of a broadly representative government, autonomous armies would be eliminated as such, and all armed forces in China integrated effectively into the Chinese National Army." He concluded by promising that, "As China moves toward peace and unity along the lines described above, the United States would be prepared to assist the National Government in every reasonable way to rehabilitate the country, improve the agrarian and industrial economy, and establish a military organization . . . [and] give favorable consideration to Chinese requests for credits and loans."[8]

---

6   The Senate Foreign Affairs Committee invited Hurley to testify, but then voted not to investigate the China issue further. Cf. H. K. Tong, *op. cit.*, p. 387.

7   U.S. Department of State, *U.S. Relations with China, 1944-1949*, pp. 605-606. For the full text see *Ibid.*, pp. 607-609; U.S. Department of State, *Bulletin*, December 16, 1945, p. 945.

8   Of the 38 members of the Political Consultative Conference, eight belonged to the Kuomintang, seven to the Communist Party, five to the China Youth Party, four to

Such were the proposals that Marshall brought to China on Truman's behalf. If the Nationalist government agreed to a cease-fire, a national conference, and the establishment of a coalition government including the Communists, Marshall was authorized to assure China that important American economic aid would be forthcoming. Should China reject the American proposals, the inference was clear, she would receive little or no help.

Marshall began his mission in China by concluding a truce between the Nationalist and Communist armies. A truce committee was set up on the initiative of the Nationalist government, chaired by Marshall, with Chang Chun representing the Nationalists and Chou En-lai the Communists. After six meetings, the committee agreed on the wording of a cease-fire order, and on January 10, 1946, both sides issued the order to their respective commanders in the field. It called for the cessation of all hostilities and troop movements throughout China, with the exception of Manchuria, on January 13. The truce was enforced by eight "truce teams," operating under the supervision of an executive headquarters in Peking, which were assigned to monitor different areas of China. The teams, as well as the headquarters itself, were tripartite bodies, consisting of one representative of the Nationalist government, one Communist, and one American.

Meanwhile, Marshall was pushing the Nationalists to establish a new coalition government with the Communists. The Nationalist government, pledged to terminate the period of "political tutelage" within a year of war's end, had already organized the Political Consultative Conference (PCC). This now became the organizational basis for negotiations between the Nationalist government and the Communists. The PCC convened in Chungking on January 10, 1946, and most of the differences between the government and the Communists were resolved over the course of the next 20 days of meetings.[9]

---

the Democratic League, two to the National Salvation Association, one to the Vocational Education Association, one to the Third Party, one to the Local Self-Government League, and nine were independent.

[9] Of the 38 members of the Political Consultative Conference, eight belonged to the Kuomintang, seven to the Communist Party, five to the China Youth Party, four to the Democratic League, two to the National Salvation Association, one to the

It was agreed that the long-postponed National Assembly should finally meet on November 12, 1946, to adopt a constitution. The nucleus of the Assembly would be the 1,200 delegates elected in 1946, but to this number would be added 150 regional and vocational delegates to represent Taiwan and Manchuria, and 700 additional delegates representing the various political parties.[10]

In the interim, authority would be vested in a State Council of 40 members, in which all parties would be represented. Chiang would continue as president, and would have veto power over all Council decisions, with a three-fifths majority required for override. The Executive Yuan should also be reorganized, and minority parties would receive portfolios. In "liberated areas" under the control of the Communists, the status quo was to be maintained until the Nationalist government was reconstituted and the armed forces reorganized and reduced in size.[11]

Progress was also made toward the integration of the Chinese Communist armies into the Chinese National Army. A military subcommittee of the PCC, comprised of Chang Chun for the government and Chou En-lai for the Communists, met with Marshall to work out the details of military reorganization. An agreement signed on February 15 provided for the reduction of the Chinese National Army to 90 divisions within the year, then to 50, and finally to 10.

An optimistic Marshall left China on March 11, 1946, to report to Truman on his progress toward his three primary objectives. No sooner had Marshall left than the Communists, in defiance of the cease-fire order, attacked the cities of Changchun, Harbin and Tsitsihar in the Northeast. The Communist forces also seized Szepingchieh, a strategic railroad junction in the south of Manchuria, effectively blocking the Nationalists from sending reinforcements. Within a few days, the whole Manchurian front was ablaze, and truce violations began to occur in

Vocational Education Association, one to the Third Party, one to the Local Self-Government League, and nine were independent.

[10] For details of the five agreements reached by the Political Consultative Conference in 1946, see Chiang Kai-shek, *Soviet Russia in China, A Summing-up at Seventy* (New York: Farrer, Straus, and Cudahy, 1968), pp. 109-112.

[11] H. M. Vinacke, *A History of the Far East in Modern Times* (6th ed. New York: Appleton-Century-Crofts, 1959), pp. 665-666.

other parts of China. On April 15 the Communists declared a state of "all-out hostilities" in Manchuria. The Marshall truce had been short-lived.

The Failure of the Marshall Mission

Marshall returned to China on April 16, one day before Changchun fell to the Communists, and resumed his efforts at mediation. On July 11, 1946, Truman appointed as U.S. Ambassador to China John Leighton Stuart, President of Yenching University in Peking. His chief task was also to assist Marshall in the peace negotiations.[12]

The situation in Manchuria slowly improved. Szepingchieh was recaptured on May 19. Retreating northward in the face of the Nationalist advance, the Communist troops evacuated Changchun on May 23. One by one, all of Manchuria's important cities were returned to the control of the Nationalist government. The Communist armies in Manchuria, although defeated, had received a generous gift from the departing Soviets: the arms and munitions of the Kwantung Army.[13] American military supplies which had arrived at Vladivostok during the later stages of the war were also transferred to the Chinese Communists.[14]

Beginning in May 1946, in support of the military action in Manchuria, Communist armies south of the Great Wall began large-scale attacks on Nationalist troops in Jehol, Chahar, Hopei and Shantung provinces. By the end of 1946 the massive infusion of Japanese and American arms began to tell in the field. The Nationalist army had lost its superiority in arms, and the balance of power began shifting to the Communists.

---

[12] For details of Stuart's role in negotiations see Stuart, *Fifty Years in China, the Memoirs of John Leighton Stuart, Missionary and Ambassador* (New York: Random House, 1954), pp. 160-175.

[13] According to Japan's own estimates, the Kwantung Army depots contained, in addition to ample supplies of rifles and munitions, 151 planes, 155 tanks, 186 armored cars, and 787 guns of various caliber's. Cited in H. K. Tong, *op. cit.*, p. 393.

[14] D. MacArthur, *Reminiscences* (New York: McGraw Hill Co., 1964), p. 320.

Neither Marshall nor the U.S. State Department had apparently learned anything about Communist perfidy from the earlier violations of the cease-fire agreement, for they sought once more to impose a truce. Undersecretary of State Dean C. Acheson set the tone of Marshall's second effort on June 28, 1946, when he declared that the U.S. was "impartial" as regards the Nationalists and the Communists. "Too much stress cannot be laid on the hope of this Government," he added, "that our economic assistance be carried out in China through the medium of a government fully and fairly representative of all important Chinese political elements, including the Chinese Communists."[15]

Both sides struggled for position, bargained for a truce, and as the truce collapsed, resumed fighting. Marshall strongly opposed the stand of many Nationalist leaders that the two sides were now so divided that the issue could only be decided by force. They responded by pointing to repeated Communist violations of truce agreements and to the openly stated intention of the Communists to overthrow the government. The Communists, for their part, bitterly attacked American "interference," protesting the limited U.S. assistance the Nationalist government continued to receive.

Criticized from both sides, Marshall strove to be increasingly impartial in the enforcement of American foreign policy. The U.S. government went so far as to announce that, in order to preserve Marshall's role as an even-handed mediator, it had ordered a ten-month embargo on the shipment of American arms to China.[16] This drastic measure virtually disarmed Nationalist forces equipped with American arms, even as Communist troops were regrouping for fresh attacks. On August 19, 1946, Truman issued a thinly veiled threat to Chiang that, unless the fighting stopped, "it will be necessary for me to redefine and explain the position of the United States to the people of America," diplomatic phraseology for a basic change in U.S. policy toward the Nationalist government.[17]

---

[15] *Ibid.*, p. 395.
[16] The prohibition was in place from August 1946 to May 1947.
[17] Truman to Chiang, U.S. Department of State, *U.S. Relations with China, 1944-1949*, p. 652.

Truman issued another statement of policy on China on December 18, 1946, distancing himself even further from the Nationalist government. "The views expressed a year ago by this Government are valid today," he maintained. "The plan for political unification agreed to last February is sound. The plan for military unification of last February has been made difficult of implementation by the progress of the fighting since last April, but the general principles involved are fundamentally sound. . . . We continue to hope that the [Nationalist] Government will find a peaceful solution. We are pledged not to interfere in the internal affairs of China. . . . While avoiding involvement in their civil strife, we will persevere with our policy of helping the Chinese people to bring about peace and economic recovery in their country."[18]

By now the Nationalist government was maintaining that the ongoing military confrontation must be halted before any further discussion on political questions could take place. The Communists, on the other hand, demanded the Political Consultative Conference immediately take up the question of the status of Communist-controlled local administrations. The Communist demand for simultaneous settlement of military and political questions was rejected by the Nationalists as unrealistic.

On November 12, 1946, the National Assembly met in Nanking. The 1355 delegates in attendance represented all of China's political parties with the exception of the Chinese Communist Party and Democratic League, whose delegates boycotted the proceedings. Chou En-lai and the Communist delegation left Nanking on November 19, terminating the negotiations begun in January. On December 25, 1947, the new Constitution was accepted by the National Assembly. Five days later, the Young China Party and the Social Democratic Party were invited to join the Nationalist Party in an interim coalition government.

While the Nationalists were complaining about the one-sided pressure being exerted on them by the U.S. government, the Communists began attacking Marshall's personal integrity. These attacks, coupled with the persistent refusal of the Communists to accept any peace proposals that Marshall could persuade the Nationalist government to make, made his position as mediator increasingly untenable. Marshall's resignation in January 1947 brought to an end U.S. efforts to bring the

---

[18] U.S. Department of State, *Bulletin*, December 29, 1946, *Ibid.*, p. 694.

Nationalists and the Communists together in a coalition government. The last contingent of American troops stationed in China was withdrawn at the same time.[19]

When Marshall departed from China on January 17, 1947, it was to succeed James F. Byrnes as Secretary of State. Soon after, he issued a statement summarizing the reasons for the failure of his mission. Marshall stated that "the greatest obstacle to peace has been the complete, almost overwhelming suspicion with which the Chinese Communist Party and the Kuomintang regard each other. . . . On the one hand, the leaders of the Government are strongly opposed to a Communistic form of government. On the other hand, the Communists frankly state that they are Marxists and intend to work toward establishing a Communist form of government in China, though first advancing through the medium of a democratic form of government of the American or British type. . . . The leaders of the Government are convinced in their minds that the Communists' expressed desire to participate in a government of the type endorsed by the Political Consultative Conference last January had for its purpose only a destructive intention. The Communists felt, I believe, that the Government was insincere in its apparent acceptance of the PCC resolution for the formation of the new government and intended by coercion of military force and the action of the secret police to obliterate the Communist Party." Marshall concluded by arguing that, since negotiations had failed, "The salvation of the situation, as I see it, would be the assumption of leadership by the liberals in the Government and in the minority parties, a splendid group of men, but who as yet lack the political power to exercise a controlling influence. Successful action on their part under the leadership of Generalissimo Chiang Kai-shek would, I believe, lead to unity through good government."[20]

---

[19] After V-J Day 55,000 U.S. Marines landed in North China to aid in the repatriation of Japanese and defend vital points from Communist attacks. All marines were promptly withdrawn, except for a guard contingent in Tsingtao, the location of the U.S. Naval Training Group engaged in training Chinese naval personnel. Cf. U.S. Department of State, *U.S. Relations with China, 1944-1949*, pp. 219-695.

[20] Text of Personal Statement by the Special Representative of the U.S. President (Marshall), January 7, 1947, in U.S. Department of State, *Bulletin*, January 19, 1947, pp. 83-85; *Ibid.*, pp. 686-689.

Responses to the Marshall statement were immediate. Chiang referred to it as "friendly and constructive."[21]   Chen Li-fu, a Kuomintang leader, complained that if Marshall had spent more time with leading figures in the Kuomintang "his appraisal of the Chinese situation in its proper breadth and depth might have been more enlightening."[22]   Chou En-lai criticized Marshall for trying to conclude a truce while American goods and troops were being used by the Kuomintang for attacks upon the Communists. According to Chou, this proved that "the American government is intentionally supporting Chiang Kai-shek in the waging of large-scale civil war."[23]

The Marshall report also produced a sensation in the United States. Many conservatives viewed it as naive and unduly favorable to the Chinese Communists, especially in its assertion that the Communists intended to set up "a democratic government of the American or British type." The U.S. should support the Kuomintang without reservation, anti-Communists argued, as a vital bulwark in the worldwide struggle against the advance of Communism. Were the Nationalists to be defeated, they predicted that a flood tide of Communism would engulf Southeast Asia.

Others in the U.S. lauded the Marshall report. Liberals thought it an even-handed presentation of the objective situation in China. Leftist sympathizers eagerly agreed with Marshall that American aid could not salvage the Nationalist government, and that the Chinese should be left alone to work out their own difficulties. A bitter war of words began between these two camps.[24]

The fundamental fallacy of the U.S. position, from the point of view of the Nationalist government, was its assumption that the Communists would ever agree to assume a subordinate role in a coalition government. With their Soviet "elder brothers" in a dominant position in Manchuria and Northwest China, the aim of the Communists after World War II

---

[21] *New York Times*, January 12, 1947. Cited in H. F. MacNair and D. F. Lach, *Modern Far Eastern International Relations.* 2nd ed. (New York: D. Van Nostrand Co., 1955), p. 538.

[22] Statement quoted in H. R. Isaacs *op. cit.*, p. 68.

[23] *Ibid.*, pp. 75-81.

[24] H. F. MacNair & D. F. Lach, *Modern Far Eastern International Relations*, 2nd ed. pp. 538-539.

was total victory. It was only for tactical advantage that they entered into negotiations at all. As long as the Americans entertained the hope of a peaceful settlement, the Communists realized, American aid to the Nationalists would not be forthcoming, at least not in the quantity needed to defeat them on the battlefield. And so the Communists toyed with Marshall, first raising his expectations that a peaceful compromise was within reach, then wrecking the negotiations by persistent defiance and truce violations. Weeks turned into months, and the Nationalist government's military superiority over Communists was slowly eroded away. The Marshall Mission, however well-intentioned, fatally weakened Chiang for his final confrontation with the Communists.

The substantial amount of American aid received after the war could not offset the harm done by the Marshall, because it delayed military action against the Communists at a time when victory was still possible. Had the Nationalists struck quickly after the Japanese surrender, and had they been supported by American financial and military aid, the Communist insurgency might have been quashed.

In his book *War or Peace*, John Foster Dulles commented on the loss of China that "The United States itself is not . . . without fault. When the Japanese surrendered on September 2, 1945 (V-J Day), the Chinese National Government shared the prestige of victory, and it had considerable military power. It was a time—perhaps the only time—when the situation might have been saved. But the United States government, in December 1945, decided that the National Government should come to terms with the revolutionary Communist elements in China, and 'that a China disunited and torn by civil strife could not be considered realistically as a proper place for American assistance' (Presidential Instructions of December 15, 1945, to General Marshall).[25]

---

[25] J. F. Dulles, *War or Peace* (New York: MacMillan Co., 1950), p. 226.

II. THE PROGRESS IN ECONOMIC RELATIONS

The Sino-American Commercial Treaty and Other Agreements

Despite the increasing civil strife in China, Sino-American diplomacy had its moments between 1946 to 1948. Negotiations were successfully carried out for a commercial and navigation treaty, an agreement for the sale of U.S. surplus property, an aviation agreement, and for the formation of the Joint Commission on Rural Reconstruction.

The Treaty of Friendship, Commerce, and Navigation between the Republic of China and the United States, which replaced the old commercial treaty of 1903, was signed in Nanking on November 4, 1946.[26] Ratifications were exchanged and the treaty entered into force on November 30, 1948. The treaty provided that U.S. nationals in China would enjoy the same rights and privileges as those enjoyed by Chinese nationals in the United States. The two countries also guaranteed that trade and commerce would be conducted on a most-favored-nation basis.

The Agreement between the United States and China for the Sale of Surplus Property was signed in Nanking on August 30, 1946.[27] The property, the procurement value of which was $900 million, was located in India, China, and seventeen Pacific Islands. It consisted in the main of small ships and marine equipment, vehicles of all types, construction equipment, airplane supplies and equipment, and a wide variety of communications and electrical equipment. The agreed-upon sale price was $175 million, of which $55 million was to be a long-term credit. The remainder was to come from the $150 million that America owed China for expenditures by Chinese government on behalf of the U.S. Army, with the difference of $30 million being used for shipping technical services arising out of the property transfer. Although this transaction involved only war surplus material, not munitions or

---

[26] Text in Ministry of Foreign Affairs, *Treaties Between the Republic of China and Foreign States, 1927-1961*, pp. 688-718.

[27] Text in *Ibid.*, pp. 683-688.

weapons, the Communists accused the U.S. government of extending large-scale military aid to the Nationalist government.[28]

The Air Transport Agreement between China and the U.S. for the reciprocal exchange of commercial air rights was signed in Nanking on December 20, 1946, and immediately took effect.[29]	Under this agreement the airlines of each country were accorded the right to operate services to the other country over three different routes, and were granted base rights there.

Joint Commission on Rural Reconstruction

In October 1945 the Chinese government proposed the establishment of a joint Sino-American mission to investigate China's agricultural problems, focusing on those commodities important in the U.S.-China trade.[30]	The mission, following field investigations in 15 provinces, submitted its final report in late 1946, outlining a comprehensive and long-range program that the Chinese government might undertake for the improvement of China's agriculture. Given the times, few of these were implemented.

Several of the recommendations of the joint mission, however, were included in the program of the Joint Commission on Rural Reconstruction (JCRR), which was established by the China Aid Act of 1948.[31]	According to notes exchanged on August 5, 1948, between Foreign Minister Wang Shih-chieh and Ambassador Stuart, the JCRR was authorized to formulate and carry out a coordinated program for the reconstruction of rural China, and that ten percent of U.S. economic aid

---

[28]	U.S. Department of State, *U.S. Foreign Relations with China, 1944-1949*, pp. 180-181.

[29]	Text in Ministry of Foreign Affairs, *Treaties Between the Republic of China and Foreign States, 1927-1961*, pp. 720-732.

[30]	As Chiang wrote to Truman, "I am keenly conscious of the fact that unless and until Chinese agriculture is modernized, Chinese industry cannot develop; as long as industry remains undeveloped, the general economy of the country cannot greatly improve." U.S. Department of State, *U.S. Relations with China, 1944-1949*, p. 228.

[31]	Notes in U.S. Economic Cooperation Administration, *Economic Aid to China under the China Aid Act of 1949* (Washington, D.C.: Government Printing Office, 1949), p. 126-129; *Ibid.*, pp. 1004-1006.

to China was to be used for this purpose.[32]   On October 1, 1948, the JCRR, comprised of three Chinese and two Americans, formally convened in Nanking, electing Chiang Monlin as its chairman. Although its program on the mainland was short-lived, in the fall of 1949 it moved to Taiwan, where it enjoyed many fruitful years.

In April 1949 the Nationalist government implemented an extensive land reform program in Taiwan province with the assistance of the JCRR. First, farm rent was limited to 37.5 per cent of the value of the primary crop. Then, the following year, the government began selling publicly-owned farmland to landless farmers. Finally, in 1953, the Land-to-the-Tiller program was implemented, allowing tenant farmers to buy the land they cultivated. By the time this program was completed, most of the island's agricultural land was in the hands of owner-cultivators. Unlike the violent program of land reform carried out by the Communists, these measures to equalize land ownership were effected peacefully.[33]   American economic aid was effectively utilized by the Nationalist government to build a stable and prosperous society in Taiwan.

III. THE DISENGAGEMENT AND THE IMPASSE

The Truman Doctrine and the Marshall Plan for Europe

After World War II, Stalin not only installed puppet regimes in Eastern Europe, but attempted to bring other states into the Communist orbit. It was Soviet designs on Greece and Turkey that finally brought about an American response. On March 12, 1947, Truman announced that the U.S. would henceforth help "free peoples who are resisting attempted subjugation by armed minorities or by outside pressures . . . to work out their own destinies in their own way," primarily by providing "economic and financial aid." Under the Truman Doctrine, the U.S.

---

[32] U.S. Economic aid to China ceased in July 1965.
[33] For details, see Chen Cheng, *Land Reform in Taiwan* (Taipei: China Publishing Co., 1961).

would actively defend the free world against Communist aggression.[34] The $400 million in U.S. aid Greece and Turkey promptly received was only the beginning of a vast program of economic assistance, intended to strengthen the economies of Western European countries, known as the Marshall Plan.

The Truman Doctrine was also, in principle at least, intended for Asia. Marshall believed, however, that China was too vast and its problems too complex for the U.S. to handle. As a result, nothing was done about China throughout much of 1947.

The Wedemeyer Fact-Finding Mission

Although the Nationalist government made one more peace offer after Marshall's departure, the Communists were interested only in a military solution. On July 18, 1946, the State Council had adopted a General National Mobilization Order for the Suppression of the Communist Rebellion. The Order had placed the Republic of China on a war footing, empowering the government to draft troops and allocating revenues for the prosecution of the war. Now they launched twin offensives in Shantung and northern Shensi, without marked success. The combination of a war-weary populace and deteriorating of military morale sapped the Nationalist effort.[35]

Alarmed over the deteriorating China situation, Truman, on July 11, 1947, appointed Wedemeyer to make a fact-finding tour of China and Korea and report his findings. Despite his vigorous opposition of Communist aggression elsewhere, Truman promised "considerable assistance" to China "only if the Chinese Government presents satisfactory evidence of effective measures looking towards Chinese recovery." The ROC nevertheless welcomed the Wedemeyer Mission, hoping against hope that it would result in immediate economic and

---

[34] F. H. Michael & G. E. Taylor, *The Far East in the Modern World* (New York: Henry Holt Co., 1956), pp. 662-663.

[35] For military campaigns in 1947-49, see F. F. Liu, *A Military History of Modern China, 1924-1949* (Princeton: Princeton University Press, 1956), pp. 243-270.

military aid to China.[36]   The Communists, not surprisingly, were bitterly hostile.

Wedemeyer spent a month in China, talking to people both inside and outside the government.[37]   On the eve of his departure on August 24, 1947, he summarized his conclusions in a public statement:

> In China today I find apathy and lethargy in many quarters. Instead of seeking solutions of problems presented, considerable time and effort are spent in blaming outside influences and seeking outside assistance. . . . the existing government can win and retain the undivided, enthusiastic support of the bulk of the Chinese people by removing incompetent and/or corrupt people who now occupy many positions of responsibility in the Government, not only national but more so in provincial and municipal structures. . . . To regain and maintain the confidence of the people, the Central Government will have to effect immediately drastic, far-reaching political and economic reforms. Promises will no longer suffice. Performance is absolutely necessary. It should be accepted that military force in itself will not eliminate communism.[38]

The government's reaction to Wedemeyer's statement was generally unfavorable. It hurt that he emphasized government corruption and incompetence to the exclusion of other, more positive aspects of China's post-war picture, a bias which Premier Chang Chun attributed to Wedemeyer's failure to seek information from impartial sources. Even the Communists fiercely attacked Wedemeyer, even though his statement was generally interpreted to mean that he would not recommend substantial American assistance to the government.[39]

When Wedemeyer submitted his report to Truman on September 19, however, it recommended a five-year program of large-scale American economic aid to China. This was to be administered by the Nationalist

---

[36] U.S. Department of State, *U.S. Relations with China, 1944-1949*, pp. 255.

[37] For the summary of the remarks made by Wedemeyer before a joint meeting of the State Council and the Ministers of the Nationalist government on August 22, 1947, see *Ibid.*, pp. 758-763.

[38] Statement of August 24, 1947 by Wedemeyer on conclusion of his mission in China, see *Ibid.*, pp. 763-764.

[39] *Ibid.*, p. 258.

government under the guidance of American advisers.[40]   To effect the necessary reforms in China's military establishment, a further advisory group of 10,000 American officers would be needed. Manchuria, by this time a Communist stronghold, should be put under a U.N. trusteeship.[41]

Wedemeyer's proposal ran directly contrary to the Truman administration's China policy, which was that no further economic aid would be given to Nanking until it ceased hostilities and entered into a coalition government with the Communists. His report was quickly shelved, and Wedemeyer himself was never again consulted about China policy.[42]

A Constitutional Government Amid Communist Offensives

Despite the ongoing civil war, China took an important step toward constitutional government on Christmas Day, 1947, when the new Constitution came into effect. As called for in the Constitution, general elections for representatives for the new National Assembly, the Legislative Yuan, and the Control Yuan were held from November 21 to 23, 1947. This was the first nationwide election ever held in China, and an estimated quarter of a billion people were theoretically eligible to vote. There were imperfections in the electoral machinery, and great disparities in voter turnout, but despite these and other problems the new Assembly was a broadly representative body.[43]

The new National Assembly convened in Nanking on March 29, 1948, and its members elected Chiang president and Li Tsung-jen vice president. Chiang appointed Weng Wen-hao to the post of premier, and selected a cabinet which included members of the Young China Party, the

---

[40] The text of Wedemeyer's report to Truman was not made public until 1949. See *Ibid.*, pp. 764-814.

[41] For discussion of Wedemeyer's idea of a U.N. Trusteeship over Manchuria, see Carsun Chang, *The Third Force in China* (New York: Bookman Associates, 1962), pp. 249-252.

[42] A. C. Wedemeyer, *Wedemeyer Reports* (New York: Henry Holt Co., 1958), p. 308.

[43] The total number of delegates to the 1948 National Assembly was to have been 2,050. Out of the 1,744 representatives actually elected, 847 were independents, 725 Kuomintang members, and 172 Young China Party members and Social Democrats.

Social Democrats, and independents. In the throes of civil war, the Republic of China had at last become a functioning democracy.

In the year 1948 all the forces which had been whirling China toward disaster came to a tragic climax. Inflation continued to skyrocket, and a new currency—the gold yuan—issued in August soon went the way of its predecessors. The military situation also grew steadily worse as the Communists went on the offensive, subjecting Nationalist forces to an endless series of ambushes, skirmishes, and attacks on isolated garrisons. Government troops defending fixed positions or critical lines of communications were especially vulnerable to such hit-and-run tactics.[44]

The spring saw a renewed Communist offensive in Manchuria. Szepingchieh, the gateway to Changchun, was occupied on March 15, and by late summer all of Northeast China was in Communist hands. By this time, according to estimates made by the Defense Minister Ho Ying-Chin, the Communists had reached military parity with the government.[45] The attack then shifted inside the Great Wall, with Tsinan, the capital of Shantung, falling on September 27. The critical encounter was the Battle of Hsuchow-Pangpu, which raged from November 7, 1948, to January 10, 1949. By its end, the government had lost 200,000 of its best troops.

Following the debacle at Hsuchow-Pangpu, a number of government leaders began clamoring for peace talks with the Communists. President Chiang resigned on January 21, 1949, and Li Tsung-Jen became Acting President. The government had to evacuate from Nanking on April 23, 1949, and soon all of China north of the Yangtze was under Communist control. The military situation was by now irretrievable.

The Nationalist government moved to Canton, then to Chungking, and finally to Taipei, all within a few months. On October 1, 1949, the Chinese Communists established the People's Republic of China with its capital at Peking. On December 7, 1949, the Republic of China established its capital at Taipei.

---

[44] For the Communist strategy, see F. F. Liu, *A Military History of Modern China,* 1924-1949 (Princeton: Princeton University, 1956), pp. 249-255.

[45] *Report of the Defense Minister, General Ho Ying-ching to the Legislative Yuan, September 24, 1948,* Cited in F. F. Liu, *Ibid.,* p. 254.

The Decision of Limited Assistance

The Truman administration viewed the mounting catastrophe with studied detachment. Many members in the U.S. Congress, concerned about the strategic implications of a Communist China, demanded that substantial military aid be given the Nationalist government. So strong was this sentiment, the administration belatedly realized, that Congress might well reject all funding for the Marshall Plan under the 1948 Economic Cooperation appropriations bill unless China were included.

On February 18, 1948, Truman reluctantly sent a message to Congress requesting $570 million for China. Noting that the request conspicuously omitted military assistance, the Congress specified that $125 million be used for this purpose, and limited the economic aid to $338 million. The Foreign Assistance Act including these provisions was signed by President Truman on April 3, 1948.[46] For a time, it seemed that the Nationalists were about to receive some belated relief.

If the American aid was to affect the course of the war, it had to reach the Nationalist forces almost immediately. Decisive battles were even then being fought in Manchuria, Shantung, and Shansi. The U.S. government was certainly capable of delivering aid to China quickly if it so chose. After the British debacle at Dunkirk in 1940, U.S. military supplies were en route to England eight days after the decision to send them had been made. China, however, was not high on Truman's or Marshall's list of priorities. Three full months were squandered in filling out the paperwork for the shipments, and the first ship loaded with munitions did not sail for China until November 9, 1948. At about the same time, two smaller shipments were made directly from Japan. U.S. military aid did not reach China until the decisive battles of the year had been fought and lost.

Marshall could not have been too disturbed by this outcome. Following the failure of his mission in January, 1947, he seems to have written China off, preferring to concentrate American aid on Europe. When Congress balked at this strategy, he agreed to grant China limited economic assistance. When he was again overridden by Congress on the

---

[46] For the details of the China Aid Act of 1948, see U.S. Department of State, *U.S. Relations with China, 1944-1949*, pp. 387-409.

question of military aid, he did not, for whatever reason, ensure that it was delivered in timely fashion. Perhaps he believed that it would only prolong a war the outcome of which was already inevitable. In any event, the result of his policies was a disaster for the Chinese people and for U.S. interests in the Far East.[47]

One contemporary evaluation of the Truman administration's failure in China was made by then-Congressman John F. Kennedy, in a speech delivered on January 30, 1949:

> Our relationship with China since the end of the Second World War has been a tragic one, and it is of the utmost importance that we search out and spotlight those who must bear the responsibility for our present predicament. . . . During the postwar period the great split began in the minds of our diplomats over whether to support the Government of Chiang Kai-shek or force Chiang Kai-shek, as the price of our assistance, to bring Chinese Communists into his government to form a coalition. Our policy in China has reaped the whirlwind. The continued insistence that aid would not be forthcoming unless a coalition government was formed was a crippling blow to the National Government. So concerned were diplomats and their advisors . . . with the imperfection of the democratic system in China after twenty years of war, and the tales of corruption in higher places, that they lost sight of our tremendous stake in a non-Communist China. This is the tragic story of China whose freedom we once fought to preserve. What our young men had saved our diplomats and our President have frittered away.[48]

The China White Paper, August 1949

Marshall left the task of responding to the critics of the Truman administration's China policy to his successor, Dean G. Acheson, who issued a 1,054-page report which placed the entire blame for the loss of China on the Nationalist government and the Kuomintang, and portrayed

---

[47] For a detailed discussion of Marshall's China policy, see T. Tsou, *America's Failure in China, 1941-1950.* (Chicago: University of Chicago Press, 1963), pp. 349-493; and H. Feis, *The China Tangle* (Princeton: Princeton University Press, 1953), pp. 413-430.

[48] Cited in D. MacArthur, *op. cit.,* pp. 320-321.

Chiang and his government as corrupt and incompetent. The official title of the report, which was released on August 6, 1949, was "United States Relations with China, with Special Reference to the period 1944-1949," but it quickly became known as the "China White Paper."[49]

Acheson's letter of transmittal summarizes his view that "The reasons for the failure of the Chinese National Government . . . do not stem from any inadequacy of American aid. Our military observers on the spot have reported that the Nationalist armies did not lose a single battle during the crucial year of 1948 through lack of arms or ammunition. The fact was that the decay which our observers had detected in Chungking early in the war had fatally sapped the powers and resistance of the Kuomintang. . . . The Nationalist armies did not have to be defeated; they disintegrated. . . . Nationalist China [received] in the form of grants and credits approximately 2 billion dollars[50] . . . [and] large quantities of military and civilian war surplus property with a total procurement cost of over 1 billion dollars, for which the agreed realization to the United States was 232 million dollars.

Acheson concluded that "the ominous result of the civil war in China was beyond the control of the government of the United States. Nothing that this country did or could have done within the reasonable limits of its capabilities could have changed that result; nothing that was left undone by this country has contributed to it. It was the product of internal Chinese forces, forces which this country tried to influence but could not."

Acheson's letter of transmittal, like the China White Paper it summarized, was a transparent and self-serving attempt to distance the Truman administration from any responsibility for the tragedy then unfolding in China. Hu Shih, the former Chinese Ambassador to the United States, jotted in the margin of his copy of Acheson's text the note "Matthew 27:24," which reads "So when Pilate saw that he was gaining nothing, but rather that a riot was beginning, he took water and washed

---

[49] U.S. Department of State, *U.S. Relations with China, 1944-1949.* Acheson's letter of transmittal is found on pp. III-XVIII.

[50] In the postwar period, the European Recovery Plan disbursed aid to Great Britain in the amount of U.S. $1,001,041,791. ECA economic aid to China was $275 million. Cited in G. Fitch, *Formosa Beachhead* (Chicago: Henry Regnery Co., 1953), p. 141.

his hands before the crowd, saying 'I am innocent of this man's blood; see to it yourselves.'"[51]   The Nationalists could expect no further help from the United States.[52]

The China White Paper was also, in critical respects, duplicitous. To give but one example, the military war surplus that Acheson makes so much of was all "demilitarized for combat use" by the U.S. government before the Chinese army received it.   The principal consignments of subsequent military supplies were not shipped until late 1948, arrived in China too late to be put to effective use on the mainland, and were detoured to Taiwan.

Opponents of Truman's "hands-off" China policy wasted no time in sharply attacking the China White Paper.   Senators Styles Bridge, William Knowland, Patrick McCarran, and Kenneth Wherry called it "a 1054-page whitewash of a wishful, do-nothing policy which has succeeded only in placing Asia in danger of Soviet conquest."[53]   Others in Congress spoke of a conspiracy in the State Department to aid the Chinese Communists.   The country was bitterly divided between those who held the Truman administration responsible for losing China, and those who believed that, whatever the U.S. did or had not done in China, a Communist victory was inevitable.

A State Department committee appointed by Acheson to review U.S. Asia policy predictably took the administration line, recommending on November 11, 1949, that China be crossed off as hopeless.   The U.S. should make no commitments to aid Taiwan in its continuing anti-Communist resistance, the committee recommended further, but rather seek to have the island placed under a U.N. trusteeship.[54]   In January 1950 the U.S. government declared that no assistance would be given to the Nationalist government, which by then had moved to Taiwan, but fortunately made no attempt to have the island placed under a trusteeship.

---

[51] Cited in Jonathan D. Spence, The Search for Modern China (New York: W. W. Norton & Co., 1990), p. 527.

[52] J. L. Stuart, *Fifty Years in China* (New York: Random House, 1954), pp. 267, 270.

[53] U.S. Congressional Record, XCV, 81st Session (1949), pp. A 5451-54. Cited in T. Tsou, *op. cit.*, p. 509.

[54] Philip C. Jessup headed the committee. Raymond E. Fosdick and Everest Case, both American educators, served as members. Cf., H. K. Tong *op. cit.*, pp. 456-457.

Chiang refused to consider publishing a reply to the China White Paper, telling Acting Foreign Minister George K. C. Yeh that such a step would cause irreparable damage to the traditional amity between the Chinese and American people, besides providing the Communists with an opportunity to sow more discord between China and America. Later, in his book *Soviet Russia in China*, he did try to set the record straight, but it was "with larger aims in view."[55]

---

[55] Chiang Kai-shek, *op. cit.*, p. 210.

10

REDEFINITION OF AMERICAN POLICY 1950–1954

I. STRAINED PARTNERSHIP

The Republic of China's Search For East Asian Alliance

After the ROC government moved to Taiwan, President Chiang thoroughly reorganized the government and took steps to build up Taiwan as a base for national recovery and reconstruction. This move gave hope to his countrymen, who were disheartened by Acheson's announcement that the U.S. would wait until "the dust settled" in Asia before making another move.

In the hope that the U.S. would change its position, Chiang determined to try a new approach. His idea was to enlist Korea, Indochina, Burma, Malaya, the Philippines, and the Republic of China—all the East and Southeast Asian countries threatened by Communism—into a kind of Asian NATO. This anti-Communist alliance could then collectively approach the U.S. for aid in containing communism within its present boundaries. Chiang flew to the Philippines at the invitation of President Elpidio Quirino, finding him warmly receptive to the proposal. The two leaders issued a joint statement on July 11, 1949, urging all independent, non-Communist Asian nations to combat "the menace of international communism" and "fight collectively as well as

individually.[1] A second trip abroad, this time at the invitation of South
Korean President Syngman Rhee, resulted in the issuance of a similar
statement on August 4, 1949. This called upon Quirino to convene "a
preliminary conference" to "bring about the birth of the proposed
union."[2]

The plan was well-conceived, but its execution hinged upon the
support of the U.S. This was not forthcoming. After Quirino visited
Washington in August 1949, both he and Rhee subsequently lost interest
in the proposed alliance, and the proposed conference was never called.
On May 18, 1950, Acheson came out in public opposition of an East
Asian anti-Communist alliance, citing the antagonism of Prime Minister
Nehru of India to such an undertaking.[3] There the matter rested.

America's Withdrawal and Hands-off Policy

By the fall of 1949, rumors abounded in Washington that the
Truman administration would soon extend diplomatic recognition to the
Chinese Communist government. These suspicions intensified after the
PRC was formally established on October 1, 1949. Acheson seemed to
rule out recognition on October 12, declaring that the U.S. only
recognizes governments which fulfill their international obligations and
rule by the consent of the governed. The Chinese Communist regime
further disqualified itself on October 24 when it placed Angus Ward, the
American Consul General in Mukden, under house arrest and jailed his
staff for a month.[4]

Britain urged the U.S. to recognize the PRC and did so herself on
January 6, 1950. Whatever the Truman administration would have
wished to do in the matter, this was now politically impossible because of

---

1   C. Y. Chang, *The Kuomintang on the March* (Taipei: China Cultural Service,
    1954), pp. 26-27.
2   *Ibid.*, p. 27.
3   Cited in H. K. Tong, *Chiang Kai-shek* (Taipei: China Publishing Co., 1953), p.
    456.
4   H. B. Westerfield, *Foreign Policy and Party Politics: Pearl Harbor to Korea*
    (New Haven: Yale University Press, 1955), cited in W. A. Williams, *The Shaping
    of American Diplomacy--Readings and Documents in America Foreign Relations,
    1950-1955* (Chicago: Rand McNally, 1956), p. 1058.

the Ward incident. Then came a further provocation: On January 13, 1950, the Communists seized the U.S. Embassy in Peking. The State Department retaliated by ordering the recall of 135 U.S. diplomats stationed in China and the closure of the remaining U.S. consulates in Tientsin, Shanghai, Nanking, and Tsingtao.

Despite Taiwan's strategic importance, the State Department's position was that U.S. forces should not be committed to its defense, and that without such assistance the island could not withstand a determined attack from the mainland. Acheson expected Taiwan to fall in 1950.[5] This hands-off policy provoked heated debate in Congress, but Truman would not be budged. The U.S. has no "intention of utilizing its Armed Forces to interfere in the present situation," he said on January 1, 1950. "Similarly, the United States Government will not provide military aid or advice to Chinese forces on Formosa. . . . The United States Government proposes to continue under existing legislative authority the present ECA program of economic assistance.[6] Acheson further delineated the administration's position on January 13, 1950, when he declared that the U.S. would take military action only to defend the perimeter running from the Aleutians to Japan, the Ryukyu Islands and the Philippines.[7] Both Taiwan and Korea were conspicuously absent from this formulation.

II. THE KOREAN WAR AND THE DEFENSE OF TAIWAN

The Neutralization of Taiwan

On June 25, 1950, the North Korean army crossed the 38th parallel.[8] The North Koreans, trained and equipped by the Soviet Union,

---

5   *The Military Situation in the Far East*, Hearings before the Senate Committee on Armed Services and the Committee on Foreign Relations, 82 Congress, 1st Session (1959), p. 1682. Concerning the State Department's "Policy Information Paper— Formosa," which was pessimistic about the future of the Nationalist government on Taiwan, see J. W. Ballantine, *Formosa, A Problem for the United States Foreign Policy* (Washington D.C. Brookings Institution, 1952), pp. 119-120.

6   Cited in *Ibid.*, pp. 120-121.

7   The text of Acheson's address, entitled "Crisis in Asia," was published in U.S. Department of State, *Bulletin*, January 23, 1950, pp. 111-118.

8   The initial division of Korea at the 38th Parallel was only intended to facilitate the Japanese surrender, not to divide the country into zones of occupation.

encountered little resistance, and advanced rapidly to Seoul. Truman's days of vacillating on Asia policy came to an abrupt end. He appointed General Douglas MacArthur Supreme Allied Commander in Korea on June 28, and ordered U.S. land, air, and naval forces to come to the aid of the beleaguered South Koreans. Taking advantage of the absence of the Soviet delegate, the U.S. even secured the sanction of the Security Council for the "Police Action" in Korea.[9]

On June 27, 1950, Truman extended U.S. protection to Taiwan, stating that "The attack upon Korea makes it plain beyond all doubt that Communism has passed beyond the use of subversion to conquer independent nations and will now use armed forces and war. . . In these circumstances, the occupation of Formosa by Communist Forces would be a direct threat to the security of the Pacific Area and to the United States forces performing their lawful and necessary functions in that area. Accordingly, I have ordered the seventh fleet to prevent any attack on Formosa. As a corollary of this action I am calling upon the Chinese Government on Formosa to cease all air and sea operations against the mainland. The determination of the future status of Formosa must await the restoration of security in the Pacific . . ."[10]

Truman had decided that Taiwan was of strategic value to the U.S. and must be defended. Overnight the attitude of the administration changed. On July 28, 1950, the State Department announced the appointment of Chargé d'affaires to the Nationalist government in Taipei.[11] MacArthur came to Taipei to meet with Chiang on July 31, and the following day announced that plans had been made for a joint U.S.-Chinese defense of Taiwan in the event of an attack by a hostile force. Such an attack, he stated with assurance, would have little chance of success.[12] MacArthur's deputy Chief of Staff, Major General A. P.

---

9   This was only possible because of the absence of the Russian delegate who had been boycotting Security Council meetings since January to protest the continuing exclusion of the PRC to the U.N.
10 U.S. Department of State, *Bulletin*, July 3, 1950, Vol. 23, p. 5.
11 After the recall of Ambassador John Leighton Stuart from Nanking to Washington in August, 1949, the American diplomatic mission was headed by a Chargé d'affaires, Lewis Clark. The mission had not, however, followed the Nationalist government to Taipei, but had remained in Hong Kong.
12 *New York Times*, August 1 & 2, 1950. Cited in J. W. Ballantine, *op. cit.*, p. 129.

Fox, arrived in Taiwan on August 4, assigned to act as liaison with the Nationalist government. In Washington, Congress allocated $71,000,000 for military aid to Taiwan. A military assistance advisory group was established in May 1951 to train and equip the Nationalist Army. New economic aid was also forthcoming.

The Nationalist government accepted the "corollary" that it would not be allowed to make attacks on the mainland, but rejected the implication of Truman's announcement that the status of Taiwan somehow awaited resolution. ROC Minister of Foreign Affairs George Kung-chao Yeh insisted upon this point on June 28, 1950. "That Taiwan is a part of the territory of China is generally acknowledged by all concerned powers," Yeh stated. "The proposal of the United States Government as contained in the above-mentioned aide memoir should in no way alter the status of Formosa as envisaged in the Cairo Declaration, nor should it in any way affect China's authority over Formosa."[13]

The Korean War probably saved Taiwan from invasion. The Communists had planned to assault the island in the summer of 1950. A large concentration of motor-driven junks had been noted in take-off ports in Fukian province, and a select force of 150,000 assault troops was standing by. The presence of the U.S. seventh fleet in the Taiwan Straits forced Peking to delay its plans.

The war went badly at first, but in September 1950, MacArthur carried out an amphibious landing at Inchon which caught the North Korean forces totally unprepared. Seoul was recaptured, and what was left of the North Korean armies retreated pellmell for the Chinese border. The Chinese Communists then intervened in force in November, sending some 200,000 "volunteers" into the fray. The vastly outnumbered American forces were driven back below the 38th parallel and Seoul was lost for a second time. The U.N. General Assembly adopted a resolution condemning Communist China's aggression in Korea on February 1, 1951.[14] The U.S. forces, reinforced from America, counterattacked in

---

[13] Cited in H. K. Tong, *op. cit.*, pp. 505-506.

[14] The General Assembly adopted Resolution 498 (V) which "finds that the Central People's Government of the Republic of China, by giving direct aid and assistance to those who were already committing aggression in Korea and by engaging in hostilities against the U.S. forces there, has itself engaged in aggression in Korea."

force in March, inflicting tremendous losses on the People's Liberation Army. Seoul was recaptured and the Communists driven north of the 38th parallel.

MacArthur wanted to bomb communist supply depots and troop concentration areas north of the Yalu—what he called the "privileged sanctuary" of the enemy—but Truman rejected these measures for fear of full-scale war with the PRC.[15]   When MacArthur spoke out publicly against the prohibition, saying that "there is no substitute for victory", Truman on April 11, 1951, relieved him of his command. His recall set off a violent debate in the U.S. over the issue of whether to limit the war to Korea or go all out against Communist China at the risk of intervention by the Soviet Union. Truman continued to give priority to the defense of Europe, and a long investigation by two Senate committees of the affair ended inconclusively. Although the administration continued to adhere to its painful policy of limited war in Korea, the war itself, combined with Communist China's intervention and public opinion, led the administration to abandon the anti-ROC attitude of the China White Paper.[16]

The new policy was first publicly enunciated by Dean Rusk, then Assistant Secretary of State for Far Eastern Affairs, in a May 18, 1951, address to the China Institute in New York.

> We recognize the National Government of the Republic of China," Rusk stated, "even though the territory under its control is severely restricted. We believe it more authentically represents the views of the great body of the people of China, particularly, their historic demand for independence from foreign control. That government will continue to receive important aid and assistance from the United States. Under the circumstances, however, such aid in itself cannot be decisive to the future of China. The decision is up to the Chinese people wherever they are, acting on behalf of China to pool together their efforts.[17]

---

[15] F. Freidel: *America in the 20th Century* (New York: Alfred A. Knopf, 1970), pp. 508-510.

[16] J. W. Pratt: *A History of United States Foreign Policy* (Englewood, N. J.: Prentice Hall, Englewood, 1965.), pp. 489-490.

[17] Cited in J. W. Ballantine, *op. cit.*, p. 131.

The Nationalist government hosted a number of U.S. Senators and Congressmen who undertook fact-finding tours to Taiwan.[18]   All were favorably impressed with the strategic importance of the island, as well as with the reforms undertaken by Chiang.   Taiwan was not only included in the huge U.S. Mutual Security appropriation of October 1951, but received the lion's share of the $535,250,000 in military funds and $237,500,000 in economic aid allotted to the Asiatic and Pacific Area not including Korea.

The Embargo on Shipments for Communist China

During the summer of 1949 the ROC had announced the closure of mainland ports to shipments of military value.   The U.S. had acquiesced in this embargo, although stipulating that it was up to the Nationalist government to make it effective.   After the onset of the Korean War, the U.S. joined in this embargo, prohibiting shipments of petroleum and other strategic materials to East Asia, including Hongkong and Macao, from June 26, 1950. [19]   On December 16, after the effective entry of the PRC into the war, Washington went further, prohibiting all trade with Communist China and North Korea and ordering the confiscation of all their U.S. assets.

The embargo was further tightened when the U.N. General Assembly on May 18, 1951, by a vote of 47 to 0, banned all shipments of strategic materials to the Chinese Communist regime.   On the very same day, U.S. Senator Kem introduced an amendment to the Supplemental Appropriation Act of 1951, prohibiting U.S. economic aid to countries which failed to carry out this U.N. resolution.[20]   The Kem Amendment

---

[18]   The important visitors to Taiwan during 1951-1952, included Thomas E. Dewey, Dan Kimball, Francis Cardinal Spellman, John Sparkman, Joseph W. Martin, William C. Bullitt, Admirals William Fechteler, Arthur Radford and General Lawton Collins.

[19]   For details see The China Handbook Editorial Board: *China Handbook 1952-1953* (Taipei: China Publishing Co., 1952), pp. 143-145.

[20]   This Act was cited as "H. R. 3587, the Third Supplemental Appropriation Act for the Fiscal Year 1951," with Section 1302 thereof commonly referred to as the Kem Amendment.

required all countries receiving U.S. aid to certify each month to the State Department that no war materials had been sold to the U.S.S.R. or its satellites.

Truman was dissatisfied with this amendment, since it interfered with his constitutional prerogative to conduct U.S. foreign policy, and a new bill was introduced by Congressman Battle to take its place. The Battle Act, as it was known, was signed into law by Truman on October 26, 1951, and prohibited shipments of strategic materials and implements of war to any country threatening the security of the U.S., including the U.S.S.R. and all countries under its domination. It further provided that no military, economic, or financial assistance would be supplied to any third country unless it applied a similar embargo to the countries of the Soviet Bloc. The decision to withhold assistance was left to presidential discretion.

On December 18, 1951, the State Department delivered an aide memoir to the ROC Embassy in Washington requesting the Nationalist government to furnish information on the embargo measures it had so far adopted, and to express its agreement with the U.S. embargo. This the ROC was happy to do, transmitting through Ambassador V. K. Wellington Koo its agreement with the general principle that the free world should refrain from supplying to regimes engaged in aggression goods and materials which might augment the strength of such regimes.[21]

In the end the U.S. government placed an embargo on some four hundred and fifty categories of exports to Communist China, or more than twice as many as were denied the U.S.S.R.

The Peace Treaty with Japan

In late 1950 the U.S. government sent memoranda to the 53 governments which had been at war with Japan, soliciting their suggestions for a proposed peace treaty. Taipei's suggestions arrived in Washington before January 6, 1951. A first draft was completed by John Foster Dulles by March, and copies were sent to the governments concerned. The ROC received its copy on April 1, and the full text was published in the Taiwan press on April 7, 1951. The British, unhappy

---

[21] Cited in *China Handbook 1952-53*, p. 145.

with the American proposal, circulated a draft of their own which sharply differed on two points: Britain's draft called for the PRC government to represent China at the forthcoming Peace Conference, and for the return of Taiwan to the PRC. The government and people of the ROC were deeply stung by this insult, which seemed to reflect a frightening attitude of abandonment on the part of the Western world.

U.S. State Department, which turned down a Soviet proposal for PRC participation in the treaty process, sought to reach a compromise with Great Britain, whose position was shared by a number of other British Commonwealth and European countries. Dulles and Kenneth Younger, the British Foreign Minister, eventually agreed that Japan should choose for herself which government of China to recognize after becoming independent. In the meantime, neither Nationalist nor Communist Chinese delegates would be seated at the peace conference.

On July 13 the text of the revised draft treaty was made public, with the ROC conspicuous by its absence from the list of participating countries. Foreign Minister Yeh immediately issued a protest, declaring that "The Chinese Government has taken strong exception with the United States Government to the version of Article 23 of the draft treaty as it now stands. The Republic of the China maintains that Article 23 of the draft treaty in its present form shall in no way affect its right and position with regard to the conclusion of peace with Japan and that it cannot reconcile itself to any agreement incompatible with recognized principles of international justice."[22]

Protests from official and civic bodies in Taiwan and from overseas Chinese poured in. A number of American senators and congressmen as well as newspapers, and some Latin American countries such as El Salvador and Cuba openly expressed their sympathy with the ROC. But the decision to exclude the ROC stood, however, and Nationalist China was not one of the 52 nations which took part in the Japan peace conference in San Francisco on September 4, 1951.

On September 11 Yeh declared for the first time that the Nationalist government was willing to enter into a bilateral treaty with Japan. On December 1, 1951, the Japanese Government sent Shiroshichi Kimura, a career diplomat, to Taipei to establish an interim office preparatory to

---

[22] H. K. Tong, *op. cit.*, pp. 528-529.

resumption of formal diplomatic relations between the two countries. On December 24, 1951, Japanese Premier Shigeru Yoshida wrote to Dulles pledging Japan to sign a bilateral peace treaty with the ROC. On January 16, 1952, when this letter was made public, Yeh promptly replied that the ROC was ready to negotiate. On January 30 Isao Kawada, a former Minister of Finance, was appointed to negotiate peace with the ROC. Yeh himself was the chief Chinese representative to the peace negotiations, with Hu Ching-yu, Vice-Minister of Foreign Affairs, his alternate.

The peace talks began on February 17 and lasted more than two months. Carl L. Rankin, the U.S. Chargé d'affaires in Taipei, quietly worked to narrow the differences between the two sides. Kawada returned to Tokyo on May 2 with a treaty more lenient in its terms than that which Japan had earlier signed with the allies. Following the lead of Chiang, who had urged generosity in dealing with Japan at the end of the war, the ROC made no demand for reparations, even those taking the form of services. The Japanese Diet approved the Sino-Japanese Peace Treaty by an overwhelming majority on July 5. The Legislative Yuan, after several weeks of heated debate, finally ratified the treaty on July 31. The instruments of ratification were signed by Chiang on August 2, 1952, and exchanged with the Japanese three days later.[23] Ambassadors were then exchanged. Japan sent Kankichi Yoshizawa, a former Minister of Foreign Affairs, as the first Japanese Ambassador to the ROC in Taipei, while the ROC sent Hollington K. Tong, a well-known newspaperman and former Information Minister, to Japan as its Ambassador.

III. THE EISENHOWER ADMINISTRATION

Dulles and the New Policy Toward East Asia

The Eisenhower administration came to office having promised, in the Republican Party's platform, to end the "neglect of the Far East", to

---

[23] The Sino-Japanese Peace Treaty of 1952 was unilaterally abrogated by Japanese Foreign Minister Masayoshi Ohira on September 29, 1972, the date of Japan's "normalization of relations" with the PRC.

repudiate all "secret understandings," and to replace "the negative, futile and immoral" policy of containment. The new Secretary of State, John Foster Dulles, was deeply convinced of the evils of Communism and clear on ways to combat it. He believed that, since most wars are the result of miscalculation, it is important for a nation to make clear in advance, even at considerable risk, exactly how it will respond to a specific provocation.[24]

Dulles came to office in 1953 convinced that the diplomatic blunders of the Roosevelt-Truman administration had lost the peace in Asia. He first purged the State Department of foreign service officers who had played a role in the loss of China, then assigned Far Eastern affairs to a Virginia gentleman named Walter Robertson. Robertson, like Dulles himself, believed that anti-Communism was the only possible moral response to the evils of totalitarianism, and that neutrality in the cold war was tantamount to immorality. The U.S. should forge alliances with other nations dedicated to freedom, especially with weaker nations on the perimeter of the Eurasian land mass which were directly exposed to the Communist threat.

Dulles shared the belief of the conservative wing of the Republican Party that Communist aggression in Asia must be met with military force and that, until this was done, further economic aid was a waste of money. The U.S. would no longer seek a modus vivendi with Communist China, but rather to isolate it. America would no longer keep its distance from Taiwan, but would work with the Nationalist government to forge a strong alliance. To check Communism's new moves, the U.S. would go to the brink of war. This renewed hostility towards the PRC was not unrequited. Within the Communist Bloc, Peking had already become America's most uncompromising enemy.

The Deneutralization of Taiwan

Eisenhower's first move in East Asia was to "deneutralize" the Taiwan Straits. In his first State of the Union Message on February 2, 1953, arguing that the free world could not indefinitely remain in a

---

[24] R. W. Leopold, *The Growth of American Foreign Policy* (New York: Alfred A. Knopf, 1962), pp. 711-713.

posture of paralyzed tension, the new president said that he was rescinding Truman's order to the U.S. Seventh Fleet to shield Communist China from attacks from Taiwan. "[T]here is no longer any logic or sense in a condition that required the United States Navy to assume defensive responsibilities on behalf the Chinese Communists, thus permitting those communists, with greater impunity, to kill our soldiers and those of our United Nations allies in Korea," Eisenhower said. "[W]e certainly have no obligation to protect a nation fighting us in Korea."[25] That same day, the U.S. Joint Chiefs of Staff dispatched an order to the commanders of the Pacific fleet and the Far East Forces rescinding "that portion of your current directive which requires you to ensure that Formosa and the Pescadores will not be used as bases of operations against China Mainland by the Chinese Nationalists."[26]

The political significance of Eisenhower's decision far outweighed its military significance. During the presidential campaign, Eisenhower had announced a "policy of liberation" to help the people behind the Iron Curtain regain their freedom. Now people in the ROC on Taiwan felt that America had recognized that their cause to recover the Mainland was morally just, whether or not the U.S. would actually assist in the counterattack.

Eisenhower's message released the ROC from the obligation, which it had voluntarily undertaken, to desist from military operations against the PRC. Chiang welcomed this move, saying on February 3 that,

> Since the participation in aggression in Korea of the Peiping Regime in November 1950, I have repeatedly maintained in public statements that the limitations placed by the United States Government on the operations of our armed forces should be withdrawn. . . . President Eisenhower's decision to lift the limitation on the operations of our armed forces is not only judicious but also militarily sound. . . . While our own plan for fighting the mainland will necessarily form, in my opinion, an important link in the general plan of the free world to combat worldwide communist aggression, I would like to assure our

---

[25] The State of the Union Message to Congress, February 2, 1953, U.S. Department of State, *Bulletin*, February 9, 1952, pp. 207-211.

[26] Cited in R. J. Donovan, *Eisenhower, The Inside Story* (New York: Harper Brother, 1956), p. 28.

friends abroad that the Republic of China will not ask aid in ground forces from any nation to achieve our own goal. . . . It is only when the Communist aggressors are made to realize that aggression does not pay that we may hope to restore peace and security in the world.[27]

Britain, India, and some Southeast Asian governments were critical, fearing a wider conflict. American military chiefs declared the decision sound, however, and one which would not contribute to the Korean War's spread. MacArthur called the Eisenhower decision a correction of "one of the greatest anomalies known to military history." There was certainly strategic benefit to the move, for no enemy can ignore a threat on his flank. The uncertainty it created in Peking—uncertainty as to the size and nature of the threat, uncertainty about American intentions in backing it up--forced the PLA to expend some of its strength to cope with the perceived danger. It remained a point of pressure against Communist China throughout the Korean War, and contributed to the Chinese Communist decision to call for a ceasefire.

The Appointment of Ambassador Rankin, and Nixon's Visit to Taiwan

Another sign of improving relations between the U.S. and the ROC was the resumption of ambassadorial-level relations. In February, 1953 Eisenhower appointed Carl Lott Rankin, who had been in Taipei for two and a half years as American Chargé d'affaires, as U.S. Ambassador to China. Rankin presented his credentials to Chiang on April 2, 1953.[28] "The significant progress which your Government has made since the removal of its seat to Taiwan in the face of tremendous difficulties is indeed heartening," he remarked on the occasion.

The situation now prevailing in free China stands in bold contrast to the suffering, privation and condition of servitude to which the

---

[27] Cited in The China Handbook Editorial Board, *China Handbook 1953-1954* (Taipei: China Publishing Co., 1953), pp. 152-153.

[28] Robert C. Strong was in charge of the U.S. Consulate in Taipei until August 8, 1950, when Rankin became head of mission.

Chinese people on the mainland are subjected by a ruthless communist oligarchy. I am confident that this contrast will become increasingly apparent to all, as the benefits accruing to free people through representative government continue to be demonstrated here. The plight of the mainland Chinese people, so long as it exists, will cause my government and the American people deep concern.[29]

Although the Eisenhower administration desired to enlist the ROC into its worldwide alignment of anti-Communist alliances, it had no intention of attempting to overthrow the Peking regime by force. Rather, its efforts were directed toward isolating and encircling the PRC, in which effort the ROC was seen as a key ally. Instead of equipping the ROC military to invade the mainland, the U.S. limited itself to strengthening Taiwan's defense capabilities and military preparedness. Its chief hope was that the application of international pressure would so deepen the Peking regime's internal crisis that the Chinese people would rise up in revolt. This was the meaning of Dulles' "policy of peaceful liberation."[30] As applied to the ROC, it meant working to enhance the international image and political influence of the Nationalist government. Dulles believed, correctly, that the ROC's continued existence on Taiwan was a source of inspiration to the people on the Chinese mainland that Communism would not last forever and that one day they, too, would be free.[31]

A visit by Vice President Richard M. Nixon to Taiwan in November 1953 was another sign of the close relations which had developed between Washington and Taipei. The manifest sympathy of this powerful anti-Communist politician for the ROC cause further bolstered the Nationalist government's confidence. Nixon's five-day sojourn was part of a 72-day goodwill mission covering 18 countries.[32] While Nixon

---

[29] Cited in *China Handbook, 1953-1954*, p. 153.

[30] The most well-known expression of this policy is a speech given by Dulles in San Francisco on June 28, 1957, entitled "Our Policies toward Communism in China," U.S. Department of State, *Bulletin*, July 15, 1957.

[31] C. Kuan, *A Review of the U.S. China Policy, 1949-1971* (Taipei: World Anti-Communist League, China Chapter, 1971), pp. 9-10.

[32] Nixon visited Taiwan from November 8 to 12, 1953. For details see E. H. C. Wang, *Nixon's State Visit to China* (Taipei: China Culture Publishing Foundation, 1953).

was in Taipei, the U.S. press misconstrued a remark by Dulles's, on the admission of Communist China to the U.N., to signal a new and softer line toward Peking. To reassure his obviously concerned hosts, Nixon responded on November 12 by asserting that

> Secretary Dulles's remarks as reported in the press state nothing new as far as the United States policy is concerned. . . . In effect, what he said was that the United States would not consider the question of recognition unless Red China quit following communist policy, and quit taking orders from Moscow. He did not announce any change in the United States position with regard to the question of admitting Communist China to U.N. membership. The position was that the United States would continue to oppose vigorously admission to the United Nations of a Government which had waged war against the United Nations, which had on its hands the blood of over 150,000 men from members of the United Nations who were fighting to carry out a United Nations policy, and which defied and obstructed the United Nations in its efforts to bring peace in Korea.[33]

The Korean Armistice

On July 27, 1953 an armistice agreement was signed ending the Korean War.[34] A short time before, Eisenhower had notified Peking that unless truce talks showed satisfactory progress, the U.S. intended to "move decisively without inhibition in its use of weapons, and would no longer be responsible for confining hostilities to the Korean Peninsula." The U.S. threat to use nuclear weapons on the Chinese mainland, even at the risk of bringing Russia into the struggle, caused a war-weary Peking to yield.

---

[33] K. L. Rankin, *China Assignment* (Seattle: University of Washington Press, 1964), pp. 187-188.
[34] General Mark W. Clark, Commanding General of the U.S. Armed Forces of the Far East, on July 27, 1953, signed a military armistice agreement between the U.N. Command and the military commanders of the North Korean and the Chinese "People's Volunteers" at Panmunjon.

In agreeing to the armistice, Peking had dropped its demand that all prisoners of war held by the U.N. be forcibly repatriated.[35]   Of the 20,000 Chinese "volunteers" captured by U.N. forces, fully 70 per cent chose to come to Taiwan rather than return to the Chinese mainland. This high percentage of defections occurred despite the efforts of the U.N. repatriation commission to adopt a stance of strict neutrality; if anything, the POWs were encouraged to return to their homeland. Moreover, most of the soldiers were peasants from Szechuan, who knew little of politics and even less about Taiwan. They knew what life was like under Communist rule, however, and refused to go back.   On January 23, 1953, 14,009 Chinese Communist POWs left Korea, arriving in Taiwan four days later as free men.   The ROC government designated January 23 World Freedom Day.

The Transfer of the Ryukyu Islands

On August 8, 1953, Dulles surprised the world by announcing in Tokyo that the Amami Oshima group of the Ryukyu Islands would be returned to Japan "as soon as necessary arrangements can be concluded with the Government of Japan."[36]   This news elicited a sharp reaction from the Chinese public. Newspapers in Taiwan editorialized against the transfer.   The Legislative Yuan passed a resolution asking the U.S. government to reconsider.

From Taipei's perspective, the American plan could not be justified on either cultural, geographic, historical or legal grounds.[37]   The inhabitants of the islands were culturally distinct from the Japanese people. The southernmost island of the Ryukyu archipelago was only 73 miles from Taiwan. The chain had been under Chinese suzerainty from 1372 to 1879, a period of 507 years. Most importantly, the projected transfer was inconsistent with the terms of the Potsdam Declaration, which provided that "Japanese sovereignty shall be limited to the islands

---

[35]   A. Nevins & H. S. Commager, *A Short History of the United States* (New York: Random House, 1969), p. 598.

[36]   The China Handbook Editorial Board, *China Handbook, 1954-55* (Taipei: China Publishing Co., 1955), p. 230.

[37]   *Ibid.*, pp. 230-231.

of Honshu, Shikoku, Hokkaido, Kyushu, and such minor islands as we determine." (emphasis added)   The ROC, as a cosignatory of the declaration, should have been consulted about the disposition of the Ryukyus.   Since this had not occurred, the Nationalist government considered the U.S. action arbitrary if not illegal.

The return of the Ryukyus to Japan also seemed inconsistent with the Japanese Peace Treaty. The treaty authorized the U.S. to administer the islands, either directly or under a U.N. trusteeship, but made no provision for the U.S. to transfer them to Japan or any other power.

The ROC view of the matter was expressed in two memoranda to the U.S. Embassy, dated November 24, and December 23, 1953.   In its response, the U.S. government denied that it was violating the terms of the Japan Peace Treaty, pointing out that this treaty did not require Japan to renounce its claim to the Ryukyu islands, over which the Japanese government is therefore considered to have "residual sovereignty."   The U.S. further stated that this question of Japan's "residual sovereignty" over the Ryukyus had been brought up by the U.S. delegate in the Second Plenary Session of the Peace Conference on September 5, 1951, and that neither the other signatories of the treaty, nor the ROC, had taken issue with it at the time.

The bulk of the Ryukyus were transferred to Japanese control on December 25, 1953.   In anticipation of the transfer, the Nationalist government issued a statement on December 24 regretting that the U.S. had not respected "the wishes of the inhabitants of the islands for self-government. . . the United States Government has failed to see its way to give the matter its reconsideration."

Dulles responded with a lengthy defense of the U.S. position, to which ROC Foreign Minister Yeh responded on February 1, 1954, by reaffirming the position of the Nationalist government with regard to the transfer of the Amami Oshima group, and expressing the hope that the ROC "will be consulted by the Government of the United States prior to any decision to be taken in the future with regard to [the remaining Ryukyu islands]."[38]

---

[38] *Ibid.*, p. 232.

IV. THE COLLECTIVE SECURITY AND MUTUAL DEFENSE TREATY

The Vietnam War and the Geneva Conference

The end of the Korean War brought neither peace nor stability to Asia, merely a shift in the focus of the confrontation between Communist China and the U.S. to Southeast Asia. In this sense, the Vietnam War was a continuation of the Korean War.

Since World War II, France had been struggling with national independence movements in each of the three Indochinese states of Vietnam, Laos, and Cambodia. Chief among these were the Communist Vietminh, heavily armed by the PRC and adept at using guerrilla tactics against the fixed encampments of the French. Despite massive American aid and the commitment of France's best troops, the conflict in Vietnam had dragged on into the fifties. Eisenhower likened the nations in Southeast Asia to a row of dominoes, leaving the press to draw the obvious implication: the first domino must not be allowed to fall.

By the time of the Korean armistice, it was apparent that France could not win without direct American participation in Vietnam. Still, when the administration proposed an air strike to aid the defenders of Dienbienphu, who were besieged by the Vietminh, there was little enthusiasm either in Congress or abroad.[39] Dienbienphu fell on May 7, 1954, and at the Geneva Conference then in progress the French agreed to complete independence for all the Indochinese states and to the partition of Vietnam. Under the terms of the Geneva Declaration which followed on July 21, 1954, these states were forbidden to join regional alliances or to allow foreign bases on their soil. The free world had compromised with Communist aggression, rather than roll it back by concerted action.[40] The U.S. did not sign this agreement, but separately

---

[39] A. S. Link, et. al., *American Epoch, A History of the United States* (New York: Alfred A. Knopf, 1967), pp. 830-831.

[40] The South Vietnamese delegation refused to sign the armistice agreement in protest against the abandonment to the Vietminh of territories still in the possession of Vietnamese troops.

declared that it would view a renewal of aggression as a serious threat to peace.[41]

SEATO and other Defense Pacts

Even before North Vietnam came under the control of the Vietminh, the U.S. had been increasing its military presence in Asia, augmenting the Seventh Fleet, strengthening existing base facilities, and building new installations. A number of mutual defense treaties had been signed with Pacific rim countries, including the Philippines (August 30, 1951), Japan (September 8, 1951)[42], and the Republic of Korea (October 1, 1953). The U.S. had also joined with Australia and New Zealand on September 1, 1951, in the United Defense Pact known as ANZUS.

After the Geneva Conference in 1954 the U.S. government adopted a policy of "strengthening China's periphery and containing communist power within the border of mainland China." Dulles declared that America would not allow Southeast Asia to be overrun, and strove energetically to build a collective security organization for the region along the lines of NATO. The British, more inclined toward a loose organization emphasizing economic ties, balked at the idea of a military arm. A compromise was reached between these two positions, and at an eight-nation conference held in Manila in September, 1954, the South-East Asia Treaty Organization (SEATO) was created.

The member nations--the U.S., the Philippines, Thailand, Pakistan, Australia, New Zealand, the United Kingdom, and France--agreed that "aggression by means of armed attack in the treaty area against any of the parties or against any state or territory which the parties by unanimous agreement may hereafter designate, would endanger its own peace and safety."[43] At British insistence, the treaty specified a northern limit of latitude 21° 30"N, thus excluding both Taiwan and Hong Kong

---

[41] F. H. Michael & G. E. Taylor, *The Far East in the Modern World* (New York: Henry Holt, 1956), pp. 682-683.
[42] On January 19, 1960, the United States and Japan signed a new Treaty of Mutual Cooperation and Security in Washington superseding the 1951 treaty.
[43] Article 4 of the SEATO Treaty.

from its jurisdiction.[44] The U.S. appended an understanding which restricted the treaty obligation to aggression of Communist origin. A separate protocol certified that Cambodia, Laos, and the Republic of Vietnam, although not signatories to the treaty, would be treated as member nations and their security guaranteed. This was designed by Dulles to throw "some mantle of protection" over the three non-Communist Indochinese states.[45]

A SEATO Council, with headquarters in Bangkok, was soon established, charged with promoting social and economic welfare and preventing invasion and subversion within the treaty area. Dulles had succeeded in building an Asian security organization, albeit one with no armed force of its own, and in a whirlwind tour of Southeast Asia in the spring of 1955 assured Thais, Laotians, Cambodians, Vietnamese, and Filipinos that SEATO would protect them against further Communist encroachments.

The Sino-American Mutual Defense Treaty of 1954

In the "mosaic"—Dulles's word—of defense pacts that America had woven in Asia, Taiwan was conspicuous by its omission. In December 1953 the ROC government proposed the conclusion of a mutual security treaty between the two countries, and submitted a draft for U.S. consideration. Preliminary talks yielded little progress. In May 1954, when Secretary of Defense Charles E. Wilson visited Taipei, President Chiang again raised the question, observing that the absence of such a pact was being interpreted, particularly in Japan, to mean that the U.S. was keeping the door open for diplomatic recognition of Communist China in the future.

The primary issue of contention was the territorial scope of the treaty, now and in the future. The U.S. was willing to assist in the defense of Taiwan and Penghu (the Pescadores), but not of the 30 other

---

[44] The ROC was no longer recognized by the U.K. and could not join for that reason. India, Burma, Ceylon and Indonesia declined to join because they were committed to neutralism.

[45] Though all three states at first welcomed SEATO protection, Prince Norodom Sihanouk of Cambodia soon rejected it for a course of neutralism. Laos followed in 1962, leaving only South Vietnam under Dulles' "mantle of protection."

Nationalist-held islands along the coast of mainland China, chief among them Quemoy and Matsu. And what of the former territory of the ROC that might be recovered in the future. Foreign Minister Yeh proposed to cover these two points by a clause applying the treaty "to all the territories which are now, or which may hereafter be, under the control of the ROC." Washington rejected this provision as too broad, although they acknowledged that limiting the pact to the territory of Taiwan and Penghu might suggest a lack of support for the ROC's aim of liberating the Chinese mainland from Communism. The Eisenhower administration shared that aim, but was concerned that the U.S. might be drawn into hostilities with the PRC by offensive operations initiated by the ROC. In June 1954 Yeh informed Washington through Rankin that, following the conclusion of a mutual defense treaty, the ROC would seek prior U.S. agreement before undertaking any important military action.[46]

Dulles stopped in Taipei on his way home from the Manila Conference, and the ongoing discussions took an important step forward. A final round of negotiations between Yeh and Dulles in the U.S. capital brought the two sides into agreement, and a joint statement was issued simultaneously in Washington and Taipei on December 1, 1954, which read in part:

"The Republic of China and the United States of America have concluded negotiations for a mutual security pact. . . . The treaty will recognize the common interest of the parties in the security of Taiwan and Penghu (the Pescadores) and of the Western Pacific Islands under the jurisdiction of the United States. It will provide for inclusion by agreement of other territories under the jurisdiction of the parties. . . . This treaty will forge another link in the system of collective security established by the various collective defense treaties already concluded between the United States and other countries in the Pacific area. Together, these arrangements provide the essential framework for the defense of the Western Pacific by the free peoples against Communist Aggression. Like the other treaties, this treaty between the Republic of China and the United States will be defensive in character."[47]

---

46 K. L. Rankin, *op. cit.*, pp. 194-197.
47 The China Handbook Editorial Board, *China Handbook 1955-56* (Taipei: China Publishing Co., 1956), p. 250.

The Mutual Defense Treaty between the Republic of China and the United States of America was signed by Yeh and Dulles on behalf of their respective governments in Washington on December 2, 1954. The instruments of ratification were exchanged by Yeh and Dulles in Taipei on March 3, 1955, after which the treaty came into force.[48]

The key provisions of the agreement were that "in order to achieve more effectively the objective of this treaty, the parties separately and jointly by self-help and mutual aid will maintain and develop their individual and collective capacity to resist armed attack and communist subversive activities directed from without against their territorial integrity and political stability" (Article II); that "each party recognizes that an armed attack in the West Pacific Area directed against the territories of the parties would be dangerous to its own peace and safety, and declares that it would act to meet the common danger in accordance with its constitutional processes" (Article V); and that, for the foregoing provisions, "the terms 'territorial' and 'territories' shall mean in respect of the Republic of China, Taiwan, and the Pescadores; and in respect of the United States of America, the island territories in the West Pacific under its jurisdiction," although said provisions may be applied to other territories "by mutual agreement" (Article VI).

Critics of the treaty, and there were some, pointed out that it was solely defensive in character. It placed the U.S. under no obligation to support an attack against the Chinese Mainland by the ROC, nor to offer assistance in case an initial attack by the ROC against the Chinese Communists led to a counterattack by the latter. They further charged that the treaty could actually be used by the U.S. to halt an attack, or even a counterattack, by the ROC against the Chinese mainland.

The source of their concern was twofold. First there was Article V of the treaty itself, which stated that all measures taken to deal with an armed attack "shall be immediately reported to the Security Council of the United Nations, and such measures shall be terminated when the Security Council has taken the necessary measures to restore and

---

[48] For the full text of the Sino-American Mutual Defense Treaty, see the Ministry of Foreign Affairs, *Treaties Between the Republic of China and Foreign States* (Taipei: Commercial Press, 1963), pp. 824-827.

maintain international peace and security. By this stipulation, all measures involving military action taken by the Republic of China including a counterattack against mainland China shall be subject to interference by the United Nations, otherwise there is the possibility of its being declared an aggressor." Skeptics argued that this tied the hands of the ROC militarily.

Then there was the exchange of notes on December 10, eight days after the treaty was signed, between Yeh and Dulles. In these notes, both parties agreed that "the use of military force is a matter of mutual agreement; therefore, all military units created through the joint efforts and contributions of the two contracting nations, unless by mutual agreement, may not leave the territories mentioned in Article VI if such departure will reduce the defensive capabilities of the said territories." The U.S. viewed this restriction as a "written guarantee" to check attack against the Chinese mainland.[49]

The position of the Nationalist government, however, was that the treaty in no way prohibited an attack, defensive or otherwise, against the mainland by the ROC. On the day the treaty was signed, Yeh made it clear that "the Sino-American Mutual Defense Treaty did not signify in any way that the Republic of China did not have the right to recover the Mainland."[50] In Taipei's view, the December 10 exchange of notes was merely an extension of Article IV, which stipulated that both nations should consult with each other from time to time concerning implementation of the treaty. Neither a secret agreement outside of the treaty, nor an appendix to the treaty, it was, properly speaking, an understanding between the two governments.[51]

The U.S. government entered into the treaty to warn Peking that it took its obligations to Taiwan seriously. It would not permit an attack on the island. Nor would it sell out Taiwan to appease the PRC. Washington nevertheless insisted upon inserting three understandings, or reservations, into the treaty. The American side maintained that the

---

[49] C. Kuan, *op. cit.*, pp. 11-13.
[50] Statement by Yeh on December 2, 1954, to Chen Yu-ching, New York-based correspondent of the *Central Daily News* of Taipei
[51] The text read: ". . . it is agreed that such use of force will be a matter of joint agreement, subject to action of an emergency character which is clearly an exercise of the inherent right of self-defense."

treaty 1) did not affect the legal status of Taiwan, which still awaited clarification; 2) did not obligate the U.S. to garrison troops in Taiwan; and 3) did not obligate the U.S. to defend Quemoy or any other offshore island.[52]

From the standpoint of the ROC, this treaty not only bolstered the security of Taiwan and Penghu, but also enhanced the international status of the Nationalist government. For the U.S., the treaty forged the final link in the chain of alliances that encircled Communist China in Asia. It further strengthened the already close relationship between the two countries, especially in the area of military cooperation. The ROC military, reequipped with American arms, soon came to occupy a prominent place in the front-line defense works of the free world. Taiwan, indeed, became a bastion of strength, and an important deterrent to Communist aggression in East Asia.

The Mutual Defense Treaty, along with continued diplomatic ties, laid the groundwork for close and positive U.S.-ROC relations throughout the 1950s. The two countries had come a long way since the turbulent year of 1950.

---

[52] See U.S. Ambassador to China Walter P. McConaughy's testimony contained in Hearings before the Subcommittee on the United States Security Agreements and Commitments Abroad of the Committee on Foreign Affairs, U.S. Senate, 91st Congress, Second Session, Part 4, November 24, 25, and 26, 1969; and May 8, 1970 (Washington, D.C.: Government Printing Office, 1970), p. 929. See also F. Greene, *U.S. Policy and the Security of Asia* (New York: McGraw Hill, 1968), pp. 80-81.

11

THE PERIOD OF CLOSE COOPERATION
1955–1960

I. THE TAIWAN STRAITS' FIRST CRISIS

The Issue of the Offshore Islands

On August 14, 1954, shortly after the conclusion of the Geneva Conference, the Chinese Communists issued a fierce denunciation of the "American imperialists" for their continued "occupation of Taiwan." This "occupation," according to Peking, had begun when the U.S. Seventh Fleet had been dispatched to defend the island, but it must now end. Taiwan would be "liberated," by force if necessary.[1] Battle-hardened Communist divisions were moved to staging areas along the Fukien Coast and MIG's appeared over the South China Sea. Tension mounted.

President Eisenhower did not back down. When the question of Communist China's war preparations came up at a press conference on August 17, he replied that he had recently reaffirmed standing orders to the U.S. Seventh Fleet to defend Formosa against any attack. "Any

---

[1] Cited in H. C. Hinton: *China's Turbulent Quest* (New York: MacMillan, 1970), p. 67.

invasion of Formosa," Eisenhower concluded, "would have to run over the Seventh Fleet."[2]

Deterred from launching a full-scale attack on Taiwan, the Communists shifted their attention to the offshore island groups controlled by the Nationalists. Chief among these were the Tachens, located midway between Shanghai and Keelung; the Matsus, ten miles off the port of Foochow and opposite the northern end of Taiwan; and the Kinmens, two miles off the port of Hsiamen (Amoy). These islands had helped maintain a fairly effective blockade of the South China coast, and had also served as intelligence gathering posts and commando bases.[3] To the Nationalist government, the offshore island were stepping stones for the recovery of the mainland. The Communists were as eager to capture the offshore islands as the Nationalists were to hold them.

On September 3 the Chinese Communists began an intense artillery bombardment of Kinmen (Quemoy) and Little Kinmen, located two miles off the port of Hsiamen (Amoy). The ROC Air Force responded by bombing mainland artillery positions. The bombardment of Kinmen alerted the world to the aggressive intentions of the Chinese Communists more effectively than anything they had done since invading Korea.

Eisenhower's advisers were divided in their response to the Kinmen crisis. Some felt that the U.S. should pledge itself to defend the offshore islands. All the service chiefs, with the exception of General Matthew B. Ridgway, the Army Chief of Staff, advocated American air strikes on Communist bases. Others called for a more flexible policy, arguing that any direct U.S. involvement could lead to a full-scale war. Eisenhower chose the latter approach, preferring to wait until an actual assault materialized and it could be seen whether the landing was limited in

---

[2] D. D. Eisenhower, *Mandate for Change, 1953-56* (New York: Doubleday, 1963), pp. 462-463.

[3] The Kinmen complex comprises Kinmen (Quemoy), Little Kinmen (Liehyu) and twelve islets. The total area of the Kinmen complex is 176.37sq. km. As of 1971, Kinmen had a population of 61,008, not including military personnel. Many natives of Kinmen have migrated to Southeast Asia over the years. The known number was 106,250 in 1971, of whom 70,000 went to Singapore and Malaysia, 23,000 went to Indonesia, and 12,000 went to the Philippines. The Matsu Island comprise Nankan and other 18 islets. The islands have an area of 27.1 sq. km. As of 1971, the civilian population was 17,057.

scope or preliminary to one on Taiwan.[4] His position—defend Taiwan but not the offshore islands—was shortly to be written into the Mutual Defense Treaty of December 2, 1954.

Now convinced that the Americans would not intervene, the Chinese Communists assaulted the northernmost island in the Tachen chain, a place called Yi Kiang Shan, on January 20, 1955. The garrison force of 720 soldiers died to the last man defending the tiny island. Eisenhower, convinced that the two remaining Tachen islands were indefensible, advised the ROC to abandon the chain, offering the U.S. Seventh Fleet to cover the evacuation of the 20,000 civilians and 11,000 Nationalist soldiers stationed there. The ROC reluctantly gave way, and relinquished control of the Tachen islands on February 6, 1955. At the same time, Eisenhower warned the Chinese Communists that the U.S. would resist an attack on the remaining offshore islands.

The U.S. Congress Joint Resolution on the Defense of Taiwan

To further clarify the American position, Eisenhower asked Congress on January 25 to pass a resolution authorizing him "to assure the security of Formosa and the Pescadores" and, if need be, other "closely related localities" which he did not identify. As the Commander-in-Chief of the U.S. Armed Forces, he went on, he had the authority to act alone, but was convinced that if the Congress stood with him in unity and firmness of purpose, the Chinese Communists would be less disposed to "precipitate a major crisis which even they neither anticipate nor desire." Learning from Truman's mistake in Korea, Eisenhower wanted to make U.S. intentions perfectly transparent.

---

4   In September, 1954, the Communists began a heavy bombardment of Kinmen. Fearing an invasion attempt, Admiral Arthur W. Radford, Chairman of U.S. Joint Chiefs of Staff; Admiral Robert B. Carney, Chief of Naval Operations; and General Nathan F. Twinning, the Air Force Chief of Staff urged that American and Nationalist Chinese's planes be used to bomb Communist bases, but General Matthew B. Ridgway, the Army Chief of Staff, opposed saying any such action was likely to involve the United States in full-scale war. President Eisenhower sided with Ridgway. See N. M. Blake and O. T. Barck; *The United States in Its World Relations* (New York: McGraw Hill, 1960), p. 751.

The Joint Resolution on the Defense of Formosa was passed by the House on a vote of 409 to 3 on February 26, and by the Senate two days later on a vote of 85 to 3. The resolution gave Eisenhower precisely what he wanted, authorization to "employ the Armed Forces of the United States for protecting the security of Formosa, the Pescadores, and related positions and territories of that area." Both the threat faced by Taiwan and the vital American interest at stake were specified with admirable clarity: "[C]ertain territories in the West Pacific under the jurisdiction of the Republic of China are now under armed attack, and threats and declarations have been and are being made by the Chinese Communists that such armed attack is in aid of and in preparation for armed attack on Formosa and the Pescadores. . . . the secure possession by friendly governments of the Western Pacific Island chain, of which Formosa is a part, is essential to the vital interests of the United States and all friendly nations in or bordering upon the Pacific Ocean."[5]

This resolution accomplished several ends. First, it cleared up the ambiguity of the Sino-American Mutual Defense Treaty, which was ratified by the Senate on February 9, 1955, specifically its area of applicability. Second, it signaled to Peking that both the U.S. Congress and the Eisenhower administration were united in their determination to resist any further aggression on its part. The Taiwan Straits crisis was left entirely in the hands of a U.S. President with extensive military experience, who promptly announced (to allay fears that local military commanders might by their actions trigger a war) that he alone would decide on when and how to use the authority Congress had bestowed on him. Third, it stated unequivocally that Taiwan was an indispensable link in the chain of U.S. mutual security agreements ringing Communist China.

---

[5] Joint Resolution on Formosa, January 29, 1955, 84th Congress, 1st Session; *United States Statutes at Large, Vol. 69* (Washington, D.C.: Government Printing Office, 1955), p. 7.

The U.N. Cease-Fire Proposal

Dulles also sought to resolve the Taiwan Straits crisis through the U.N., as he made clear when he visited Taipei on September 9, 1954.[6] His plan was to have New Zealand introduce a resolution in the Security Council, with American and British support, calling for a cessation of hostilities. The ROC readily consented to Dulles's request that it, as a member of the Security Council, support this course of action. If, as expected, the Soviet Union vetoed the resolution, then the Communists would have declared themselves before the court of international opinion to be warmongers. The free world would have gained a public relations victory.

Leslie K. Munro, New Zealand's representative to the United Nations, on January 28, 1955, proposed to the Security Council a resolution calling for a cease-fire in the Taiwan Straits. The U.S. and U.K. concurred, and Communist China was invited to join in the discussion. The PRC had in 1950 accepted a similar invitation from the Security Council to discuss the Korean hostilities. This time, however, the U.N. invitation was rejected by Communist China on the grounds that the U.N. had refused either to seat it or to take any action on its repeated complaints of American "aggression."[7] In his reply of February 3 PRC Premier Chou En-lai went so far as to declare the offer an unwelcome intervention in China's internal affairs, and to demand, in language that was as insolent as it was arrogant, that the U.S. get out of Taiwan. The Soviet reaction was also uncompromisingly negative. Dulles had scored procedural points against the Communists, but U.N. would not be of any further help in restoring the peace in East Asia.

The use of force had given the Communists nothing except an insignificant chain of islands and a virtual promise of heavy U.S. retaliation in the event of any further attacks. The shelling of Kinmen and Matsu came to an abrupt end, as did the feverish preparations for an

---

6   J. R. Beal, *John Foster Dulles, A Biography* (New York: Harper Brothers, 1957), p. 225.
7   On October 10, 1954, the Chinese Communists, alleging American "aggression" against Taiwan, had asked to the General Assembly to call for a complete American withdrawal from the area.

assault on the islands. At the Bandung Conference, held in Indonesia from April 17 to 24, 1955, Chou En-lai suddenly proposed direct negotiations with the U.S. for a relaxation of tensions across the Straits.[8] A number of factors were at work, including troubles in the PRC, pressure from the new Bulganin-Khrushchev regime in the U.S.S.R., and the hope of enlisting the support of neutral nations. But Dulles was undoubtedly correct in maintaining that his willingness to go to the brink of war was primarily responsible for Peking's change of attitude.

Dulles responded on April 26 by indicating his willingness to talk with the Chinese Communists about a cease-fire in the Taiwan Straits. He stressed that these talks would not imply official diplomatic recognition of the Chinese Communist regime, nor would the U.S. discuss the interests of the ROC "behind its back." By the end of May, an informal cease-fire existed on the Taiwan Straits.[9] Talks between the U.S. and the PRC began in Geneva and continued for months, but no settlement was ever reached.

The Chinese Communists continued to build up their military establishment opposite Taiwan, and a number of new airfields were constructed. For its part, the ROC fortified the offshore islands, and reinforced the garrisons stationed there. Nevertheless, three years were to pass before the PRC tried again to wrest the offshore islands away from the ROC.

---

[8] In April 1955, the Prime Ministers of Burma, Ceylon, India, Indonesia, and Pakistan, the Colombo Powers, invited a total of twenty-nine countries to an Asian-African Conference at Bandung in Indonesia. In addition to the sponsoring countries, there were Afghanistan, Cambodia, Communist China, Egypt, Ethiopia, the Gold Coast, Iran, Iraq, Japan, Jordan, Laos, Lebanon, Liberia, Libya, Nepal, the Philippines, Saudi Arabia, Sudan, Syria, Thailand, Turkey, North Vietnam, South Vietnam, and Yemen. The list included countries allied with the Western Powers, Communist countries, and neutral countries. The list did not include the Republic of China, North and South Korea, and Israel, which were regarded as being too controversial, and South Africa, which was barred on the grounds of its racial policies. The conference provided a platform for the expression of the anti-colonial meeting of Asian powers, however, strong public statements were made by several Asian leaders against Communist imperialism.

[9] D. D. Eisenhower, *op. cit.*, p. 482.

II. THE CONTAINMENT POLICY ON MAINLAND CHINA

The Geneva Talks, 1955

On July 25, 1955, the U.S. and the PRC announced that discussions between the two countries, which had been carried on sporadically in Geneva since 1954, would be elevated from a consular to an ambassadorial level. This change in status did "not involve diplomatic recognition," the State Department stressed, but was undertaken "in the hope that this would bring about agreement on the return of American civilians detained in China and facilitate further discussions and settlement of other practical matters."   U.S. Ambassador to Czechoslovakia, U. Alexis Johnson, was thereafter to hold regular meetings in Geneva with PRC Ambassador to Poland Wang Ping-nan.

The "number of American civilians in China is small and their question can be easily settled," Chou En-lai responded on July 30. He went on to complain about "the extremely unjust policy of blockade and embargo," saying it should be possible "to remove such barriers so that peaceful trade between all countries will not be hindered." Two days later the PRC announced the release of 11 American fliers who had been imprisoned as spies.

Dulles observed on August 2 that Chou En-lai had gone further than ever before in renouncing the use of force. "What we hope to arrive at by progressive steps," he went on to say, "is a situation where the Chinese Communists will have renounced the use of force to achieve their ambitions. If they want to use force . . . that will almost surely start up a war, the limits of which could not be defined in advance." Two weeks later, however, Dulles was expressing disappointment that the Geneva talks had still not resulted in the release of the 41 American citizens held in China. In the light of Chou's speech, he said, he had hoped that matter would be "promptly settled."[10]   On September 6 came word through Geneva that Peking would release 12 of the 41 Americans. The State Department called this news "encouraging," but reaffirmed the U.S. demand that the remaining 29 be released as well. On September 10

---

[10] Cited in T. N. Schroth et., al., *China and U.S. Far East Policy, 1946-1967* (Washington, DC: Congressional Quarterly Series, 1967), pp. 74-75.

Wang Ping-nan told Ambassador Johnson that all Americans would be released, if the U.S. agreed to higher-level discussions. Johnson replied that the U.S. would consider the matter only after the Americans had actually been released.

On January 21, 1956, the State Department released a report on the Geneva talks, detailing U.S. efforts to gain the PRC's acquiescence to a mutual renunciation of the use of force. Peking had refused to agree to a joint declaration unless the "internal affair" of Taiwan was excluded, to which Washington responded that Peking was trying to exclude those areas which it planned to seize by force. Unless and until there was agreement on a declaration renouncing the use of force "generally, and particularly in the Taiwan area," the State Department concluded, little progress toward an overall settlement could be expected.

The State Department report also complained that, four months after the PRC had promised their release, "13 Americans are still held in Communist prisons." These prisoners should be immediately released "not only for humanitarian reasons but because respect for international undertaking lies at the foundation of a stable international order." Peking called the charges concerning the detention of Americans in mainland China "groundless," and further alleged that "the great majority" of "tens of thousands of Chinese in the United States," because of "obstruction and threats," had "not been able or had not dared to apply to return to China." At the time, Dulles remarked dryly that "Negotiations with the Chinese Communists are usually slow and prolonged," but "we are planning to go ahead."[11] The talks went laboriously on.

The ROC government, while sympathetic to the efforts of the U.S. to secure the release of the American citizens that the PRC was holding hostage, believed that this objective could better be achieved through the pressure of world opinion. Time was to bear this out, since a number of American citizens still languished in Communist prison cells after more than a year of marathon talks. Direct, high-level negotiations were also a propaganda windfall for the Chinese Communists. The Geneva talks enhanced the prestige of the PRC and created the impression, especially in Asia, that the U.S. was moving toward at least de facto recognition. Moreover, the U.S. found itself obliged to discuss "other practical

---

[11] *Ibid.*, pp. 76-77.

matters" which had nothing to do with its chief concern, the repatriation of American nationals.

The ROC was adamantly opposed to the inclusion in the Geneva talks of any political subject that would unfavorably affect its interests or weaken the solidarity of the free world in its struggle against Communism. Both in its public utterances and private assurances, the Eisenhower administration tried to reassure the ROC that the talks did not imply "any degree of diplomatic recognition of the Chinese Communists," nor would they, in their subject matter, "involve the claims, rights or essential interests of the government of the Republic of China."[12] As the Geneva talks continued interminably, however, Taipei began to have serious misgivings about their scope and direction. At the very least, they served to confuse the issues and divide the free nations.

The Chinese Communists succeeded in bringing to the conference table their request for direct negotiations between foreign ministers, and in raising the question of a relaxation of the U.N. embargo, although the U.S. did not accede to either. For its part, Washington continuously pressed for a joint renunciation of the use of force in the Taiwan area. Peking balked at making such a specific promise, favoring a vague pronouncement on behalf of world peace, and this only in exchange for ministerial-level talks. Seventy-three sessions were held in all, but this impasse was not resolved.

The Policy of Non-Recognition vs. The "Two-Chinas" Concept

The PRC was recognized immediately by eight Communist countries upon its founding, and by thirteen additional states, including India and the United Kingdom, in 1950. The outbreak of the Korean War put an end to Peking's diplomatic inroads, as nearly all non-Communist states adhered to the U.N. boycott of the Chinese mainland. The notorious "five-anti" campaign against capitalists and foreigners also generated much international rancor, as many expatriots were arrested and forced to confess to espionage. Chinese employees of Western-owned businesses filed exorbitant wage and pension claims against their employers, which were then upheld by the courts. Until every such claim

---

[12] Cited in *China Handbook, 1955-56*, pp. 269-270.

against them had been settled, foreigners could not shut down their businesses, however serious their losses, or obtain exit visas. By the end of the war, over two billion dollars worth of American and European investments had been confiscated. More millions had to be paid by the parent firms to ransom their representatives in China.

The PRC's policy toward the U.S. was driven by its obsessive anti-Americanism. Chou En-lai once remarked that all nations fell into one of four categories. Communist allies constituted the highest category, while the second was comprised of potentially friendly Afro-Asian states. European "imperialists" fell into a third category. The lowest category was occupied by a single country, the United States of America, which was the arch-enemy of Communism and the leader of the "imperialist" camp. Not surprisingly, there had been a series of incidents involving American and Communist Chinese forces. American patrol planes had been shot down, and their pilots given lengthy prison sentences.

This deep antagonism was in part ideological, in part strategic, and in part domestic politics. Marxist-Leninist theory demands the defeat of reactionaries, which internationally were identified with the "imperialist" forces led by the United States. Peking's efforts to spread Communism abroad were frustrated by repeated U.S. intervention, which even helped keep alive a rival regime on Taiwan. In the midst of almost continuous domestic turmoil and purges, the Chinese Communists tried to focus the attention and wrath of the people outward and, here again, the most conveniently available target was the U.S. Finally, this anti-American policy was a convenient excuse to isolate Chinese intellectuals from politically subversive foreign contacts. It was Peking which thwarted U.S. plans to establish diplomatic relations in 1949 by mistreating American diplomatic personnel. Later, it was Peking's intervention in Korea which set the seal on their mutual hostility. The antagonism which came to characterize U.S.-PRC relations in the fifties resulted less from American anti-Communism than from the extreme anti-Americanism of the Chinese Communists.[13]

The U.S at first hesitated to extend diplomatic recognition to the PRC because of its brutal mistreatment of American nationals, which

---

[13] H. C. Hinton, *Communist China in World Affairs* (Boston: Houghton Mifflin, 1966), pp. 491–492.

continued during and after the Korean War. A second reason for withholding recognition, cited by Dean Rusk in 1951, was the conviction that the Nationalist government more authentically represented the views of the people of China. Another reason, which became prominent in U.S. policy as the fifties continued, was Dulles' belief that Chinese Communism, and indeed Communism in general, was "a passing and not a perpetual phase," and that non-recognition would contribute to its demise. Diplomatic recognition, on the other hand, and the U.N. seat that would certainly follow, would so increase PRC's prestige and influence in Asia, and "so dishearten our allies there, that the Communist subversive efforts would almost surely succeed."[14]

The U.S. policy of non-recognition of the PRC received strong support from the American people, who had willingly assumed heavy burdens in order to check further Communist aggression in East Asia. This support was reflected in the Congress, where in 1956, for example, a joint resolution opposing a U.N. seat for Communist China passed without a single dissenting vote.

So popular was this non-recognition policy that even its critics did not attack it directly. They merely suggested that over time it would serve U.S interests less and less well. As an alternative, they usually offered some variant of the "two-Chinas" concept. Under this scheme, the PRC regime would obtain universal diplomatic recognition and a U.N. seat as the representative of the Chinese people on the mainland, while the ROC government would retain recognition and a U.N. seat but only as the representative of the people on Taiwan. It would either be considered a new independent state or be placed under some form of U.N. trusteeship.[15]

The principal flaw of the "two-Chinas" proposal was that it was repeatedly and vehemently denounced by both Taipei and Peking. Certainly the vast majority of the Chinese people were opposed to the idea of splitting their homeland into two separate parts. Taiwan was

---

[14] J. W. Pratt, *A History of United States Foreign Policy* (New York: Prentice Hall, 1961), p. 508.

[15] For details see R. N. Clough, "United States China Policy," *The Annals of the American Academy of Political and Social Science, Vol. 321* (January 1959), pp. 24-25.

viewed as an integral part of China, not a separate territory which could be internationalized or made into an independent state at will. As the leader of the free world and the dominant power in the Pacific, the U.S. faced a fundamentally different set of problems in the Far East than did, say, Great Britain or France. Indeed, Great Britain's hasty recognition of the PRC did not prevent the later expulsion of its nationals and expropriation of its investments. United States recognition of the PRC would create a raft of problems. The morale of the ROC would be destroyed, along with America's reputation as a dependable ally. The policy of containment would have to be abandoned, in practice if not in theory, and not just Taiwan but other Asian nations would be exposed to Communist aggression. Neither would it facilitate negotiations between Washington and Peking, for the Geneva talks demonstrated that, "where negotiation was desired on both sides, recognition was not necessary to negotiate on substantive questions."[16]

On August 8, 1958, the State Department issued a memorandum reaffirming the non-recognition policy. "One day Communist rule in China will pass," the memorandum asserted, and by "withholding diplomatic recognition from Peking, the United States seeks to hasten that passing." The "two China" theory was rejected on the ground that the ROC government "would not accept any diminution of its sovereignty over China." The U.S. would only "readjust its present policies" if the situation in the Far East were to change so fundamentally as to warrant "a radically different evaluation of the threat Chinese Communist policies pose to the United States."

Shortly before the beginning of his 1960 presidential campaign, Vice President Richard M. Nixon once responded to the question of recognition by saying that the U.S. should not "take the naive attitude that by recognizing Red China and elevating them to the status of a respected member of the community of nations, we are hereby going to get better treatment from the Red Chinese at a time when their policies are obviously aggressive—much more so, as a matter of fact, than those of the Soviet Union. . . . I can think of nothing which would be more detrimental to the cause of freedom and peace to which we are dedicated

---

16 H. C. Hinton, *op. cit.*, p. 493.

than to recognize Red China and admit it to the United Nations at this time. . . . our present policy of non-recognition must be continued."[17]

China and the United Nations

In a variety of parliamentary guises, "the question of the representation of China" was raised at every session of the U.N General Assembly after 1950. On September 27, 1949, the Nationalist government filed a complaint with the U.N. against the Soviet Union for its aid to the Chinese Communists. Because of the lukewarm attitude of the Truman administration, this complaint was initially sent to committee for review. In the meantime, hostilities had erupted on the Korean Peninsula. In January 1951 the U.S. asked the General Assembly to condemn the Chinese Communist regime as an aggressor in the Korean War. The U.S. proposal was adopted by the General Assembly on May 18, along with an embargo of strategic materials to Communist China and North Korea.[18]

The ROC complaint against the U.S.S.R. was once more brought before the General Assembly in 1951, this time with American support. On February 1, 1952, the Assembly adopted Resolution 505 (VI) which, "finding that the U.S.S.R. obstructed the efforts of the National Government of China in reestablishing Chinese national authority in the three eastern provinces (Manchuria) after the surrender of Japan and gave military and economic aid to the Chinese Communists against the National Government of China, determines that the U.S.S.R., in relations with China since the surrender of Japan, has failed to carry out the Treaty of Friendship and Alliance between China and the U.S.S.R. of August 14, 1945." In light of its findings, the General Assembly should have determined that the U.S.S.R. had committed an act of aggression against the ROC, but its failure does not alter this fact.

The Soviet Union first challenged the representation of China in the U.N. by the Nationalist government in January, 1950. When this effort

---

[17] R. M. Nixon, *The Challenge We Face*—Compiled and Edited from the Speeches and Papers of Richard M. Nixon (New York: McGraw Hill, 1960), pp. 122-127.

[18] For details, see U.N. General Assembly Resolutions 498 (V), 337 (V) Section D, and 500 (V), May 18, 1951.

failed, Soviet Ambassador Jacob Malik walked out. He returned to the Security Council on August 11, taking the chair for his scheduled one-month term as Council President. Malik immediately ruled that the Nationalist delegation could not participate in Council deliberations because it did not represent China. He was overruled by the other members of the Security Council. Having failed to obtain its objective by procedural means, the Soviet Union then tried to have the substantive question of China's representation placed on the Council agenda. This effort, too, was defeated.

Following these failures in the Security Council, the Soviet Union attempted to have the question of China's representation taken up by the General Assembly. In each session from 1950 to 1955 the Soviet representative raised a point of order, calling for the PRC delegation to be seated in preference to the ROC delegation. India took the lead beginning in 1956, but instead of raising a point of order, the Indian representative requested that the "question of the representation of China" be included in the agenda. The invasion of Tibet and border clashes along the Sino-Indian border gradually cooled India's ardor, and by 1960 it was the Soviet representative, not the Indian, who requested the inclusion of this agenda item. In 1963 the U.S.S.R. yielded this role to Albania, having fallen out with Peking over questions of Communist ideology.

The position of the U.S., both in the Security Council meeting and the 1950 session of the General Assembly, was that as long as the Chinese Communist regime was at war with the U.N., reconsideration of the question of China's representation was out of the question. The U.S. did accept a Canadian proposal, offered in the General Assembly, for the establishment of a committee to study the question.[19] That committee was unable to make any recommendations, however, having been sabotaged by Poland, one of its members. Thereafter, from 1951 to 1960, the General Assembly voted to postpone consideration of the question.

The U.S. government had powerful support at home in its efforts to bar the PRC from the U.N. "You can't shoot your way into the U.N.," Americans told one another. "The United Nations is not a reform school

---

[19] The Canadian proposal was adopted as Resolution 490 (V) on September 19, 1950.

for delinquent Governments," Dulles was fond of saying. On at least six occasions dating from January 1953 the House or the Senate formally and by overwhelming margins voiced disapproval of the PRC's efforts to join the U.N.[20] If the Chinese Communists were seated by the U.N., some elected representatives were ready to pull the U.S. out. Senator William Knowland told the Senate on July 1, 1954, that if Communist China were admitted to the U.N. he would resign as majority leader and devote all his efforts canceling American membership in, and financial support of, the United Nations.[21] Six years later, Nixon would still say, "I can think of nothing which would be more detrimental to the cause of freedom and peace than to recognize Red China and admit it to the United Nations at this time. . . will [this position] never change? The answer is: it will change, but only when the policies of the Communist Chinese government change."

International support for the U.S.-ROC position was gradually eroded away by time. The motion to postpone the question of China's representation, which carried by 81.5 per cent in 1953, passed by only a 55.3 per cent margin in 1960. Nations once opposed to the inclusion of this item in the agenda, now felt that a full debate on the question might serve to clarify the basic issues, particularly for new members. Beginning in 1961 the U.S. and the ROC were forced to adopt new tactics.

III. THE SECOND TAIWAN STRAITS CRISIS

The Battle of Kinmen, 1958

Following a meeting between Nikita Khrushchev and Mao Tse-tung in Peking, the Chinese Communists suddenly unleashed a fierce bombardment of Kinmen on August 23, 1958. Some 42,000 artillery

---

[20] For example, in 1953, Public Law 195, 83rd Congress, Department of State Appropriation Act, 1954, Section III stated: "It is the sense of Congress that the Communist Chinese Government should not be admitted to membership in the United Nations as the representative of China."

[21] Cited in R. J. Donovan, *Eisenhower, The Inside Story* (New York: Harper Brothers, 1956), p. 132.

rounds rained down on the island within the first two hours.[22] Communists jets strafed the island, while torpedo boats attacked Nationalist convoy and transport ships.

On August 29, Radio Peking announced that an amphibious landing on Kinmen was imminent. The 100,000-man Nationalist army on the island stood ready to repel the invaders, but the threatened attack did not materialize. Instead, torpedo boats swarmed about the island, and PLA gunners began concentrating their fire on Kinmen's landing beach and airstrip. The blockade was complete, and it was only a matter of time before the garrison force, deprived of reinforcement from Taiwan, would be starved out.

As later became known, the Communist plan was to isolate Kinmen and Matsu through bombardment and blockade, and then seize the islands once the U.S. was convinced not to intervene. They hoped to hoodwink the U.S. into believing that their ambitions were limited to the offshore islands by strictly avoiding any mention of Taiwan in their propaganda, thereby forestalling American military involvement.

At the outset of the crisis, the U.S. stood firmly by the ROC. Realizing that the ultimate objective of the Communist Chinese remained the capture of Taiwan itself, Eisenhower publicly warned Communist China not to attempt to invade the offshore islands. "Let us suppose that the Chinese Communists conquer Quemoy," he remarked in a radio address, "Would that be the end of the story? . . . They frankly say that their present military effort is part of a program to conquer Formosa. . . this plan would liquidate all of the free world positions in the Western Pacific."[23]

Dulles stressed that the security and defense of Kinmen and Matsu had increasingly become related to security and defense of Taiwan. In a letter to Congressman Thomas E. Morgan, acting Chairman of the House Foreign Affairs Committee, concerning the situation of Taiwan and the Offshore islands, Dulles pointed out on August 23 that the ties between

---

22 *China Yearbook 1958-59*, pp. 214-215.
23 President Eisenhower preferred that the Seventh Fleet merely patrol the Taiwan Straits rather than provide escorts for conveys. He assented to escort, with the proviso that American vessels should halt three miles off the unloading beaches, remaining in international waters.

the offshore islands and Taiwan had become closer and that their interdependence had increased. In a veiled threat to Peking, he stated that it would be highly hazardous for anyone to assume that, if the Chinese Communists were to attempt to change the situation by force and conquer these islands, this could remain a limited operation.

On August 24, 1958, Chinese Foreign Minister Huang Shao-ku commended Dulles for his "correct appraisal of the interdependence between Taiwan and the offshore islands. The importance of these islands is not merely of a military character. Psychologically and politically, they stand as the strategic outpost of freedom, not only for the Republic of China but also for the whole democratic world. Any attempt by the Chinese Communists to seize these islands will be a challenge to the determination and ability of the free nations in resisting aggression. In view of the enemy's heavy artillery shelling, air strafing, and other hostile activities against the island of Kinmen, the Chinese Communists have now definitely posed this challenge. Only by an unequivocal and concrete demonstration of firmness and preparedness on our part and on the part of our allies can the aggressor be deterred from plunging into large-scale adventure."[24]

To demonstrate its commitment to the defense of Taiwan, the U.S. immediately shipped a host of modern weapons to the island, including super-saber jets, Nike-Hercules ground-to-air missiles, and eight-inch caliber guns. To further underscore the point, Chinese and American marines staged a large-scale amphibious landing in southern Taiwan on September 8.

The blockade of Kinmen continued for two weeks. Then, on September 7, a convoy of Nationalist supply ships, escorted by warships of the U.S. Seventh Fleet and the ROC Navy, steamed directly for beleaguered Kinmen. The U.S. naval squadron escorted the supply ships to a point three nautical miles from Kinmen, then stood off while they continued on to land and unload their cargo. The commander of the U.S. squadron had permission to return fire if fired upon, but the Communist guns were silent. Eisenhower and Dulles had gone to the brink, and the Communists had blinked.

---

24 *China Yearbook, 1958-59, op. cit.*, pp. 214-215.

Frustrated in their plan to seize Kinmen by force, the Chinese Communists fell back on political maneuvers, and requested talks with the U.S. Eisenhower, anxious to avoid a repetition of the explosive confrontation of September 7, agreed. On September 15 talks between the U.S. and the PRC were resumed in Warsaw after a hiatus of nearly a year.[25] Concerned that the Communists were reverting to their old tactic of trying to gain at the conference table what they had failed to win on the battlefield, Foreign Minister Huang immediately declared that the ROC would not recognize any agreements detrimental to its sovereign rights and interests that resulted from these talks.

On September 18, 1958, Dulles told the U.N. General Assembly that debate on the Taiwan and Kinmen-Matsu dispute should be postponed while the Warsaw talks were continuing. The following day, Premier Chen Cheng told the Legislative Yuan in Taipei that the government would not accept any resolution reached in Warsaw that might prejudice the rights of the ROC. "Nobody has the right to make us demilitarize these islands," he added. "Communist occupation of Kinmen and Matsu would pose a serious threat to the security of all the East Asian region."

Once the talks began, Dulles softened his policy toward the Communist Chinese somewhat, asserting that the offshore islands were not worth risking a nuclear war, and that the problem could only be resolved through negotiation. At a press conference on September 30 he summarized his new approach in the following five points:

1. The Warsaw talks between the United States and the Chinese Communists prevented a deterioration of the situation in the Taiwan area.

2. If a cease-fire was reached, the Republic of China should reduce its forces on the offshore islands. If the cease-fire was effective, the Republic of China should abandon the offshore islands to reduce the possibility of renewed hostilities.

3. The United States did not believe that the Armed Forces of the Republic of China had sufficient strength to recover the mainland by force.

---

[25] The earlier talks in Geneva had dealt with the release of American prisoners and other matters.

4. The United States did not view the Taiwan Straits crisis as a civil war or purely as the internal affair of another nation, because both the Nationalists and the Communists had treaty obligations with the United States and the Soviet Union respectively.
5. The possibility existed for a major change in the American policy if the Chinese Communists reacted favorably.[26]

Dulles's statement, though conciliatory in tone, did not lead Peking to make any concessions in turn. U.S. proposals for a mutual renunciation of the use of force across the Taiwan Straits met with PRC demands that the U.S. in return abandon Taiwan, withdraw the Seventh Fleet, and lift the ban on trade. The Communist representatives even demanded talks at the ministerial level, an obvious step toward diplomatic recognition. Since the majority of these demands were unacceptable to the U.S., no agreement on a cease-fire was reached, and the intermittent bombardment of Kinmen continued.[27] Neither did the U.S. insist that the ROC reduce the size of its garrison on the offshore islands.

On October 5, after 45 days and 444,433 artillery rounds, Peking suddenly announced a week-long cease-fire on the Kinmen front and offered direct peace talks with Taipei. The Communist peace-offensive was ignored, for, as the ROC government pointed out, it was nothing but a camouflage for bigger military adventures. After extending the truce for another two weeks, the Communists broke their own cease-fire on October 20, the eve of Dulles' arrival in Taipei.

Dulles's Visit and the Joint Communiqué

Dulles had already visited Taiwan once during 1958, to speak at the U.S. Far East Chiefs of Mission Conference, which opened in Taipei on March 14. He had met with Chiang on that occasion, and reaffirmed that the ROC would continue to receive steadfast U.S. support. Now, for discussion on the Taiwan Straits crisis with Chiang and his new cabinet, headed by Premier Chen Cheng, he paid a second visit. Three days of talks led to a Joint Communiqué, issued on October 23, which read:

---

[26] U.S. Department of State, *Bulletin*, October 20, 1958, pp. 579-604.
[27] J. W. Pratt, *op. cit.*, p. 507.

The consultations have been arranged to be held during the two weeks when the Chinese Communists had declared a ceasefire on Quemoy. It had been hoped that under these circumstances, primary consideration could have been given to a measure which would have contributed to stabilizing an actual situation of non-militancy. However, on the eve of the consultations, the Chinese Communists, in violation of their declaration, resumed artillery fire against the Quemoys. In the light of these developments, the consultations necessarily dealt largely with the military aspects of the situation. It was recognized that the defense of Quemoy, together with the Matsus, is closely related to the defense of Taiwan and Penghu.

The two Governments reaffirmed their solidarity in the face of the new Chinese Communist aggression now manifesting itself in the bombardment of the Quemoys. This aggression and the accompanying Chinese Communist propaganda have not divided them, as the Communists have hoped. On the contrary, it has drawn them closer together. They believe that by opposing aggression, they serve not only themselves but the cause of peace. As President Eisenhower said on September 11, 1958, the position of opposing aggression by force is the only position consistent with the peace of the world. . . .

The United States recognizes that the Republic of China is the authentic spokesman for free China and of the hopes and aspirations entertained by the great mass of the Chinese people. . . . The two governments reaffirmed their dedication to the principles of the United Nations. They recalled that the treaty under which they are acting is defensive in character. The Government of the Republic of China considers that the restoration of freedom to its people on the mainland is its sacred mission. It believes that the foundation of this mission resides in the minds and hearts of the Chinese people and that the principal means of successfully achieving its mission is the implementation of Dr. Sun Yat-sen's Three People's Principles (Nationalism, Democracy, and Social Well-being) and not the use of force.

The consultations which took place permitted a thorough study and re-examination of the pressing problems of mutual concern. As such, they proved to be of great value to both governments. It is believed that such consultations should continue to be held at appropriate intervals.[28]

To correct the misimpression, widespread at the time, that Chiang had pledged to Dulles not to use force under any circumstances, George Kung-chao Yeh, the recently appointed ROC Ambassador to the United States, said on October 27 that "we will not give up military might for legitimate and self-defense purposes." While the most important achievement of his talks with Chiang, Dulles remarked the following day, was "a fresh formulation of the mission of the Government of Free China" with "the emphasis on winning through peaceful processes," he denied asking Chiang to unilaterally renounce the use of force against the Peking regime. "Certainly we do not nor have we ever asked anybody else to do that," he explained. The issue was further clarified on October 31 when State Department Spokesman Lincoln White told a news conference that the ROC's renunciation of force did not apply in cases of "self-defense or in the case of a large-scale uprising" on the Communist mainland.[29]

In the meantime, the ROC accepted the American suggestion that the offshore islands need not be so heavily garrisoned, and that having so many troops in forward positions was actually detrimental to Taiwan's security. Discussions between the military staff of the two countries, Chiang indicated, would probably result in some units being redeployed to Taiwan.

Meanwhile, Peking's bizarre behavior continued. A so-called "even-day" cease-fire was announced on October 25, but was broken when the shelling continued the next day. After several days of sporadic shelling, the "even-day" ceasefire gradually took effect, becoming a regular part of island life. On even days, convoys could arrive without being challenged. On odd-days, the attack continued, but with ever-lessening intensity. The tactic was condemned by the Taiwan press as a cruel game. Eisenhower called it a Gilbert and Sullivan war. Dulles told a press conference that

---

[28] The China Handbook Editorial Board, *China Handbook, 1959-1960* (Taipei: China Publishing Co., 1960), pp. 244-246. Also, U.S. Department of State, *American Foreign Policy: Current Documents, 1958* (Washington, D.C.: Government Printing Office, 1962), p. 1185.

[29] T. N. Schroth, et. al., *op. cit.*, p. 90.

the odd and partial truce proved that "the killing is done for political purposes and promiscuously," and that the Communists "are trying to save themselves from a loss of face and a defeat in the effort which they had initiated but had been unable to conclude successfully."

The ROC armed forces acquitted themselves well in the conflict. Thirty-one MIG-17s were shot down, 16 torpedo boats and gunboats were sunk, and a large number of PLA artillery batteries were destroyed.[30] A total of 576,636 rounds of high explosives had fallen on Kinmen by November 22, resulting in some 3,000 civilian and 1,000 military casualties. Many thousands of homes were destroyed.[31]

The Taiwan Straits crisis eventually passed. The failure of the Great Leap Forward and the ensuing famine turned the attention of the Communists to their growing domestic problems for a time.[32] The Eisenhower-Dulles policy of facing down Communist aggression wherever it might occur, along with the resolve of the Nationalist government, had carried the day. The Chinese Communists would never again challenge the Nationalist government over the offshore islands.

To the end of his term, Eisenhower stood just as firm on the defense of Kinmen and Matsu as he had consistently been on the defense of Taiwan and Penghu. On May 11, 1960, Eisenhower declared that, regardless of "the actual value of Matsu and Quemoy, of course we must remember how much [their abandonment would seem] a complete surrender, abject surrender. So, it is a factor to consider for anyone who talks about the abandonment of these sets of islands."

The defense of Kinmen and Matsu also became an issue in the presidential campaign of 1960. In his second television debate with Nixon in October 1960 Kennedy declared that U.S. strategy in the Pacific should not be tied to the offshore islands, but only to the defense of Taiwan itself. Nixon denounced this as "woolly thinking," insisting that the U.S. must not surrender one inch of territory inside the "area of

---

[30] In the aerial battles some of the Nationalists' fighter planes, equipped with new Sidewinder air-to-air missiles, took a heavy toll against the Communists' planes.

[31] *China Yearbook 1958-1959, op. cit.*, pp. 3-4.

[32] In 1958, the Chinese Communists adopted the policy of "three red banners"— general line, big leap forward and people's communes. However, the "three red banners" movement was a failure as was the ill-fated campaign of "letting one hundred flowers bloom and one hundred schools of thought contend," in 1957.

freedom." Kennedy shot back that Nixon was trigger-happy. Nevertheless, when Kennedy became president, the Eisenhower-Dulles policy toward the offshore islands remained in place. In June 1962, when Peking once again began building up its forces opposite Kinmen and Matsu, and another crisis appeared imminent, Kennedy forcefully emphasized that U.S. policy on the Taiwan Straits remained just what it had been since 1955.[33]

IV. OTHER ISSUES FROM 1955-1960

Chinese Immigration Under the Refugee Relief Act, 1953

The Communist revolution caused millions of refugees to flee the Chinese mainland and seek sanctuary abroad in Taiwan, Hong Kong, Macao, and other cities in Southeast Asia. With the exception of Taiwan, where extensive efforts were made at resettlement, they faced miserable conditions in their new homes. To alleviate the plight of at least a few of these refugees, Congress in due course passed the Refugee Relief Act of 1953, as it was commonly known, which was signed into law by Eisenhower on August 7, 1953.

This law defined a "refugee" as "any person in a country or area which is neither Communist nor Communist-dominated who, because of persecution, fear of persecution, natural calamity or military operations, is out of his usual place of abode and unable to return thereto, who has not been firmly resettled, and who is in urgent need of assistance for the essentials of life or for transportation."

There were three provisions of the Refugee Relief Act under which Chinese might apply for admission into the United States: (1) Section 4 (A), paragraph (13) of the Act provided for the issuance of "two-thousand visas to refugees of Chinese ethnic origin whose passports for travel to the United States are endorsed by the Chinese National Government or its authorized representatives." (2) Section 4 (A), paragraph (12) provided for "the issuance of three-thousand" visas to

---

[33] A. de Conde, *A History of American Foreign Policy* (New York: Charles Schribner's, 1971), p. 834.

refugees residing within the district of an American consular office in the Far East: provided that such visas shall be issued only in said consular office district and only to refugees who are indigenous to the area described in this paragraph." (3) Section 5 provided for the issuance of visas within the quota of four thousand to orphans who were under ten years of age.[34]

In response, the ROC government promulgated on April 16, 1954, "regulations governing application and screening of refugee emigrants to the United States." A screening committee composed of representatives of the Ministry of Interior, the Ministry of Foreign Affairs, the Overseas Chinese Affairs Commission, and the Taiwan Peace Preservation Headquarters was established to issue endorsed passports under the first provision mentioned above. The committee adopted a policy of facilitating family reunification, giving preferential consideration to applicants who were relatives of Chinese already residents in, or citizens of, the United States. Most such applicants were living in Hong Kong, since most of the early emigrants to the U.S. came from adjacent Kwangtung province. The number of endorsed passports issued to applicants in Taiwan was comparatively small, totaling no more than 800 by the end of 1956.[35]

The number of Chinese applicants for immigrant visas under the first and second provisions of the Refugee Relief Act quickly exceeded the quota, reaching over 20,000 in 1955 alone. Additional bills were introduced in Congress in early 1956 to expand the quota, but did little to bring down the huge number of waiting Chinese refugees.

President Eisenhower's Visit to Taiwan

Near the end of his term in office, Eisenhower undertook a tour of East Asia, including the Republic of China on his itinerary.[36] During his

---

[34] *China Handbook, 1954-1955*, pp. 232-233.
[35] According to the regulations, those eligible were the Chinese parents of naturalized U.S. citizens, the spouses or unmarried sons or daughters of Chinese admitted to permanent residence in the U.S., and the brothers, sisters, sons or daughters of U.S. citizens.
[36] Eisenhower's original itinerary had included Japan, where the Communist and Socialist parties were demonstrating against a new U.S.-Japan security treaty. As

stay in Taipei, which began on June 18, 1960, he met twice with Chiang. The conversation ranged from ongoing security cooperation under the Sino-American Mutual Defense Treaty of 1954 to the international situation following the recent collapse of the Paris summit. Chiang emphasized the high priority that Soviet planners gave to East and Southeast Asia, which they viewed as the Achilles heel of the free world. The talks were satisfying and reassuring, with Eisenhower pledging the "steadfast solidarity" of the U.S. with the ROC[37]

Then there was Eisenhower's public address to a crowd estimated at 65,000 people. The U.S. would stand fast behind free China in resisting Communist aggression, Eisenhower said amongst thunderous cheers. The U.S. did not recognize the claim of the "warlike and tyrannical Communist regime" in Peking to speak for all the Chinese people. As Eisenhower spoke, the Communist Chinese were saluting him in their own inimitable way. During the twenty-four hours Eisenhower was in Taipei, Kinmen was given its heaviest pounding ever by the PLA artillery batteries. An incredible 174,854 rounds fell upon the island.

The Joint Communiqué was issued at the conclusion of Eisenhower's visit contained few surprises. It took note of the "continuing threat of Communist aggression against the free world in general and the Far Eastern free countries in particular," and pledged that both "governments would continue to stand solidly behind the Sino-U.S. Mutual Defense Treaty in meeting the challenge posed by the Chinese Communists in this area." It "deplored the outrageous and barbaric practice of the Chinese Communists in shelling and ruthlessly killing Chinese people on alternative days and noted that this practice emphasized the necessity for continued vigilance and firmness in the face of violence." It concluded with a discussion of the importance of Taiwan's continued economic progress and a promise of additional U.S. assistance.[38] It may serve as

---

the demonstrations grew larger and more violent, the Kishi government asked him not to come. But he received an enthusiastic welcome in Taipei, Manila, and Seoul.

[37] D. D. Eisenhower, *Waging Peace, The White House Years, 1956-1961* (New York: Doubleday Co., 1963), pp. 564-565.

[38] China Yearbook Editorial Board, *China Yearbook 1960-1961* (Taipei: China Publishing Co., 1961), p. 272-273.

an apt summary of the official attitude of the U.S. government towards the ROC and the Chinese Communists in the later 1950's.

Tibet, India and Laos

In 1959 the militant Chinese Communists shifted their attention to other fronts. For several years there had been unrest in Tibet over the failure of the Peking regime to respect Tibetan autonomy as it had earlier promised. Tibetans found their distinctive culture, religion, and political organization under assault. In the late fifties, PLA troops had destroyed a large number of monasteries and killed many Lamas. Other monks and officials were forced into work gangs and employed in the construction of roads in China. Finally, the Tibetans rose up in revolt.

On March 25, 1959, after heavy fighting, Chinese Communist troops occupied Lhasa, the capital of Tibet. Peking announced that its army had "swiftly put down the rebellion in Lhasa and was mopping up the rebels in some other places in Tibet." The Tibetan government under the Dalai Lama was dissolved, and replaced by a puppet regime headed by the 21-year-old Panchen Lama. Peking had been forced to take these steps, Chou En-lai charged, because Tibetan officials had "colluded with imperialism, assembled rebellious bandits, carried out rebellion," and "put the Dalai Lama under duress."

Nobody believed him. The U.S. State Department on March 28 accused Communist China of a "barbarous intervention" and of attempting to "destroy the historical autonomy of the Tibetan people." Nehru charged on March 30 that the Chinese Communists had broken pledges to allow Tibet "full autonomy." India sympathized with the Tibetan rebels, he said, and would admit refugees from Tibet on an individual basis. On March 31, after a 300-mile journey over the southern mountains of Tibet, the Dalai Lama and his party of eighty officials reached India. He charged that Communist China was bent on the "complete absorption and extinction of the Tibetan race," and that

65,000 Tibetans had been slain since 1956.[39]   The ROC, while maintaining that Tibet was a part of China, also condemned Peking.[40]

On September 9 the Dalai Lama accused Communist China of aggression and urged immediate U.N. intervention. The State Department welcomed the "initiative of the Dalai Lama in bringing the plight of the Tibetan people directly to the attention of the United Nations." The debate on the question was lengthy and acrimonious, and it was not until December 20 of the following year that the U.N. General Assembly voted 56-11, with 29 abstentions, to demand the "cessation of practices which deprive the Tibetan people of their fundamental human rights and freedoms."

After quelling the Tibetan revolt, Chinese Communist troops continued their march southward, crossing India's northern border in early September 1959 and seizing two important mountain passes which guarded approaches to Sikkim and India. The clash of arms on the Sino-Indian border began. It made no difference that India had often sided with the PRC in international affairs. The Indian delegation at the U.N. was arguing passionately on behalf of Communist China's admission to the General Assembly, even as PLA troops were pouring across the border.

On September 4 an obviously nonplused Nehru announced that the Chinese Communists had accused India of "aggression" and demanded that India evacuate Chinese territory. At first he indicated that he would be willing to make some minor revisions to the border, calling the dispute "rather absurd." But Nehru was soon to admit that the Chinese claim was "much more serious" than he originally thought and "quite impossible for India ever to accept." He declared that India had "undertaken the defense of Sikkim and Bhutan, and anything that happens on their borders is the same as if it happened on the borders of India." Meanwhile, border skirmishes continued.

After the Tibetan revolt, Peking also began manifesting a new militancy toward countries in Southeast Asia. The "Bandung Spirit," which Peking had invoked in peacefully wooing non-aligned nations in

---

[39] T. N. Schroth, et. al., *op. cit.*, p. 92.
[40] See H. T. Tu, "The Legal Status of Tibet," *The Annals of the Chinese Society of International Law*, Taipei, No. 7 (August 1970), pp. 1-31.

the region, was a thing of the past. Instead, Communist China began to act in accordance with an ancient Chinese diplomatic principle, *yuan chiao chin kung*, meaning "to appease distant countries while attacking those nearby."[41]   Faraway Canada, Italy, Belgium, Chile, and Mexico were courted for diplomatic recognition, while neighboring countries like Burma, Indonesia, Thailand, India, and Laos were attacked in word, and sometimes, in deed.

Laos, one of the three Indo-China States covered by SEATO protection, was a particular target.   Although small in size and population, the country was important because of its strategic location between the PRC, North Vietnam, and the non-Communist states of Burma, Thailand, Cambodia, and South Vietnam.   A Communist guerrilla group, the Pathet Lao, began receiving increasing amounts of military aid in the late fifties.   The U.S. countered with an expanding program of military and economic assistance.   The conflict intensified in 1959 as North Vietnam sent military units across the border to reinforce the Pathet Lao.   On September 4 Laos appealed to the U.N. to dispatch an emergency force to counter aggression by North Vietnam.   The U.S. responded by warning both the Soviet Union and Communist China that it would help counter any new danger to peace in the region.   China responded by stepping up its aid to the Pathet Lao.

The PRC campaigns of the late fifties against its close neighbors were characterized by limited objectives, careful probing, and restricted military engagements.   By causing repeated crises over territories where Western commitment was doubtful, Peking hoped to expand its influence abroad.   Both the Indian and Kinmen campaigns met these operational criteria and netted some political gains.[42]

Traveling farther afield, Chou En-lai went to Africa to offer economic aid and preach revolution.   His fundamental goal was not merely to win friends for the PRC, nor even to create a worldwide anti-colonial and anti-imperialist movement directed at the U.S., though these

---

41   This theory of "yuan chiao chin kung" was advocated by a scholar-strategist Fan Sui of the state of Ch'in during the Period of the Warring States (481-221 B.C.) in ancient China.

42   F. Greene, *U.S. Policy and the Security of Asia* (New York: McGraw Hill, 1968), p. 210.

were important aims. Rather, it was to encourage other underdeveloped nations to carry out their own Communist revolutions, using China as a model. Communism, Chou told the leaders of Africa's emerging states, was the wave of the future. Capitalism, on the other hand, was tantamount to colonialism. Many were interested. The problems of underdevelopment and poverty that Communist China claimed to have solved were exactly what they faced in their own countries. The experience of the U.S., or even the Soviet Union, seemed far remote.

At the close of the fifties, the U.S. was faced with a paradox. America was by far the most wealthy and powerful country the world had ever seen. The growth of its industries, combined with its amazing technological achievements, had given its military the capability to obliterate any nation on the globe. At the same time, everything for which America stood—democracy, liberty, and peace—was under intense attack in many quarters by the partisans of a hostile ideology. Its arsenal of nuclear weapons had little deterrent effect on the aggressive and subversive activities of Communist China, a nation that did not as yet even possess such weapons. Against the U.S.S.R., with its rapidly expanding nuclear strength, the threat of massive nuclear retaliation was even less effective.[43] As Eisenhower had remarked, Quemoy and Matsu were not worth a nuclear war.

---

[43] R. N. Current, T. H. Williams, F. Freidel, *op. cit.*, p. 867.

12

A DECADE OF MULTIPOLARITY
1961–1968

I. KENNEDY AND JOHNSON'S POLICIES TOWARD CHINA

Reappraisal of Containment

Although the idea of a "two-China" policy had been discussed in U.S. policy circles for some time, the first official mention of the idea came during the 1954-55 Taiwan Straits crisis. President Eisenhower stated at a press conference on January 19, 1955, that one of the approaches being considered to achieve a cease-fire was the adoption of a "two-China" policy.[1]   This proposal was strongly condemned by the ROC, but to no avail.   On August 1 of that year the U.S. and the PRC entered into direct talks.   These interminable discussions were to continue for the next 16 years, even though the two sides were never able to reach agreement on a single issue of substance.[2]

The ROC consistently opposed these talks, fearing that they would lead over time to a softening of the American attitude toward Communist China and eventually to diplomatic recognition.   Taipei also maintained that the talks violated the spirit, if not the letter, of the Sino-American

---

1   *New York Times*, January 20, 1955.
2   For details of US-Chinese Communists talks, refer to Kenneth T. Young, *Negotiating with the Chinese Communist, the United States Experience, 1953-1967* (New York: McGraw Hill, 1968).

Mutual Defense Treaty of 1954, since ROC officials were not consulted prior to the commencement of the talks, nor informed afterward as to their content.[3]   The U.S. was sympathetic to the ROC position, but refused to forsake its own designs.

In late 1959 the "two-China" question once again became a matter of public debate in the U.S. with the release of the Conlon Report. This report, which was released by the Senate Foreign Relations Committee on November 1, proposed that the trade embargo against mainland China be lifted and the ROC's permanent seat on the U.N. Security Council be turned over to the PRC.[4]   The following month another survey of U.S. foreign policy, this one largely orchestrated by Dean Rusk, then President of the Rockefeller Foundation, asserted that no responsible Communist state should be barred from membership in the international community of nations. While not proposing that the U.S. immediately recognize the PRC or support its admission into the U.N., Rusk's report did call for a reassessment of mainland China's position in the modern world and cautioned against permitting "emotion or differences of ideology" to stand in the way of improved relations with the people of the Chinese mainland.[5]

John F. Kennedy's election as President of the United States, and his selection of Dean Rusk as his secretary of state, augured major changes for U.S. China policy. Kennedy accepted that Communist China would continue to exist for many years to come, and thought the current state of U.S.-PRC relations "irrational." Though he hoped to gradually improve relations between the two countries through the use of friendly gestures, he was a cautious man. He did not imagine that admission to the U.N. would work any miraculous conversion in Communist China, and he had

---

3   C. Kuan, *A Review of the U.S. China Policy, 1949-1971* (Taipei: World Anti-Communist League, China Chapter, 1971), pp. 19-20.

4   The Conlon report, entitled *Studies of United States Foreign Policy in Asia*, was part of a general survey of U.S. foreign policy. Part 4, Section D, of the report was entitled "The Chinese Communists and Taiwan," and was written by Professor Robert A. Scalapino of the University of California at Berkeley.

5   For details, see *Rockefeller Panel Reports: Prospect for America* (New York: Doubleday, 1961). The report was prepared by a 14-man panel headed by two former U.S. assistant secretaries of state, Dean Rusk, president of Rockefeller Foundation; and Adolph A. Berle, Jr.

no doubt that the international gains of admission, if any, would be far outweighed by the domestic uproar it would cause. No less a figure than Eisenhower himself had warned Kennedy before his inauguration that, while he hoped to support the new administration on all foreign policy issues, he would return to public life if Communist China threatened to enter the U.N.[6] Kennedy, who had only won election by the tiniest of margins, felt that he could not tackle the China problem in 1961.[7] Significant policy changes would be reserved for his second term of office.

So it was that Kennedy, in his first State of the Union address to Congress on January 29, 1961, took a hard-line approach.[8] "In Asia," he declared, "the relentless pressures of the Chinese Communists menace the security of the entire area, from the border of India and South Vietnam to the jungles of Laos, struggling to protect its newly won independence. . . . Our greatest challenge is still the world that lies beyond the Cold War, but the first great obstacle is still our relations with the Soviet Union and Communist China. We must never be lured into believing that either power has yielded its ambitions for world domination, ambitions which they forcefully restated only a short time ago. . . . To meet this array of challenges, to fulfill the role we cannot avoid on the world scene, we must reexamine and revise our whole arsenal of tools: military, economic and political. . . . One must not overshadow the other. On the Presidential coat of arms, the American eagle holds in his right talon the olive branch, while in his left he holds a bundle of arrows. We intend to give equal attention to both."[9]

On February 6 Secretary of State Rusk insisted that the U.S. commitment to the ROC was firm even though Communist China considered Taiwan a "major obstacle" to reaching an accommodation with the United States. The U.S. was studying ways to include Communist China in disarmament discussions, Rusk revealed, adding

---

6   A. M. Schlesinger, Jr., *A Thousand Days, John F. Kennedy in the White House* (Boston: Houghton Mifflin, 1965), pp. 479-480.

7   Kennedy won the popular vote by a little more than 100,000.

8   President Kennedy's address in 1961 was a masterpiece of rhetoric, but it crumbled in the agonies of a cruel and bitter war.

9   Cited in J. W. Gardner, *President John F. Kennedy: To Turn the Tide* (New York: Harper Brothers, 1962), pp. 23-25.

that "it will not be easy to achieve any realistic or effective disarmament unless all those countries that are capable of producing large armed forces are brought within the system."

History would now repeat itself. As in 1949, just as an American president was prepared to reconsider U.S. policy toward China, Peking began behaving with increasingly belligerence toward not merely America, but the world.[10]　During the Kennedy years the Communist Chinese became more militant, attacking the West, their neighbors, and even the Soviet Union.

This was immediately evident when the Warsaw talks resumed on March 7, 1961. American Ambassador to Poland Jacob D. Beam proposed discussions on the exchange of newsmen and the release of imprisoned Americans. Wang Ping-nan immediately rejected both proposals, saying that nothing could be negotiated until the U.S. withdrew its forces from Taiwan. The next day, Kennedy accused the Chinese Communists of being "extremely belligerent towards us, and . . . unfailing in their attacks upon the United States. Of course, I think part of that has been because they recognized that the United States is committed to maintain its connections with other countries, committed to its own defense and the defense of freedom. . . I would like to see a lessening of tension. . . . But we are not prepared to surrender in order to get a relaxation of that.[11]

Vice President Johnson's Visit

To further underscore this point, Kennedy sent his Vice President to Taiwan on May 14-15, 1961.[12]　Johnson had two talks with Chiang, the first relating to the Sino-American cooperation under the Mutual Defense

---

[10] In November 1961, John F. Kennedy defined one central aspect of the world crisis bluntly: "We must face the fact that the United States is neither omnipotent nor omniscient, that we are six percent of the world's population, and we cannot right every wrong or reverse each adversity, and that therefore there cannot be an American solution for every world problem."

[11] Cited in T. N. Schroth, et. al., *China and U.S. Far East Policy, 1945-1967* (Washington, D.C.: Congressional Quarterly Service, 1967), pp. 102-103.

[12] Vice President Johnson was accompanied by Jean and Stephen Smith, President Kennedy's sister and brother-in-law.

Treaty of 1954, and the second concerning the international situation following the Vienna summit meeting, at which Kennedy took Khrushchev's measure. The joint communiqué which resulted expressed the "complete agreement on the common purpose of the Republic of China and the United States of America to maintain the integrity of free Asia. There was candid exploration and consideration of the strategies required to assure effective action. . . . The Vice President, on behalf of President Kennedy, assured President Chiang that: The United States means to stand by her allies in the Asian area; the United States has no intention of recognizing the Peiping regime; the United States opposes seating the Peiping regime in the United Nations and deems it important for the Republic of China to maintain her position in the United Nations; the United States will continue to work with the Republic of China in support of its accelerated growth program. . . . The President and the Vice President joined in expressing their common concern over the conditions of famine on Mainland China and the mass suffering under Communist rule."[13]

These sentiments seemed to reflect Johnson's actual views, since he was soon to report to Kennedy that he was "pleasant[ly] surprised" by the ROC. "I had long been aware of the criticisms against Chiang Kaishek and his government and cognizant of how these feelings influence our U.S. policy," he wrote. "Whatever the cause, a progressive attitude is emerging there. Our conversations with Chiang and Madame Chiang were dominated by discussions of measures of social progress, to my gratified surprise. As with the Republic of Germany in Western Europe, so I believe we might profitably and wisely encourage the Republic of China in Asia to export talents, skills, and resources to other Asian lands to assist in the program of progress."[14]

In late July 1961 Vice President and Premier Chen Cheng paid a reciprocal visit to the U.S. to discuss the U.N. situation. He hoped to map out a joint strategy on the perennial U.N. debate on Chinese representation and to reach some kind of understanding on the thorny question of the admission of Mongolia, which the ROC regarded as

---

[13] *China Yearbook 1961-1962*, pp. 272-273.
[14] *China Yearbook 1961-1962*, p. 242.

Chinese territory, not an independent state. The August 2 communiqué that resulted from his discussions with Kennedy "reiterated firm United States support for the continued representation of the Republic of China in the United Nations, of which she is founding member. . . [and] reaffirmed the United States determination to continue to oppose the admission of the Chinese Communist regime to the United Nations."

The communiqué also noted that "Communist mismanagement, unworkable agricultural policies, and the commune system have brought serious food shortage and grave hardships to the Chinese people. They noted that reports from refugees and visitors indicate the magnitude of the apathy, discontent and disillusionment of the mainland of China. They agreed that these developments provide vivid proof that the Communist regime cannot meet the genuine needs and desires of the Chinese people for economic and social progress."

On the question of Mongolia, however, the differences had been too great to be easily bridged. The communiqué spoke of a "candid and comprehensive exchange of views" on "the pending applications for U.N. membership of Outer Mongolia and Mauritania."[15]

It was the Soviet Union which had linked the admission of the two countries. Earlier, in 1955, the ROC had used its power as a permanent member of the Security Council to successfully veto the U.N. application of Mongolia. This time around, the Soviets had made it clear, if the ROC used its veto against Mongolia, it would retaliate by vetoing Mauritania's application. If this happened, the Kennedy administration feared that other African states might decide to support the admission of Communist China. Let Mongolia into the U.N., Kennedy told Chen Cheng, so that we might easier solicit votes, or at least abstentions, to keep Communist China out. Kennedy understood the ROC's concerns about the so-called "People's Republic of Mongolia," but sought to persuade a reluctant Nationalist government not to use its veto.[16]

15 *China Yearbook 1961-1962*, pp. 270-271.
16 A. M. Schlesinger, *op. cit.*, pp. 480-481.

The Third Taiwan Straits Crisis

After the 1958 crisis, the Chinese Communists had continued their military build-up along the Taiwan Straits and the shelling of Kinmen on alternate days.[17]   There had been a period of tension in the Taiwan Straits in mid-1959 at the time of the Tibetan and Sino-Indian border crises, but no serious fighting took place. Now, in mid-1962, a third crisis erupted.

By this time a brutal famine had descended upon the Chinese mainland, one which would eventually take over 40 million lives. Food shortages were particularly acute in Kwangtung, where the authorities nonetheless continued to export large quantities of foodstuffs to Hong Kong to earn foreign exchange. Popular unrest grew, and in May some 100,000 refugees flooded across the border into Hong Kong.[18]

In June the Chinese Communists began to make obvious preparations for an attack on the offshore islands, moving a number of army divisions to points directly opposite Kinmen, Matsu, and Taiwan. Speculation was rampant in the American press over the position the Kennedy administration would take with regard to the defense of the offshore islands. On June 27 Kennedy clarified his position, telling newsmen that the U.S. would take any action necessary to "assure the defense of Formosa and the Pescadores [Penghu] provided for in the 1955 Congressional Resolution," if Communist China were to take "aggressive action against" Kinmen and Matsu. "Any threat to the offshore islands," he declared, "must be judged in relation to its wider meaning for the safety of Formosa and the peace of the area."[19]   Kennedy left no doubt that an attack upon Kinmen would be viewed as an attack upon Taiwan.

---

[17] A total of 906,000 Communist artillery shells had hit Kinmen in twenty years.

[18] On May 21, 1962, the Government of the Republic of China offered to accept all refugees who wished to live in Taiwan. On May 23, 1962, President Kennedy announced that the United States would admit, under provisions of the McCarran-Walter Act, "several thousand" Chinese refugees from Hong Kong. Despite these efforts, most of the refugees were detained and deported back to the PRC.

[19] In the 1960 presidential campaign, Kennedy charged that the Eisenhower administration had tried to persuade Chiang to withdraw from Kinmen and Matsu. Nixon denied this allegation, saying that no one had tried to persuade Chiang "to withdraw from and thus to abandon" the offshore islands. The Robertson-Radford

During the fifties and early sixties, the Chinese Communists concentrated their forces along their long, essentially maritime, frontier from Korea down to the Gulf of Tonkin. Their strategic thinking was dominated by the tension between their determination to achieve their aggressive designs, on the one hand, and their fear of the U.S., on the other. They were strengthening their forces along the Taiwan Straits not to deter a Nationalist counterattack, but to capture Taiwan, the last stronghold. If they succeeded, they would have removed not only a hostile and competing government, but the Seventh Fleet from the Taiwan Straits as well. They would have secured a large part of their maritime frontier, and driven a wedge between American forces in Japan and the Philippines. Ultimately, the PRC hoped to eliminate all American bases from East Asia and the Western Pacific, though it intended to use political stratagems rather than military force to gain this end.

The American containment of the PRC made sense not only because that country espoused a form of government inimical to democracy, but because of its long-term strategic aims. Communist China's insistence upon changing the status quo in Asia, no less than the methods of Communist insurgency she relied upon in that effort, more than it justified America's resort to a policy of isolation and containment. The U.S. had to maintain a credible counterweight to Communist China's new power and aggressiveness, or retreat from Asia altogether.

The Two-China Proposals

Still, beginning in the spring of 1961, liberals in the U.S. began to get respectful hearings when they proposed various forms of the "two-China" policy, causing much strain on U.S.-ROC ties.[20] One specific proposal

---

discussions in Taipei, he stated, sought only a better deployment of Nationalist ground forces among Taiwan, Penghu, Kinmen, and Matsu.

[20] Numerous other proposals intended to "resolve the Taiwan problem" appeared at this time, such as the "country of China Taiwan" proposal of Chester Bowles, Assistant Secretary of State during the Kennedy Administration, which appeared in "The China Problem Reconsidered," *Foreign Affairs*, Vol. 38, No. 3, April, 1960. See also Adlai E. Stevenson's "national self-determination" proposal in "Put First Things First, A Democratic View", *Foreign Affairs*, Vol. 38, No. 2, January 1960.

that was advanced was the establishment of diplomatic relations with the Outer Mongolian regime. Mongolia would be an excellent listening post, some State Department officials maintained, especially given that the Soviet Union was conducting a series of nuclear tests at a site not far form it. The ROC was at pains to point out that Mongolia was not an independent state. Moreover, it had opposed the U.N. forces in the Korean War. For the U.S. to recognize such a regime would adversely affect the morale of the free world. Ultimately, the Kennedy administration decided against recognition, although it successfully urged the ROC not to use its veto when the issue of Mongolia's admission came before the U.N. Security Council in 1961.[21]

As late as August 1, 1963, Kennedy could still say that Communist China, with its 700 million people, with its "Stalinist internal regime," with its willingness to view war "as a means of bringing about its ultimate success," and with its future potential as a nuclear power, might present, by the seventies, a "potentially more dangerous situation than any we faced since the end of the Second World War."[22] It was perhaps the magnitude of the future threat posed by the PRC that led him to hold out an olive branch once again.

Just one week before he was assassinated, Kennedy intimated that a new effort to reach an understanding with the PRC was in the works. At a press conference in November 1963 he stated that the U.S. would not stick stubbornly to a policy hostile toward the Chinese Communists. If the Peking regime expressed a willingness to coexist peacefully with other countries, then the U.S. would reconsider its China policy.[23]

This policy was further elaborated the following month, when Assistant Secretary of State for Far Eastern Affairs Roger Hilsman indicated to the Chinese Communists that the "door was open." Because Peking was wedded to "a fundamentalist form of Communism which emphasizes violent revolution, even if it threatens the physical ruin of the civilized world," they must be met by firmness and strength, so that they

---

21 On December 13, 1955, the ROC vetoed Mongolia's application for membership in the U.N. and the Soviet Union retaliated by vetoing Japan. Sixteen other states were admitted, and Japan came in the following year. Mongolia remained out of the U.N. until 1961.

22 T. N. Schroth et. al., *op. cit.*, p. 125.

23 *New York Times*, November 15, 1963.

would not "subvert or commit aggression" against China's "free world neighbors." At the same time, Hilsman averred that "We are determined to keep the door open to the possibility of change, and not to slam it shut against any developments which might advance our national good, serve the free world, and benefit the people of China." As to how this hoped-for change in China's attitude might come about, he mentioned the coming to power of more pragmatic second-generation leaders.[24]   This speech, which may be regarded as a probe by the newly installed Johnson administration of the PRC's flexibility on the "two China" question, elicited only disdainful hostility from Peking.

Relations between Peking and Moscow also deteriorated badly during these years. In 1960 the Soviet Union had suddenly demanded the repayment of its loans and the repatriation of its technicians. In 1962 the PRC had virtually accused Khrushchev of cowardice for agreeing to remove the missiles he had secretly installed in Cuba.[25]   The militarization of the Sino-Soviet border was an all-too-obvious harbinger of future troop clashes. The Chinese Communists, eager to spread their ideology to neighboring states, made plain their intent to support revolutionary movements abroad. The Soviets were pursuing a more cautious line in their dealings with the Western powers which Peking mocked as "revisionist." Communist Chinese aggressiveness locked it into a confrontation with the U.S. that affected every nation in Asia, regardless of its size, power, or political attitude.[26]

---

[24] *New York Times*, December 14, 1963, Roger Hilsman's speech delivered at the Commonwealth Club of San Francisco three weeks after Kennedy's assassination, may be regarded as a probe toward the Chinese Communists by the Johnson Administration.

[25] During the Cuban missile crisis Kennedy forced Khrushchev to remove the missiles he was installing in Cuba. Khrushchev agreed, on condition that Kennedy not invade Cuba. Kennedy accepted with reservations.

[26] Former White House Special Consultant for National Security McGeorge Bundy had called this confrontation "an unfinished contest of power, purpose and policy." Cited in *NBC News, American White Paper, U.S. Foreign Policy* (New York: Random House, 1967), p. 83.

U.S. Congress Hearings on China, 1966

The containment of the PRC continued to be a cardinal doctrine of U.S. foreign policy under Kennedy's successor, President Lyndon B. Johnson. Both allied and non-aligned states accepted, even supported, American efforts to contain Chinese Communist expansion and subversion, but increasingly balked at American efforts to isolate China and boycott its goods. They wanted to engage in trade with the Chinese mainland, and establish channels of communication, even diplomatic relations, with the Peking regime. By 1964 it appeared that the PRC, despite continued U.S. opposition, would soon be admitted to the U.N.

On January 27 of that year France established diplomatic relations with the PRC. The ROC government reacted by breaking diplomatic relations with France on February 10. The State Department called the French move "an unfortunate step, particularly at a time when the Chinese Communists are actively promoting aggression and subversion in Southeast Asia and elsewhere." The U.S., for its part, would "stand firmly by its commitments" to the ROC, Vietnam, and other countries endangered by the Communist Chinese.

But these sentiments were not shared by everyone. On March 25 Senator J. William Fulbright, Chairman of the Senate Foreign Relations Committee, criticized U.S. policy toward East Asia as "inflexible," calling for its thorough reevaluation.[27] "I do not think that the United States can or should recognize Communist China or acquiesce in its admission to the United Nations under present circumstances," Fulbright said. "It would be unwise to do so because there is nothing to be gained by it so long as the Peking regime maintains its attitude of implacable hostility towards the United States. I do not believe, however, that this state of affairs is necessarily permanent. . . Is it not possible that in time our relations with China will change again, if not to friendship, then perhaps to 'competitive coexistence.' It would therefore be an extremely useful thing if we could introduce an element of flexibility, or, more precisely, of the capacity to be flexible, into our relations with Communist China."

---

[27] Cited in T. N. Schroth, et. al., *op. cit.*, pp. 136-137.

Fulbright asserted that "there are not really 'two-Chinas' but only one, Mainland China, and that is ruled by Communists and likely to remain so for the indefinite future." He expressed hope that "a generation of leaders" both in Nationalist China and Communist China "may put a quiet end to the Chinese civil war."

Rusk visited Taipei in April 1964 and, unlike his predecessors, conspicuously failed to refer to the ROC government as "the only Chinese government which legally represents China." Instead, he stressed America's treaty obligations toward the ROC, and opposed handing over the ROC's seat in the U.N. to the Chinese Communists. That is to say, the U.S. no longer objected to the PRC's admission into the U.N. as long as this did not result in the ROC's expulsion. Taipei found this new U.S. policy unacceptable, and no joint communiqué resulted from Rusk's visit. Relations between Washington and Taipei took a nose-dive.[28]

On October 15, 1964, Soviet Premier Nikita Khrushchev was ousted from power in the Kremlin, and the following day Communist China exploded its first nuclear device in Sinkiang. Johnson immediately cautioned against overestimating its military significance. The test came as "no surprise," he said, and had been "fully taken into account" in the U.S. defense commitments in Asia. The U.S. would continue to support the 1963 limited nuclear test-ban treaty and would work to end all nuclear tests and prevent the spread of nuclear weapons. Johnson assured "nations that do not seek national nuclear weapons" that "if they need our strong support against some threat of nuclear blackmail, then they will have it."

On October 20, 1964, Peking proposed, to the leaders of all governments, an international summit meeting on nuclear disarmament. United Nations Secretary General U. Thant seconded that idea two days later, saying that it would be "very worthwhile" for the U.S., the U.S.S.R., the U.K., France and Mainland China to hold disarmament

---

[28] A 1964 public opinion study of attitudes toward China found that a large majority of Americans were concerned about Communist China because of its perceived aggressive intentions and strength. Majorities favored closer contacts, but opposed the sale of wheat, or its admission to the U.N. *The American Public's view of U.S. Policy toward China* (New York: Council on Foreign Relations 1964), Tables 2, 3, 7, 10 and 16.

talks.   The U.S. State Department responded that "channels for a dialogue are open" if Communist China had "anything worthwhile to say."   Communist China would have to participate in negotiations "at some stage," noted a State Department spokesman, "if such agreements are to have any real meaning."

Subsequently, an air of appeasement began to spread in the U.S. and abroad, and the Johnson administration pulled out all the stops in an effort to improve relations with the PRC. Some in Washington began to nurture the illusion that, given the increasingly public split between Peking and Moscow, that Mao might imitate Tito of Yugoslavia in resisting the Soviet Union.[29]   When the U.N. vote that year on the PRC's admission came down to a tie, the cries for Communist China's acceptance into the international community grew even more strident.

These developments, combined with mounting anxiety over American involvement in Vietnam, led to public protests by students and pacifist groups.   The increasing boldness of the PRC aroused fear in many quarters that, as in Korea, the PLA would sooner or later intervene in force in Vietnam, this time armed with nuclear weapons. Reflecting these shifts in attitude, the fabric of restraints on trade with the Communist bloc also began to erode away.   In May 1965 China exploded a second atomic bomb.[30]

Johnson sent his Vice President, Hubert H. Humphrey, to Taiwan on January 1, 1966, to reassure that Nationalist government of American support.   "We are bound together by solemn treaty and alliance: the Mutual Defense Pact or Treaty," Humphrey said.   "I want you to know that this treaty is a sacred obligation. We do not enter into these matters

---

[29] Former U.S. Vice President Richard M. Nixon stated in his address to the American Society of Newspaper Editors, Washington on April 20, 1963: "Red China and Russia are having their differences.   But we cannot take too much comfort in the fact that what they are debating about is not how to beat each other but how to beat us.   They are simply arguing what kind of a shovel they should use to dig the grave of the United States." Cited in P. D. Hall, *The Quotable Richard M. Nixon* (Anderson, S. C.: Drake House, 1967), p. 21.

[30] In mid-April 1965, President Johnson assigned Ambassador Henry Cabot Lodge as his personal representative to visit the ROC and five other Asian countries to exchange views on the Vietnam situation.   The visit tried to bring about closer cooperation between the U.S. and its Asian allies.

lightly. And you may rest assured, you and your people, that the United States of America fulfills its commitments; that the United States of America is a nation of honor and recognizes its obligation once a compact or a treaty has been arrived at." The American Vice President was also impressed by the ROC's progress. "What has happened here," he said, "can serve as an example and an inspiration for any part of the world."[31] Conspicuously absent was any criticism of the PRC.

Spurred on by liberal groups and the hope of a rapprochement with the Chinese Communists, both the Senate and the House of Representatives in 1966 scheduled hearings on the question of U.S. China policy. Hearings in the Senate Foreign Relations Committee opened on March 8, with Fulbright announcing that "The immediate purpose of these hearings is educational. At this stage perhaps the most effective contribution the Committee can make is to provide a forum for recognized experts and scholars in the field of China. I hope that hearings in this way will increase the knowledge of China, our knowledge in Congress and the public's knowledge."

Among the first to testify was A. Doak Barnett, a professor at Columbia University, who set the tone for the hearings. Barnett argued that the attempt to isolate Mainland China had been unwise and unsuccessful, and should be abandoned. In its place, he proposed a policy which he called "containment but not isolation." The Chinese military or subversive threat should be checked, but at the same time "maximum contacts" should be fostered. To this end, he urged recognition of the Chinese Communist regime as the *de facto* government of the Chinese mainland, increased trade in non-strategic goods with China, and American acceptance of some formula to provide seats in the U.N. for both Chinas.

John K. Fairbank, director of the East Asian Research Center at Harvard University, followed this new line on March 10. The burden of his testimony was that the Chinese Communists were merely acting out their history and culture. "The problems they face and the methods they use are in large part inherited," Fairbank argued, "I think we need more perspective on the Chinese style of political behavior. . . . China's remarkable feeling of superiority, its cultural isolation, and its classical

---

[31] *China Yearbook 1966-1967*, p. 212.

doctrines of social order . . . [are] reflected in the current Communist regime as well as in its foreign policy. . . . We should not get too excited over Peking's vast blueprints for the onward course of Maoist revolution." He concluded by sympathetically psychoanalyzing Peking's leadership: "Containment alone is a blind alley unless we add policies of constructive competition and international contact. . . . Peking's rulers shout aggressively out of manifold frustrations. . . . Isolation intensifies their ailment and makes it self-perpetuating, and we need to encourage international contact with China on many fronts."[32]

On March 20 nearly 200 American academics issued a joint statement calling for the PRC to be admitted to the U.N., recognized by the U.S., and allowed to trade freely with America and the world. The statement cautioned, however, that these steps should be taken "without prejudice to the maintenance of relations" with the ROC government.

A hint of a shift in official U.S. policy had come a few days before, on March 9, when the State Department announced that scholars and journalists would be allowed to visit Communist China. Then, on April 14, it was further announced that American universities would be permitted to invite Communist Chinese scholars and scientists to the U.S. While expressing the hope that these scholarly visits would be on a reciprocal basis, the State Department made clear that this was not a condition of U.S. approval. Peking wasted no time in rejecting the proposed visits, on the grounds that the U.S. government had followed "a policy of hostility toward China."[33]

The hint became official when Rusk testified before the House Foreign Affairs Committee on March 16. Rusk acknowledged that the Chinese Communists had established a stable political force on the Chinese Mainland, which the U.S. had no intention of overthrowing by force. Should the Chinese Communists renounce their belief that "force is the best means of resolving disputes," and also abandon their goal of a violent world revolution, then the U.S. would welcome the establishment

---

[32] For the proceedings of the hearings, refer to U.S. Policy with Respect to Mainland China, Hearing before the Committee on Foreign Relations, United States Senate, 89th Congress 2nd Session, March 8, 19, 16, 19, 21, 28-30, 1966 (Washington, D.C.: Government Printing Office, 1966).

[33] U. S. Department of State, *Bulletin*, April 14, 1966.

of friendly relations between the two nations. Rusk spelled out the new policy in ten points:

1. The U.S. should firmly resolve to offer American aid in resisting Chinese aggression.
2. The U.S. should continue to assist Asian nations in establishing viable governments, striving for progressive economic and social policies.
3. The U.S. must solemnly fulfill its commitments to the ROC and the people of Taiwan, who do not desire to be ruled by Communism, to continue the defense of Taiwan, and to persuade the Chinese Communists to reach an agreement with the U.S. against the use of military force in the Taiwan area.
4. The U.S. will continue in its efforts to prevent the expulsion of the ROC from the U.N. and its affiliate organizations. If the Chinese Communists persist in their present policies, the U.S. will oppose their admission into the U.N.
5. The U.S. should continue to assure the Chinese Communists that the U.S. has no intention of attacking the Chinese mainland. The U.S. does not need a war, has no intention of touching off one, and there is no reason to believe in the inevitability of a war between the U.S. and the Chinese Communists.
6. The U.S. must realize that Chinese Communist policies and attitudes are not immutable.
7. Under the cardinal rule of not endangering its own self interest, the U.S. should seek more opportunities for unofficial contacts with the Chinese Communists, if such contacts are beneficial in changing the Chinese Communist attitude toward the U.S. The U.S. must believe that contacts and intercourse are not contrary to a firm policy of encirclement.
8. The U.S. should continue to maintain direct diplomatic contacts in Warsaw with the Chinese Communists in the hope that such contacts will pave the way to fruitful discussions.
9. The U.S. is prepared to negotiate with the Chinese Communists and other countries on such problems as disarmament and limiting the proliferation of nuclear weapons. The nations of the world should urge the Chinese

Communists to change their position of refusal to all such proposals and invitations.

10. The U.S. must continue to collect and analyze intelligence materials on the Chinese Communists in order to formulate a realistic policy.[34]

This ten-point statement, especially the last six items, in effect outlined a new approach to dealing with Chinese Communists. Major administration figures, such as Secretary of Defense Robert McNamara and Vice President Hubert H. Humphrey, began to advocate "bridge-building" with the Chinese Communists.[35] Elaborating on Rusk's fourth point, U.S. Ambassador to the U.N. Arthur Goldberg disclosed on April 19 that Washington would not oppose Communist China's admission if they dropped their demand (1) that the ROC be expelled, (2) that the U.N. apologize for aiding South Korea during the Korean War and, (3) that the U.N. Charter be revised. Peking must agree to abide by the U.N. Charter, Goldberg asserted, especially in regard to renouncing the use of force to resolve disputes. At the same time, State Department spokesman Robert J. MacClosky made no secret of the fact that the U.S. was working on a "two-China" policy in the U.S.[36]

The Foreign Affairs Committee of the House followed with its own report on May 20, questioning the U.S. capacity and wisdom to continue to undertake "heavy responsibilities in Asia with only marginal assistance and cooperation from our allies in Europe." Peace in Asia was said to depend on "deterring Communist aggression and on helping independent Asian nations to develop economically, to mature politically and, in time, to establish viable relations with Mainland China." The administration was urged to expand "peaceful contacts" with Communist China despite

---

[34] *New York Times*, April 17, 1966.
[35] Refer to a May 18, 1966, speech by Robert McNamara before the Newspaper Editors Association, *New York Times*, May 19 1966, and a speech by Hubert H. Humphrey at West Point Military Academy, *New York Times*, June 9, 1966.
[36] C. Kuan, *op. cit.*, p. 25, p. 63. In December 1966, the State Department formed a China study group, composed of A. Doak Barnett, John K. Fairbank, R. A. Scalapino, A. Eckstein, G. E. Taylor, R. L. Powell, Lucian W. Pye, P. A. Varg, P. D. Sprouse, J. C. Holmes and others. The National Committee on U.S.-China Relations was formed this same year.

repeated rebuffs, and to refrain from attacking North Vietnam for fear of a "violent" response from Communist China.

Johnson himself indicated on July 12 that, from now on, U.S. "policy toward the Chinese Communists would be firm but flexible."[37]   He explained that his administration was making a concerted effort to reach a rapprochement with the Chinese Communists, although he ruefully acknowledged that all of his proposals to date had been rejected by the other side.

In the ROC, Washington's new overture to Peking was viewed as tantamount to appeasement. Civic organizations on Taiwan sent a flurry of telegrams to Washington in protest.[38]   An "open letter to the American people," signed by over 1,500 Chinese professors and scholars, pointed out that the new approach was based on a series of false assumptions:

1.   "Mao Tse-tung Thought" was not "a manifestation of Chinese traditions."
2.   Chinese Communism was not "a manifestation of Chinese nationalism."
3.   The Chinese Communists are not powerful enough in reality to crush the U.S. and the free world.
4.   The Chinese Communist regime does not effectively control the people on the Chinese mainland.
5.   The policy of "containment but not isolation" is a contradiction, for isolation must result from containment.
6.   There is no guarantee of the "peaceful evolution" of the Communist system under the next generation of Communist leaders.[39]

---

[37]   Refer to a July 12 speech by President Johnson before the American Alumni Council at White Sulphur Springs, West Virginia, and a nationwide telecast, both reported in the *New York Times*, July 13, 1966.

[38]   For example, 34 members of the Legislative Yuan sent a joint letter to American Congressmen; 64 members of the Control Yuan sent a letter to the U.S. Congressmen; 65 civic organizations and universities sent a joint letter to President Johnson indicating that appeasement would lead to disaster and that the United States should adopt a firm position.

[39]   Refer to *Central Daily News*, Taipei, May 16, 1966.

These points illustrated the serious differences of opinion that now divided the ROC and the U.S. where the Chinese Communists were concerned. Rusk attempted to reassure ROC leaders about U.S. intentions, visiting Taipei twice during the second half of 1966, but his efforts only served to underscore the new divide.[40]

"Building Bridges"

The isolation of Mainland China, which had never been wholly successful, had depended on a trade embargo by the U.S. and the West, on Asia and Africa remaining politically indifferent, and on the assistance of the ROC. By the late 1960s, only the ROC government remained resolute in its determination to isolate the PRC. The focus of U.S. strategic thinking had shifted to the three-power rivalry now unfolding between itself, the U.S.S.R., and Communist China. While America was still seeking to contain Communist China, militarily and otherwise, the Soviet Union had begun to practice a kind of containment policy, too, this designed to limit Peking's political and ideological gains throughout the world. Both wanted to achieve their objectives without creating a major advantage for the other. For its part, the PRC was bent on establishing its ideological superiority to the Soviet Union, and perhaps even to detach some Soviet territory, without giving the U.S. a decisive politico-military advantage.[41] The triangular relationship that was to characterize international relations for the next two decades had emerged.

On January 11, 1967, in his annual State of the Union address, Johnson dourly predicted "more cost, more loss and more agony" in the Vietnam War. At the same time, he held out the hope for "a reconciliation between the people of Mainland China and the world community . . . including working together in all the tasks of arms control." Peking responded that spring by repeatedly denouncing the U.S. for "escalating" the Vietnam War, reiterating its firm support of North Vietnam, and lodging a series of protests against American planes for allegedly "crossing the Chinese border."

---

[40] Rusk's visits to Taipei took place on July 3, and December 7, 1966.
[41] R. E. Osgood, *America and the World* (Baltimore: John Hopkins Press, 1970), pp. 407-408.

These incidents may have stiffened Johnson's resolve where the ROC was concerned, for in May 1967, when Vice President and Premier Yen Chia-kan visited the U.S., he was warmly received by senior administration officials. Yen's three-week visit was the most important trip by a Nationalist leader to Washington since Vice President Chen Cheng's 1962 visit. Although the main purpose of his trip was to confer with Johnson, Yen took advantage of the opportunity to crisscross the U.S. Yen made 48 speeches and held 20 press conferences in 20 days.

The joint communiqué that resulted on May 10 reflected Johnson's concern that Communist China might act on its threat to intervene in the Vietnam War. Johnson and Yen "exchanged information and views on the conditions existing on the Chinese mainland resulting from the Cultural Revolution. They agreed that the struggle for power is far from over and that developments on the Chinese mainland are closely related to the peace and security of Asia. They further agreed to hold consultations on the future developments on the Chinese mainland." Yen reaffirmed that the ROC would continue its vigorous support of the U.S. policy of opposing Communist aggression in Vietnam.

It then shifted to the perennial question of Chinese representation in the U.N.: "They noted the favorable outcome of the 21st General Assembly when efforts to expel the Republic of China from the United Nations and seat the Chinese Communists were decisively defeated." President Johnson reaffirmed that the United States firmly supported the Republic of China U.N. seat."[42]

On June 17, 1967, two years and eight months after detonating its first nuclear device, Peking announced that it had successfully tested its first hydrogen bomb. The announcement was calculated to dramatize the power of Communist China. American strategic dominance in Asia was now being challenged not only by the Soviet Union, but also by China. There was a renewed clamor for the PRC's admission to the U.N., for progress on arms control, and for diplomatic recognition.

The proposals now advanced continued to be variations on the "two-China" formula. Advocates generally argued that recognition of the new Chinese "reality" was inevitable, advantageous, or both. Sooner or later

---

[42] Government Information Office, *Vice President C. K. Yen visits the United States* (Taipei: China Publishing Co., 1968), pp. 18-19

those in power in Peking would have to be recognized, the first argument ran, so why not establish relations now. Furthermore, argued proponents of the second, recognition would reduce tension in Asia, influence the Chinese Communists, drive a wedge between Moscow and Peking, and improve relations between the U.S. and countries sympathetic to Communist China.

Neither of these arguments was persuasive, particularly as a justification for the "two-China" concept. It was and remains realistic to deal, when necessary, with those who actually rule an area. The U.S. did this with the Japanese in Manchuria, but without finding it either necessary or desirable to recognize "Manchukuo." For years the U.S. had negotiated with the Chinese Communists at Panmunjom, Geneva and Warsaw, again without finding it necessary or desirable to accord them diplomatic recognition. As far as the inevitability argument was concerned, there was ample evidence from the uprisings in Eastern Europe in the fifties, that Communism would not long endure. Why accept Communism's own flawed eschatology that its worldwide success was somehow inevitable? There was no need for the U.S. to yield to this erroneous view of the events.

Refusal to recognize another government despite its obvious viability is far from unusual. Spain and the Soviet Union, the Arab states and Israel, most of the African states, Indonesia and Malaysia had all used recognition as a discretionary instrument of national policy, rather than simply a recognition of "reality." China was not the only divided country with two competing governments. The cases of Germany, Korea and Vietnam had all forced all other nations to view diplomatic relations as more than just a simple recognition of the "facts on the ground." A superpower, in particular, may wish to keep its options in terms of recognition open, and not foreclose them by acting in haste or prematurely.

Up to 1968 the U.S. policy of opposition to the admission of Mainland China into the U.N. had remained unchanged. Undersecretary of State Nicholas B. Katzenbach, in a speech delivered on May 22 of that year, stressed that the U.S. could not accept the demands of Communist China that it be admitted into various international organizations and that the ROC be expelled. During his visit to Taipei in July 1968 George Ball, U.S. Permanent Representative to the U.N., indicated that the

Johnson administration would continue to support the legal position of the ROC in the U.N.[43]

II. DEVELOPMENTS IN THE REPUBLIC OF CHINA

Economic and Political Progress in Taiwan

In December 1963 Chen Cheng, for reasons of ill health, resigned as premier after holding the post for five years. The new cabinet was headed by Yen Chia-kan, who took over the helm at a time when the economy of Taiwan was taking off. The land reform had been peacefully and successfully concluded, and three successive four-year economic development plans had brought Taiwan the second-highest living standard in Asia.[44] Premier Yen praised the former cabinet for laying a firm economic foundation for the fight against Communism and for the recovery of the mainland. He pledged to carry out the nation's unfinished tasks.[45]

The people in Taiwan closed ranks behind their government following France's recognition of the Peking regime in 1964, and the ROC successfully weathered this diplomatic storm. Contrary to some predictions that difficult times lay ahead, most of the African states did not rush to follow the French example. Indeed, the Malagasy government soon announced that it was establishing an embassy in Taipei. There were other diplomatic successes as well. The fear that the U.S. would abandon the ROC for a rapprochement with Peking proved to be unfounded, and were soon put to rest entirely by President Johnson, who remarked on April 20, 1964, that none should "doubt our unalterable

---

[43] *China Yearbook 1968-1969*, pp. 375-376.

[44] Since 1963, the Republic of China launched three successive four-year economic development plans. The efforts had paid off in the rapid growth of national economy. From 1962 to 1966, annual net national income had on the average increased by 7.6% and annual net per capital income by 4.2%. The rates of annual increases in agricultural and industrial production were 6.1% and 13.2%, respectively.

[45] China Yearbook Editorial Board: *China Yearbook, 1963-1964* (Taipei: China Publishing co., 1964), p. 1.

commitment to the defense and liberty of free China. Meanwhile we will say to our historic friends, the talented and courageous people on the Chinese mainland, that just as we opposed aggression against them, we must oppose aggression by their rulers and for the same reasons."[46]

Rusk weighed in on March 25, criticizing Communist China for refusing to renounce the use of force in the Taiwan Straits. He cited Chinese Communist mischief making in South Vietnam, Africa and South America, as well as its policy of military aggression, as further obstacles to the U.S. recognition of the Peking regime.[47] Also in 1964, the U.S. House and Senate reaffirmed that the Communist Chinese regime should not be admitted to U.N. membership as China's representative.

In June 1965 Chow Shu-kai, then Chinese Ambassador to Spain, succeeded Tsiang T'ing-fu as the Chinese Ambassador to the United States. Two months later, Madame Chiang Kai-shek went to the U.S. for an extended lecture tour, speaking in Washington, New York, Chicago, Detroit and other cities. As with her visit to the U.S. during World War II, these speeches helped the American public to better understand Nationalist China and the base character of the Chinese Communists. Madame Chiang did not return to Taiwan until the following October.

To bring the ROC viewpoint home to Americans, President Chiang used the following analogy in a 1965 interview with a UPI correspondent:

> If Communism suddenly took over the American mainland and the U.S. government were forced to establish a central headquarters in Hawaii, what actions would the American people take? Would the American government and people not actively endeavor against Communism in the hope that some day the Communists would be driven out, so that they could return to their homes on the American mainland? Would the American people not long for their old homes, their friends, and their enslaved compatriots on the mainland, or would they be content with a status quo in which Hawaii be the only free piece of American soil? I cannot believe this would be the case. We believe that each and every American would long for the day

---

[46] T. N. Schroth et. al., *op. cit.*, p. 138.
[47] China Yearbook Editorial Board: *China Yearbook, 1964-1965* (Taipei: China Publishing Co., 1965), p. 278.

when the aggressive Communists were driven out. Without a doubt, they would assert that their sacred right is to return to their homeland and wrest back their legal property. This is exactly how the Chinese people feel at the present time.[48]

Following his election to a fourth six-year term as President, Chiang promised in his inaugural address on May 20, 1966, that he would lead the people of China to final victory over the Communists, the recovery of the mainland, and the reconstruction of the nation under the Constitution and the ROC government. That same month, underlining the importance that Johnson attached to Taiwan, Walter P. McConaughy, then American Ambassador to Pakistan, was named to succeed Admiral Jerauld Wright as the U.S. Ambassador to China.

U.S. Economic Aid Comes to a Close

When U.S. economic and military aid to Taiwan was resumed in 1951 the economy was in a critical position. Food, clothing, and basic necessities were scarce as a result of the wartime loss of production facilities. Heavy military spending was producing large deficits in the national budget. Inflationary pressures were threatening to set off the same tragic sequence of events that had contributed to the Communist takeover on the mainland. The initial priorities of the aid program were (1) to achieve economic stability and control inflation; (2) to support the military effort; and (3) to improve Taiwan's capacity for self-support. By the time the Sino-American Mutual Defense Treaty of 1954 was signed, inflation had been curbed and per capita income had begun to increase.

The years of 1956-1960 were marked by heavy U.S. aid commitments to infrastructure and industrial projects. The infrastructure improvements included increased power generation, better transportation, improved communications, and the like. Industrial projects relied more on private investment, which was more easily obtainable because of the "multiplier effects" of external aid. A condition of U.S. aid for such

---

[48] A talk of President Chiang Kai-shek with a UPI journalist, *Central Daily News*, Taipei, April 29, 1965.

projects was that its local sponsors had to raise a certain percentage of the cost, which helped to stimulate local capital formation and contributed, albeit indirectly, to the economic conditions that induce private investment.

By 1961 the goals of U.S. aid had shifted again. Now the emphasis was on fostering private enterprise, promoting exports, and terminating congressional assistance. It was becoming clear that Taiwan would not require U.S. assistance for much longer.

During the first five years of the U.S. assistance program, from 1951 to 1955, all aid took the form of outright grants. Beginning in the late fifties, these were gradually replaced by interest-free development loans and farm surplus loans, to be repaid in Taiwan dollars over a period of twenty to forty years. After 1962 development loans decreased and terms of repayment were in U.S. dollars with interest. The amount of U.S. aid ranged from $80 to 120 million per year in the 1950s, and thereafter tapered off until it was terminated in mid-1965. The total amount of American aid was $1.52 billion.[49]

By the time U.S. aid ended on June 30, 1965, Taiwan was economically self-sufficient and its GNP was expanding at the rate of 7.2 percent a year. The ROC was ready to go it alone. In his report to the Legislative Yuan of September 1964 Premier Yen said: "U.S. economic aid constituted 13 percent of our GNP fourteen years ago. At present it constitutes of only 2.4 percent. After deducting farm surplus, pure economic aid constitutes only 0.7 percent. Owing to the strength of our present economic situation, it will not be difficult to make up this difference."

Although the economic aid program was terminated, the U.S. continued to provide military assistance and surplus farm products. The latter were partly gifts and partly loans under the provisions of the U.S. Agricultural Trade Development Assistance Act (Public Law 480).[50] The ROC and U.S. governments had also decided, prior to the end of the

---

[49] From 1951 to 1965, U.S. economic aid included $950 million in grants, U.S. $220 million in development loans, and U.S. $350 million in farm surplus.

[50] Under the Sino-American Agricultural Commodity Agreements signed in 1964 and 1967, Taiwan was to be provided with agricultural commodities amounting to $66.3 million and $37.5 million respectively for the subsequent years.

aid program, to establish a Sino-American Fund for Economic and Social Development. The Fund was a consolidation of existing counterpart funds, new counterpart funds to be deposited by the ROC government, interest and loan payments, and funds for loans to be provided by the U.S. under the agricultural commodities agreements. The Fund would be used to promote the economic and social development in Taiwan and to supplement the Republic of China's international technical cooperation programs. After June 30, 1965, U.S. approval on each project or program was no longer required.[51]

The U.S aid program was a spectacular success by any measure. Over the course of 15 years Taiwan's economy, long subordinated to Japan's and devastated by the war, was rebuilt, self-reliant, and well on its way to be industrialized. U.S. aid had helped move Taiwan from a position of economic weakness to one of sustained progress. Viewed as an instrument of national security, the U.S. aid program had reinforced America's defensive perimeter in East Asia by creating a strong, secure, and stable ally in East Asia. The cost of this achievement had been exceedingly reasonable. The U.S. spent less than 5 percent of its aid budget in Taiwan during the years from 1951 to 1965, ranging from a high of 4.9 percent in 1955 to a low of 1 percent in 1964.

The effectiveness of U.S. economic aid to the ROC was due to the following: (1) the high degree of cooperation between the Chinese and American officials; (2) the relative autonomy of the principal Chinese organizations of aid administration, such as the Economic Stabilization Board, the Council for U.S. Aid, and the Joint Commission on Rural Reconstruction, from government control; (3) the unusual continuity of these institutions and their personnel, which permitted cumulative increases in their efficiency. Other factors contributing to Taiwan's economic success were the land reform program, the influx of technical, professional, and administrative personnel from the Chinese mainland, and the Chinese legacy of hard work, discipline, and social order.

The ROC had not only made excellent use of U.S. foreign aid, it was soon to itself embark upon a foreign aid program of its own. Johnson, in the joint communiqué of May 10, 1967, "expressed admiration for the

---

[51] The Sino-American Development Fund Agreement of 1965, scheduled to expire on June 30, 1970, was amended and renewed in 1970 until June 30, 1975.

continuing progress made by the Republic of China in developing Taiwan's economy since the conclusion of the United States economic aid program in 1965. He also noted the sharp contrast between the economic conditions in Taiwan and on the Chinese mainland. The President congratulated Vice President Yen on the remarkable success of the Republic of China's technical cooperation program in the friendly countries, particularly in the field of agriculture, and noted that the Republic of China was making a most significant contribution to the collective war on hunger."[52] The ROC had come of age economically.

---

[52] Government Information Office, *Vice President C. K. Yen visits the United States* (Taipei: China Publishing Co., 1968), pp. 18-19.

13

THE PERIOD OF INNOVATIVE POLITICAL MANEUVERS 1969–1974

I. AN ERA OF NEGOTIATION

Nixonian Detente

Richard M. Nixon assumed the presidency determined to effect a breakthrough in relations with the Chinese mainland. He had made clear his intentions as early as 1967, in an article published in *Foreign Affairs*, entitled "Asia after Vietnam."[1] "Any American policy toward Asia must come urgently to grips with the reality of China," wrote Nixon. "This does not mean, as many would simplistically have it, rushing to grant recognition to Peking, to admit it to the United Nations and to ply it with offers of trade—all of which would serve to confirm its rulers in their present course. It does mean recognizing the present and potential danger from Communist China, and taking measures designed to meet that danger. Taking the long view, we simply cannot afford to leave China

---

[1] Nixon first disclosed this "negotiation instead of confrontation" foreign policy slogan in his nomination acceptance speech at the 1968 Republican Convention. Nixon stated that the cold war existing since the end of the Second World War had now drawn to a conclusion. For a theoretical analysis of this policy, refer to Richard M. Nixon, "Asia after Vietnam," *Foreign Affairs*, October, 1967.

forever outside the family of nations. We must. . . persuade China that it must change."[2]

His foreign policy, as Nixon later said in accepting the Republican nomination for president, would be based on "negotiations instead of confrontation." While he conceded that there was a "long road" to travel before normal diplomatic relations with Communist China could be established, he left little doubt that he was eager to begin the journey.

Nixon possessed, of course, impeccable anti-Communist credentials. He was first elected to Congress in 1946 by portraying his opponent, a liberal Democrat by the name of Jerry Voorhis, as soft on Communism. Following his arrival in Washington, he quickly made a name for himself on the House Committee on Un-American Activities, in 1948 co-sponsoring the Mundt-Nixon bill which placed restrictions on the activities of communists. He moved to the U.S. Senate in 1950, and two years later was chosen by Dwight D. Eisenhower as his running mate in the 1952 presidential campaign. As vice president, Nixon continued his crusade against Communism, repeatedly charging over the years that the Democrats recognized neither the danger that Communist infiltration posed to America, nor the magnitude of the Communist threat to the international order.

In the 1960 race, which he narrowly lost to John F. Kennedy, Nixon stressed the necessity of defending Asia, and specifically Taiwan, from the Communists. During the sixties he visited the ROC on several occasions, meeting with President Chiang, whom he always found cordial, and giving speeches. On one such trip in November 1964 for instance, Nixon addressed the 10th Conference of the Asian People's Anti-Communist League (APACL) in Taipei, declaring that the struggle with Communism in Asia would continue even if the war in Vietnam were won because of "the tremendous power center that [Communism] has on the mainland of China."

Nixon's victory in the 1968 presidential race was one of the greatest comebacks in the history of American politics. Never before had a candidate, defeated in one presidential race and then denied re-nomination four years later, been able to capture the White House subsequently. A look at Nixon's campaign speeches of that year reveals no basic change

---

[2]   R. M. Nixon, "Asia After Vietnam," *Foreign Affairs*, October, 1967, p. 121.

in his staunch anti-Communism. He stuck to his past convictions and won the presidency. Whatever he did as president, it would be difficult to accuse him, as he had accused so many others, of being soft on Communism.

After his election, Nixon continued to speak publicly of the normalization of relations between the U.S. and Communist China as a long-range U.S. goal. But in fact he moved with great speed, even abandonment, toward this end. On February 1, 1969, less than two weeks after assuming the presidency, he secretly directed the head of his National Security Council, Henry Kissinger, to give "every consideration" to bringing about better relations with Communist China.[3] Exactly a month later, in Paris, he had asked French President Charles de Gaulle to transmit to Peking his desire to move toward the normalization of relations. At the same time, although there was no public mention of these confidential approaches, senior American officials began voicing their hope for high-level contacts with the Chinese Communists.

The Nixon Doctrine and China Policy

Six months after his inauguration, Nixon set out upon a ten-day trip that would take him to the Philippines, Indonesia, Thailand, Vietnam, India, Pakistan and Romania. At the same time, his Secretary of State, William P. Rogers, was to visit Japan, Korea, the Republic of China, and other countries in the region. The trip was billed as a fact-finding tour to gather the information necessary to prepare a new policy for America in Asia. In reality, Nixon knew before leaving Washington the precise direction in which he wanted to go.

The first stop on Nixon's Asia trip was Guam, where he welcomed the Apollo 11 astronauts home from their successful lunar landing. Nixon took advantage of the occasion to hold an impromptu press conference on July 5, 1969, at which he outlined the principles that would

---

3   Refer to President Richard M. Nixon's "State of the World" messages to Congress, February 9, 1972.

henceforth guide American foreign policy.[4]   His approach—which inevitably became known as the Nixon doctrine—was fundamentally defensive in character. The U.S. would no longer be the sole guarantor of freedom in the world, he made clear, but would rather seek to preserve a balance of power.

Nixon was even more emphatic in his "State of the World" address to Congress on February 18, 1970. The U.S. "will participate in the defense and development of allies and friends," he avowed, "but America cannot and will not conceive all the plans, design all the programs, execute all the decisions, and undertake all the defense of the free nations of the world. We will help where it makes a real difference and is considered in our interest." Other nations "now have the ability and responsibility to deal with local disputes which once might have required our intervention," he continued. For the U.S. "to insist that other nations play a role is not a retreat from responsibility; it is a sharing of responsibility."[5]

Nixon was convinced that the ongoing difficulties between the Soviet Union and Communist China provided an opening for the U.S. to drive a wedge between the two Communist powers.[6] In April 1969 Secretary of State Rogers declared that the U.S. would pursue a prudent and neutral policy with regard to the Peking-Moscow conflict, but Nixon's ambitions were in reality much more grandiose. He imagined that the U.S. would replace the Soviet Union as the principal foreign supporter of Communist China's industrialization, which over time would pull it into the U.S. orbit.   At the very least, Nixon believed, improved relations with Communist China would widen the rift between it and the Soviet Union. The triangular relationship that he envisaged puzzled those accustomed to

---

[4]   As reporters were not allowed to quote Nixon directly, discrepancies appeared in the published reports. Refer to Joel Blocker's report which appeared in the August 28, 1969, *Newsweek*, and to S. T. Hwang, "On President Nixon's Asia Trip and His New Concept," *Asian Outlook*, Taipei, September 1969, pp. 16-18.

[5]   Nixon's two State of the World messages outlined a foreign policy for the seventies. The first, subtitled "A New Strategy for Peace," was issued on February 18, 1970. The second, subtitled "Building for Peace," was released on February 25, 1971.

[6]   E. Mazo & S. Hess, *Nixon, A Political Portrait* (New York: Harper & Row, 1968), p. 311.

a bipolar world, but it struck Chinese strategists as neither novel nor strange. "Checking the foreigner with a foreigner," was an ancient principle of Chinese statecraft.

Nixon's first public move in his game of geopolitical chess took place on July 21, 1969, when the State Department announced that passports for travel to the Chinese Mainland for certain categories of persons would be automatically issued, and that all U.S. citizens traveling abroad would be allowed to purchase limited quantities of PRC goods.[7] The ROC protested these moves as breaches of free world solidarity, but to no avail.[8] Other measures followed, designed to facilitate people-to-people contact between the Mainland Chinese and American people. In December of that same year, for example, Washington announced that foreign firms whose products used American components would be offered export licenses to the PRC for goods judged non-strategic. Beginning in August 1970, American oil companies were allowed to bunker China-bound ships.

Nixon further upped the ante when, in an address to the U.N. General Assembly on September 18, 1969, he appealed to "the various Communist powers" to come to terms with the U.S. on a "broad front of issues." Officials in Washington stressed that, while the U.S. had no intention of turning away from its traditional ties with the ROC, these ties would not be allowed to stand in the way of a rapprochement with Communist China.

The Chinese Communists were unmoved. By 1970 the U.S. State Department had issued more than 1,000 passports to Americans who wished to visit the PRC. Peking deigned to issue entry visas to only three.[9] No Chinese from the mainland, Communist or otherwise, were permitted to visit the U.S.

The first sign of a thaw came on January 8, 1970, when the U.S. and the PRC agreed to resume ambassadorial-level talks in Warsaw. The initial session, held on January 20, was a disappointment, however. The Communist Chinese representative, Lai Yang, demanded in effect that the U.S. completely abandon the ROC as a condition of improved relations

---

7   U.S. Department of State, *Bulletin*, Vol. LXI, No. 1573, August 18, 1969, p. 126.
8   *Express News*, Taipei, July 23, 1969.
9   U.S. Department of State, *Bulletin*, Vol. LXIV, No. 1956, March 22, 1971, p. 384.

with the PRC. However eager Nixon was to achieve this end, this was too high a price to pay. Rogers blandly reported that, although this first meeting had seen new proposals, these had not been of far-reaching consequence. The ROC's persistent opposition to the talks, on the grounds that they would lead neither to a relaxation of tensions nor to other constructive results, seemed to be vindicated.

Nixon, undaunted, continued in his efforts to woo Peking throughout 1970. Washington ceased pressuring its allies to withhold recognition from the PRC. Canada and Italy promptly joined fellow NATO members Britain and France in posting ambassadors to Peking. Despite Peking's lack of response, Nixon stated at a press conference on December 10, 1970, that the U.S. would continue its initiative in relaxing trade and travel restrictions.[10]

By 1971 Nixon, sensing that he would have to go even further to elicit a response from Peking, was ready to espouse openly what he had earlier only hinted at: a two-China policy. The occasion was his second State of the World address, which was delivered to the U.S. Congress on February 25. In it, he expressed the desire to normalize relations with the Chinese Communists, stating that existing ties between the U.S. and the ROC should not be an obstacle to this effort. While Nixon asserted that the U.S. would continue to oppose any attempt to deprive the ROC of its seat in the U.N., it was clear that the U.S. would no longer oppose China's efforts to enter that organization with any vigor. The previous 22 years of antagonism between the U.S. and Communist China were, in his words, "a grave mistake."[11]

Perhaps the biggest surprise of Nixon's speech, other than the two-China policy itself, was his use of names: for the first time, Communist China was referred to by a President of the United States as the "People's Republic of China." The Republic of China, on the other hand, on

---

[10] There are some indications that, at the very outset of the Nixon Presidency, the Chinese Communists were intrigued by his speeches indicating that he would like to see less confrontation and more friendship, and considered extending a feeler. But his firm policy in Vietnam and Cambodia caused them to draw back.

[11] *United States Foreign Policy for the 1970's, Building for Peace, A Report by President Richard Nixon to the Congress, February 25, 1971* (Washington, D.C.: Government Printing Office, 1971).

several occasions became merely "Taiwan."[12]   From the standpoint of international law, merely to call Communist China by the name it had chosen for itself did not imply recognition, de facto or otherwise. Rhetorically, however, his use of the "People's Republic of China" greatly softened his message.

Nixon went on to express the sanguine view that the differences between Taipei and Peking, about which the American government could do little, would be resolved by peaceful means over time. In the meantime, the U.S. would "recognize realities" and treat the ROC and the PRC as two separate entities.

Other steps to distance the U.S. from the ROC, its long-time ally, were taken as well. Military aid was slashed, and the provision of more sophisticated weapons was stopped altogether. The patrolling of the Taiwan Straits, which had been reduced by December 1969, was now halted altogether.[13]   The ROC itself was pressured to halt commando raids against the mainland. When ROC naval commando forces sank three Chinese Communist gunboats at the mouth of the Minkiang River at Fukien on July 2, 1969, State Department spokesman Robert J. McCloskey revealed that the U.S. had raised the incident with the Nationalist authorities on the basis of the Sino-American Mutual Defense Treaty.[14]

The Republic of China Reaction

Nixon's calculations paid off, at least where the PRC was concerned. Beijing reacted to his overtures not with its accustomed hostility but with a wary cordiality that became known as "smiling diplomacy." In the Republic of China, however, there were few smiles.

---

[12] It was in the State of the World message that the two-China policy was openly and clearly stated for the first time by President Nixon.

[13] When State Department Spokesman Robert M. McCloskey was questioned on reports of declining number of patrols on December 24, 1969, he said he could not confirm them. But, according to a UPI wire story, he admitted that "Recent U.S. naval budgetary reductions have required changes in the deployment of our forces." *China News*, Taipei, December 25, 1969.

[14] Refer to *International Herald Tribune*, Paris, July 4, 1969, p.2.

The Nixon administration, of course, had gone out of its way to earlier reassure Taipei concerning its intentions. Secretary of State Rogers, during his 1969 visit to the ROC, asserted that "Our policy towards the Republic of China is going to remain constant. . . We intend to continue to work very closely with the Republic of China in the future, and nothing that we do in Vietnam or other areas is going to affect our relationship with the Republic of China."[15] While recognizing the ROC on Taiwan and Communist China on the mainland as facts of life, the U.S. would continue to meet its treaty obligations to the ROC.[16]

These sentiments were reaffirmed by Vice President Spiro T. Agnew, who visited Taiwan in January and August of 1970. On the first occasion, Agnew took note of the ROC opposition to American attempts to develop a "meaningful dialogue" with Communist China for fear that this would come at the expense of the ROC and its security. "We intend to honor our defense commitments to the Republic of China and other allies in East Asia," he reassured his hosts.[17]

Agnew did not reveal, and presumably did not know, that Nixon had already decided to send his national security advisor, Henry Kissinger, to China as soon as possible. On February 20, 1970, when the Warsaw talks resumed, U.S. Ambassador to Poland, Walter J. Stoessel, Jr., confidentially broached the idea to PRC Ambassador Lai Yang. More than a year passed before Peking gave its consent to the visit. Not until July 1971 did Kissinger, aided by Pakistan President Yahya Khan, slip into China for several days of talks with Chou En-lai.

Meanwhile, the Nixon administration continued to publicly stress its regard for the ROC. On October 6, 1970, Assistant Secretary of State for East Asian and Pacific Affairs Marshall Green testified before the House Foreign Affairs Committee. Speaking of "anomalies in our present attitude toward the immensely complex China question," Green averred that U.S. policy toward the PRC could not be considered "in isolation" from U.S. relations with the ROC. He spoke of the continued

---

[15] "Answers to Press Queries by Mr. William P. Rogers," *Asian Outlook* (Taipei) August, 1969, pp. 46-46. This particular comment was made at a press conference in Taichung on August 3, 1969.
[16] "Growing Role for Secretary Rogers," *U.S. News and World Report*, August 25, 1969, pp. 13-14.
[17] *China Yearbook*, 1970-1971, p. 4.

U.S. commitment to assist in the defense of Taiwan and the Pescadores under the terms of the Mutual Defense Treaty of 1954 and continued U.S. support for the ROC government internationally. "However one may view the [ROC's] claim to be the only legitimate Government of China," he concluded, "the record of accomplishment on Taiwan and the constructive role which that government and the people on Taiwan are playing internationally merit, we believe, a rightful place for the Republic of China in the community of nations."[18]

Despite these public assurances, the ROC remained skeptical about U.S. intentions. In April 1970 ROC Vice Premier Chiang Ching-kuo visited the U.S. and left no doubt about his government's position.[19] The ROC opposed any contact between its allies and Maoist China, he declared, for such contacts merely encourage this tyrannical, oppressive regime to engage in aggressive acts. Neither would the ROC abandon its efforts to recover the mainland, using a stable and prosperous Taiwan as a base, for only when the ROC is successful will peace be restored to Asia and the world. From the U.S., Chiang stated, the ROC asked only spiritual, moral, and material support, not troops.

This message was reinforced by Premier Yen Chia-kan, who called on President Nixon and Vice President Agnew in October 1970, while visiting the U.S. in connection with the 25th anniversary of the United Nations. Yen's response to Nixon's speech of February 25, 1971, was unequivocal. He chided the American President for using the term "People's Republic of China" and reasserted the ROC government's firm opposition to any two-China arrangement. Republic of China Ambassador Chow Shu-kai filed a formal protest with the U.S. government.

Ping Pong Diplomacy

Peking's reaction was very different. During the 31st annual world tournament of table tennis, held at Nagoya, Japan in April 1971, Chinese Communist representatives invited teams from the U.S., Canada, Colombia, Britain, and Nigeria to visit China. After playing exhibition

---

[18] *News Backgrounder* (Taipei: USIS), No. BG-71, January 4, 1971.
[19] C. Kuan, *op. cit.*, pp. 34-35.

matches in Peking, Shanghai, and Canton, the 15 American players, accompanied by three American journalists, were invited to meet with Chou En-lai on April 13. Chou, the consummate diplomat, received the American delegation warmly, telling them that "a new page" was opening between their countries.[20]

Nixon, gratified that Peking had at last responded to his many overtures, could hardly restrain his exuberance. "Now it is up to them," he excitedly told newsmen on April 16. "If they want more trade we are ready. If they want to have Chinese come to the United States we are ready. We are also ready for Americans to go there. Americans in all walks of life. We are going to proceed in these substantive fields of exchange of persons and also in the field of trade."[21]

The American President moved quickly to make further concessions. Secretary of State Rogers announced on May 21, 1971, that, despite the absence of diplomatic relations between the PRC and the U.S., the scientists and scientific organizations of the two countries would henceforth be free to exchange unclassified scientific and technical information. State Department officials later admitted that the U.S. had started offering unclassified scientific and technical information to the Chinese mainland some time before. The following month, on June 10, the U.S. embargo on trade with the Chinese Communists was lifted. White House Press Secretary Ronald Ziegler distributed to reporters a long list of American goods and commodities approved for export to the PRC.

As a concrete gesture of goodwill the list was impressive, but it proved to have little commercial importance, at least initially. For all its huge size, China's two-way volume was only $4.2 billion in 1970, about the same as it had been in 1959. Moreover, American businessmen who rushed to Hong Kong found that the PRC was not yet prepared to engage in direct trade with capitalistic America. Trade between the two countries in 1971 remained a paltry $4 million, all handled by

---

[20] Shortly thereafter Tillman Durdin, a *New York Times* correspondent with extensive experience in China, was granted a one month visa, the first issued to an American reporter for regular news coverage since the early 1950's.

[21] *International Herald Tribune*, Paris, April 19, 1971, p.1.

middlemen. The following year the total grew to $92.5 million, but this included a huge purchase by Peking of 400,000 tons of American wheat. Peking was more interested in honing its image. The U.S. media had played up the American table tennis team's visit to the Chinese mainland to an almost unbelievable degree. Pleased with the impact the visit had on American public opinion, Peking began to issue other visas to Americans.[22]   Between April 1971 and December 1972 some 2,000 Americans traveled to the PRC, among their number influential U.S. Congressmen and journalists, as well as scholars, scientists, and students.

The "Status of Taiwan" and Treaty Obligations

For the rest of the world, it was an odd sight: American table tennis players enjoying "friendly" matches and sightseeing tours in China even as American soldiers were fighting and dying in neighboring Vietnam. But the ROC had too much at stake to be long captivated by this bizarre spectacle. Its very existence was soon to be called into question.

On April 28, 1971, Charles W. Bray, press officer of the Department of State, publicly urged the ROC government to enter into direct negotiations with the Peking regime. "In our view," Bray said, "sovereignty over Taiwan and the Pescadores is an unsettled question, subject to future international resolution." While Nixon backpedaled at a press conference held the following day, saying that it was "completely unrealistic" to expect the ROC and the Chinese Communists to settle their differences by negotiation, he did not retract Bray's statement that the status of Taiwan was an "unsettled question."

The damage was done. Taipei buzzed with rumors about why a representative of the U.S. government had raised questions about the status of Taiwan. Most people came to believe that the U.S., in calling the sovereignty of the ROC government over Taiwan into question, had buckled under to a secret Communist demand.

Legally and historically, there was absolutely no uncertainty surrounding Taiwan's status. The island had been restored to the ROC on October 25, 1945, and had since been administered as one of its provinces. President Truman had declared on January 5, 1950, that the

---

[22]   U.S. Department of State, *Bulletin*, Vol. LXLV, No. 1668, June 14, 1971, p. 767.

purpose of the Cairo Declaration of December 1943 was to return to China the territory seized by Japan, including Formosa, and that the Potsdam Proclamation of July 1945 was designed to accomplish this. This position was accepted by Japan when it signed its peace treaty with the Allied Powers on September 8, 1951. Three years later, in 1954, the ROC and the U.S. had signed a mutual defense treaty in which the word "territory," as applied to the ROC, was considered by the two sides to refer to Taiwan and the Penghu Islands.[23]

Underlining the importance that the ROC attached to relations with the U.S.—especially now that its huge ally seemed to be calling the fundamentals of this relationship into question—Ambassador Chow was recalled from Washington in April to succeed Wei Tao-ming as Minister of Foreign Affairs. A new Ambassador to the U.S., James Chien-hung Shen, was appointed and presented his credentials to Nixon on May 18, 1971.

Meanwhile, the Ministry of Foreign Affairs in Taipei did not let Nixon's efforts to woo Peking pass unnoticed. Lifting the trade embargo, commented a foreign ministry spokesman, was like using wood to put out a fire. It would strengthen the hand of the Chinese Communists, fill them with *hubris*, and lead to more acts of aggression. When some in Taiwan suggested that the ROC should be more flexible in its foreign policy, even attempting to win over nations in the enemy camp, this was immediately rejected by the government. The ROC would never enter into talks with the Communists or otherwise compromise its principles.

The worrisome new drifts in U.S. policy elicited a strong reaction from President Chiang himself. On June 15, 1971, he delivered a hard-hitting speech, entitled "The Stand of our Nation and the Spirit of Our People," to the National Security Council of the ROC government. Some countries were myopic, he told his audience. Seduced by the prospect of short term advantages, they became irrational and cast their honor aside. "These nations talk of peace but actually are engaging in actions which destroy peace," Chiang said. "We are checkmating the Chinese

---

[23] Ministry of Foreign Affairs, *Treaties Between the Republic of China and Foreign States, 1927-1961* (Taipei: Commercial Press, 1963), pp. 824-827.

Communists. The destiny of Asia hinges on our efforts. No one can take our place, change us, or shake us in this vital stand."[24]

When asked by CBS journalist Morley Safer if he thought that the U.S. had stabbed China in the back, Chiang answered: "Traditional Chinese philosophy teaches us that in dealing with friends we should be loyal and faithful. In all of our relations with friendly nations, we have been strictly adhering to these principles of loyalty and faithfulness. Of course, we expect our friends to do the same to us."[25]

That October, on the occasion of the 60th anniversary of the founding of the Republic of China, yet another emissary of Nixon arrived in the ROC. Special Presidential Envoy Ronald Reagan, then governor of California, came with "assurances of the continued relations between the Republic of China and the United States despite the American initiative towards Communist China. . . . We intend to continue honoring our treaty commitments for the security of our Asian allies, among which is the Republic of China. We believe the Republic of China will remain in the United Nations and we will bend every effort to see that is so."[26]

Back in Washington, however, the buzzword was "change." Asia had changed since the Korean War, and friendly relations with Communist China were now deemed extremely desirable. This attitude would soon have even more serious repercussions for the ROC.

Nixon's Visit to China and the Shanghai Communiqué

On July 15, 1971, Nixon stunned the world by announcing his plans to visit the PRC. Kissinger had just returned from a secret visit to Peking, he revealed, bearing an invitation from Chou En-lai, which he had accepted with pleasure. Nixon promised that, in seeking a new relationship with the Chinese mainland, old friends would not be sacrificed. His trip would be a "journey for peace—peace not just for the present but for future generations as well."

---

24 Government Information Office, *President Chiang Kai-shek's Selected Speeches and Messages in 1971* (Taipei: China Publishing Co., 1972), pp. 30-36.

25 Answers to Questions submitted by Morley Safer of CBS News, April 29, 1971. *Ibid.*, p. 21.

26 *China News*, Taipei, October 12,1971, p. 8.

The reaction in East and Southeast Asia was mostly negative. The ROC deemed the proposed visit "an unfriendly act," and lodged a formal protest. If Nixon's visit actually took place, commented Premier Yen Chia-kan on July 16, it would be very damaging. In Japan it was the "Nixon shock," and Foreign Minister Takeo Fukuda likened it to a stab in the back. Amid unprecedented economic prosperity, Tokyo began to chart a more independent course in foreign policy. Thailand, Vietnam, and the Philippines, among other countries in the region, privately expressed great alarm at Nixon's abandonment of his anti-Communist principles. "How far would the U.S.-China thaw go?" U.S. Asian allies wondered.

A few sought closer relations with the PRC, although most of the major Southeast Asian states remained wary. In the past, Peking had stepped up its assistance to Communist insurgents within Indonesia, the Philippines, and other Southeast Asian nations, at the very time that it was trumpeting its "friendship" for these countries.[27]   To many, neutrality now seemed a more viable option. Prime Minister Abdul Razak of Malaysia proposed that ASEAN (comprised of Indonesia, Malaysia, Singapore, the Philippines and Thailand) declare itself a neutral zone, free from the rivalries and interference of the big powers. This resulted in the Kuala Lumpur Declaration of November 27, 1971, which stated that the Asian states were "determined to. . . secure the recognition of the respect for Southeast Asia as Zone of Peace, Freedom and Neutrality, free from any form or manner of interference by outside powers."

The Soviet Union also expressed displeasure at Nixon's overtures, and Nixon went out of his way to reassure Moscow that the U.S. was not trying to pit the two Communist powers against each other. Kissinger publicly decried this approach as the "most foolish thing we could

---

[27] Communist China began providing assistance to the Malayan Communists after World War II and was still supporting a Communist insurgency in Sarawak in North Borneo in the early seventies. Peking was behind the abortive coup instigated by the Indonesian Communists in September, 1965, which resulted in the slaughter of many Indonesians of Chinese descent. The Philippines was grappling with a Maoist rebellion in the south in the 1970s spearheaded by the Maoist-inspired "New People's Army (NPA).

do."[28]   The proposed visit nevertheless created a new international configuration which, on its surface at least, was more unfavorable to the U.S.S.R. than the old had been. Uncertainty was injected into the strategic calculations of the Soviet leaders. Were Peking and Washington secretly conspiring against them? If World War III broke out, would they have to fight on two fronts? The Soviet Union reacted by launching a drive for increased power and influence in Asia. Already the chief source of war supplies for North Vietnam, North Korea, and India, it sought to draw closer to these and other neighbors of Communist China. It also encouraged India to occupy East Pakistan, later Bangladesh, in December 1971, reducing Pakistan, which was a major ally of the Chinese Communists, to a weak country.

Nixon justified his decision to go to Communist China on the grounds that the trip would help establish a "balance of power." "[W]e must remember that the only time in the history of the world that we have any extended period of peace is when there has been a balance of power," he posited. "[I]t will be a safer world and a better world if we have a strong, healthy United States, Europe, Soviet Union, China, Japan—each balancing the other, not playing one against the other, an even balance."[29]

Many were unconvinced. The five powers Nixon mentioned were anything but equal. Moreover, balance-of-power politics had only been successful when the majority of the states were prepared to form shifting coalitions to prevent any of their number from tilting the balance. This classic diplomatic game could best be played by autocratic regimes, whose decisions were unchecked by public opinion or parliaments. The final weakness of Nixon's formulation was that it meant the abandonment of the grand strategy, followed by the U.S. since the end of World War II, of encircling and containing the Soviet Union and, to a lesser extent, Communist China. No longer would Washington rely on firm alliances with its European and Asian partners to maintain absolute dominance. Instead, Washington would court, and be courted in turn by,

---

[28] Kissinger's interview with CBS News in February, 1973 is cited in "Worldgram," *U.S. News & World Report*, February 26, 1973, p. 2.

[29] G. W. Ball, "Who Balances Whom?" *Newsweek*, April 3, 1972, p. 52.

Moscow and Peking, maintaining only enough strength so that neither of the two could easily upset the balance.

The opening to China encountered other obstacles, among them a series of outrageous demands by the Chinese Communists. A thoroughly chastened Kissinger returned from his second trip to China in October 1971 to report that Chou had demanded a complete American withdrawal from Indochina as a condition of peace. What other demands had Peking made, the people on Taiwan wondered? Would Nixon use the ROC as a "bargaining chip" to ensure the success of his negotiations with the Chinese Communists?

The months leading up to Nixon's visit to China were difficult ones for Taiwan. Even before Air Force One landed in Peking the ROC had suffered a series of setbacks as a result of the new U.S. policy.

The Republic of China's Withdrawal from the U.N.

The first year of the Nixon administration saw no change in the long-standing U.S. policy of opposing the PRC's admission to the U.N. American policy on China in the U.N. would remain unchanged, reaffirmed Secretary of State Rogers on April 21, 1969, calling attention to the responsible and constructive role played by the ROC in the international community.[30]

The issue resurfaced the following year, given further impetus by the Canadian démarche towards the Chinese mainland. The two governments went on to establish relations on October 13, 1970, with Italy and Belgium, it was clear, soon to follow. Despite this incipient shift in the Western diplomatic stance toward the PRC, the General Assembly in 1970 again barred its entry. As usual, an American-backed "important question" resolution requiring a two-thirds majority for any change in the Chinese representation had passed handily, on a vote of 66 to 52 with 7 abstentions. The actual vote on the pro-Peking Albanian resolution was 51 in favor and 49 against with 25 abstentions, far short of the two-thirds majority Communist China needed.

But the momentum was in Peking's favor. On April 26, 1971, a U.S. presidential commission, headed by former U.S. Ambassador to the

---

[30] *China Yearbook 1969-1970*, p. 387.

U.N Henry Cabot Lodge, recommended to the White House that Communist China be admitted to the U.N., even though both the U.S. and that international body might find so doing "awkward and discordant." At the same time, the fifty-member commission advised that the continued U.N. membership of the ROC was imperative. Under no circumstances should the U.S. agree to the Nationalist government's expulsion. This position, which was in effect a "two-China" policy, came to be adopted by the Nixon administration.

Admission to the U.N. was a priority of Chou En-lai's foreign policy agenda, and during their July 1971 talks he pressed Kissinger hard on this subject. Kissinger revealed that, although the public stance of the Nixon administration was to oppose the PRC's admission, in fact it now intended to support Peking's application for entry into the U.N. and a seat on the Security Council. Kissinger went on to say that, while the U.S. would back the Nationalist government's effort to remain in the U.N., he "did not know" if this effort would succeed. What Nixon's chief foreign policy advisor intended to convey by this damaging admission is not clear, but Chou took it as an oblique signal that the U.S. would merely be "shadow boxing" when the question came up in the General Assembly, not fighting hard to prevent the ROC's expulsion.

The first public disclosure of this new policy came from Secretary of State Rogers on August 2. "The United States would support the seating of the People's Republic of China in the United Nations," Rogers announced, and on the question of China's seat in the Security Council "would abide by the majority vote of the members of the United Nations."

Then he made what can only be considered a major diplomatic blunder. Instead of vigorously asserting the ROC's right to keep its U.N. seat, Rogers said only that "the United States considered the expulsion of the Republic of China an important question which required a two-thirds majority vote of the General Assembly for passage." This seemed to suggest that the U.S. would not go all-out on behalf of its long-time ally, but merely fight a rearguard action.

Sensing weakness, Peking responded on August 20 by denouncing Rogers's "two-China" policy. Unless Taiwan was expelled from the U.N., a Communist Chinese spokesman asserted, the PRC would not accept a seat.

Had Nixon at that point launched a vigorous campaign on behalf of the ROC, its seat in the U.N. might still have been saved. But it was not until September 15 that the U.S., without consulting its allies, declared its strategy: dual representation for China. Nationalist China would stay in the General Assembly as the representative of the "14 million persons" living in Taiwan. In return, the U.S. and its allies would vote to seat Communist China in the General Assembly as the representative of "more than 700 million persons" on the mainland and, more importantly, to assign to it China's permanent seat on the Security Council.

Two American draft resolutions were prepared. The first would seat Communist China in the United Nations as a permanent member of the Security Council. The second would save the ROC's membership in the General Assembly by treating the proposal for its expulsion as an "important question," requiring a two-thirds majority for passage.

Washington's long period of indecision alarmed its allies. Japan, in particular, hesitated to co-sponsor the "two-China" resolution until Rogers publicly warned that its failure to do so would be detrimental to the ROC's cause. Only on the eve of the 26th Session of the General Assembly, scheduled to convene on September 21 did the governments of Japan, Australia, and New Zealand announce they would co-sponsor the American resolutions.

On September 22, 1971, Australia, Costa Rica, Colombia, Japan, Liberia, the Philippines, and sixteen other states joined the United States in submitting the "important question" draft resolution, Resolution No. 1, which read as follows:

The General Assembly, recalling the provisions of the Charter of the United Nations, decides that any proposal in the General Assembly which would result in depriving the Republic of China of representation in the United Nations is an important question under Article 18 of the Charter.

The same day, a slightly different consortium of nations, including Australia, Chad, Gambia, Japan, Lesotho, New Zealand, Thailand, Uruguay, and other ten states, joined the United States in submitting the second American resolution, this one on "dual representation." Resolution No. 2 called upon the General Assembly to:

(1) affirm the right of representation of the People's Republic of China and recommends that it be seated as one of the five permanent members of Security Council; (2) affirm the continued right of representation of the Republic of China; and (3) recommend that all United Nations bodies and the specialized agencies take into account the provisions of this resolution in deciding the question of Chinese representation.[31]

An opposing resolution had been submitted by the Albanians on July 15, 1971. Co-sponsored by Algeria, Cuba and nineteen other African, Asian, and Eastern European states, it requested that the Secretary-General include on the agenda of the General Assembly an item it called the "Restoration of the lawful rights of the People's Republic of China in the United Nations."

As soon as the General Assembly convened, the Albanians moved to prevent debate of the U.S. Resolution No. 1. This was defeated on September 24 by a vote of 65 to 47, with 15 abstentions. This result encouraged many to believe that the U.S. would be successful in its effort to defend the ROC's seat. The American strategy was simple: the passage of Resolution No. 1 would effectively defeat the Albanian resolution, giving the American proposals priority. The passage of Resolution No. 2 would assure the continued membership of the ROC, and also seat the PRC.

The ROC's diplomatic representatives worked around the clock to shore up the support of friendly nations. Special envoys from the ROC, including Vice Foreign Ministers Yang Hsi-kun and Tchen Hiong-fei and Ambassador Hsueh Yu-chi, arrived in New York to add their efforts to those of their colleagues already stationed there. Within the U.S., the Committee of One Million Against the Admission of Red China to the United Nations, headed by Walter Judd and Lee Edwards, redoubled its efforts. The Committee published pamphlets by the hundreds of thousands, mailed newsletters to its tens of thousands of supporters, and ran advertisements in some of America's largest newspapers.[32] While its

---

[31] For details see *China Yearbook 1971-1972*, pp. 360-362.
[32] The Committee of One Million re-organized itself as the Committee for a Free China in Washington on February 15, 1972. The Chairman was Walter H. Judd

representatives and supporters endorsed the U.S. effort to protect the ROC's U.N. membership, the ROC government remained steadfastly on record as opposing a "two-China" policy.

Then came an unexpected blow to the ROC's cause. Kissinger again went to Peking. Chou had cleverly scheduled the visit to coincide with the U.N. vote, hoping thus to sway nations still in the undecided column. He even went so far as to delay Kissinger's planned departure from Peking by two days just in case a "slip-up" occurred. Kissinger's presence in the PRC's capital during the crucial hours before the final vote on Resolution No. 1 spoke volumes, effectively undercutting the efforts of American Ambassador to the U.N. George Bush.

The drive to seat the PRC as China's sole representative had, by now, built up such momentum that it was virtually unstoppable. Nations traditionally friendly to the ROC, such as Turkey and Iran, indicated that they would switch their votes. Even Asian countries strongly opposed to the PRC like the Philippines, Thailand, and Malaysia began reconsidering their policies.

After a week of debate, the General Assembly voted on U.S. Resolution No. 1 on October 25. The "important question" resolution was defeated by a narrow margin. The vote was 55 in favor to 59 against, with 15 abstentions and 2 absentees. The subsequent vote on the Albanian Draft Resolution—76 in favor, 35 against, 17 abstentions, and 3 absentees—was not even close, as many nations switched their vote to avoid offending the newest member of the U.N. Security Council. The ROC delegation walked out of the General Assembly, and the Communist Chinese delegation was seated in its place. The belated U.S. effort to help the ROC retain its U.N. membership had failed.

At a hastily convened press conference, ROC Foreign Minister Chow Shu-kai announced that the ROC had "decided to withdraw from the organization which it helped establish." In a prepared statement, he elaborated the Nationalist government's position:

---

and the Executive Secretary was Lee Edwards. The members of its steering committee included Paul H. Douglas, H. Alexander Smith, Joseph C. Grew, Charles Edison, Francis E. Walter, Anna Chen Chennault and others. The International Council of Christian Churches led by Dr. Carl McIntyre also organized several parades in Washington, D.C. in support of the ROC's U.N. effort.

For twenty-six years the Republic of China has faithfully discharged its Charter obligations. It has played not a negligible part in the decolonization process. It has cooperated with other members of the United Nations in the economic, social, cultural, educational and health fields. No one can gainsay the fact that the Republic of China has been a loyal member of the Organization. To deny the Republic of China of its rightful position in the United Nations, is to violate the Charter and negate the noble and sacred purposes upon which the United Nations was founded.

Those who advocate the seating of the Chinese Communist regime base their argument on what was regarded as realism. But the existence of the criminal Communist regime is one thing and the acceptance of that criminal regime as a member of the United Nations is quite another. The purpose of the United Nations is to suppress the crime of aggression and not to allow the aggressor to get away with impunity, still less to bow before force and thus forfeit its own raison d'être.

The Chinese Communist regime is oppressive at home and aggressive abroad. It has publicly proclaimed that it intends to "thoroughly reform" the United Nations or else to establish a new one. Once it has been seated both in the General Assembly and on the Security Council, it will surely transform the United Nations into a Maoist front and battlefield for international subversion. It will use the veto as an instrument for the protection of its subversive activities and for undermining the Western democracies. The United Nations would then be a center for the promotion of war and aggression.

There are those who think the participation of the Communist regime will enhance the prospect of peace. The idea is to subject the aggressive regime to the discipline of international public opinion. This is dangerous nonsense. It is like tying a tiger with a straw rope. The Republic of China cannot let the majestic headquarters of the United Nations become the place where justice and law yield to lawlessness and injustice. It has therefore decided to withdraw from the Organization of which it was one of the founders. The responsibility for this state of affairs must be borne by those who have sacrificed the lofty principles of the Charter on the altar of expediency. They will have to answer to the judgment of history and posterity.

The Government of the Republic of China wishes to take the opportunity to express its profound appreciation of the support given to it by friendly governments during the past twenty-two years. It can assure them that it will continue to struggle for the realization of the purposes and principles enshrined in the Charter.

The Government of the Republic of China, in order to realize the aspiration of the Chinese people, will struggle on until the Communist regime is overthrown. The admission of the Communist regime to the United Nations will in no way affect the determination of my Government to liberate the Mainland.

The Republic of China is fighting for law and justice. It has done so many times before, often without outside aid. It is our firm conviction that right will eventually triumph over might and justice will sooner or later prevail over injustice.[33]

The following day, President Chiang issued a message of encouragement to the Chinese people at home and abroad. "Neither the government of the Republic of China nor the Chinese people," he said, "will ever recognize the validity of an illegal resolution adopted by the current United Nations session in flagrant violation of the provisions of its own Charter. . . . The Chinese Communists may occupy the Mainland for the present. But the Government of the Republic of China, with its base in Taiwan, Penghu, Kingmen and Matsu, is the true representative of the 700 million Chinese on the Mainland, expressing their common will, heeding their anguished outcries and inculcating within them a maximum of courage and hope with which to struggle against the violence of the Mao regime and win back their human rights and freedom."[34]

The streets of Taipei were calm, but the people were coldly angry at the callous way their country had been unjustly deprived of an important part of its international representation. Nor was this the last shock they were to face. Just a few months later, in January 1972, rumors began circulating in Washington and Taipei that the Sino-American Mutual Defense Treaty of 1954 would expire in 1974 and would not be renewed.

---

[33] *Ministry of Foreign Affairs Weekly*, Taipei, No. 1071, November 2, 1971, pp. 1-4.

[34] For the full text of President Chiang's message on the Republic of China's Withdrawal from the U.N. see *Issues & Studies*, Taipei, Vol. 8, No. 3, (December 1971), pp. 2-5.

On January 31 State Department press officer, Charles W. Bray, was at pains to point out that the treaty had no expiration date. It would continue in force indefinitely. "The American position," said Bray, "is that eventually the Red Chinese and the Nationalists must settle their own dispute. If and when such a settlement is made, there would be little reason for a U.S.-Taiwan security treaty. Until then it is needed."[35]

The rumors were not entirely groundless, however. As it later became known, in exchange for finalizing his invitation to visit the Chinese mainland, Nixon had at about that time agreed to reduce the American military presence on Taiwan. Actually, this presence was already minimal, consisting of a military advisory group, the Taiwan Defense Command, and a small U.S. Air Force operations unit. Nevertheless, it was further reduced.

Despite the feeling of betrayal in Taipei, Secretary of State Rogers, in his Foreign Policy Report to Congress of March 7, 1972, stated that relations between the U.S. and the ROC had continued to be close in 1971. The American effort to normalize relations with mainland China, Rogers said, "understandably caused concern and has been the major development affecting U.S. relations with Taipei." He noted that the U.S. had a commitment "to meet any external attack against Taiwan and the Pescadores."

The U.N. debacle aside, the fundamental American commitment to the ROC, a friendly government in the midst of remarkable social and economic progress, remained strong. In his eagerness to embark on a dialogue with Communist China, Nixon had not totally forgotten this long-time U.S. ally. He maintained diplomatic relations with the ROC, stood ready to fulfill U.S. treaty obligations for the defense of Taiwan, and continued to encourage private American investment in the island.

Nixon Goes to China

Nixon, long reviled as the leader of the Western imperialists, arrived in Peking on February 21, 1972. "Affairs in the world require consultations," explained Mao Tse-tung to his puzzled compatriots.

---

[35] "Official Size-up of the World's Top Problems," *U.S. News & World Report*, February 14, 1972.

"They must not be decided by the two big powers." During the course of his week in the PRC, Nixon spent 15 hours in meetings with Communist leaders—one hour with Mao on the day of his arrival, and more than 14 hours with Chou En-lai. It was the first time that an American President had ever negotiated on the soil of a country with which the U.S. did not have diplomatic relations.[36]

The meetings, intended to bridge the vast differences in outlook between the U.S. and the PRC, did not succeed. In the end, these differences were acknowledged, defined, and catalogued, but they were not bridged. The resulting communiqué, issued in Shanghai on February 27, was notable for its dearth of delicate diplomatic phrasings. Nixon and Chou exchanged their views on the international situation "candidly" in "earnest, extensive and frank" discussions. "The United States supports individual freedom and social progress for all the peoples of the world," the Shanghai Communiqué read, "free of outside pressure or intervention. . . . No country should claim infallibility and each country should be prepared to re-examine its own attitudes for the common good. The United States stressed that the peoples of Indochina should be allowed to determine their destiny without outside intervention; its constant primary objective has been a negotiated solution."

Even so, the Shanghai Communiqué must be judged a victory for Chou En-lai, and a defeat for Nixon. For Chou, while eight times reaffirming the PRC's "firm support" of its allies in his part of the Communiqué, would not allow Nixon to do the same. Unless Nixon committed himself to the eventual withdrawal of all American forces and military installations from Taiwan and Indochina, Chou threatened, there would be no joint communiqué. On this point, through a week of hard bargaining, the Communist Chinese stood firm. In the end Nixon and Kissinger blinked. On these points the Communiqué read:

> In the absence of a negotiated settlement the United States envisages
> the ultimate withdrawal of all U.S. forces from [Indochina],

---

36 Two American Vice Presidents, John Nance Garner in 1935, and Henry Wallace in 1944, made trips to China during their terms in office. General Ulyses S. Grant toured Peking, Shanghai, and Canton in 1879, two years after he left the presidency. President Eisenhower visited Taiwan in 1960. But no incumbent American President had ever set foot on the Chinese mainland.

consistent with the aim of self-determination for each country. . . . The
United States acknowledges that all Chinese on either side of the
Taiwan Straits maintain there is but one China and that Taiwan is a
part of China. . . . It reaffirms its interest in a peaceful settlement of
the Taiwan question by the Chinese themselves. With this prospect
in mind, it affirms the ultimate objective of the withdrawal of all U.S.
forces and military installations from Taiwan. In the meantime, it
will progressively reduce its forces and military installations on
Taiwan as the tension in the area diminishes.[37]

The Ministry of Foreign Affairs of the ROC was quick to denounce
the Shanghai Communiqué, on February 28 declaring "null and void any
agreement [between the U.S. and the PRC], published or secret, involving
the rights and interests of the government and people of the Republic of
China." As far as the "Five Principles of Peaceful Coexistence"
enunciated by Peking were concerned, these were merely a "smoke screen
emitted by the Chinese Communists to help them carry out their plan of
infiltration, subversion, and aggression against other countries. . . .
United front tactics lay behind the efforts of the Chinese Communists to
enter into trade, scientific, technological, cultural, sports, journalistic and
other contacts and exchanges with the United States. The invitation to
President Nixon to visit the Mainland was intended to drive a wedge
between the democratic nations and the United States."[38] The
government, then and later, ruled out any form of "coexistence" with the
PRC.

Stung by criticism from the right, Nixon hastened to reassure
congressional leaders upon his return to the U.S. on February 29 that he
was not abandoning the Republic of China. The Shanghai Communiqué
had contained no reference to the U.S. treaty commitment to Taiwan and
there had been "no secret deals of any kind." Putting the best face on the
situation, some Washington observers noted that subsequent American
pledges to abide by the U.S.-ROC mutual defense treaty had elicited no

---

[37] *U.S. News & World Report*, March 13, 1972, pp. 86-87. The real work of
negotiating was done by two men—Henry Kissinger and Chiao Kuan-hua, a deputy
foreign minister of the PRC and the man who led its first delegation to the U.N.
General Assembly in 1971.

[38] Press Release, Ministry of Foreign Affairs, Taipei, February 28, 1972.

protest from Peking. For the time being at least, they argued, Peking had accepted a continuing U.S. commitment to Taiwan.

Closer Ties Between America and Mainland China

After Nixon's visit, there was a period of rapid progress in the normalization of relations between the U.S. and the PRC. People-to-people exchanges were expanded, barriers to trade were removed, and official contacts were increased. To minimize opposition in the U.S. Congress, Peking invited both Democratic and Republican leaders, including Mike Mansfield, Hugh Scott, Hale Boggs, and Gerald Ford, to visit the Chinese mainland.

Nixon's trip had also made the PRC a hot travel destination. Thousands of Americans applied for tourist visas during 1972 and 1973, but Peking condescended to approve visits only for individuals of some influence or renown. Senators, congressman, scholars, journalists, and important businessmen headed the list.[39]

Nixon's most important initiative, one which was not mentioned in the Communiqué at all, was the establishment of a "communication belt" between the two countries. In March 1972 U.S. Ambassador Arthur K. Watson entered into talks with his Communist Chinese counterpart, Huang Chen, in Paris. Unlike the Warsaw talks, which saw little progress, these new discussions quickly produced agreements on travel, exchange programs, and trade procedures, as Huang sought to take advantage of the concessions that Nixon had made in Peking. In June 1972 Kissinger ventured to China for his fourth visit in less than a year.

The payoff for Peking was immediate. American communications technology enabled the PRC to dramatically expand its ability to talk and listen to the rest of the world. By the end of 1973 Peking had access to communications satellites which could reach every large nation and most smaller ones. Other links were established following the lifting of the 22-year-old ban on the travel of American aircraft and ships to the Chinese mainland on November 22, 1972, which would lead to the eventual

---

[39] The U.S. State Department estimated that some 1,500 Americans visited Mainland China in 1972. Perhaps twice that number had been granted visas by mid-1973. Only 200 Chinese from the PRC visited the U.S. during this same period of time.

establishment of regular air and sea services between the U.S. and the PRC.

Trade got off to a slower start. Since June 1971, when Washington removed a large number of items from its embargo list, the only sizable American sales to Mainland China had been a $29 million deal for a communications satellite station in Peking by RCA Corporation and 10 Boeing 707 jetliners and associated equipment for $150 million.

1972 had been the year of Richard Nixon, a year in which the U.S. President extended his authority at home and his power abroad with each successive victory. Elected to a second term in the White House by a landslide, beholden to nobody, Nixon stood at the pinnacle of his power when he gave his second Inaugural Address on January 20, 1973:

> This past year saw far-reaching results from our new policies for peace. By continuing to revitalize our traditional friendships, and by our missions to Peking and Moscow, we were able to establish the base for a new and more durable pattern of relationships among the nations of the world. Because of America's bold initiatives, 1972 will be remembered as the year of the greatest progress since the end of the World War II toward a lasting peace in the world. . . . We shall respect our treaty commitments. We shall support vigorously the principle that no country has the right to impose its will or rule on another by force. We shall continue, in this era of negotiation, to work for the limitation of nuclear arms, and to reduce the danger of confrontation between the great powers. We shall do our share in defending peace and freedom in the world.[40]

The Establishment of Liaison Offices

On February 4, 1973, Democrat Senator Henry M. Jackson, seconded by Republican Senator Edward Brooke, publicly urged the U.S. to sever diplomatic relations with the ROC and recognize Communist China "without delay." The Nixon administration responded that such a step was premature, especially in view of U.S. commitments to the ROC,

---

[40] *American News Digest* (Maseru: U.S.I.S.), Vol. 5, No. 22, (January 29, 1973), pp. 1-5.

but there were soon indications that some in the administration did not view that particular "obstacle" as insurmountable.

Kissinger paid his fifth visit to Peking in February 1973 to secure Communist China's cooperation in reaching a cease-fire in Vietnam, and incidentally to nudge forward the normalization of relations. With the end of the Vietnam War in sight, and bilateral ties proliferating, Peking was ready to move forward. Strengthening ties with the U.S. would provide valuable insurance against Soviet pressure. As a goodwill gesture, Peking agreed during Kissinger's visit to release three Americans—two American pilots who had strayed across the PRC border and been shot down, and a CIA agent who had languished in Communist Chinese jails since 1952.

The joint communiqué that resulted from this visit on February 22 contained startling news. "The two sides agreed that the time was appropriate for accelerating the normalization of relations," it read. They would "broaden their contacts in all fields" and, "in the near future, each side would establish a liaison office in the other's capital.[41] The new liaison offices, it was soon clear, would have virtually all the plenipotentiary powers of regular embassies. They would be able to promote trade relations, arrange cultural exchanges, maintain code communications, and present formal and informal messages to their host governments. As German Chancellor Willy Brandt was fond of remarking, "It is not what is on the label but what is inside the bottle that counts."

The triangular relationship that Nixon had been angling to establish was finally taking shape. Peking and Washington had different views on the issue of Taiwan, Kissinger stated upon his return to the U.S., but Peking understood that the U.S. would continue to maintain diplomatic relations with the ROC. The PRC's willingness to compromise on this critical point testified to its eagerness to improve relations with the U.S. In the past, Communist China had refused to station its diplomats in capitals where the ROC enjoyed diplomatic recognition.

---

[41] For details see W. L. Chu, "A Survey of New Developments in Peiping-Washington Relations," *Issues and Studies*, Taipei, Vol. 9, No. 7, (April 1973), pp. 2-5.

The Nationalist government, fearing that formal diplomatic ties between the U.S. and the PRC were just around the corner, was not mollified. It repeated on February 23, 1973, what it had said earlier, namely, that it considered "null and void any agreement which had been reached between the United States and the Chinese Communist regime, because the regime now occupying the Chinese mainland is a rebel group, having no right whatsoever to represent the Chinese people." The announcement concerning the "so-called liaison offices," it continued, "contravenes the wishes of the Chinese people. The Government of the Republic of China hereby reiterates its firm and resolute position set forth in the statement of February 17, and 28, 1972. [The ROC government is] the legitimate government elected the people of China in accordance with the Constitution. . . any move taken by the United States and the Chinese Communist regime shall under no circumstances affect [its] firm stand. . . to fight against communism and to recover the Chinese mainland.[42]

This protest was swallowed up in the excitement surrounding the U.S.-PRC Detente like a stone thrown into the ocean. Nixon announced on March 15 that the first head of the Liaison Office in Peking would be David K. E. Bruce, a veteran American diplomat. Alfred Lee S. Jenkins and John H. Holdridge were appointed as his deputies.[43]

Feelings in Taipei ran high against this American action, and ROC Ambassador to Washington, James C. H. Shen, was recalled to Taipei for consultations. In Washington, Congressmen Trent Mott, Edward J. Derwinski, Robert L. F. Sikes, Bill Chappell, Dan Daniel and others, on May 8, 1973, requested a special order to discuss the matter in the House of Representatives. A bipartisan group of seventy congressmen stressed the necessity for continued American support of the ROC. A demonstration against the establishment of the liaison offices drew some 700 Chinese and American participants to D.C. streets on May 13, 1973.

---

[42] Press Release, Ministry of Foreign Affairs, Taipei, February 23, 1973.

[43] Bruce, then 75, had helped to create the Office of Strategic Services, the forerunner of the CIA, in Europe during World War II. He had served as Ambassador to France, Germany, and Great Britain, and more recently as the chief delegate to the Paris peace talks with North Vietnam in 1970-1971. "We called him out of retirement," Nixon explained, "because I thought it was very important to appoint a man of great stature to this position."

David Bruce, before leaving Hong Kong for Peking on May 14, stated that his goal would be to "try to foster friendship between the citizens of China and the United States—a traditional goal" he noted, "that had been interrupted by almost a generation." He assumed that "in the course of time" the U.S. mission would be upgraded to full embassy status.[44]   Two weeks after the U.S. Liaison Office opened its doors in Peking, on May 30, 1973, the PRC opened its Liaison Office in Washington, D.C., Huang Chen, one of Communist China's most senior diplomats, was appointed to head the office and Han Hsu became his deputy.[45]   Hoping to profit from closer U.S.-PRC ties, a group of American business executives set up a National Council for U.S.-China Trade. The group, which included David W. Packard, who served in the Nixon's Defense Department, had been assured of the President's support for their initiative.[46]

Had America's improved ties with the PRC given it an edge in the ongoing superpower rivalry with the Soviet Union, or had the all-too-obvious Vietnam syndrome so sapped its international resolve that a rapprochement with Peking was necessary to stave off further Soviet advances in Asia? As long as the Soviets and the Chinese Communists remained implacably hostile, the new triangular relationship seemed to work in Washington's favor. But numerous concessions of both principle and practice had been necessary to its establishment. Nixon had made a pact with a lesser devil in order to constrain a greater one.

To be sure, the United States and Communist China in 1973 seemed to have more interests in common than not, particularly in the Western Pacific region. While Peking objected in principle to the dozens of U.S. military bases around the world, it tacitly conceded the necessity for a

---

[44]   An AP May 14 cable from Hongkong, *China News*, Taipei, May 15, 1973.

[45]   Huang Chen, then 64, was one of Communist China's senior diplomats. He had served as ambassador to Hungary, Indonesia, and France. Han Hsu, who later became the PRC's representatives in the U.S., was at the time director of protocol in Peking's foreign office.

[46]   The National Council for U.S.-China Trade was established on Washington on May 31, 1973. Mike Blomfield of the Westinghouse Corporation was elected chairman, while David Rockefeller of Chase Manhattan Bank and David W. Packard of Hewlett-Packard Corporation were elected vice-chairmen. The council set up its own Trade Liaison office in Peking to facilitate contact between American businessmen and Communist Chinese trade representatives.

continued American military presence in Japan for the same reasons that it accepted the major American presence in Western Europe. Once the Vietnam cease-fire was signed, Communist China even welcomed the American decision to retain a military presence in Thailand. Were America to precipitously withdraw, Peking feared, Soviet encroachments would surely follow. And the Soviet Union was by far the more dangerous adversary, since its power was on the ascendant, while the U.S. was in irreversible decline. Or so Peking thought.

China watchers argued that, with the PRC's political economy and diplomacy in total disarray after the chaotic Cultural Revolution, a detente with the United States offered a number of advantages. It brought Peking's international isolation to an end. It raised the prospect of American technical assistance for Peking's fourth and fifth five-year plans. Most importantly, it effectively neutralized the growing military threat from the Soviet bear.

But Peking's aims were not merely defensive in character. The Chinese Communists hoped to utilize the contradictions which divided their principal enemies, Washington and Moscow, to take the diplomatic offensive in the two so-called "intermediate zones." The "First Intermediate Zone," as defined by the Communist Chinese, were Afro-Asian and Latin American developing countries. The "Second Intermediate Zone" consisted of second-echelon capitalist countries such as Great Britain, France, Australia, Canada, and Japan."[47] What many in the West took to be a softening of Peking's anti-capitalist attitudes was in reality deliberate deception. Peking had adopted a "two-faced revolutionary policy"—one face for the Americans and one face for the Soviets—designed to intensify the struggle between the two "enemies of the people of the world," that is, the two superpowers. Peking's "smiling diplomacy" represented only a shift in tactics, not a change in heart. Mao Tse-tung still dreamed about a world revolution that would "bury" imperialism for all time.

Peking's new tactics produced both gains and losses during the early seventies. In all, diplomatic relations were established or restored with 35 nations in Europe, Asia, Africa, and the Americas. Many Asian nations, taking their cue from the United States and interested in trade,

---

[47] *People's Daily* editorial, January 21, 1964.

set out to improve relations with their giant neighbor. Only India and Singapore remained standoffish, India because of its recent, unhappy experience with Communist Chinese aggression, Singapore because its feared subversion among its largely Chinese population.

The PRC had a more difficult time making headway in Africa. It had earlier supported radical revolutionary movements throughout the continent, making enemies of the heads of many independent African states. At the same time, the ROC had won many friends through its economic assistance programs. Under the imaginative and energetic leadership of Vice Foreign Minister Yang Hsi-kun, Taipei sent 2,000 agricultural technicians and other experts to various African countries from the late fifties onwards, helping them to become self-sufficient in food production.

To overcome the resistance of African states, Communist China began practicing dollar diplomacy on a massive scale in Africa. Its aid budget for 1972 came to an incredible 0.33 per cent of its total annual GNP. By December 31, 1972, the number of African states which recognized the PRC had doubled to 31. Worldwide, the PRC had diplomatic relations with 94 countries recognized by the end of 1972.

Peking's attempt to play the Americans against the Russians was not well received in the Communist world, however. Reflecting Soviet fears, Czechoslovakia, Hungary, Bulgaria, and other states criticized the PRC for its detente with the NATO powers.[48]

Communist China also turned its deceptively smiling face toward Nationalist China. No longer did Communist broadcasters angrily shout that the island of Taiwan would be "liberated" by force. Instead they spoke of "peaceful negotiations between the Kuomintang and the Chinese Communist Party" resulting in "the peaceful reunification of the motherland." Now that the U.S. was no longer a reliable ally of the Nationalist government, the broadcasts implied, the island had better make its separate peace with the Mainland. While some overseas Chinese, unfamiliar with duplicitous "united front tactics," were swayed

---

[48]   See M. H. Yao, "The Changing Foreign Policy of the Chinese Communists," *Issues & Studies*, Taipei, Vol. 9, No. 3, (December 1972), pp. 49-62.

by this propaganda, few in Taiwan gave it any credence.[49]   "We in Taiwan will never allow ourselves to be deceived by the Chinese Communist united front tactic of 'peaceful negotiation'," Premier Chiang Ching-kuo remarked on numerous occasions. "We learned the hard way and paid a heavy price for our past negotiations with them."

Chinese refugees continued to pour into Hong Kong, despite Peking's efforts to seal the border. In 1972 alone an estimated 28,500 refugees crossed the border into the colony. A sizable number of these refugees were later resettled in Taiwan with the help of the Free China Relief Association headed by Ku Cheng-kang. Altogether, the Association had helped 256,258 Chinese find a new home on the island, including 55,071 from Hong Kong and 30,102 from South Vietnam.

II. TRYING YEARS FOR THE REPUBLIC OF CHINA

Diplomatic Activities of the Republic of China

The early seventies were trying years for the Republic of China. The U.N. withdrawal, Nixon's visit to Peking, Japan's recognition of the PRC, and the loss of embassies and diplomatic missions in over a dozen countries around the globe all cut deeply. Friends of the ROC suggested that its policy of breaking off relations with any country that established diplomatic ties with the Peking regime was too inflexible. The national interest of the ROC would be better served, they argued, by compromise. This way, the ROC's membership in the U.N. and its specialized agencies could have been saved, and bilateral relations with many friendly countries preserved. Others urged that the ROC give up all hope of recovering lost territory and make its own way in the world, declaring itself independent of the Chinese mainland.

During this difficult time, the people of the ROC bore themselves well. They took to heart the traditional admonitions contained in President Chiang's exhortation of June 15, 1971: "Don't be anxious in times of adversity." "Be resolute with dignity and self-reliant with

---

[49] For details see C. T. Wu, *Mao's United Front and China's Reunification* (Taipei: Current Event Weekly Inc., 1972).

strength." When the U.N. blow fell in October 1971 the free Chinese were ready. There was dismay but no despair. Indignation was followed not by outburst but by a renewed sense of national purpose. There was, the people realized, no reason for panic. The ROC could not be conquered—the Chinese Communists were not strong enough for that— nor would it be sold out. The people of Nationalist China would control their own destiny.

Towards the U.S.-PRC rapprochement, the people of the ROC maintained a certain degree of cynicism. The general attitude was that the Metternichean game of choosing between friendly and malevolent dictatorships could only disguise, not replace, the fundamental confrontation between the superpowers. The ideological and systemic chasm between the Free World and the Communists was too deep to be papered over with alliances of convenience.

The Nationalist government responded to these diplomatic setbacks by redoubling its efforts to cooperate with friendly nations. Though given the cold shoulder by the Nixon administration, the strengthening of its overall relations with the U.S. remained a paramount foreign policy goal. The mutual defense treaty which united the two countries, in order to be efficacious, had to be backed by a mutual resolve to enforce its provisions. On this point, however, the evidence was at best ambiguous.

While Nixon averred that he intended to fulfill all U.S. security commitments to the ROC, his actions sometimes suggested otherwise. After reassuring Vice President Yen Chia-kan on January 5, 1973, of his intention to continue diplomatic relations with the ROC, for instance, his "State of the World" report to Congress, issued five months later on May 3, made no mention of this commitment.[50] Later that month, Senator Mike Mansfield caused further shudders in Taipei by declaring that "Treaties are not chiseled in stone; much less are executive agreements. The defense treaty with the Republic of China on Taiwan obviously

---

[50] Yen visited Washington twice in January 1973 to attend the funerals of former U.S. Presidents Harry S. Truman and Lyndon B. Johnson. His talks with Nixon and Agnew took place on January 5, 1973.

needs to be re-examined in the light of the President's initiative with regard to Peking."[51]

Despite his fondness for geopolitical schemes, Nixon realized that he could extend diplomatic recognition to Communist China only if he was ready to write off Taiwan. But this would require abrogation of the mutual security treaty, a step which would entail a long and fractious fight with Congress. What would such an attempt say to other U.S. allies in the region about American reliability? Then there was the domestic factor. Nationalist China, as Nixon well understood, enjoyed a deep reservoir of goodwill and sympathy among the American people. This is why the American President, even as he was preparing to visit Peking, spoke of loyalty to old friends and underlined the continued friendship of the U.S. with the Republic of China.

The Nationalist government understood that it had an American constituency as well. After Nixon's visit to Peking, it sought to build on this base, expanding its political, economic, and cultural relations with the American people. The Ministry of Foreign Affairs reinforced its Embassy staff and opened four new consulates across America.[52] The Chinese people themselves, ever more involved in the world of international trade and commerce, in many ways bolstered these official efforts.

Political Renovation and New Elections

Whatever reverses the ROC had suffered in the field of diplomacy were more than compensated for by its stunning economic growth and increasing political maturity. On March 21, 1972, the National Assembly elected Chiang Kai-shek to an unprecedented fifth term as

---

51 M. Mansfield, "Congressional Action Needed to Cement U.S.-China Relations," *Denver Post*, Denver, May 6, 1973.

52 The ROC maintained ten consulates general in the U.S. (New York, San Francisco, Chicago, Los Angeles, Boston, Honolulu, Houston, Seattle, Atlanta and Calexico) and two in American territories (Guam and American Samoa). It had information services in New York and in Los Angeles.

president.[53]   Here was a man who had been present at the birth of the Republic of China a half century before, who had played a formative role in the evolution of the first republic in the history of Asia. In the years following, he had led his country through foreign invasion and civil war. He had fought communism at every turn for more than four decades and had served in the ROC's highest office for more than twenty years. "For the remainder of my life," Chiang pledged to the Assembly on March 25, "I shall endeavor to do my very best to extinguish the evil sources of Maoist treachery and violence internally, while externally endeavoring to ensure welfare, peace and justice in free Asia." No one doubted that the acknowledged elder statesmen of the Free World meant exactly what he said.

But new faces were appearing in the ranks of senior government officials as well. A new premier, Chiang Ching-kuo, took over the Executive Yuan on June 1, 1972. Known for his ability and integrity, the younger Chiang immediately launched a campaign to simplify the structure of government, improve its efficiency, and improve its image among the people. On the most important domestic and foreign policy questions his views were virtually identical to those of his father. "In the past months, the world has witnessed many perverse changes," he told the Legislative Yuan on February 23, 1973. "These changes appear deceptive and treacherous to the eyes of a country which stands firmly on the principle of justice. The principles on which we insist are these: We shall always oppose the Communists and never compromise with them. We shall fight for democracy and freedom and never deviate from their course. In the light of such guidance, we shall never lose our sense of diplomatic direction or hesitate while complex changes are taking place in the world."

Premier Chiang's specific proposals for working around the ROC's increasing diplomatic isolation were two: 1.) Accentuate total diplomacy in every way so as to strengthen our relations with other free nations, promote friendships, and tie our strength with that of the free world. 2.) Take advantage of all favorable elements to promote our international

---

[53] Chiang was elected by the National Assembly for the first time in Nanking on April 19, 1948, then subsequently in Taipei on March 20, 1954, March 22, 1960, and March 21, 1966.

activities in order to further understanding and friendship in the world and smash the Chinese Communists' efforts to create a united front.[54]

In normal course of events, the governments of countries under great external stress tend to become politically authoritarian, even dictatorial. The Republic of China proved to be an exception to this rule, for as the seventies unfolded the people of Taiwan became increasingly scrupulous about the democratic process. The accent of the 1972 elections was on youth and education. Nearly 80 per cent of the newly elected representatives were under forty-five years of age.

During these years, economic development also continued apace. The economic policies adopted in the early sixties at the urging of the U.S. improved the climate for private investment and continued to pay dividends in terms of accelerated economic growth. The private sector was helped by such measures as a noninflationary fiscal and monetary policy, tax reform, unification of foreign exchange rates, liberalized exchange controls, establishment of a utilities commission and investment banking machinery, the sale of government enterprises to private owners, the encouragement of savings and private investment, the removal of subsidies, an increase in public utility rates, and liberalized trade regulations. Despite the loss of its U.N. seat, the economy of Taiwan continued growing at the record-setting clip of 10 per cent a year.

Taiwan's modern agricultural sector, in particular, was an important element in the Nationalist government's continuing efforts to win foreign friends and became a magnet for visitors from around the globe. Some 7,500 agricultural officials, scholars, technicians and farm leaders from Asia, Africa, Latin America, and Europe visited Taiwan during these years to participate in briefings and observation sessions arranged by the Joint Commission on Rural Reconstruction. An additional 3,000 agricultural technicians, most from Southeast Asian countries, underwent technical training through JCRR programs. A number of collaborative programs between the JCRR and the agricultural ministries of foreign countries sprang up as a result of these visits.

---

[54] Premier Chiang Ching-kuo's Report to the First Meeting of the 51st Session of the Legislative Yuan, February 23, 1973 (Taipei: Government Information Office, 1973), pp. 1-18.

Overseas Chinese also assisted the cause of Free China. Of the 15 million Chinese in Southeast Asia, a majority supported the ROC, pouring money into Taiwan's economy and sending their children to study there. Investment from overseas Chinese totaled $300 million by 1972, and by that year over 10,000 ethnic Chinese from Southeast Asia were studying in the island's universities.

With sustained growth in Taiwan's gross national product, per capita income climbing by 10 per cent or so a year, and private and semiofficial support from around the world, the ROC had weathered the storm of diplomatic derecognition. But there was more rough weather ahead.

14

THE PERIOD OF COOLING RELATIONS
1975-1979

I. FORD: LOW PROFILE RELATIONS WITH TAIPEI

During his first visit to Peking in 1972, Nixon reportedly told Mao Tse-tung and Chou En-lai that he would complete the process of the "normalization" of relations with the PRC in his second term. After handily winning re-election later that year, however, the unfolding Watergate scandal forced him to resign under threat of impeachment 18 months later. Gerald Ford, who had replaced Spiro T. Agnew as Vice President in 1973, became the thirty-eighth President of the United States.

Although time would reveal Nixon's successor a little more than a caretaker president, undertaking no major foreign policy initiatives during his brief 30 months in office, Ford's decision to retain Kissinger as Secretary of State initially caused concern in Taipei. Few doubted that the architect of Nixon's China policy would continue to work for closer relations with Peking. After all, Kissinger himself had assured the Chinese Communists during his November 1973 visit that, no matter what happened to the Nixon administration, the American rapprochement with Peking would continue. Not long after his reappointment by Ford, Kissinger headed back to the Chinese mainland once again in November 1974, angling for a breakthrough in Washington-Peking relations. But he was faced with the dilemma: How could he find a way of normalizing relations with Peking without totally abandoning Taiwan and the Mutual Security Treaty which bound it to the United States?

America's shifting China policy was disconcerting to Taipei, which wanted to leave no doubt where it stood on the question of relations with Peking. The ROC would never negotiate with the Chinese Communists, Premier Chiang Ching-kuo declared on January 1, 1974, going on to list four other absolutes:

> (1.) The democratic system of the Republic of China as established under Article 1 of the Constitution would never change. (2.) The overall goals of anti-Communism and national recovery of the Republic of China would never change. (3.) The Republic of China would always align itself with the democratic bloc. Its duty to uphold justice and its will to safeguard the peace of the world would never change. (4.) The resolute position of the Republic of China of never compromising with the Chinese Communist rebel group would never change.[1]

President Chiang died on April 5, 1975, and Vice President Yen Chia-kan assumed the presidency the following day as provided for by the constitution. Chiang Ching-kuo continued as premier. While deeply mourning the passing of their country's father-figure, the people of the ROC were reassured by the smooth transfer of power. Unlike the political turmoil which followed the death of Mao on the mainland, there would be no succession struggle in Taiwan. Chiang's state funeral was attended by dignitaries from around the world, including Nelson Rockefeller of the U.S., who came on Ford's behalf. He brought with him a message from the American president reaffirming U.S. support for the ROC.

Less than a week later, however, in his first "State of the World" address to Congress, Ford made no mention of this pledge, or of the Mutual Security Treaty. Rather, he declared that Sino-American relations were firmly fixed on the course established by the 1972 Shanghai Communiqué. Though there was no hint of any plans to extend

---

[1] Premier Chiang's Administrative Report to the 53rd Session of the Legislative Yuan, *Gazette of the Legislative Yuan* (Taipei: Legislative Yuan), Vol. 61, No. 78, p. 12.

diplomatic recognition to Peking any time soon, Ford left little doubt that he would like to accelerate the process of improving relations with the PRC. The ROC's Ministry of Foreign Affairs, anticipating Ford's visit to the PRC the following month, issued a statement on November 4, 1975.

The Government of the Republic of China has repeatedly made known its firm and resolute stand against the dealings between the United States Government and the Chinese Communist regime. The stand is hereby reiterated in regard to the forthcoming visit to the Chinese Mainland by President Gerald R. Ford of the United States of America. The Chinese Communist regime unconstitutionally seized the mainland by the use of force and has sustained itself in power by terror and repression. The ever-growing turmoil and unrest in many parts of the mainland clearly indicates the increasing resistance against the Chinese Communist regime by the masses, and the intensification of a general movement to overthrow the reign of tyranny. As friend and ally, the United States must not allow itself to be lured into doing anything prejudicial to the interests of the Republic of China and the Chinese people.[2]

Ford's Visit to Peking

Ford went to Peking in December 1975, more than a year after Chinese Communist leaders first invited him to visit. His PRC hosts were reportedly displeased when they discovered that he intended to visit Indonesia and the Philippines on the same trip, since this seemed to reduce the significance of his stopover in Peking, although they had little choice but to accept his travel plans.

In Ford's discussions with Chinese Communist leaders, they reportedly expressed the hope that the U.S. would consider using the Japanese formula, under which Washington would establish diplomatic relations with Peking while retaining nonpolitical ties with Taiwan through a quasi-official organization set up for this purpose. Kissinger himself lent credence to this report at his press conference of December 4, 1975, when, in response to a question about the future U.S.

---

[2]   Press Release No. 185, Ministry of Foreign Affairs, Taipei, November 4, 1975.

relationship with Taiwan, he had replied: "We will work out the modalities on the Japanese model over a period of time." This led reporters to ask if the U.S. government had decided upon the Japanese model, whereupon Kissinger became evasive. "I think that will have to be decided when the normalization in fact takes place," he responded. In the end, there was no normalization to be announced, at least not at that time.

Following Ford's trip, Philip Habib, Assistant Secretary of State for East Asian and Pacific Affairs, was dispatched to Taipei. The highest U.S. State Department official to visit the ROC since Marshall Green's stopover of March 1972, his presence was meant to reassure the Chinese people that the U.S. administration, though committed to improving relations with the Chinese Communists, would not abandon Taiwan. The discussions between Ford and Communist Chinese officials, according to Habib, had focused on the international situation rather than on bilateral relations. Washington and Peking were one in opposing hegemony—that is, the Soviet Union—but disagreed on many other issues, including the question of Korea. The question of when and how the U.S. government was going to normalize its relations with the Chinese Communists remained to be decided, and the U.S. government anticipated no dramatic developments in the near future. Whatever happened, Habib assured Taipei, "the U.S. government would act carefully and responsibly when it came to matters concerning the security, prosperity, and well-being of the Taiwan people." This was to remain the standard response of State Department officials to questions about Washington-Taipei-Peking relations until the eve of Carter's announcement of December 15, 1978.[3]

Most people on Taiwan took Ford's 1975 visit in stride, having resigned themselves to the geopolitical realities of the Sino-American relationship. The fear that the U.S. would simply dump Taiwan, which had been so prevalent at the time of Nixon's first visit, had dissipated. In its place was a growing sense of self-confidence. Even if they were abandoned by the U.S., people told each other, their island nation would not only survive, but prosper.

---

[3]   J. C. H. Shen, *The U.S. and Free China, How the U.S. Sold Out Its Ally* (Washington, D.C.: Acropolis Books Ltd., 1983), p. 199.

The principal reason for the people's newfound confidence was the island's burgeoning foreign trade, especially with the U.S. America had become Taiwan's largest trading partner, and two-way trade between the two countries was running at a level more than eight times that between the U.S. and China. There were other reasons as well, having to do with the widespread support that the ROC enjoyed in the U.S. A November 1975 Gallup poll revealed that no less 70 percent of the American people opposed recognizing China if this meant breaking diplomatic ties with Taiwan. And, on the eve of Ford's departure for Peking, almost half of the U.S. House of Representatives, some 210 out of 435 members, signed a resolution calling for the continued support of Taiwan. Most people on Taiwan were convinced by these sentiments that, even if the U.S. replaced its embassy with a liaison office, she would still stand by them if they were threatened.

Although Ford had not achieved the breakthrough in U.S.-PRC relations that he sought, the ROC was not in a position to capitalize on his failure. Its own relations with the U.S. seemed to be in a state of slow decline, with Washington taking an ever lower profile. The U.S. Congress in 1974 repealed the 1955 Formosa Resolution, with the apparent acquiescence of the State Department. Military aid to the ROC was terminated that same year. The withdrawal of American air force squadrons of C-130, KC-135 and F-4 fighter-bombers, which had begun in early 1972, was complete by June 1975. American forces in Taiwan, which had numbered 9,000 in 1972, were down to 1,100 by 1977. Perhaps most disturbing, no senior American officials had visited Taipei since the Shanghai Communiqué had been signed. The repeated requests of the ROC ambassador for such meetings in Washington had been uniformly denied.

One of the few bright spots in the U.S.-ROC relationship was the extension of the Sino-American Scientific and Technological Cooperation Agreement. The purpose of the agreement, first signed on January 23, 1969, was to facilitate contact and cooperation between scientists, engineers, scholars, and research institutes of the two countries. On January 23, 1975, Foreign Minister Shen Chang-huan and Ambassador Leonard Unger exchanged notes for the renewal of the pact for five more years.

Ford's December 1975 trip to Peking marked the high-water mark of his efforts to improve U.S.-PRC relations. The aftermath of Watergate and the debacle in South Vietnam, which occurred at the end of April 1975 proved major distractions. Moreover, he was afraid that recognizing the PRC might so anger the Soviets that a Strategic Arms Limitation Treaty (SALT) would be out of reach. By 1976 he was caught up in the presidential election campaign, and was reluctant to undertake any major initiative toward the PRC for fear of domestic criticism.

The leaders of the PRC, unimpressed by Nixon's successor, were also unwilling to move the relationship forward. They demanded diplomatic recognition on their own terms. They openly criticized American efforts to reach an arms control agreement with the Soviets, instead urging Washington to take a tougher line against Soviet "hegemony." The death of Chou En-lai in January 1976 and Mao Tse-tung in September of that year sent China into a major political convulsion, as the purge of the so-called "Gang of Four" the following month was made clear to the world.

II. CARTER: THE SEVERING OF DIPLOMATIC RELATIONS

Nationalist Chinese leaders greeted Jimmy Carter's ascension to the presidency with cautious optimism, hopeful that he would break with Nixon's policy. But Carter proved every bit as eager to play the "China card" as his predecessor had been. He lacked Nixon's skills as a strategist, however, and where China was concerned proved to be hopelessly naive. To make matters worse, Zbigniew Brzezinski, the chief architect of his foreign policy, nursed a personal, nationalistic grudge against the Soviet Union. Once installed as National Security Advisor, he abandoned the "balance of power" principle that had led Kissinger to keep Washington equidistant from both Moscow and Peking, tilting towards the latter.

For a time, other thorny foreign policy questions took precedence for the Carter administration. The first was Vietnam, but talks on establishing diplomatic relations stalled when Hanoi demanded extensive economic aid as a precondition. The second was the Panama Canal

Treaty, which involved the new president in a bruising political battle with the U.S. Senate, well as with Republican presidential hopeful Ronald Reagan. Stung by criticism that the Panama Canal turnover was a betrayal of the national interest, Carter put off the expected confrontation over China policy, much to the PRC's dismay.

The question of how to handle the break with Taiwan was a particularly thorny issue. Peking had always insisted that, upon the normalization of U.S.-PRC relations, Washington must derecognize Taiwan, terminate its military presence on the island, and abrogate the 1954 Mutual Security Treaty. Carter was ready to take the first two steps, but the third posed a problem. If the U.S. unilaterally abrogated these defense commitments, with no reciprocal pledge from the PRC to avoid the use of force, U.S. security arrangements with Japan, South Korea, and the Philippines might be called into question.

In an effort to resolve this difficulty and move toward full relations, Carter announced that he was dispatching Secretary of State Cyrus Vance to Peking. This move generated a firestorm of criticism from Chinese in the United States and Taiwan and the White House, the State Department, and the U.S. Senate was deluged with letters, telegrams and phone calls voicing opposition. At the last minute, Carter changed the purpose of the Vance trip from "negotiation" to "exploration."

Secretary of State Cyrus Vance arrived in Peking on August 22, 1977, for three days of "exploratory talks." In sessions with Premier Hua Kuo-feng, Vice-Premier Teng Hsiao-ping, and Foreign Minister Huang Hua, he proposed that normalization be modeled on the Japanese formula. The U.S. and Peking would establish full diplomatic relations, with the U.S. allowed to maintain an informal liaison office in Taiwan. This ostensibly private mission and its ROC counterpart in Washington would be staffed by "retired" diplomats empowered to conduct diplomatic, economic, and cultural affairs. The U.S. was willing to abrogate the defense treaty it maintained with Taiwan, Vance told his hosts, but Peking must publicly pledge not to use force to "liberate" the island. The PRC refused.

Carter portrayed the failure of the Vance mission in the most positive terms possible. "I don't feel under any constraint in this instance to act precipitously just to get an agreement. . . . We do not intend to act hastily. When we do make a decision about China, if we make one of recognition, it is undoubtedly going to be well into the future and it will be based on what I consider to be in the interest of our country and one which I think the American people will support."[4]

Vice-Premier Teng Hsiao-ping took a more dour view of the visit, telling an AP correspondent on September 6, 1977, that Vance's trip had actually been a setback for the "normalization of relations." According to Teng, Vance had proposed upgrading the U.S. liaison office in Peking to embassy status while downgrading the U.S. embassy in Taipei to a liaison office. He had had no choice but to reject this proposal, Teng claimed, since it meant that government-to-government relations between Washington and Taipei would continue.

By the spring of 1978, with the passage of the Panama Canal Treaty alleviating his concern about a possible domestic political backlash, Carter felt strong enough to make another attempt. On April 26 the White House announced that Brzezinski would visit China the following month. The purpose of the trip, according to the announcement, was not to normalize relations, but to "consult" with the Chinese leadership on a broad range of issues. But, as subsequent developments were to prove, the understandings reached on this trip led directly to U.S.-PRC diplomatic relations later in the year.

Brzezinski, arriving in Peking on May 20, wasted no time in reassuring his hosts that the U.S. did not view its relationship with Peking merely as a tactical expediency, but as a component of a long-term strategy "to resist the efforts of any nation which seeks to establish global or regional hegemony. . . . Only those aspiring to dominate others have any reason to fear the further development of American-Chinese relations. . . . The President of the United States desires friendly relations with a strong China. He is determined to join you in overcoming the remaining obstacles in the way to full normalization of our relations within the framework of the Shanghai Communiqué. The United States has made up its mind on this issue."[5]

---

4   M. Schaller, *The United States and China in the Twentieth Century* (New York: Oxford University Press, 1990), pp. 203-204.
5   J. J. Cheng, ed., *R.O.C.-U.S.A. Relations, 1979-1989* (Taipei: Institute of American Culture, Academia Sinica, 1991), pp. 30-31.

Following the Brzezinski visit, a high-level U.S. government science and technology mission was dispatched to Peking to lay the ground for cooperative, scientific, and technological projects. A short time later, the Carter administration announced that it "will no longer object to sales of nonthreatening or 'defensive' arms to China by its NATO allies," although U.S. companies would still not be allowed to supply weapons to China.

In June, Carter told the Trilateral Commission, an influential foreign policy study group, that he intended to press for full diplomatic relations with Peking, although no deadline had been set for this step. He assured his audience that Taiwan's future would be safeguarded by three "conditions" which Peking had to meet prior to the establishment of relations: 1.) U.S. trade and aid to the ROC would continue, and would include military assistance. 2.) The U.S. embassy in the ROC would be closed. 3.) Communist China would make clear, through a formula yet to be agreed upon, that it would not use force in seeking to reunite Taiwan with the Chinese mainland. Only the third of these so-called "conditions" called for any compromise on Peking's part and, as events were later to demonstrate, even on this point Carter was to capitulate.

Nor was Carter any more forceful when, on September 19, 1978, he received Chai Tse-ming, who headed Peking's liaison office in Washington. The American president reportedly told Chai that, in the event of the normalization of relations, the U.S. would insist on maintaining commercial and cultural relations with Taiwan.

In early October 1978 the Carter administration picked January 1 of the following year as the target date for the normalization of relations with Peking. Leonard Woodcock, chief of the U.S. liaison office in Peking, entered into secret negotiations with Teng and made rapid progress. From the standpoint of the administration, there were two key questions to be answered—Would Peking agree to publicly pledge not to attack Taiwan? What would Peking's attitude be if the U.S. should insist on supplying Taiwan with defensive arms after recognition?

Teng refused Carter's request for a pledge, but promised not to contradict the U.S. president if he expressed his hope, or even expectation, that the Taiwan question would be resolved peacefully. Peking would publicly object, Teng said, if the U.S. insisted on continuing to sell arms to Taiwan, but added that this would not prevent the normalization of relations.

Carter accepted all of Teng's demands without much resistance, insisting only that he be allowed to abrogate the Mutual Defense Treaty properly by serving the required one-year notice. Teng accepted this condition in exchange for Carter's promise not to consider new arms sales to Taiwan during the one-year "extension" ending on December 31, 1979. This concession was made in secret, although it was later revealed in early 1979 during congressional hearings on the Taiwan Relations Act.

Teng received Woodcock on December 13 and told him that Peking was ready to normalize relations with the U.S. "on the basis of the American terms." The following day, acting on Carter's instructions, Woodcock made a last effort to secure Peking's agreement to continued U.S. arms sales to Taiwan. He was unsuccessful. On the morning of December 15, Brzezinski and Chai Tse-ming "agreed to disagree" on this issue.[6]

With the last obstacle thus removed, Carter impetuously decided to break the news that same day. A news conference was hastily scheduled for 9:00 p.m. that evening.

Carter began by reading a joint U.S.-PRC communiqué, the crux of which was that the U.S. recognized the government of the PRC "as the sole legal government of China" and that the two countries would "exchange ambassadors and establish embassies on March 1, 1979." The communiqué also reaffirmed the principles agreed on by the two sides in the Shanghai Communiqué and set out further points of agreement between the two countries: 1.) Both wish to reduce the danger of international military conflict. 2.) Neither should seek hegemony in the Asia Pacific region or in any other region of the world, and each is opposed to efforts by any other country or group of countries to establish such hegemony. 3.) Neither is prepared to negotiate on behalf of a third party or to enter into agreement or understanding with the other directed

---

6 Premier Hua Kuo-feng, at his press conference in Peking on December 16, 1978, insisted that Taiwan remained a part of China and that Peking firmly opposed the U.S. plan to provide defensive arms for the island. He acknowledged that Peking had endorsed the normalization deal with full knowledge that the United States would continue to make arms available to Taiwan.

at other states.   4.) The government of the United States of America acknowledges the Chinese position that there is but one China and that Taiwan is a part of China.   5.) Both believe that normalization of Sino-American relations is not only in the interest of the Chinese and American peoples but also contributes to the cause of peace in Asia and the world.

The only reference to the ROC in the communiqué was the following: "[W]ithin this context the people of the United States will maintain cultural, commercial, and other unofficial relations with the people of Taiwan." Nor was the U.S. statement, which Carter then went on to read, any more reassuring to the ROC. The U.S. government, it said, would notify Taiwan of its decision to terminate diplomatic relations as of January 1, 1979, and the Mutual Defense Treaty as of January 1, 1980. In the future the American people and the people of Taiwan would maintain commercial, cultural, and other relations without official government representation and without diplomatic relations. American laws and regulations would be readjusted wherever necessary to permit such non-governmental relationships to be continued. On the question of Taiwan's security, a subject on which Carter and his officials had spoken so eloquently and earnestly, the U.S. statement had only this to say: "The United States is confident that the people of Taiwan face a peaceful and prosperous future. The United States continues to have an interest in the peaceful resolution of the Taiwan issue and expects that the Taiwan issue will be settled peacefully by the Chinese themselves."

During the entire period leading up to the break in relations the Carter administration had kept the ROC entirely in the dark. Even the way that Carter finally broke the news to Taipei was arrogant and undiplomatic. United States Ambassador Leonard Unger called President Chiang Ching-kuo in the middle of the night of December 16, 1978, waking him at 2:30 a.m. to deliver the bad news.

Immediately after Carter's announcement, President Chiang issued a strong statement of condemnation:

The decision by the United States to establish relations with the Chinese Communist regime has not only seriously damaged the rights and interests of the government and people of the Republic of China, but also has a tremendously adverse impact upon the entire free world. For all the consequence that might arise as a result of this move, the Government of the United States alone should bear the full responsibility.

In the last few years, the United States Government has repeatedly reaffirmed its assurances to maintain diplomatic relations with the Republic of China and to honor its treaty commitments. Now that it has broken the assurances and abrogated the treaty, the U.S. Government cannot expect to have the confidence of any free nation in the future.

The United States, in extending diplomatic recognition to the Chinese Communist regime, which owes its very existence to terror and oppression, is not in keeping with her professed position of safeguarding human rights and strengthening the capabilities of democratic nations to resist totalitarian dictatorships. Such a move is tantamount to dashing the hopes of the hundreds of millions of people enslaved on the Chinese mainland for an early restoration of freedom. Viewed from whatever aspect, the move by the United States constitutes a great setback to human freedom and democratic institutions. It will be condemned by all freedom-loving and peace-loving people throughout the world. Recent international events have proven that the United States' pursuit of "normalization" with the Chinese Communist regime did not protect the security of free Asian nations.

It has further encouraged Communist subversion and aggressive activities and hastened the fall of Indochina into Communist hands. The Government and people of the Republic of China firmly believe that lasting international peace and security can never be established on an unstable foundation of expediency.

Regardless of how the international situation may develop, the Republic of China as a sovereign nation will carry on in the light of her glorious tradition by rallying all her people, both civilian and military, at home and abroad, to continue to make progress in social, economic, and political fields . . . Our late President Chiang Kai-shek had repeatedly instructed our people to be firm and strong and to face adversity with dignity and to press on till the task of national recovery and reconstruction is completed.

The Government and people of the Republic of China are determined to do their utmost in their fight against Communist tyranny and aggression and in cooperation with other free peoples and democratic countries. Henceforth, we shall remain calm and firm, positive and hard-working. All our citizens are urged to work fully with the Government, one heart and one soul, united and determined to tide over this difficult moment in our history. Under whatever circumstances, the Republic of China will neither negotiate with the Chinese Communist regime, nor compromise with Communism. Our nation will never give up its sacred dual task of recovering the Chinese mainland and delivering our compatriots there from Communist enslavement. This firm position of ours will remain unchanged for all time to come.[7]

Despite ROC protests, the die was cast. Washington had unilaterally terminated the diplomatic relations it had enjoyed with the ROC from 1928. A long-time and faithful ally was ditched for expediency.

To negotiate the form that unofficial relations between the ROC and the U.S. would take in the future, Carter sent a delegation, led by Undersecretary of State Warren Christopher, to Taipei on December 27, 1978. Other members of the delegation were Admiral Maurice Weisner, Commander-in-chief of U.S. forces in the Pacific; Herbert Hansell, Chief Legal Advisor of the State Department; Michael Armacost, Deputy Assistant Secretary of Defense; Dean Moran, Deputy Assistant Secretary of Commerce; John Cannon, a State Department spokesman; and Roger Sullivan, Deputy Assistant Secretary of State for East Asian and Pacific Affairs.

Reflecting the mood of betrayal in Taipei, Christopher and his party were greeted by angry demonstrators upon their arrival. A few of the more agitated demonstrators even tried to smash the windows of the cars with wooden sticks. Fortunately, the police intervened in time, and no one was injured. The government quickly apologized and took steps to guarantee the personal safety of Christopher and his party.

President Chiang Ching-kuo received Christopher and his party on December 29. Future relations between the two countries, he asserted, should rest on five principles: reality, continuity, security, legality, and governmentally. The existence of the Republic of China is an international reality, not subject to change simply because some country decides to recognize the Chinese Communist regime. The U.S. should

---

7   *China Yearbook, 1979* (Taipei: China Publishing Co., 1979), pp. 343-344.

continue to recognize and respect the legal status and international personality of the ROC.

On the questions of continuity and security, Chiang was equally assertive. "While it is unfortunate that the two countries have broken diplomatic ties, the two peoples should continue to strengthen their cooperation and promote their friendship. This is especially important because the situation in the Western Pacific region remains unstable, and the danger of Communist invasion and subversion is ever present. The ROC President expressed the hope that "the United States can continue to provide an effective guarantee of our security and remain committed to the sale of defensive weapons we need. . ."

On the question of legality, the ROC president insisted that "the private interests of both Chinese and American citizens require the protection of definite legal provisions as well as government policy guidance. . . The United States has. . . said that, except for the Mutual Defense Treaty, all of the more than 50 other treaties and agreements will remain in full force and effect. These commitments and pledges and establishment of proposed government representation and all other relations can be effectively carried out and preserved only through legislation."

Finally, given the entire range of U.S.-ROC activities to be managed, from arms sales and foreign trade to cultural, scientific, and technological relations, Chiang asserted that it was "essential that government-to-government representation be established in Taipei and Washington to administer all relations." He rejected the suggestion that "any private organization or any individual" could carry out activities of such a complex nature.[8]

The Christopher delegation left Taipei on December 30, 1978, without any agreements having been reached. James C. H. Shen, the last ROC Ambassador to the United States, left San Francisco the following day. On January 1, 1979, diplomatic relations between the Republic of China and the United States ended.

Negotiations continued in Washington with the ROC represented by H. K. Yang, ROC Vice-Minister of Foreign Affairs for Political Affairs.

---

[8] Press release, Government Information Office, Taipei, December 29, 1978, cited in *China Post*, Taipei, December 30, 1978.

To enable Yang to deal with U.S. State Department officials, he was given the title of President Chiang Ching-kuo's Personal Representative. Over the course of several meetings, agreement was reached on most points. All the existing treaties and agreements between the two countries, except the Mutual Defense Treaty, were to remain in force and military sales would continue. Both sides agreed to establish new instrumentalities for the conduct of relations, the personnel of which would be accorded the privileges and immunities as necessary for the performance of their functions.[9]

Washington rejected Taipei's bid for continued government-to-government relations, however, insisting that these new "instrumentalities" meant "unofficial relations." The impasse persisted for some time, with Washington maintaining that the newly established American Institute in Taiwan (AIT) was a nongovernmental body incorporated in the District of Columbia, while Taipei claimed that the functions of the Coordination Council for North American Affairs (CCNAA) were official in character.

Though shrouding his plans in secrecy, Carter was not entirely able to escape criticism for his decision to terminate both diplomatic relations and the Mutual Defense Treaty with the ROC without appropriate prior consultation with Congress. Republican Senator Barry Goldwater, joined by fourteen other U.S. lawmakers, filed suit against Carter and Vance in federal court. They charged the defendants with violating U.S. law and ignoring precedent by failing to consult with the U.S. Congress on the termination of the treaty.

Goldwater specifically charged that Carter had ignored the Dole-Stone Amendment, contained in the International Security Assistance Act of 1978, which he himself had signed into law on September 26, 1978. The amendment stipulates that "there should be prior consultation between Congress and the executive branch on any proposed policy changes affecting the continuation of the Mutual Defense Treaty of

---

[9] See *Taiwan Hearings Before the Committee on Foreign Relations, United States Senate* (Washington, D.C., 1979), p. 11, cited in A. James Gregor, "The United States, the Republic of China, and the Taiwan Relations Act." Symposium on ROC-U.S. Relations 1980, p. 56

1954."[10]   "Just as the President alone cannot repeal a law," Goldwater pointed out, "he cannot repeal a treaty, which in itself is a law. He must ask Congress, or at least the Senate, which was a partner with him in ratifying a treaty, for approval to cancel it."

The suit claimed that "under past practice" presidents had acted with the U.S. Senate or the whole U.S. Congress to end treaties. Of the 48 treaties that had been terminated, the suit noted, 44 had been ended by congressional legislation or resolutions and only four by presidents alone. These latter presidential actions had gone unchallenged, the suit noted, only because they had occurred "under circumstances where it became impossible to perform the obligations specified in those treaties. . ." The lawsuit went all the way up to the U.S. Supreme Court, where it ended in dismissal in December, 1979.

IV. THE TAIWAN RELATIONS ACT (TRA)

After the end of diplomatic relations, the ROC ceased to exist insofar as the Carter Administration was concerned. Henceforth there were only "the people on Taiwan," with whom the United States would continue to have commercial, cultural, and other relations on an unofficial basis. To provide a legal underpinning for this relationship, the Carter administration submitted the so-called Omnibus Bill to the U.S. Congress on January 26, 1979. The most important provision of this bill, S. 245, concerned the establishment of a private organization, later known as the American Institute in Taiwan, to carry on the relationship with and through an instrumentality to be established by the people on Taiwan. This latter, of course, was the Coordination Council for North American Affairs.

The Senate Committee on Foreign Relations was not long in expressing its dissatisfaction with S. 245. Senator Frank Church, who chaired the committee, found the bill "woefully inadequate to the task, ambiguous in language, and uncertain in tone." Senior Republicans on the committee, such as Senators Jacob K. Javits and Charles H. Percy, agreed. They insisted that the bill must be rewritten in precise and

---

[10]   For a more detailed descriptions, see J. C. H. Shen, *op. cit.*, pp. 269-272.

definite language before it could be adopted by Congress.[11]   The end result of these changes was the Taiwan Relations Act (TRA), which was passed by the U.S. House of Representatives on March 28 and by the U.S. Senate the following day. Carter signed it into law (Public Law 96-8) on April 10, 1979.

The Taiwan Relations Act contained 18 sections, the most important of which, Section 2(b), declares that it is the policy of the U.S.:

> to preserve and promote extensive, close and friendly commercial, cultural, and other relations with Taiwan; to declare that peace and stability in Taiwan are in the political, security, and economic interests of the United States and are matters of international concern; to make clear that the U.S. decision to establish diplomatic relations with the PRC is on the expectation that the future of Taiwan will be determined by peaceful means; to consider any effort to determine the future of Taiwan by other than peaceful means, including boycotts or embargoes, is a threat to the peace and security of the Western Pacific area and of grave concern to the United States; to provide Taiwan with arms of a defensive character; to maintain the capacity of the United States to resist any resort to force or other forms of coercion that would jeopardize the security or the social or economic system of the people of Taiwan.

Section 3(a) of the Taiwan Relations Act commits the U.S. to make available to Taiwan such defense articles and defense services in such quantity as may be necessary to enable Taiwan to maintain a sufficient self-defense capability. Section 3(b) stipulates that "the President and Congress shall determine the nature and quantity of such defense articles and services based solely upon their judgment of the needs of Taiwan, in accordance with procedures established by law. Such determination of Taiwan's defense needs shall include review by United States military authorities in connection with recommendation to the President and Congress." In addition, Section 3(c) directs the President "to inform Congress promptly of any threat to the security or to the social or

---

[11] S. M. Goldstein and J. Mathews, *Sino-American Relations After Normalization, Toward the Second Decade* (Headline Series, No. 276, Foreign Policy Association, New York, 1985), pp. 26-27.

economic system of the people of Taiwan and any danger to the interests of the United States arising therefrom . . . the President and Congress shall determine, in accordance with constitutional processes, appropriate action by the United States in response to any such danger."

Other sections state, with admirable clarity, that "the absence of diplomatic relations or recognition shall not affect the application of U.S. laws with respect to Taiwan" [Section 4(a)]; "the continuation in force of all treaties and other international agreements, including multilateral conventions, entered into by the United States and the governing authorities on Taiwan recognized by the United States as the Republic of China prior to January 1, 1979" [Section 4(c)]; and asserts "that nothing in this Act may be construed as a basis of supporting the exclusion of Taiwan from continued membership in any international financial institution or any other international organization" [Section 4(d)].

Another section of the Act, which was to become a bone of contention between the ROC and the Carter administration: under Section 10(b) the president was "requested to extend to the instrumentality established by Taiwan the same number of offices and complement of personnel as were previously operated in the United States by the government authorities on Taiwan recognized as the Republic of China prior to January 1, 1979."

Before the severing of relations, the ROC had, in addition to its embassy in Washington, D.C., 11 consulates-general (New York, Boston, Atlanta, Houston, Chicago, Kansas City, Seattle, San Francisco, Los Angeles, Calexico, Honolulu) and three consulates (Portland, Guam, American Samoa). But in the negotiations which followed, the U.S. State Department insisted that CCNAA limit itself to eight offices in addition to its main office in Washington, D.C. As a consequence, the ROC was forced to abandon its consulates-general in Boston, Calexico, and Kansas City and its consulates in Portland, Guam, and American Samoa. Following the passage of the TRA, the U.S. State Department repeatedly denied ROC requests to reopen these offices.[12]

---

[12] For a more detailed analysis, see K. Y. Chang, ed., *ROC-US Relations under the Taiwan Relations Act: Practice and Prospects* (Taipei: Institute of International Relations, 1988).

Another indication that the Carter administration had its own ideas about implementing the TRA came in August 1979 when Vice President Walter Mondale announced at a news conference in Canton that the Carter administration had decided to abrogate the ROC-U.S.A. Air Transport Agreement of 1946. This would pave the way, he informed his PRC hosts, for the conclusion of an official Washington-Peking air transport agreement. As for Taiwan, a new, unofficial air transport agreement would be signed between the AIT and CCNAA. The Carter Administration, in its eagerness to please its new friends in Peking, seemed to be going out of its way to antagonize its former allies in Taiwan. But its behavior raised legal questions as well: How could it justify this decision when Section 4(c) of the TRA clearly provided for "the continuation in force of all treaties and other international agreements. . . entered into by the United States and the governing authorities on Taiwan. . . ?" And why had the Carter administration not consulted the U.S. Congress?

The Asia-Pacific Subcommittee of the Senate Foreign Relations Committee decided to hold hearings on the question. Richard Holbrooke, Assistant Secretary of State for East Asian and Pacific Affairs, appeared before the Subcommittee on September 27, 1979. Although Holbrooke denied that the State Department intended as a matter of policy to replace all 59 existing treaties and agreements with the ROC with informal and unofficial ones, he did admit that there were plans to revise several of them.

The Carter administration, undeterred, proceeded with its plans. On November 13 the AIT suddenly notified the CCNAA, its counterpart, that the U.S. intended to terminate the air transport agreement in a year. Negotiations began on a new agreement, which was signed on March 5, 1980, by Konsin C. Shah, representing the CCNAA, and David Dean, Chairman of the Board and Managing Director of the AIT. The agreement went into effect immediately.

The U.S. seemed to have been co-opted into playing Peking's game, which was to reduce, at every possible opportunity, the status of Taiwan to that of a mere province of China. Peking's goal was to completely destroy any claim that the ROC might have to be a separate and distinct international personality. If this were to occur, the U.S. would have no right under international law to "intervene" in the internal affairs of

China by affording military protection to Taiwan, its government, and its people. The TRA's assertion of such rights would be a dead letter. Indeed, it seemed as if some in the Carter administration were already treating it as such.

Another area of concern was U.S. arms sales to Taiwan, but the implementation of this provision of the TRA, too, got off to a bad start. Carter had secretly acceded to Peking's demand for a one year moratorium on such sales. Though this did not affect items already in the pipeline, it caused a great deal of apprehension in Taipei, where officials were concerned that the moratorium might be extended in response to pressure from Peking.

This anxiety did not dissipate until January 3, 1980, when the State Department announced that the U.S. would sell Taiwan about $280 million worth of arms. On the whole, the announcement came as good news, though there was some disappointment when the actual list of items approved for sale was released. The Carter administration had carefully selected only defensive weapons, such as anti-tank and anti-aircraft missile systems. Conspicuously absent from the list were the advanced fighter planes which the ROC desperately needed.

The Carter administration also seemed to be inching its way toward supplying Peking with arms. During his visit to Peking in early January 1980, U.S. Secretary of Defense Harold Brown indicated to his hosts that the U.S. might agree to transfer defense-related American industrial know-how to Red China. On March 11, 1980, the State Department gave general approval for U.S. manufacturers to sell Peking six categories of military equipment, including communications equipment, certain kinds of early warning radar, training equipment, trucks, and certain types of helicopters, and cargo aircraft. Then in June 1980 the U.S. Department of Defense announced that it would authorize U.S. companies to build electronics and helicopter factories on the Chinese mainland.

During the entire first year of the TRA, the Carter administration failed to consult with the U.S. Congress on its implementation. In a public hearing in mid-May 1980 Senator John Glenn, chairman of the Senate Subcommittee on East Asian and Pacific Affairs, openly voiced his dissatisfaction with this lack of consultation, particularly with regard to arms sales. The U.S. policy on arms sales, he complained, seemed to be dictated by the PRC. Kenneth Fasick, director of the international division of the General Accounting Office, also testified that the executive branch had made little effort to explain to Congress what specific plans there might be for future arms sales to Taiwan.

It was clear that the Carter administration could not be trusted to implement the TRA faithfully. The ROC's only hope was that the U.S. Congress, which under the TRA was to be consulted on its implementation, would exercise its right to hold public hearings on the TRA and insist on its full implementation.

15

A DECADE OF PRAGMATISM
1980–1989

I. THE SHANGHAI COMMUNIQUÉ, AUGUST 17, 1982

The election of Ronald Reagan as 40th President of the United States was greeted with enthusiasm by the people and government of the Republic of China. During the campaign, Reagan had made no secret of his friendly feelings for Free China, and had more than once faulted Jimmy Carter for the way in which he had established diplomatic relations with Peking. Immediately after he moved into the White House January 20, 1981, relations between Taipei and Washington improved. There was no repetition of the deliberate humiliations that the Carter administration had inflicted upon the ROC and its representatives. Instead, consultations between the ROC's unofficial representatives in Washington and the State Department became frequent and cordial.

While the Nationalist government did not expect that Reagan would reestablish formal diplomatic relations between the U.S. and the ROC, it was hopeful that the sale of advanced aircraft and other sophisticated armaments of a defensive character would be speedily approved. Lists of requested weapons were submitted—with advanced aircraft at the top of the list—and the decision of the Reagan administration awaited with bated breath.

The first clear statement on the China policy of the new administration came in mid-June of 1981, when Secretary of State Alexander M. Haig, Jr., paid a three-day visit to Peking. Haig told the

Chinese Communists that President Reagan intended to treat the PRC as a friendly nation, with which the U.S. was not allied but with which it shared many interests. The success of this policy, he added, "foreshadows the prospect that President Reagan's administration will be marked by a major expansion in friendship and cooperation between Peking and Washington." Haig also disclosed that he had extended an invitation from President Reagan to Premier Chao Tse-yang to visit the U.S. the following year and that Chao had accepted. As far as a visit by American president to the PRC, this would be discussed further at a later date. On the critical question of arms sales, he told his PRC hosts that the Reagan administration had decided in principle to sell them lethal arms, although any sales would have to be approved on a case-to-case basis after consultations with the U.S. Congress and possibly other nations. No mention was made of arms sales to Taiwan.

The U.S. decision to sell weapons to the PRC was a bitter blow to Taiwan, though it was immediately softened by President Reagan himself. Speaking at a Washington press conference that same day, Reagan declared that "I have not changed my feelings about Taiwan. We have an Act. . . called the Taiwan Relations Act that provides for defense equipment being sold to Taiwan. . . and I intend to live up to the Taiwan Relations Act."[1]

Still, many in the ROC felt threatened by this turn of events, and were impatient for Reagan to act on his promise of arms sales to the ROC. President Chiang Ching-kuo issued a statement on July 15, 1981, urging his countrymen to show patience.

> All of us are greatly concerned about recent developments in the relations with the United States. On the basis of what President Reagan has said and done since his inauguration, I think he is a statesman of ideals, principles, and moral courage. He is an anti-communist. He believes that Communism and its influence is the greatest scourge of humankind. . . . We must be aware that the U.S. government faces many urgent problems, all waiting to be solved. We should, therefore, stick to our established policy and principles and move ahead with maximum patience and total perseverance. I

---

[1] J. C. H. Shen, *The U.S. and Free China, How the U.S. Sold Out Its Ally* (Washington, D.C.: Acropolis Books Ltd., 1983), pp. 283-284.

am certain that the mutually beneficial relationship between the two countries will improve as time goes by.[2]

Later that year, there were several auspicious signs. When Reagan met PRC Premier Chao Tse-yang on October 21, 1981, during the North-South Summit Conference at Cancun, Mexico, Chao raised objections to the continued sale of American arms to Taiwan. Reagan told Chao in no uncertain terms that the U.S. would maintain its obligations to Taiwan as stipulated in the Taiwan Relations Act. When PRC Foreign Minister Huang Hua called on the American President at the White House on October 30, 1981, Reagan told him that he would honor the U.S. commitment toward the ROC as stipulated in the TRA.

Huang Hua then went to Secretary of State Haig, who was thought to be more sympathetic to the PRC's position, and threatened to downgrade relations with Washington if the U.S. sold advanced arms to the ROC. Peking had used this same threat earlier in 1981, when the Dutch government was considering whether to approve the sale of arms, including two submarines, to the ROC. The sale had been approved anyway, and Peking had retaliated by replacing its ambassador with a chargé d'affaires.

This threat was apparently taken to heart, for on January 11, 1982, the Reagan administration informed Taipei that advanced aircraft would not be on the list of arms approved for sale. Rather, Taiwan's F-5E fighters would be replaced with "comparable aircraft." Although clearly a concession to the PRC, the Chinese Communist leaders refused to be mollified. Instead, they directed a stream of threats and protests at the Reagan administration that *any* arms should be sold to Taiwan.

At that point, Reagan decided to take the unusual step of writing personal letters to Chinese Communist leaders. The first letter, dated April 5, 1982, was addressed to Teng Hsiao-ping, Vice-Chairman of the Chinese Communist Party. Reagan's letter to Teng declared that the U.S. "firmly adheres to the positions agreed upon in the joint communiqué on the establishment of diplomatic relations between the United States and China. There is only one China. We will not permit

---

2   President Chiang Ching-kuo's Remarks on Current Development at the weekly meeting of the Central Standing Committee of the Kuomintang, July 15, 1981.

the unofficial relations between the American people and the people of Taiwan to weaken our commitment to this principle." This paragraph sent shock waves through the ROC, since it implied that in the future Peking would have veto power over relations between Washington and Taipei.

Another key paragraph also raised concerns, since it concerned Peking's "nine-point proposal," which was a united front tactic designed to lead to reunification of Taiwan and the Mainland on the PRC's terms. "We fully recognize the significance of the nine-point proposal of September 30, 1981," Reagan's letter read, "and the policy set forth by your government as early as January 1, 1979. The decisions and the principles conveyed in my instructions to your government on January 11, 1982, reflect our appreciation of the new situation created by these developments."

A second letter, also dated April 5, 1982, was sent to Premier Chao. This also made reference to the "the nine-point initiative," adding ominously that "in the context of progress toward a peaceful solution [of the question of reunification], there would naturally be a decrease in the need for arms by Taiwan."

On May 3, 1982, Reagan wrote a third letter, this time addressed to Hu Yao-bang, Chairman of the Chinese Communist Party. In it he informed Hu that "Vice President Bush is visiting China as my personal emissary," adding that "among the issues the Vice President will discuss in his April 23-May 9 visit to Peking is the question of U.S. arms sales to Taiwan."

The wording and phraseology of Reagan's three letters bore marks of input by the State Department. Secretary Alexander Haig had made no secret of his intention to appease Peking for geopolitical reasons, even if it meant sacrificing Taiwan's security.[3] And Peking was vigorously pushing for a cut-off date for arms sales to Taiwan, and for U.S. acceptance of Peking's claim of sovereignty over Taiwan. Haig was circulating drafts of an agreement, which would later be known as the "Shanghai Communiqué No. 2," which came dangerously close to adopting Peking's point of view, even though the Communist leadership stubbornly refused to renounce the use of force against Taiwan.

---

[3]   J. C. H. Shen, *op. cit.*, pp. 289-291.

Several things happened to delay the issuance of the second Shanghai Communiqué, and to moderate its substance. Bush was unable to reach an agreement with Peking during the course of his visit. He was followed by Senate Majority Leader Howard Baker, who visited Peking between May 30-June 10, 1982, at the invitation of the Standing Committee of the National People's Congress. Baker reported that, while he had originally thought that Peking was definitely prepared to downgrade its relations with the U.S. if arms sales to Taiwan should continue, after his visit he was convinced that this issue was not as critical and difficult as he had imagined. Baker's report strengthened the hand of those who were not willing to go as far as Haig in officially appeasing Peking.

Then came Haig's sudden resignation on June 25, 1982. George Schultz was chosen as his successor, but the Senate confirmation process caused a further delay of several weeks. The second Shanghai Communiqué was not issued until August 17, 1982.

The U.S.-PRC Joint Communiqué of 1982

The text of the joint communiqué which the U.S. and PRC governments issued called for a gradual reduction and eventual termination of U.S. arms sales to Taiwan:

1. In the Joint Communiqué on the Establishment of Diplomatic Relations on January 1, 1979, issued by the Government of the United States of America and the Government of the People's Republic of China, the United States of America recognized the government of the People's Republic of China as the sole legal Government of China, and it acknowledged the Chinese position that there is but one China and Taiwan is part of China. Within the context, the two sides agreed that the people of the United States would continue to maintain cultural, commercial, and other unofficial relations with the people of Taiwan. On this basis, relations between the United States and China were normalized.

2. The question of the United States arms sales to Taiwan was not settled in the course of negotiations between the two countries on establishing diplomatic relations. The two sides stated that they would raise the issue again following normalization. Realizing

that this issue would seriously hamper the development of United States-China relations, more meetings took place between President Ronald Reagan and Premier Chao Tse-yang and between Secretary of State Alexander M. Haig, Jr. and Vice-Premier and Foreign Minister Huang Hua in October, 1981.

3. Respect for each other's sovereignty and territorial integrity and non-interference in each other's internal affairs constituted the fundamental principles guiding United States-China relations. These principles were confirmed in the Shanghai Communiqué of February 28, 1972, and reaffirmed in the Joint Communiqué on the Establishment of Diplomatic Relations which came into effect on January 1, 1979. Both sides emphatically stated that these principles continued to govern all aspects of their relations.

4. The Chinese Government reiterated that the question of Taiwan was a matter of China's internal affair. "The Message to Compatriots in Taiwan" issued by China on January 1, 1979 promulgated a fundamental policy of striving for peaceful reunification of the motherland. The Nine-Point Proposal put forward by China on September 30, 1981, represented a further major effort under this fundamental policy to strive for a peaceful solution to the Taiwan question.

5. The United States Government attached great importance to its relations with China, and reiterated that it had no intentions of infringing on Chinese sovereignty and territorial integrity, nor interfering in China's internal affairs, nor pursuing a policy of "two Chinas" or "one China, one Taiwan." The United States Government understood and appreciated the Chinese policy of striving for a peaceful resolution of the Taiwan question as indicated in China's "Message to Compatriots in Taiwan" issued on January 1, 1979, and the Nine-Point Proposal put forward by China on September 30, 1981. The new situation which had emerged with regard to the Taiwan question also provided favorable conditions for the settlement of United States-China differences over United States arms sales to Taiwan.

6. Having in mind the foregoing statement of both sides, the United States Government stated that it did not seek to carry out a long-term policy of arms sales to Taiwan; that its arms sales to Taiwan would not exceed, either in qualitative or in quantitative terms, the level of those supplied in recent years since the establishment of diplomatic relations between the United States and China; that

it intended gradually to reduce its sale of arms to Taiwan, leading over a period of time, to a final resolution. The United States acknowledged China's consistent position regarding the thorough settlement of this issue.

7. In order to bring about, over a period of time, a final settlement of the question of the United States arms sales to Taiwan, which is an issue rooted in history, the two Governments would make every effort to adopt measures conducive to the thorough settlement of this issue.

8. The development of United States-China relations is not only in the interest of the two peoples but also conducive to peace and stability in the world. On the principle of equality and mutual benefit the two sides were determined to strengthen their ties in the economic, cultural, educational, scientific, technological, and other fields. They would exert strong, joint efforts for the continued development of relations between the governments and peoples of the United States and China.

9. In order to bring about the healthy development of the United States-China relations, to maintain world peace, and to oppose aggression and expansion, the two Governments reaffirmed the principles agreed on by the two sides in the Shanghai Communiqué and the Joint Communiqué on the Establishment of Diplomatic Relations. The two sides would maintain contact and hold appropriate consultations on bilateral and international issues of common interest.[4]

In Paragraph 6 of the communiqué, the Reagan administration had made a major concession to Peking on the question of arms sales to Taiwan. Many felt it had done so in direct contravention of the Taiwan Relations Act, which stipulates that "The United States will make available to Taiwan such defense articles and defense services in such quantity as may be necessary to enable Taiwan to maintain a sufficient self-defense capability." Nothing in this language would seem to permit a quantitative or qualitative cap on arms sales to Taiwan, nor a secular reduction over time in arms sales.

Yet in his statement on the August 17 Communiqué, Reagan claimed that the new policy was fully consistent with the TRA. "Arms sales will

---

4   *Beijing Review*, No. 34, Peking, August 23, 1982, pp. 14-15.

continue in accordance with the Act," he insisted, "and with the full expectation that the approach of the Chinese government to the resolution of the Taiwan issue will continue to be peaceful."

Realizing the apprehension that the Communiqué had caused in Taiwan, Reagan sent assurances through appropriate channels that the fundamental U.S. position on Taiwan had not changed. "The U.S.," he made it known, "has not agreed to set a date for ending arms sales to Taiwan; has not agreed to hold prior consultations with the Chinese Communists on arms sales to Taiwan; will not play any mediation role between Taipei and Peking; has not agreed to revise the Taiwan Relations Act; has not altered its position regarding sovereignty over Taiwan; will not exert pressure on Taiwan to enter into negotiations with the Chinese Communists."[5]

Because of these assurances, the statement issued by the ROC on August 17 concerning the Communiqué took a rather mild tone. Taipei objected that:

> The supply of adequate defensive weapons to the Republic of China is an established arms sales policy of the United States of America, formulated by the executive within the stipulations of the Taiwan Relations Act. Now the United States Government has mistaken the fallacious 'peaceful intention' of the Chinese Communists as sincere and meaningful and consequently acceded to the latter's demand to put ceilings on both the quality and quantity of the arms to be sold to the Republic of China. It is in contravention of the letter and spirit of the Taiwan Relations Act, for which we must express our profound regret.

"The Chinese Communists," the statement continued,

> are exerting all efforts in waging an international united front campaign, with a view to further isolating the Republic of China. They are seeking all possible means to pave the way for their military invasion of this country. . . . We earnestly hope that the United States government will not be deceived by but will see through the Chinese

---

5   Report on R.O.C.-U.S. Relations, 1981-1983 (Taipei: Institute of American Culture, Academia Sinica, 1984). p. 129.

Communists' plot in attempting to annex our base of national recovery and to divide the free world. We also hope that the United States, upholding her spirit of freedom and justice, will fully and positively implement the Taiwan Relations Act to continue providing us with defensive arms so as to maintain the stability of the Republic of China and to safeguard the peace and security of the Asian-Pacific region.[6]

The August 17 Communiqué did succeed in reducing, however briefly, the tensions which the PRC had deliberately created in the U.S.-ROC relationship in the hope of wresting some major concessions from Washington regarding Taiwan. When the Reagan administration finally announced, two days after the release of the Communiqué, its intention to allow Taiwan to continue co-producing F-5E fighters, Peking limited itself to a note of protest. It did not carry out its threat to downgrade relations.

For its part, Taipei was relieved that the Reagan administration had finally kept its promise of January, 1982, to allow the ROC to continue its co-production arrangement with the Northrop Corporation to produce 60 new F-5E fighters. While the ROC military would have preferred a more sophisticated fighter, such as the F-5G or the F-16, five wings of upgraded F-5E would assure the ROC of continued air superiority over the Taiwan Straits for several years to come.

No sooner was the August 17 Communiqué signed than Washington and Peking openly aired their different interpretation of some of its provisions. Peking said that it had not agreed to renounce the use of force to reunite Taiwan with the mainland, and would not tolerate any outside interference on this question. The U.S., on the other hand, claimed that the "fundamental policy" of the PRC, as indicated in its 1979 "message to compatriots in Taiwan," was that of "striving for a peaceful resolution of the Taiwan question." It would seek to hold Peking to this standard, Washington said.

Still, some dangerous commitments had been made. Washington had promised to sell weapons to the PRC if it continued to show peaceful intentions, and to gradually decrease the supply of weapons to the ROC.

---

[6]   *China News*, Taipei, August 18, 1982.

Under an administration not well-disposed towards Taiwan, these pledges could be maneuvered by the PRC to the great disadvantage of its Nationalist rival. Fortunately for the ROC, the private assurances that Taipei had received from the Reagan administration were to be kept. Time would reveal that Reagan was determined to keep his commitments to Free China, and that he had a far more realistic understanding of the limited utility of the PRC in checking Soviet designs than had Carter.

II. THE REAGAN ADMINISTRATION AFTER THE 1982 SHANGHAI COMMUNIQUÉ

The Chinese Communists fully expected to build on their successes in the August 17 Communiqué to choke-off the supply of American arms to Taiwan. They expected that the amount approved for sale to Taiwan in FY 1983 would be significantly less than the $600 million the U.S. had sold to the ROC in FY 1982, and would perhaps even fall to the FY 1981 level of $295 million. Once the ROC saw the handwriting on the wall, they were confident, it would soon succumb to their threats and blandishments. This is why they had pushed so hard for an absolute cut-off date for arms sales and, failing that, had demanded gradual reductions.

Peking reacted with anger and dismay when the Reagan administration revealed in March 1983 that it intended to sell the ROC some $800 million in arms in FY 1983. In response to Peking's protests that this violated the August 17 Communiqué, State Department officials calmly explained that arms sales to Taiwan had been indexed for inflation, with FY 1979 chosen as the "base year" against which the gradual reduction in sales would be calculated. The $598 million in sales in 1979 was, after taking inflation into account, equal to $830 million 1983 dollars. The U.S. had complied with the Communiqué by reducing FY 1983 arms sales from 830 million to 800 million. Moreover, in each subsequent year, sales would be reduced by a further $20 million, so that in FY 1984 sales would drop to $780 million. Of course, additional allowances for inflation might have to be made for the future.[7]

---

[7] *The Washington Post*, March 23, 1983, Washington, D.C.

Neither was the August 17 Communiqué allowed to limit the sale of more advanced weapons. In June, 1984 the U.S. announced that twelve C-130H transport planes and 262 Chaparral surface-to-air missiles were being sold to Taipei to replace obsolete planes and air defense guns. These sales demonstrated that, according to Washington's interpretation of the Communiqué, new models of arms could be sold to Taipei to replace out-of-date models.

The Reagan administration also generously interpreted the August 17 Communiqué to permit the transfer of military technology to the ROC. By 1986 American firms were assisting the Nationalist air force to develop an indigenous fighter plane. In mid-1987 the blueprint and data package necessary to build FFG-7 Oliver Hazard Perry-class frigate was approved for sale to the Nationalist navy. Peking's protests of these transactions were brushed off by the Reagan administration, which maintained that the earlier agreement dealt solely with arms sales, not technology transfers. Communist Chinese efforts to reopen discussions of the August 17 Communiqué were likewise rejected. The Communiqué stood on its own, Washington declared in an August 1986 note to Peking, and there was no need to reinterpret or renegotiate it.[8]

Even before this, Washington's efforts to help the ROC remain in the Asian Development Bank (ADB) had gone a long way towards restoring mutual trust between the two countries. In February 1983 Peking expressed its desire to join the ADB, but publicly demanded that the ROC first be ousted. The State Department responded that, although it welcomed the PRC's participation in the ADB, any move to expel the ROC would have an adverse impact on America's continued support for that organization. Taken aback by Washington's strong opposition, Peking retreated, though it still lobbied to have the ROC's status as a full member of the ADB downgraded to associate member.

At this point the U.S. Congress intervened, passing an amendment to the International Monetary Fund (IMF) appropriation bill on November 17, 1983, stipulating that "Taiwan, the Republic of China, should remain a full member of the Asian Development Bank, and that its status in that body should remain unaltered no matter how the issue of the People's

---

[8]   K. Y. Chang, ed., *ROC-US Relations Under the Taiwan Relations Act: Practice and Prospects* (Taipei: Institute of International Relations, 1988), pp. 35-37.

Republic of China application for membership is disposed of." The amendment further instructed that the "President and the Secretary of State should express support for Taiwan, the Republic of China, making it clear that the United States will not countenance attempts to expel Taiwan from the Asian Development Bank."[9]

Peking lodged a strong protest against this amendment, accusing the U.S. of "creating two Chinas," but this protest fell on deaf ears. Instead, under heavy pressure from Japan and the U.S., the PRC was forced to abandon its attempt to downgrade the ROC's status in the ADB. It stubbornly insisted, however, that the ROC's name be changed to "Taipei, China." Although the U.S. Senate resolved that both the status and the name of the ROC should remain unchanged, the administration gave in on the latter point. With Washington's acquiescence, the ADB decided to change the ROC's name to "Taipei, China."

On April 26, 1984, Ronald Reagan finally traveled to Peking, putting aside his familiar anti-communist rhetoric for the occasion. He and his wife were models of decorum, although once, following a visit to a thriving farmer's market, he could not restrain himself. He announced with obvious glee that China had discovered the virtues of capitalism.

Once reelected in 1984, Reagan devoted little attention to China policy. Instead, he and his administration concentrated their energies upon the ongoing arms negotiations with the Soviet Union.

Relations between Taipei and Washington were generally good during the remainder of the Reagan administration, although there was recurrent friction over trade. High-handed American behavior in the Sino-American trade talks aroused strong protests from Taiwan's farmers and generated ill-feeling among members of the Legislative Yuan.

U.S. Arms and Technology Sales to Mainland China

In July 1978 the U.S. and the PRC held discussions in Peking on science and technology cooperation. These resulted in the Agreement on Cooperation in Science and Technology, which was signed in January 1979 by Vice Premier Teng Hsiao-ping during his visit to the U.S., and

---

9   *The Economic Daily*, Taipei, November 20, 1983.

extended for three more years in January 1984 by then-Premier Chao Tzu-yang on a subsequent visit. This agreement contained no fewer than 23 protocols, which were to be implemented and supervised by a newly established Joint Science and Technology Policy Commission, comprised of representatives from the U.S. Office of Science and Technology Policy and the PRC's State Science and Technology Commission.

In part to defuse continuing PRC opposition to arms sales to Taiwan, in June 1983 President Reagan announced that he would amend U.S. export control procedures to recognize the PRC's status as a "friendly, non-allied country." This revision of U.S. export control regulations, which took effect that November, moved China into country Group V, where it joined other Asian, African, and European countries. Detailed technical guidelines—so-called "green lines"—were established to describe several categories of products that would routinely be approved for export to acceptable end-users in China. These categories included certain computers, computerized instruments, microcircuits, electronic instruments, recording equipment, and semi-conductor production equipment. License applications for products falling within these guidelines were no longer subjected to a time-consuming interagency review. The new U.S. policy allowed American exporters to participate in China's modernization program while retaining controls on certain advanced technology and equipment.

Another motivation for the liberalization of export controls was the Reagan administration's desire to support private sector involvement in China's modernization program. Here State Department optimism over China's future course won out over Reagan's anti-communist views. State believed that economic development, by creating a more modern and open China, would contribute to stability in Asia. The risk of such a strategy—the creation of a powerful Communist state with interests antithetical to those of the U.S.—was seen as minimal. China was considered to be at best a regional power, whose economic development would have limited impact on the international balance of power.

Under the new policy, the dollar value of export licenses approved for Mainland China by the U.S. Department of Commerce rose from $523 million in 1982 to $2 billion in 1984. Included in this amount, of course, were all items requiring a validated export license, including technical data and commercial aircraft.

In April 1986 the Reagan administration announced the biggest military deal yet: $550 million worth of high-tech aviation equipment would be sold to the PLA air force. Washington was responding to the expanding Soviet military presence in Asia, and hoped by means of this arms sale to cement a military relationship with the PRC. The Soviets, in turn, proposed a Sino-Soviet summit to discuss helping China to build nuclear power plants, among other things. Peking rejected both suitors, making clear that it would continue to practice a policy of "superpower neutrality."

Despite Peking's unwillingness to informally ally itself with the U.S., in September 1988 Reagan approved the Chinese launch of three American-made communications satellites. The Department of Transportation strongly opposed this decision, on the grounds that sharing such sensitive technology was not in the interests of U.S. national security. Secretary of Defense Frank Carlucci disagreed, however, stating that the fundamental issue was not technology transfer but trade. Peking was, needless to say, delighted at this opportunity to examine state-of-the-art satellite communications equipment.

To raise money for the modernization of its own backward forces, which were saddled with a lot of obsolete Soviet technology, the PRC had earlier decided to go into the arms export business. Eight large import-export corporations had been formed for this purpose in the early 1980s. Virtually overnight, the PRC became one of the Third World's major arms and nuclear technology suppliers. Sales increased from $1.2 billion in 1980 to $2.6 billion in 1987 to $5.2 billion in 1990. Over the course of the eighties, Peking earned more than $12 billion in the arms trade, of which almost half came from sales to both belligerents in the 1980-1988 Iran-Iraq War. Anything and everything appeared to be on the block. In 1988 the PRC shocked the world by selling a number of CSS-2 missiles to Saudi Arabia, the first time an intermediate range ballistic missile system had been transferred from one country to another. The sales price was one billion dollars.

When U.S. Secretary of State George Schultz visited mainland China from March 2-5, 1987, one of his goals was to convince the PRC to stop shipping arms to Iran. PRC Chairman Li Hsien-nien responded by criticizing the U.S. for its continuing arms sales to the Republic of China. Schultz' efforts to convince his hosts to respect human rights was similarly to no avail. Not only was the much-touted "open-door" policy of the Chinese Communists not synonymous with "Westernization," he discovered, but Peking still insisted upon "taking the socialist road." The only two issues on which he and PRC officials found themselves in agreement were the need for a Soviet withdrawal from Afghanistan and a Vietnamese withdrawal from Cambodia.

III. THE CHANGING OF THE GUARD IN THE ROC

The Taiwan Factor

Following the death of President Chiang Kai-shek, Taiwan entered a period of rapid economic and political change. Wisely rejecting a fortress mentality, Chiang Ching-kuo, his successor, strove to assure Taiwan's survival by building its economic strength and encouraging foreign trade. Through adroit diplomacy, Taiwan forged strong commercial, and informal diplomatic links, with nearly all the one hundred or more nations that had switched their diplomatic recognition to the PRC.

The younger Chiang also opened up the domestic political process, hoping to avoid the political turmoil which was then besetting authoritarian regimes in South KoreaError! Bookmark not defined. and the Philippines. Taiwan-born citizens were allowed to play a larger role in the Nationalist Party, and opposition activity was tolerated. Beginning in the mid-1980s, opposition parties were allowed to compete in local, provincial, and national elections. These parties won seats in the national legislature, although it remained under the control of the Nationalist Party. In 1986 Chiang lifted martial law, which had been imposed 38 years before. More flexible laws were passed permitting greater freedom of speech, assembly, and the press.

There were also changes in the policy of the ROC toward private contacts with the Chinese mainland. Students from the two parts of China mixed freely in American and other foreign universities and Taiwan businessmen began traveling quietly to mainland China. By early 1985 Taipei acknowledged that the total amount of two-way trade, carried on indirectly through third countries, had reached perhaps 500 million dollars. It would not seek to prohibit such trade, the ROC government announced in May of that year.

In 1987 the government announced that Taiwan residents would be permitted to visit relatives on the mainland. More than a half million Chinese made the pilgrimage home during the first two years alone. Indirect trade, conducted mostly through Hong Kong, reached the $3 billion by 1988. Slowly and cautiously economic ties were developing.

Under President Chiang's leadership, however, Taipei continued to resist official overtures from Peking. The PRC stopped shelling the offshore islands of Kinmen and Matsu in January, 1979, and proposed reunification on the grounds that the "status quo" on the island would be respected for at least 50 years, and that "reasonable policies and measures" would be pursued in eventually settling the issue. The ROC did not deign to respond to this vague proposal.

Throughout the eighties the PRC alternately threatened and cajoled Taiwan. United front slogans came and went: "Three Links, Four Exchanges," "Talk on an Equal Footing," "Cooperation between the Kuomintang and the Chinese Communist Party," "Autonomy as a Special Region Without a Change of System," and "The Hongkong Model." Once the Sino-British agreement was signed in the spring of 1984, Peking touted the "one country, two systems" formula to be used in Hong Kong as a solution to the "Taiwan problem." Taiwan, like Hongkong, could be a capitalist society within a socialist China.

Subsequently Peking elaborated that Taiwan would be a "special administrative region with full autonomous power in its internal affairs" and could retain its armed forces; that the "current political and economic system and way of life would remain unchanged" after reunification, and that economic relations with foreign countries would be permitted; that individuals from Taiwan would be welcome to travel to the mainland; and that businessmen from Taiwan would be welcome to invest in mainland China. All it had to do was drop its claim to speak for all of China and accept the status of a "special administrative region." When Teng Hsiao-ping met Zbigniew Brzezinski on February 22, 1984, he insisted that "Taiwan can still practice capitalism after China's reunification, while the mainland keeps to socialism. Neither side will harm the other."

Taipei rejected the "one China, two systems" formula. Direct, government-to-government negotiations with Peking on the question of reunification, Taipei said, were out of the question. Frustrated by Taiwan's refusal to negotiate, Teng grew testy. When he met Reagan on April 28, 1984, Teng declared that "We have made the two different systems to exist within a unified country, but we will never abandon our sovereignty over the island." By 1988 he was threatening to launch small-scale military operations if peaceful approaches continued to elicit a negative response. Peking declared that it would invade Taiwan if the island: (1) experienced domestic turmoil; (2) declared independence from the mainland; (3) entered into a military alliance with the Soviet Union; or (4) deployed nuclear weapons.[10]

Lee Teng-hui Takes Office

The nation was saddened by the death of President Chiang Ching-kuo on January 13, 1988, but took the news calmly. Vice President Lee Teng-hui was sworn in as President of the Republic of China the following day without incident. At the Thirteenth Nationalist Party Congress, held later that year in July, Lee also inherited Chiang's post as chairman. As expected, he continued his predecessor's policies of liberalizing and democratizing ROC's political system, promoting younger, reform-minded leaders to positions of responsibility in both the party and the government. He formulated a flexible foreign policy, and continued the cautious and unofficial opening to the Chinese mainland that the late president had initiated.

The ROC had, by 1988, become an economic powerhouse. It had amassed $75 billion, the second largest foreign currency reserves in the world. Its total foreign trade of $110 billion ranked it 13th among the trading nations. Its trade surplus with the U.S. had also grown, however, and at $20 billion was second only to Japan's. As a trade-dependent economy with very little political clout, Taiwan was extremely vulnerable to foreign pressures. Its very isolation was becoming a danger to its continued economic growth.

---

[10] M. Schaller, *The United States and China in the Twentieth Century* (New York: Oxford University Press, 1990), pp. 219-221.

Fundamental changes in the ROC's external strategic environment also posed new challenges. For nearly four decades Taiwan—the unsinkable aircraft carrier—had been on the front lines of the American-led global cold war against communism. Now that struggle, at least as far as the U.S.-U.S.S.R. confrontation was concerned, was drawing to a close. With the Sino-Soviet rapprochement, the Vietnamese intervention in Cambodia, and the overture of the Republic of Korea toward the PRC, the line between "socialism and capitalism" began to blur elsewhere as well. By the late 1980's, many of the reasons that had once justified Taiwan's quarantine of the Chinese mainland and its rigidly anti-communist foreign policy elsewhere in the world had lost their relevance. The battle with the PRC over diplomatic recognition seemed increasingly futile, and the ROC found itself with only a few friends to call upon in an emergency.

President Lee began to reconsider how best to protect and promote Taiwan's interests in the face of these changing circumstances. It was clear to him that, if the ROC continued to refuse to deal directly with its trade rivals and insisted upon being recognized as the "Republic of China," Taiwan's isolation would continue. As a trade-dependent nation, the ROC must find a way to overcome Peking's opposition and take a more active international role. After a great deal of anguished debate, the ROC leadership undertook several bold foreign policy initiatives.

In April 1988 ROC delegates returned to the Asian Development Bank for the first time since that body admitted the PRC in 1986. Although its delegates proudly wore the ROC insignia, the delegation as a whole was known as "Taipei, China." A major push was launched, using the same formula, to join the General Agreements on Tariffs and Trade (GATT), the World Bank, and the International Monetary Fund. It was logical that the ROC should seek membership in these organizations, despite the PRC's objections, given Taiwan's economic standing.[11] Under the "Chinese Taipei" formula, the ROC participated in the 1984 and 1988 Olympics in Los Angeles and Seoul.

---

[11] A. J. Kane, ed., *China Briefing, 1989* (Boulder: Westview Press, 1989), pp. 95-96.

Managing the "Taiwan Question"

One of the ROC's principal foreign policy concerns was that the PRC might somehow enlist the U.S. into its effort to embark on cross-straits negotiations. Since the August 17 Communiqué, Peking had continued to press Washington on what came to be called the "Taiwan question." Fortunately, the Reagan administration stood fast on its principles. It had no intention of interfering in China's internal affairs, it maintained. Rather, it wanted to see the "Taiwan question" solved by the two parties themselves and would accept any outcome as long as it was not one that was imposed by force.

In the meantime, as Washington repeatedly asserted, it had the right to maintain a full range of economic and social relations with the island through the nominally unofficial American Institute in Taiwan. Whether or not U.S. arms sales to Taiwan would be terminated in the future depended upon eventual peaceful reunification. Washington brushed off Peking's objections that, by imposing conditions on unification and the termination of arms sales, it was violating the principle of noninterference.

To Peking's way of thinking, the full range of U.S.-Taiwan relations bore little resemblance to noninterference. The already close economic relationship between the two countries continued to deepen in the eighties. Two-way trade between the U.S. and ROC reached $20 billion in 1984, three times that of U.S. trade with the PRC. Investment by American corporations such as General Motors, General Electric, and others played a significant role in Taiwan's economic growth.

Most objectionable was the ongoing U.S.-ROC security relationship. Not only did the Taiwan Relations Act imply that the U.S. would come to the defense of Taiwan if she were attacked, U.S. arms sales to the island continued. Although Washington had not violated outright its promise to gradually reduce the level of arms sales pending a "final resolution" of the Taiwan question, Peking found the rate of decrease—20 million a year from a base of 800 million dollars—maddeningly slow.

While PRC leaders remained convinced that American support was a critical component of Taiwan's unwillingness to discuss reunification, they gradually ceased provoking confrontations over the Taiwan question. Instead of calling for Taiwan's "liberation," they spoke of the need for a "peaceful resolution" of the problem. One reason for this more conciliatory approach was a realization on Peking's part that any use of force against Taiwan would probably fail. Equally importantly, it would also hurt the PRC's reputation as a "responsible" member of the world community and dry up the sources of foreign investment capital that the PRC needed for economic development.

The U.S. was careful to allow the "Taiwan question" to remain dormant. As Reagan moved into his second term, his administration exercised greater care in its statements on Taiwan. The error made by Haig on his 1981 visit to China—linking progress on U.S.-PRC relations to PRC concessions on Taiwan—was not repeated.

Peking continued to use every means at its disposal to elicit a response from Taipei. Invitations were issued to Nationalist Party leaders to visit China. Travel regulations were relaxed to encourage travel from Taiwan to the mainland. Peking ministries attempted to contact their counterparts in Taipei to facilitate cross-straits trade and investment. The Chinese Red Cross, taking a page from the Korean Red Cross, sought to initiate talks with Taiwan on the question of family reunification. Peking even began giving prominence to Nationalist individuals, holidays and organizations that were prominent in the decades before they came to power. All these efforts were to no avail. Taipei stood firm on its so-called "three no's" policy—no contact, no talks, and no compromise.[12]

Instead, the ROC continued to look abroad. In 1988-1989 the new "flexible diplomacy" began to pay dividends. Relations with Canada, France, Britain, and Australia were strengthened by establishing trade offices that functioned as *de facto* consulates. Progress was also made in relations with the Philippines, which was considering passing its own "Taiwan Relations Act" to form the basis for ties.

---

[12] S. M. Goldstein and J. Mathews, *Sino-American Relations After Normalization, Toward the Second Decade* (Headline Series, No. 276 Foreign Policy Association, New York, 1985), pp. 28.

Peking was not pleased. In a statement released in December 1988 Peking accused ROC authorities of using flexible diplomacy to push for a "two China" or a "one China, one Taiwan" policy. While it did not object to Taiwan's unofficial ties with the rest of the world in economic, trade, and cultural exchanges, Peking asserted, it would not tolerate any move toward independence.

16

INTO THE NINETIES

I. TIANANMEN SQUARE AND ITS AFTERMATH

Bush Visits Peking

George Bush became the forty-first President of the United States on January 21, 1989. The death in the same month of Japanese Emperor Hirohito, the last surviving World War II leader, brought symbolic closure to that era when Washington, Tokyo, and Moscow had fought to control China's destiny. President Bush, who had served as Washington's *de facto* ambassador to Peking in the mid-1970s, decided to attend Hirohito's funeral in person and continue on to Peking afterwards.

President Bush's meetings with Chinese Communist officials on February 25-26 were brief, more courtesy calls than summit meetings. The most notable event was a negative one: PRC police prevented mainland China's leading dissident, astrophysicist Fang Lizhi, from attending a U.S.-sponsored banquet. Fang and his supporters expressed disappointment that American officials did not intervene more actively on his behalf, contributing to the impression that Bush was weak on China.

On April 15, 1989, former Communist Party General Secretary Hu Yao-bang died of a heart attack. Scapegoated after the 1986 student demonstrations and forced to resign, Hu was a sympathetic figure to many students. They now took to the streets, praising Hu as a martyr to the cause of political reform. This "democracy movement," as it came to be called, advocated freedom of the press and an end to excessive bureaucratism and corruption in government.

The arrival of Mikhail Gorbachev in Peking on May 15 further invigorated the protest movement. The reform-minded Soviet leader was seen as a symbol of new Communist political thinking, and many of the demonstrators who filled Tiananmen Square to welcome him held signs pleading that he intercede on their behalf with China's leaders.

On May 16-17, 1989, over one million demonstrators paralyzed central Peking. Factory workers, civil servants, policemen, and even soldiers joined the students, whose demands had now escalated to include "democratic reforms." Three thousand of them announced a hunger strike, pledging themselves to fast unto death unless such reforms were speedily enacted. Some even called for the forced retirement of Teng and Premier Li Peng, who had come to be seen as the biggest obstacles to change.

A division within the leadership prevented the Chinese Communist Party from immediately moving against the students. Communist Party General Secretary Chao Tzu-yang had emerged as an unexpectedly strong advocate of political reform, meeting with the students and calling publicly for an open dialogue with the regime's critics. Teng and Li rejected this conciliatory approach, but were not able to force Chao out of power immediately. In the meantime, foreign news coverage encouraged the protesters, who in turn gained foreign and especially American sympathy by erecting a Statue of Liberty (christened the "goddess of democracy") on Tiananmen Square.

By May 20, with Chao now out of the way, martial law was declared. Columns of troops and tanks were ordered to retake Tiananmen Square peacefully, but were stopped in their tracks by massive crowds. After two weeks of hesitation, the order to use deadly force was given. On June 4, heavily armed troops fought their way into Peking and occupied the Square, driving off the remaining students. At least 1,000 students were killed and as many as 10,000 wounded in this brutal massacre. In the months following, Teng and his hard-line allies purged the government and party of reformers and continued their harsh repression of dissidents in society at large.

The Political Aftermath

At the outset of the Tiananmen demonstrations, Bush appealed to both sides for moderation, expressing his strong support for democratic reform while praising the principle of nonviolent protest. The American president deliberately avoided criticizing China's leaders or offering any specific encouragement to the students, fearing that this would lead to charges of meddling. He also believed, perhaps wrongly, that the outcome of this political struggle was unlikely to have much effect on U.S.-China relations.

Following the massacre, Bush condemned the violence in the strongest possible terms and announced that he was suspending military ties and high-level contacts with China. Stung by this criticism, and further angered by the decision of the American Embassy to grant asylum to Fang Lizhi and his wife, Peking charged that the U.S. was interfering in China's internal affairs. When former President Richard Nixon visited China in October, he was rebuffed by the Peking leadership.

In the aftermath of Tiananmen, Bush appeared eager—too eager in the view of some in the U.S. Congress—to mend the rift in U.S.-China relations. He vetoed a bill granting permanent residence to 40,000 Chinese students in the U.S., although he later extended their visas by one year. He opposed the package of sanctions which Congress passed in early November suspending trade preferences and banning the export of certain high technology items, although Bush stopped short of vetoing it. In violation of his own ban on high-level contacts, he sent National Security Advisor Brent Scowcroft and Deputy Secretary of State Lawrence Eagleburger to Peking in early December in an effort to improve relations. In the fallout from that trip, which accomplished little, it came out that this had been Scowcroft's second trip to the Chinese capital since the massacre. He had earlier paid a secret visit to Peking in July. This news further exacerbated tensions between the U.S. Congress and the White House.

Bush's eagerness to repair relations with China arose in part from his fondness for a country to which he had served as envoy in 1976-77. But he also believed that it was important not to isolate a country of China's size, strategic location, and economic potential. He argued to everyone who would listen that political reform in China could best be achieved by private diplomacy rather than public criticism.

The collapse of communism in Eastern Europe, especially the bloody counterrevolution in Romania, shocked the Peking leadership. Even so, by early January 1990 China's deepening economic crisis led her elderly rulers to lift martial law and free 573 people who had been imprisoned for participating in the democracy movement. Although these moves generated little applause in Congress, Bush called the end of martial law a "very sound step" and began dismantling the sanctions. Other nations such as France and Japan followed suit. As China's foreign trade rebounded and loans from the World Bank and other international agencies resumed, China's post-Tiananmen slump was over.

II. TAIWAN'S EVOLVING MAINLAND POLICY

The Tiananmen demonstrations were initially viewed on Taiwan as a potential harbinger of political change on the mainland and an opportunity to advance the ROC's interests there. Already in 1987 the ban on travel to the mainland had been relaxed, and Taiwan investment capital had begun to flood into China's coastal provinces. Now in April 1989 Lien Chan, then serving as ROC Foreign Minister, spoke for the first time of a possible "one country, two governments" formula. The following month, as the demonstrations spread to other Chinese cities, President Lee Teng-hui announced that the ROC was willing to enter into negotiations with the PRC on an equal basis provided that the latter pursued an internal policy of political democratization and economic liberalization, renounced the use of force against Taiwan, and abandoned its efforts to isolate Taiwan internationally.

Peking, of course, did none of these things. Instead, in an act designed to terrorize its own population, it struck out against the student demonstrators with deadly force. The fundamental weaknesses of China's closed society—the enormous chasm between rulers and ruled, a dictatorial regime's inability to compromise in a crisis situation—were revealed for all the world to see. Taiwan, no less than the community of nations, drew back in horror.

Not until the opening months of 1990, with public feeling over the massacre beginning to subside somewhat, did the ROC government again reconsider its mainland policy. In March, Taipei lifted its ban on business travel across the Taiwan Straits and allowed its businessmen to participate in PRC trade fairs. At the same time, lower-echelon government employees and mid-ranking Kuomintang party officials were added to the categories of those officially permitted to visit their families on the mainland. The possibility of allowing direct investment in the mainland also began to receive serious consideration. In May 1990 two groups of ROC legislators, from the Legislative Yuan and the National Assembly, visited Peking. Later that year, Taipei set up an unofficial foundation, the Straits Exchange Foundation, to open channels of communication with Peking. Republic of China officials stated publicly that the Legislative Yuan should draft and pass laws governing the people-to-people links that were developing. Taken together, these developments raised doubts about whether the official "three no's" policy towards the PRC—*no* contact, *no* negotiations, and *no* compromise— would be maintained indefinitely.

Peking's reaction to these overtures was mixed. The new infusion of Taiwan capital was clearly welcome, coming as it did when other sources of foreign currency were drying up. The hundreds of thousands of tourists who flooded across the Taiwan Straits also met with a warm greeting, since foreign tourists were staying away in droves after Tiananmen. At the same time, Peking ruled out direct "government-to-government" talks, on the grounds that this would violate its one-China policy. Peking instead called for "party-to-party" contacts. Also rejected was President Lee's insistence that the PRC meet certain conditions, such as the renunciation of the use of force against Taiwan, before the opening of official contacts. Reunification talks, Peking argued, should begin without prior conditions.

President Lee's acknowledgment of the reality of a divided China, which was widely acclaimed in Taiwan, aroused the rancor of the Peking authorities, who wrongly saw it as the opening wedge of a drive for Taiwan independence. Peking accused the ROC leader of abandoning the "substantive diplomacy" of the late President Chiang Ching-kuo in favor of a "pragmatic" or "flexible" diplomacy. While the former was based on a "one-China policy," the latter would inevitably lead to "two-Chinas;

or one China, one Taiwan." By this means, Peking claimed, and with Washington's secret backing, Taipei hoped to (1) elevate its ties with other nations to at least the level that it enjoyed with the U.S.; (2) use the Asian Development Bank "dual seat" formula as a means of reentering other international organizations; and (3) establish formal diplomatic ties with other countries using a "dual recognition" approach.

Thus was the Peking's eagerness to reap the benefits of economic interaction with Taiwan combined with continued hostility towards its freely elected political leadership.

The ROC's "Guidelines for National Unification"

The ROC government was determined that the eventual reunification of China take place in a peaceful and reasonable fashion, under conditions of equality and reciprocity, and that it result in the establishment of a free and democratic country in which wealth was equitably distributed. To draw up a long-range plan to accomplish this, the National Unification Council of the ROC was established under the authority of the Office of the President. After some months of deliberation, the council on February 23, 1991, approved the "Guidelines for National Unification."

The "Guidelines" outlined three stages in the unification process, which it stressed should be peaceful, reasonable, and equitable. During the first stage, efforts would be made to promote mutual understanding with reciprocal exchanges in order to eliminate any enmity still existing between Taiwan and the mainland. To achieve this end, Taiwan would set up a nongovernmental organization to carry out various kinds of bilateral exchanges and to protect the rights and interests of the people on both sides.

During the second stage, efforts would be made to establish direct government-to-government links. Direct flights, trade and postal service would be permitted, and reciprocal visits by high-ranking public figures from both sides would be encouraged. Both sides would help each other to participate in international organizations, and would jointly develop the southeastern coastal area of the mainland in order to narrow the gap in living standards between the two sides.

During the third and final stage, an organization would be established to carry out consultations with the mainland on unification in accordance with the principles of democratic practice, economic freedom, social security, and the nationalization of military forces. These consultations would be followed by discussions on a constitutional system which would establish a free and democratic country in which wealth would be equitably distributed.

These Guidelines for National Unification differed in two principal respects from the unification policy of the Chinese Communists. The most important difference concerned the question of peaceful unification, for Peking had never ruled out the use of force against Taiwan.[1] Although they professed to be committed to peaceful unification, they had at the same time made it clear that they would resort to arms in case of foreign intervention in the unification process or if Taiwan should declare its independence.

The insistence of the Chinese Communists on reserving the right to use force was widely criticized on Taiwan, for it smacked of intimidation. Voluntarily accept our terms for unification or else we will recover Taiwan by force of arms, their posture seemed to imply. How can you say you are sincerely committed to peaceful unification, the ROC government responded, if you do not reject the use of force under any and all circumstances? But Peking was unwilling to accept Taipei's challenge and demonstrate its sincerity in the only way that really mattered.

Another key difference between the policies of the two sides was that Peking explicitly rejected the principle of equality. Under its formula of "one country, two systems," Peking would remain the central government, while Taipei would be downgraded to the status of a local government. Peking promised that Taiwan would continue to enjoy, for a certain period of time, a high degree of autonomy as a special administrative region, including the right to practice *San Min Chu I* (The

---

[1] Chien Wei-chang, Vice Chairman of the Political Consultative Conference of the PRC, stated on December 9, 1990, at Maçao, that three factors would trigger the invasion of Taiwan: delay in re-unification talks, "independence movement" activity, and foreign interference in Taiwan affairs. *China Post* (Taipei), December 13, 1990.

Three Principles of the People). This autonomy would not extend to questions of national defense or foreign relations, however, which Peking would strictly control.

Peking's "one country, two systems" formula also meant that unification would not occur on democratic terms. The PRC government was a self-avowed one-party dictatorship, and likely to remain so. Unification on its terms would subject the increasing freedom and democratic rights enjoyed by the people on Taiwan to the whims of Communist Party leaders.

The End of Emergency Rule in Taiwan

In 1948, as the Chinese civil war reached its climax, President Chiang Kai-shek had declared a "Period of National Mobilization for the Suppression of the Communist Rebellion." Under the emergency constitutional provisions passed by the First National Assembly in May, 1948, legislators elected the previous year were to serve in office indefinitely. As the decades passed, these provisions increasingly hindered the ROC's political progress, and made any reconsideration of mainland policy difficult. In 1987 the ROC government lifted martial law and embarked on a series of political reforms. These culminated on May 1, 1991, when the Period of National Mobilization was officially ended by presidential decree. The ROC had, by anyone's standards, become a full-fledged democracy.

III. ROC-U.S. TRADE AND INVESTMENT RELATIONS

Tensions in Trade Relations

If contacts between Taiwan and the mainland were growing in intensity, the ROC's most important external relationship remained that with the U.S.. Taiwan's economy was heavily dependent on foreign trade, so much so that in recent years approximately three-quarters of its

GNP has derived from this source.[2] Among the ROC's trading partners, none was more important than the U.S., which in 1986 took 48 percent of Taiwan's total exports. The value of bilateral trade, which increased more than 300 times in the four decades following 1950, reached $34.35 billion in 1990.

The problem was that, by the 1980s, Taiwan's exports to the U.S. were far outpacing her imports from that country. In 1987, for example, the ROC racked up a bilateral trade surplus with the U.S. of $16 billion. Its overall foreign trade surplus that year, nearly all of which arose from its U.S. trade, was equivalent to no less than one-sixth of its gross domestic product (GDP). Not surprisingly, the ROC's foreign exchange reserves soared, reaching $76 billion by the end of 1987 and continuing to climb.

Neither the growing trade imbalance nor the ROC's expanding foreign exchange reserves pleased Washington, which began to exert pressure on Taipei to reduce its trade surpluses. Since the ROC was heavily dependent upon the U.S. in a number of areas, including the supply of credit, foreign investment, access to advanced technology, the purchase of military equipment, and support in international affairs, Taipei entered into negotiations with the U.S. from a position of relative weakness.[3]

Such negotiations were initiated by the U.S. whenever it decided that the principle of fair trade had been violated, and specific changes in trade practices were demanded in no uncertain terms. This occurred with increasing frequency in the late eighties and early nineties, as the U.S. sought to pressure not only Taiwan, but China, Japan, South Korea, and other countries as well, to abide by the principles of fair trade and open their domestic markets to U.S. goods.

---

2 In 1990, Taiwan's total export earnings amounted to $67.2 billion and imports $54.7 billion. Taiwan had a gross national product of $161.5 billion and a per capita income of $7,990 in 1990.

3 Over the 15-year period of the U.S. Economic Aid to Taiwan Program, the United States provided $1.5 billion to ROC from 1950 to 1965. Thereafter the ROC. received continuing economic assistance in the form of grants, loans, technical assistance, and surplus agricultural commodities. The ROC. also received U.S. military assistance between 1951 and 1973 totaling about $1.5 billion.

The ROC government was eager to resolve the frictions which had arisen over trade. Taipei also agreed in principle that further trade liberalization was desirable, and that Taiwan's economy should be internationalized. The pace of change should be moderate, however, since the ROC was already in the midst of a sweeping transformation. Too much change to the political and economic system in too short a period of time might prove destabilizing. Taiwan needed time. Time for individual businesses to adapt to changing economic circumstances. Time to educate the people of Taiwan's responsibilities as an important member of the international economic community.

Washington, impatient for trade surpluses to be reduced, was unmoved by such arguments. In January 1988 President Ronald Reagan announced that the economies of Taiwan, South Korea, Singapore, and Hong Kong were sufficiently developed to "graduate" them from the preferential tariff rates they had received as "developing nations" under the Generalized System of Preferences (GSP). After January 2, 1989, these countries would pay the same tariff rates as other developed countries.

Taipei's efforts to reduce its trade surplus in the late eighties included the opening of its domestic markets to American tobacco and wine, as well as the reduction or elimination of tariffs on a number of other imported goods. These steps were taken in the face of sometimes substantial public opposition. Taiwan farmers took to the streets, for example, to protest government concessions on the import of American turkey parts.

In other moves, the ROC government granted exclusive rights to American contractors to bid on construction contracts for Taipei's subway, and for the first time allowed American insurance companies and brokerage houses to operate in Taiwan. The practice of sending special procurement missions to the U.S., which had begun in 1977, was expanded. The $12 billion in American goods which had been purchased from 1977-87 was a significant offset to the trade surplus. The ROC also tried, with some success, to reduce its overdependence on the U.S. market. Exports to the U.S., which accounted for 48 percent of total exports in 1986, had fallen to 38.7 percent of total exports in 1988.

Under U.S. pressure, the Taiwan economy went through a rapid restructuring. Beginning in September 1985 and continuing over the next several years, the New Taiwan (NT) dollar appreciated more than 40 percent. Starting at NT$40 against the U.S. dollar, it had reached NT$28.1 by the end of 1988. This drastic rise forced many small- and medium-sized enterprises to either close their doors or move to the mainland or to Southeast Asia in search of lower labor costs. Yet Washington continued to demand further appreciation, bringing protests from Taipei that its export-dependent private sector was already under severe stress. Taiwan capital began to flow to countries with more stable currencies, or which were less susceptible to U.S. pressure. Over the eighties, according to unofficial figures, Taiwan investors invested more than $8 billion abroad in Southeast Asia and the U.S.

Simultaneous with this severe currency appreciation, the once-protected domestic market was opened to a wide array of U.S. products. In 1988 tariffs were cut by an average of 50 percent on 3,800 imported items. In 1989 tariff rates fell further, with nominal rates dropping from 12.5 percent to 10.25 percent, and effective rates declining from 5.2 percent to 4.7 percent. Other changes in the Taiwan economy included improved capital flow, reduced tariff rates, and the dismantling of non-tariff barriers. Restrictions on the operation of foreign service-related businesses were ended, intellectual property rights began enjoying increased protection, and controls over foreign exchange reserves were removed.

All of these changes produced the desired result. By end of 1988 the ROC's trade surplus had fallen to $10.4 billion on a total trade of $36.4 billion.[4] By 1990 it was only $9.1 billion. The ROC-U.S. trade imbalance had been reduced almost by half, although it was still a source of considerable friction.[5]

---

4 Thomas B. Gold, "Taiwan in 1988: The Transition to a post-Chiang World," in A. J. Kane, *China Briefing, 1989* (Westview, 1989), pp. 97- 98.
5 Another factor was the actual difference in the size of two markets. The U.S. was a market with 240 million people while the ROC was only a market of 21 million people a difference in size of 12 to 1. It could not be expected there two markets would absorb the same amount of goods, one from the other. In 1986, each person in Taiwan spent $300 on American products (about 8 percent of ROC GNP). While each person in the U.S. spent about $90 on products from ROC (about 0.6 percent of U.S. GNP).

Other proposals concerning ways to reduce the trade deficit were vetoed by the U.S. When Taipei sought to increase its purchases of advanced weapons systems, the U.S. refused on the grounds that this would violate the "Second Shanghai Communiqué," which called for a gradual reduction in the amount of arms sold to Taiwan. The U.S. was willing to allow technology transfers by private firms like General Dynamics, which was helping Taiwan to develop its own jet fighter, but such transfers were relatively inexpensive and hence did little to solve the trade deficit.

The ROC government also suggested in November 1988 that the U.S. enter into a free-trade agreement with Taiwan comparable to those recently signed with Canada and Israel. American officials gave this idea a cool reception, pointing out that the lack of diplomatic ties constituted a significant barrier to the establishment of a free trade area. Neither were they convinced that non-tariff barriers to American products would come down as a result. Taipei's proposal to establish a ROC-U.S. arbitration organization also fell on stony ground.

The ROC was enthusiastic about assuming more responsibilities in the international economic arena. To aid developing nations, the government established an International Economic Cooperation Development Fund (IECDF) in 1989. The initial amount available for international economic assistance was $1.1 billion. The ROC also applied to join the World Trade Organization (WTO) so that it would be treated as an equal in future international trade talks.

American Investment in Taiwan and Its Impact

The ROC government made strenuous efforts to attract foreign investment from almost the beginning of its tenure on Taiwan. The stable political environment, high quality labor force, extensive legal protection, a five-year tax holiday for industrial investment, and ready repatriation of profits gradually attracted an increasing number of foreign investors. Foreign investments increased from $57 million in 1964 to $5.9 billion by the end of 1987. In that year alone, reacting to the political liberalization and the internationalization of the Taiwan economy, some 363 new foreign ventures totaling some $1.2 billion in capital were approved by the government.

Investors from the U.S. had more capital invested in Taiwan than any other foreign group, although the Japanese, who tended to make smaller investments, ranked first in terms of the total number of foreign investments. By the end of 1987 the total American investment of $2.3 billion in 635 different enterprises accounted for over one-third of total foreign investment. Something less than half of the total American investment capital, or $1 billion, had gone into the electronic and electrical manufacturing businesses. As a result of this investment, and the transfer of advanced American technology which it entailed, this sector of the economy had grown in importance, and by the late 1980s provided the largest share of Taiwan's exports.

Taiwan's infrastructure, which had been severely strained by the rapid economic growth of the eighties, was undergoing a major overhaul in the nineties. Under the Six-Year National Construction Plan the ROC is spending more than $300 billion from 1991-96 on infrastructural improvements to enhance Taiwan's industrial potential, increase national income, promote balanced growth, and improve the quality of life. American and other foreign companies are participating in the 775 projects which have been undertaken, covering everything from communications and transportation to environmental protection and flood prevention. The goal, as outlined by President Lee, is nothing less than the transformation of Taiwan into one of the Asian-Pacific's premier financial, high-technology, and shipping centers.

The Rising Tide of Taiwan Investments in America

In the closing years of the eighties Taiwan's foreign investment shifted away from its traditional Southeast Asian destinations towards the U.S. While U.S. economic growth and political stability, and Taiwan's desire to acquire advanced technology played a role in this shift, two factors stood out. First, the depreciation of the U.S. dollar lowered the cost of U.S. assets. Second, the ROC government eased its controls over foreign exchange and allowed its citizens to remit $5 million out of the country annually.

Taiwan investors flocked to America. The U.S. Commerce Department put the total amount of Taiwan investment in the U.S. by the end of 1989 at $620 million, or nearly double that of the previous year.

By the end of the following year, according to the Coordination Council for North American Affairs (CCNAA), total direct Taiwan investment in the U.S. had reached $1.32 billion. The real figure was considerably higher, CCNAA officials added, since many Taiwan companies reinvested their U.S. profits through their North American subsidiaries without going through government channels.

Of the more than 1,400 ROC firms operating in the U.S. as of 1991, approximately half were located in California (733), with smaller numbers in New York (166), New Jersey (101), Texas (84), and Massachusetts (29). These firms were active in the electronics, electrical, and chemicals industries, and in computer manufacturing, trading, banking, and real estate.

Although Taiwan's investments in the U.S. remain fairly modest compared to those of Great Britain, which has over $125 billion invested, or Japan, with some $78 billion invested, their growth over the past decade has been dramatic. This growth will continue, as Taiwan firms continue to push beyond their domestic markets and tap U.S. expertise in high technology.

U.S.-ROC economic ties remain very close. The ROC, which ranks fourteenth among the trading nations of the world, was the sixth most important trading partner of the U.S. throughout the early 1990s. Taipei's reserves, estimated at $90 billion in 1992, remain the second largest in the world. A substantial portion of these foreign reserves is kept in the U.S., largely because foreign trade is denominated in U.S. dollars and North America is seen as a safe haven. Although the percentage kept in American banks has fallen from 65 percent to something over 50 percent in recent years, it remains important in helping to finance the U.S. budget deficit.

The China Factor

Taiwan's future is inextricably linked to, and extensively affected by, its relationship with the United States on the one hand, and with the China mainland on the other. While U.S. influence appears to be on the wane in Asia, the PRC, with its booming economy and growing military strength, is casting an ever longer shadow.

The collapse of the Soviet Union removed a major threat from the PRC's northern and western borders, leaving it second only to Russia as the dominant power on the Asian mainland. Drawing upon its increased economic and military strength, Peking appears bent on establishing regional hegemony over Southeast Asia. The portents are many. In September 1993 New Delhi signed a treaty with Peking accepting China's territorial gains in the 1962 Sino-Indian War.[6] Burma has become a virtual tributary state, while Vietnamese officials are increasingly nervous about the intentions of their giant neighbor. Farther afield Peking also scored successes, establishing diplomatic ties with Israel and South Korea in 1992. Hong Kong will return to the embrace of the motherland in June 1997 with Macao to follow in 1999. That will leave only the territory controlled by the ROC outside Peking's writ.

Despite the disappearance of the Soviet Union as a strategic threat, and the gradual drawdown of American forward-deployed forces in the Pacific, the PRC continues its arms buildup. Advanced Su-27 fighters and other weapons systems have been purchased from Moscow and air-to-air refueling technology has been acquired from Iran. Work continues on the East Wind 25, a new intercontinental ballistic missile. The PRC continues to maintain more men under arms than any other country in Asia, and its military budget continues to expand at a double-digit clip.

It remains true that mainland China's economic gains could easily be lost to political instability. Although the Communist elite appears to have reached consensus on the importance of continued market-oriented reforms, Teng's death may shatter this apparent unanimity. It is by no means certain that Teng's hand-picked successor, Chiang Tse-min, and the pragmatic technocrats he has installed as vice-premiers and as state councilors, will emerge victorious from the power struggle that will follow Teng's death.

Facing an unpredictable future, the ROC government has behaved with great prudence. Under the general oversight of the National Unification Council, the Mainland Affairs Council sets mainland policy, with the Straits Exchange Foundation, a nonofficial body, serving as the actual channel of communication. This three-tiered organizational

---

6   See Ross H. Munro, "China's Waxing Spheres of Influence," *Orbis* (Fall 1994), p. 11.

structure has helped the ROC establish and maintain a clear and consistent policy toward mainland China based on the principles of peace, reciprocity and equality. If Peking would respond in a similarly rational and equitable manner, and refrain from threatening Taiwan's security, then the two sides could gradually gain confidence in each other.

Since this has not yet happened, and in the face of the continuing PRC arms buildup, Taiwan has countered with its own military modernization program. The single most important element in this program is the purchase of 150 F-16s from the U.S. This sale was approved by President Bush on September 2, 1992, with the rather transparent political aim of winning votes in Texas. His decision to approve the $6 billion deal was nevertheless a correct one, for it provided the ROC with badly needed military insurance against the PRC which has still not renounced the use of force. In reversing the decade-long U.S. policy of not selling advanced arms to the ROC, Bush also in effect encouraged other Western nations to follow suit. France, for one, approved an ROC order for 60 Mirage 2000s soon after.

The paradox of cross-straits relations—growing economic ties combined with residual political hostility—can in the final analysis only be resolved by changes in mainland China. As long as the political structure of the PRC remains a one-party dictatorship, perpetuating the errors of China's feudal past, then there is little hope for actual unification. Only after China becomes a democracy can true mutual respect, economic complementarity, and a common political identity be achieved. There is little that Taiwan can do directly to bring about this necessary change in China, but the power of its example as the first Chinese state in all of history to modernize and democratize should not be underestimated. Taiwan is China's future.

17

CONCLUSION

I. IN RETROSPECT

From the arrival of the Empress of China at the port of Whampoa in Canton on August 28, 1784, to the daily international flights that now link American and Chinese cities, the two-century relationship between China and the U.S. has had its triumphs and its tragedies. The U.S., to its credit, remained neutral in the Opium Wars, gaining the gratitude of the Chinese government and great benefits through the most-favored-nation treaty. American missionaries opened many modern centers of learning in China, while Chinese laborers helped build railroads across the Western U.S. The remission of the Boxer indemnity established the U.S. as the principal destination for Chinese going abroad to study, so much so that by the early 1990s there were more than 52,000 Chinese students studying in the U.S., many of whom would remain in America to make significant contributions to their adopted country.

Perhaps the greatest triumph in Sino-American relations was the "Open Door" policy, which preserved China's territorial integrity, and was eventually adopted by the signatories of the Nine Power Treaty in 1922. The U.S. also took the lead in extending diplomatic recognition to the newly established Republic of China on March 2, 1913, ignoring the objections of the other powers. When the Japanese invaded Manchuria on September 18, 1931, Washington announced that it would not recognize territorial changes created by force, although it was not until

Pearl Harbor that the U.S. joined the ROC in actively resisting Japanese aggression.

The remarkable wartime solidarity between the U.S. and the ROC was marred by a series of missteps as this war came to an end. The single most serious lapse in U.S. policy came at Yalta when, over the objections of the ROC government, Roosevelt endorsed the Soviet occupation of Manchuria. This greatly assisted the Chinese Communists in their rebellion against the Nationalist government, partially negating the otherwise outstanding efforts of the U.S. military to return to Nationalist government control all of the territories held by the Japanese at the close of the war. The Marshall mission, through its endless and ineffective efforts at mediation, gave further encouragement to the Communists to continue their civil war. When this conflict reached its unhappy end, the U.S. Department of State issued its infamous White Paper, placing all of the blame for the "loss of China" on the Nationalist government.

A new era in U.S.-ROCrelations was opened by the Korean War. Truman reversed his decision to abandon the Nationalist government and sent the U.S. Seventh Fleet to patrol the Taiwan Straits, although as much to keep the Nationalist government from counterattacking the Communists as vice versa. American aid, which was to eventually total some $1.5 billion, helped lay the foundation for Taiwan's rapid economic progress. An American ambassador was accredited to Taipei and the Mutual Defense Treaty was signed.

The U.S. maintained formal diplomatic ties with the ROC until the end of the seventies, although the relationship was under increasing strain. The Chinese Communists began to practice "smiling diplomacy" in the early seventies, inviting the U.S. Table Tennis team, Henry Kissinger, and finally Richard Nixon himself to visit Peking. As the U.S. position towards the PRC weakened, the ROC, one of the founding member of the United Nations, was forced to leave that organization. Finally, on January 1, 1979—one of the darkest days in ROC diplomatic history—the U.S. abandoned the ROC in favor of ties with the PRC.

Many in the U.S. were unhappy with this turn of events, and worked to ensure passage of the Taiwan Relations Act, which was approved by both Houses of Congress and signed into law by President Carter on April 10, 1979. The TRA has allowed substantive relations between the

ROC and the U.S. to continue through nominally private organizations, the AIT and the CCNAA, and helped to ensure the security of Taiwan and hence of the Western Pacific. Relations between the ROC and the U.S., albeit "unofficial," are perhaps closer now than they have ever been. The ROC on Taiwan has joined the ranks of the developed countries and is a full-fledged democracy.

Reviewing the record, one would have to conclude that the relationship between China and the U.S. has seen more ups than downs. The Chinese people take a generally sanguine view of this relationship, for despite the inevitable disappointments, the U.S. was the only Western Power which from the beginning sought to deal with China on a basis of equality. The desire of the two nations, expressed in the first Sino-American Treaty signed in 1844, "to establish firm, lasting and sincere friendship" has been realized.

II. THE FUTURE

In the past, relations between the U.S. and China have necessarily been somewhat one-sided. While the U.S. has consistently been one of China's most important diplomatic partners, the opposite has not been true. Well into the twentieth century, America's most important ties were across the Atlantic, not the Pacific. Relations with China were considered of secondary, even tertiary, importance.

It was only during the bleak years of World War II, in the course of a common struggle against Japanese aggression, that the U.S. finally began to perceive China as an important ally. This carried over into the post-war world, when China found herself elevated to a status equal to that of the other major powers, expected to participate in the United Nations and elsewhere in the creation of a peaceful international order.

Then came the Communist takeover of the mainland, and the inward-looking policies adopted by the Peking regime. China ceased being regarded by the major powers as one of their own. When the U.S. began to court the PRC in the late sixties, it was with the intention of using China as a counterweight to an expansionist Soviet Union. By the time this rationale disappeared with the dissolution of the Soviet Union, the Communists had loosened economic controls to the extent that the natural entrepreneurial ability of the Chinese people began to assert itself.

The disintegration of the Soviet Union and the collapse of Communism in Eastern Europe led many to conclude that similar political changes would soon come to China. This has not happened, in part because China enjoys a much higher degree of territorial and ethnic integrity than the former Soviet Union, in part because the Cultural Revolution instilled in the Chinese people a fear of rapid political change.

Communism is fading in China, however, just as it earlier did in Europe, albeit in a piecemeal fashion. Teng Hsiao-ping's stress on development over ideology has been welcomed by the people, who see his "four cardinal principles" as nothing more than a pretentious slogan, and "peaceful evolution" in the direction of a more open society as a worthwhile goal. The ROC's successful development into a free-market democracy is a powerful example for many on the mainland.

The "open-door" policy has not only created an economic boom, but has also brought in many hundreds of thousands of visitors from Taiwan and Hong Kong, as well as allowing many thousands of mainland residents to travel abroad. The increasingly cosmopolitan outlook of many mainland Chinese will eventually be reflected in the thoughts and actions of the ruling elite.

Among the scenarios for China after Teng, the most probable is a continuation of the status quo. In the future Peking will face not civil war but a continued devolution of political power to the provinces. The marketization of the economy will proceed apace, and will bring in its train gradual democratization, especially in the coastal provinces. Economic interdependence across the Taiwan Straits will draw the two sides together over time, in the same way that the Prussian customs union in 1828 led to the unification of Germany in the 1850s. Overseas Chinese will continue to pour in investment capital, and their renewed ties with their fatherland will create the necessary conditions for a Greater China economic community. Other Asian-Pacific countries may be drawn into such a community as well, as mutual investment, trade, tourism, and cultural exchanges create a sense of a common Asian-Pacific homeland.

Within a short period of fifteen to twenty years, China surely will be a militarily-strong economic power to be reckoned with in international affairs. As a consequence of this auspicious development, two dangerous trends are emerging, which will need skillful and cautious handling. The first is China's drive for industrialization which, when fully developed, will endanger her own existence and threaten the world environment. The industrialization of China will come sooner or later and will raise the standard of living of its people. To maintain it at the world average, and to feed its 1.2 billion population of China is a not insignificant problem. Here the United States, with its technological know-how, must lend a helping hand and work with China on a concerted effort for development, production and trade.

The second dangerous trend is China's behavior in the international forum. Even though she has time and again denied her intention of seeking hegemony, her actions of large arms acquisitions, intensified weaponry research, together with an anomalous foreign policy, point to exactly the opposite conclusion. Furthermore, in her urge to act as a big power—rightfully so, after more than one and a half century of bitter and humiliating experiences in dealing with the outside world—she may show a vindictive and overly assertive attitude in international affairs, as her economic, military and intellectual level grows. In her quest for superpower status, China must consider whether her resources, natural and otherwise, will allow her to reach that status while providing a decent living for her citizens. History has taught us that when a government is covetous, events sometimes turn out the opposite of what had been planned.

Some observers see the present trend of decentralization of power, and the preoccupation of the People's Liberation Army with profit-generating activity in non-military fields as a safety valve limiting excessive military activism. At the same time, the United States, as the leading benevolent power in the world, should work with countries on China's periphery to avert any perilous developments. The Republic of China on Taiwan can play an important role in Chine through its trade, investments, and technical know-how, as well as other economic and diplomatic tools, to induce and encourage changes in the right direction. These efforts also should aim to reorient the views of those in power in Peking, letting China's transformation process follow a natural course of evolution. Peaceful coexistence should become a universally accepted principle in a rapidly integrating world.

As the world is rendered increasingly interdependent by global communications, financial networks, advanced military technology, and universal values, it is expected that relations among nations will move beyond traditional military alliances and toward more productive arrangements. It is certain that upon the attainment of peaceful reunification, China will undoubtedly become a great power, politically as well as economically, in the forthcoming century. Regardless of who will reign over the country, an enlightened China will dwarf Japan's aspirations for dominance and render United States-China relations more constructive, thus setting the stage for a new model in international relations. Diplomatic initiatives in the Sino-American relationship will no longer be troubled by prejudices or misconceptions. Instead, China will be in a position to extend aid and assistance to others.

APPENDIX I-A

Chinese Heads of State, Premiers, Ministers of Foreign Affairs and Official Representatives Accredited to the U.S.A.

Ch'ing Dynasty 1644 - 1991 Emperor	Reigning Years	Minister of Foreign Affairs	Term of Office	Official Representative Accredited to U.S.A.	Term of Office
Wen-tsung (Hsien Feng)	1851 - 1861	Prince Kung, Yi Hsin*	1861		
Mu-tsung (T'ung Chih)	1862 - 1874	Prince Kung, Yi Hsin*	1862 - 1874		
Te-tsung	1875 - 1908	Prince Kung, Yi Hsin*	1875 - 1884	Chen Lan-ping Cheng Chao-ju	1878 - 1880 1881 - 1885
(Kuang Hsu)		Prince Ch'ing, Yi K'uang*	1884 - 1894	Chang Yin-huan Tsui Kuo-yin	1885 - 1889 1889 - 1893
		Prince Kung, Yi Hsin*	1894 - 1898	Yang Ju	1893 - 1896
		Prince Ch'ing, Yi K'uang	1898 - 1900	Wu T'ing-fang	1896 - 1902
		Prince Tuan, Tsai Chi*	1900		
		Prince Ch'ing, Yi K'uang	1901 - 1908	Liang Chen Wu T'ing-fang	1903 - 1907 1907 - 1909
Hsuan-T'ung	1909 - 1911	Prince Ch'ing, Yi K'uang	1909 - 1911	Chang Yin-t'ang	1909 - 1912

*Tsung-Ling Ta-chen (Chief Minister of Tsungli Yamen)

387

APPENDIX I-B

Chinese Heads of State, Premiers, Ministers of Foreign Affairs and Official Representatives Accredited to the U.S.A.

Republic of China President	Term of Office	Premier	Term of Office	Minister of Foreign Affairs	Term of Office	Diplomatic Representative Accredited to U.S.A.	Term of Office
Sun Yat-sen	1912			Wang Chung-hui	1912		
Yan Shih-k'ai	1912-1916	Tang Shao-yi Lu Cheng-hsiang Chao Ping-chun Hsiung Hsi-ling Hsu Shig-chang	1912 1912 1912 1913-1914 1914-1915	Liang Ju-hao Lu Cheng-hsiang	1912 1912-1915	Hsia Chieh-fu (M) Vi-kyuin Wellington Koo (M)	1913-1915 1915-1920
Li Yuan-hung	1916-1917	Tuan Ch'i-jui Li Chin-hsi	1916-1917 1917	Tang Sabo-yi Wu T'ing-fang Lu Cheng-hsiang	1916 1916-1917 1917		
Feng Kuo-chang	1917	Wang Shih-cheng Tuan Ch'i-jui	1917 1917-1918	Lu Cheng-hsiang Yen Wei-ching	1918-1920 1921-1922		
Hsu Shing-chang	1918-1922	Chin Yun-peng Liang Shih-yi	1919-1921 1921	Vi-kyuin Wellington Koo Wang Cheng-t'ing	1922 1922		
Li Yuan-hung	1922-1923	Yen Wei-ching Wang Chung-hui Chang Shao-tseng	1922 1922 1923	Vi-kyuin Wellington Koo Wang Cheng-t'ing Tang Shao-yi	1923-1924 1924 1924		
Tsao K'un	1923-1924	Sun Pao-chi Yen Wei-ching	1924 1924	Yen Wei-ching	1925-1926		
Tuan Ch'i-jui	1924-1926	Yen Wei-ching Vi-kyuin Wellington Koo	1926 1927	Vi-kyuin Wellington Koo	1926-1927	Sze Sao-ke	1920-1929

(M) Envoy Extraordinary and Minister Plenipotentiary

APPENDIX I-C

Chinese Heads of State, Premiers, Ministers of Foreign Affairs and Official Representatives Accredited to the U.S.A.

Republic of China President	Term of Office	Premier (President of Executive Yuan)	Term of Office	Minister of Foreign Affairs	Term of Office	Official Representative Accredited to U.S.A.	Term of Office
Chiang Kai-shek	1928 - 1931	T'an Yen-kai	1928 - 1930	Wang Cheng-t'ing	1928 - 1931	Wu Chao-chu (M)	1929 - 1931
		Chiang Kai-skek	1930 - 1931	Vi-kyuin Wellington Koo	1931	Yen Wei-ching (M)	1931 - 1933
Lin Shen	1932 - 1943	Sun Fo	1932	Chen Yu-jen	1932	Sze Sao-ke (M)	1933 - 1935
		Wang Ching-wei	1932 - 1935	Lo Wen-kan	1932 - 1933		
				Wang Ching-wei	1934 - 1935		
		Chiang Kai-shek	1936 - 1937	Chung Chun	1935 - 1937	Sze Sao-ke (A)	1935 - 1937
		Kung Hsiang-hsi	1938 - 1939	Wang Chung-hui	1937 - 1941	Wang Cheng-t'ing (A)	1937 - 1938
		Chiang Kai-shek	1940 - 1944	Quo Tai-chi	1941	Hu Shih (A)	1938 - 1942
				Soong Tse-vung	1942 - 1945	Wei Tao-ming (A)	1942 - 1945
Chiang Kai-shek	1943 - 1947	Soong Tse-vun	1945 - 1947	Wang Shih-chien	1945 - 1948	Vi-kyuin Wellington Koo (A)	1946 - 1956
		Chang Chun	1947				
Chiang Kai-shek	1948 - 1949	Wong Wen-ho	1948	Wu Teh-chen	1948 - 1949		
		Sun Fo	1948 - 1949	Yeh Kung-chao	1949 - 1958		
Li Tsing-jen (acting)	1949	Ho Ying-chin	1949				
		Yen Hsi-shan	1949 - 1950				
Chiang Kai-shek	1950 - 1975	Chen Cheng	1950 - 1954	Huan Shao-ku	1958 - 1960	Hollington K. Tong (A)	1956 - 1958
		Yui Ong-Kyuin	1954 - 1958	Shen Chang-huan	1960 - 1966	Yeh Kung-chao (A)	1958 - 1961
		Chen Cheng	1958 - 1963			Tsiang Ting-fu (A)	1962 - 1965
		Yen Chia-kan	1963 - 1972	Wei Tao-ming	1966 - 1971	Chow Shu-kai (A)	1965 - 1971
				Chow Shu-kai	1971 - 1972	James Chien-hung Shen (A)	1971 - 1978
		Chiang Ching-kuo	1972	Shen Chang-huan	1972 -		

APPENDIX I-C (continued)

Chinese Heads of State, Premiers, Ministers of Foreign Affairs and Official Representatives Accredited to the U.S.A.

Republic of China President	Term of Office	Premier (President of Executive Yuan)	Term of Office	Minister of Foreign Affairs	Term of Office	Official Representative Accredited to U.S.A.	Term of Office
Yen Chia-Kan	1975 - 1978	Chiang Ching-kuo	1978	Shen Chang-huan	1978		
Chiang Ching-kuo	1978 - 1988	Sun Yun-suan Yu Kuo-hwa	1978 - 1984 1984 - 1988	Tsiang Yieh-si Chu Fu-sung Mou-shih Ding	1978 - 1979 1979 - 1987 1987 - 1988	Konsin C. Shah (R) Tsai Wei-ping (R) Fredrick F. Chien ®	1979 - 1981 1981 - 1982 1983 - 1988
Lee Teng-hui	1988 -	Lee Huan Hau Pei-tsun Lien Chan	1989 - 1990 1990 - 1993 1993 -	Lien Chan Fredrick F. Chien	1988 - 1990 1990 -	Mou-shih Ding (R) Benjamin Chao-Chung Lu ®	1988 - 1994 1994 -

(M)   Envoy Extraordinary and Minister Plenipotentiary
(A)   Ambassador Extraordinary and Plenipotentiary
(R)   Representative, Coordination Council for North American Affairs (CCNAA), Office in U.S.A.

APPENDIX II

U.S. Presidents, Secretaries of State, and Official Representatives Accredited to China

United States of America President	Term of Office	Secretary of State	Term of Office	Official Representative Accredited to China	Term of Office
George Washington	1789 - 1797	Thomas Jefferson	1790 - 1793		
		Edmund Randolph	1794 - 1795		
		Timothy Pickering	1795 -		
John Adams	1797 - 1801	Timothy Pickering	- 1800		
		John Marshall	1800 - 1801		
Thomas Jefferson	1801 - 1809	James Madison	1801 - 1809		
James Madison	1809 - 1817	Robert Smith	1809 - 1811		
		James Monroe	1811 - 1816		
James Monroe	1817 - 1825	John Quincy Adams	1817 - 1825		

391

APPENDIX II (continued)

U.S. Presidents, Secretaries of State, and Official Representatives Accredited to China

United States of America President	Term of Office	Secretary of State	Term of Office	Official Representative Accredited to China	Term of Office
John Quincy Adams	1825 - 1829	Henry Clay	1825 - 1829		
Andrew Jackson	1829 - 1873	Martin Van Buren	1829 - 1831		
		Edward Livingstone	1831 - 1833		
		Louis McLane	1833 - 1834		
		John Forsyth	1834 -		
Martin Van Buren	1837 - 1841	John Forsyth	- 1841		
William Henry Harrison	1841 -	Daniel Webster	1841 -		
John Tyler	1841 - 1845	Daniel Webster	- 1842	Caleb Cushing (C)	1843 - 1844
		Hugh S. Legare	1843 -	Alexander H. Everett (C)*	1845 - 1847
		Abel P. Upshur	1843 - 1844	James Biddle (C)**	1845 - 1846
		John C. Calhoun	1844 - 1845	John W. Davis (C)	1848 - 1850

APPENDIX II (continued)
U.S. Presidents, Secretaries of State, and Official Representatives Accredited to China

United States of America President	Term of Office	Secretary of State	Term of Office	Official Representative Accredited to China	Term of Office
James K. Polk	1845 - 1849	James Buchanan	1845 - 1849		
Zachary Taylor*	1849 - 1850	John M. Clayton	1849 - 1850		
Millard Fillmore	1850 - 1853	Daniel Webster	1850 - 1852	Thomas A. R. Nelson (C)	1851 -
		Edward Everett	1852 - 1853	Humphrey Marshall (C)	1852 - 1854
Franklin Pierce	1853 - 1857	William L. Marcy	1853 - 1857	Robert M. McLane	1854 - 1855
				Peter Parker (C)	1856 - 1857
James Buchanan	1857 - 1861	Lewis Cass	1857 - 1860	William B. Reed (M)	1858
		Jeremiah S. Black	1860 - 1861	John E. Ward (M)	1859 - 1860
Abraham Lincoln	1861 - 1865	William H. Seward	1861 -	Anson Burlingame (M)	1862 - 1867
				J. Ross Browne (M)	1868 - 1869

APPENDIX II (continued)

U.S. Presidents, Secretaries of State, and Official Representatives Accredited to China

United States of America President	Term of Office	Secretary of State	Term of Office	Official Representative Accredited to China	Term of Office
Andrew Johnson	1865 - 1869	William H. Seward	- 1869		
Ulysses S. Grant	1869 - 1877	Elihu B. Washburne	1869 -	Frederick F. Low (M)	1869 - 1873
		Hamilton Fish	1869 - 1877	Benjamin P. Avery* (M)	1874 - 1875
				George F. Seward (M)	1876 - 1880
Rutherford B. Hayes	1877 - 1881	William M. Evarts	1877 - 1881	John F. Swift (C)***	1880
				William H. Trescott (C)***	1880
James A. Garfield*	1881 -	James G. Blaine	1881 -		
Chester A. Arthur	1881 - 1885	James G. Blaine	- 1881	John Russel Young (M)	1882 - 1885
		Frederick I. Frelinghuysen	1881 - 1885		
Grover Cleveland	1885 - 1889	Thomas F. Bayard	1885 - 1889		

U.S. Presidents, Secretaries of State, and Official Representatives Accredited to China

United States of America President	Term of Office	Secretary of State	Term of Office	Official Representative Accredited to China	Term of Office
Benjamin Harrison	1889 - 1893	James G. Blaine	1889 - 1892	Charles Derby (M)	1885 - 1898
		John W. Foster	1892 - 1893		
Grover Cleveland	1893 - 1897	Walter G. Gresham	1893 - 1895		
		Richard Olney	1895 - 1897		
William McKinley	1897 - 1901	John Sherman	1897 - 1898	Edwin H. Conger (M)	1898 - 1905
		William R. Day	1898 -	William Woodville Rockhill (C)	1898 - 1901
		John Hay	1898 -		
Theodore Roosevelt	1901 - 1909	John Hay	- 1905	William Woodville Rockhill (M)	1905 - 1909
		Elihu Root	1905 - 1909		
		Robert Bacon	1909 -		

APPENDIX II (continued)

U.S. Presidents, Secretaries of State, and Official Representatives Accredited to China

United States of America President	Term of Office	Secretary of State	Term of Office	Official Representative Accredited to China	Term of Office
William Howard Taft	1909 - 1913	Philander C. Knox	1909 - 1913	William J. Calhoun (M)	1910 - 1913
Woodrow Wilson	1913-1921	William Jennings Bryan	1913 - 1915	Paul Reinsch (M)	1913 - 1919
		Robert Lansing	1915 - 1920		
		Bainbridge Colby	1920-1921		
Warren G. Harding*	1921 - 1923	Charles Evans Hughes	1921 -	Jacob Gould Schurman (M)	1921 - 1925
				John Van Antwerp MacMurray (M)	1925 - 1929
Calvin Coolidge	1923 - 1929	Charles Evans Hughes	- 1925		
		Frank B. Kellogg	1925 - 1929		
Herbert C. Hoover	1929 - 1933	Henry L. Stimson	1929 - 1933	Nelson Trusler Johnson (M)	1930 - 1935
				Nelson Trusler Johnson (A)	1935 - 1941

U.S. Presidents, Secretaries of State, and Official Representatives Accredited to China

United States of America President	Term of Office	Secretary of State	Term of Office	Official Representative Accredited to China	Term of Office
Franklin D. Roosevelt	1933 - 1945	Cordell Hull	1933 - 1944	Clarence E. Gauss (A)	1941 - 1944
		Edward R. Stettinius, Jr.	1944 -		
Harry S. Truman	1945 - 1953	Edward R. Stettinius, Jr.	- 1945	Patrick J. Hurley (A)	1944 - 1945
		James F. Byrnes	1945 - 1947	John Leighton Stuart (A)	1946 - 1949
		George C. Marshall	1947 - 1949		
		Dean G. Acheson	1949 - 1953		
Dwight D. Eisenhower	1953 - 1961	John Foster Dulles	1953 - 1959	Karl Lott Rankin (A)	1953 - 1957
		Christian A. Herter	1959 - 1961	Everett F. Drumright (A)	1958 - 1962
John F. Kennedy*	1961 - 1963	Dean Rusk	1961 -	Allan Goodrich Kirk (A)	1962 - 1963
Lyndon B. Johnson	1963 - 1969	Dean Rusk	- 1969	Jerauld Wright (A)	1963 - 1965
				Walter P. McConaughy (A)	1966 - 1974

397

APPENDIX II (continued)

U.S. Presidents, Secretaries of State, and Official Representatives Accredited to China

United States of America President	Term of Office	Secretary of State	Term of Office	Official Representative Accredited to China	Term of Office
Richard M. Nixon	1969 - 1974	William Rogers	1969 - 1973		
		Henry A. Kissinger	1973 -	Leonard Unger (A)	1974 - 1979
Gerald R. Ford	1974 - 1977	Henry A. Kissinger	- 1977		
James E. Carter	1977 - 1981	Cyrus Roberts Vance	1977 - 1980		
		Edmund S. Muskie	1980 - 1981	Charles T. Cross (R)	1979 - 1981
Ronald W. Reagan	1981 - 1989	Alexander M. Haig, Jr.	1981 - 1982	James R. Lilley (R)	1982 - 1984
		George P. Schultz	1982 - 1989	Harry E. T. Thayer (R)	1984 - 1986
				David Dean (R)	1987 - 1989

APPENDIX II (continued)
U.S. Presidents, Secretaries of State, and Official Representatives Accredited to China

United States of America President	Term of Office	Secretary of State	Term of Office	Official Representative Accredited to China	Term of Office
George H. W. Bush	1989 - 1993	James A. Baker, III	1989 - 1992	Thomas S. Brooks (R)	1990 - 1993
		Lawrence S. Eagleburger	1992 - 1993		
William J. Clinton	1993 -	Warren M. Christopher	1993 -	B. Lynn Pascoe (R)	1993 -

*   Died in office.
**   Commodore James Biddle was Commander U.S. East India Squadron and exchanged the ratified Treaty of Wanghia, 1844, negotiated by Caleb Cushing.
***   Angell, Swift and Trescott formed a commission sent by President Rutherford B. Hayes to China in 1880; James B. Angell later succeeded George F. Seward as Envoy.
(A)   Ambassador Extraordinary and Plenipotentiary.
(C)   Commissioner Plenipotentiary.

(M)   Envoy Extraordinary and Minister Plenipotentiary.
(R)   Representative, American Institute in Taiwan (AIT)

399

BIBLIOGRAPHY

I. SOURCE MATERIALS IN CHINESE

Bibliographical Guides and Research Aids

Primary Sources

Secondary Works

Books and Manuscripts

Annuals, Journals and Periodicals

II. SOURCE MATERIALS IN ENGLISH

Bibliographical Guides and Research Aids

Primary Sources

Secondary Works

Books and Manuscripts

Annuals, Journals and Periodicals

China Yearbooks

I. SOURCE MATERIALS IN CHINESE

Bibliographical Guides and Research Aids

Chang, Li-ho, et. al., ed., *Chung-Kuo jen-min ta tzu-tien* (Encyclopedia of Chinese Biographical Names), 4th ed. Taipei: Commercial Press, 1966.

Chen, Chin-chi, *Chung-kuo tai-shih nien-piao* (Chronology of Important Events in China). Taipei: Commercial Press, 1963.

Chen, Tsong Y., et. al., eds. *Mei-kuo Ch'u-baan chih Chung-kuo Yen-chiu Liin-chu Hsiin-cheh* (Digest of Books and Articles on U.S. China Studies). New York: Chinese Information and Cultural Center, 1973-1992.

Cheng, Ho-sheng. *Chin-shi Chung-hsi shihjih tui-chao piano* (Comparative Tables of Sino-Western Historical Dates in Modern Times). Shanghai: Commercial Press, 1936.

Hsieh, Jen-chao. *Pien-nien Chung-wai tai-shih chi* (Chronology of Important Events Affecting Sino-Western Relations). Taipei: Chung Mei Cultural Publishing Co., 1966.

Kuo, Ting-yee. *Chin-tai Chung-kuo shih jih chi* (Chronology of Historical Events in Modern China). 2 vols. Taipei: Commercial Press, 1941.

Wai Chiao Pu (Ministry of Foreign Affairs). *Chung-kuo chu-waiko Ta Kung Shih- kuan li-jen Kuan-ch'ang Hsuan-ming Nien-piao* (List of Heads of Chinese Diplomatic Missions in Foreign States). Taipei: Commercial Press, 1969.

Wai Chiao Hsueh Hui (Chinese Diplomatic Science Society). *Wai-chiao ta Tzu-tien* (Diplomatic Dictionary). Reprint. Taipei: Wen Hai Publishing Co., 1965.

Primary Sources

Chang, Kwei-yung, Chia-mu Huang and Fu-ching Huang (eds.).*Chung-mei kuan- hsi shih-liao: Chia Ch'ing, Tao Kuang, Hsien Feng Ch'ao and T'ung Chih Ch'ao* (Collection of Historical Documents on Sino-American Relations 1805-1861; 1862-1874). 3 vols. Taipei: Institute of Modern History, Academia Sinica, 1968.

Chin, Hsiao-yi, ed. *Chung-hua Min-kuo Jung-yau Shih-liao Chu-pien* (Digest of Important Historical Material of the Republic of China). 3 vols. Taipei: China Cultural Service, 1981.

Kuo, Ting-yee, Yu-shu Lee and Fu-ching Huang, eds. *Ch'ou-pan I-wu shih-mo, pu-yi: Tao Kuang, Hsien Feng Chiao* (History of the Management of Barbarian Affairs during Tao Kuang and Hsien Feng reign, supplement, 1842-1861). Taipei: Institute of Modern History, Academia Sinica, 1966.

Lo, Chia-lun, ed. *Ke-ming wen-hsien* (Documents of the Revolution). Taipei: Cheng Chung Book Co., 1953.

Pao Chun, et. al., ed. *Ch'ing-tai Ch'ou-pan I-wu shih-mo* (The Beginning and End of the Management of the Barbarian Affairs in the Ch'ing Dynasty, 1836- 1850, 1851-1861; 1862-1874). Peiping: National Palace Museum, 1929-30.

Sun, Tung Hsun, Chung Tung Cheng, et. al., ed. *Chung-Mei Kuan-Hsi Pao-Kao* (Report on ROC-US Relations). Taipei: Institute of American Culture, Academia Sinica, 1981, 1882, 1984, 1986, 1988.

Tsiang, Ting-fu, ed. *Chin-tai wai-chiao-shi tzu'u-liaoSchi-yao* (Collection of Materials on Modern Chinese Diplomatic History). 2 vols. Shanghai: Commercial Press, 1931-1934.

Tso, Shun-sheng, ed. *Chung-kuo chin-pai-nien-shih tziu-liao* (Collection of Materials on Chinese History of the last Hundred Years). 2 vols. Shangai: Chung Hwa Book Co., 1928.

Wai Chiao Pao Shen. Wai Chiao Pao chi-pein (Collection of Foreign Affairs Bulletin). 14 vols. Reprint. Taipei: Kwang Wen Book Co., 1964.

Wai Chiao Pu (Ministry of Foreign Affairs). *Chung-wai t'iao-yueh chi-pien* (Treaties between the Republic of China and Foreign States, 1927-1957; 1958-1961; 1962-1964). 3 vols. Taipei: Commercial Press, Central Printing Co., Chung Hwa Book Co., 1958, 1963, 1965.

Wai Chiao Pu (Ministry of Foreign Affairs). *Pai-P'i-shu* (White Papers). Nanking, Chungking, Taipei: Ministry of Foreign Affairs, 1931, 1992.

Wai Chiao Pu (Ministry of Foreign Affairs). *Wai-Chiao-Pu' KungPao* (Ministry of Foreign Affairs Bulletin). Nanking, Chungking, Taipei: Ministry of Foreign Affairs, 1931.

Wang, Liang, ed. *Ch'ing-chi wai-chiao shih-liao* (Diplomatic Documents of the Ch'ing Dynasty). 8 vols. Peiping: *Wai-chiao Shih-liao Pien-ch'uan-ch'u*, 1932-1935.

Yu, Num-moo, Yueh-pao Huang, and Li-jen Pao, eds. *Chung-wait'iao-yueh hui- pien* (Collection of Treaties between China and Foreign States). Shanghai: Commercial Press, 1935.

Secondary Works

Books and Manuscripts

Chang, Chi-yun. *Mei-kuo wen-hua yu Chung-mei kuan-hsi*
(American Culture and Sino-American Relations). Taipei:
Chung-yang Wan-wu Kung-ying she (Chinese Cultural
Service), 1957.

Chang, Chi-yun, ed. *K'ang-Jih chan-shih* (History of China's
War of Resistance against Japanese Aggression). Taipei:
United Publishing Co., 1966.

Chang, Chung-fu. *Chung-Hua Min-kuo wai-chiao shih* (History
of Foreign Relations of the Republic of China). Reprint.
Taipei: Cheng Chung Book Co., 1943.

Chang, Kwei-yung. *Can-sheng you Chung-Mei Kuan-hsi* (Nelson
Johnson and Sino-American Relations). Taipei: Commercial
Press, 1968.

Chang, Tao-shin. *Chung-wai T'iao-yueh Sung-lun* (Treaty
Relations between China and Foreign Powers). Taipei: Woo
Chow Press, 1969.

Chang, Tsun-wu. *Kuang-hsu san-shih-i-nien Chung-Mei Kung-
yuehfeng-ch'ao* (Chinese-American Dispute of 1905
concerning the Immigration of Laborers). Taipei: Institute of
Modern History, Academia Sinica, 1965.

Chen, Edward I-hsin. *Tun-chiao hao ti Chung-mei Kuan-hsi,
1979-1994* (ROC-U.S. Relations Since 1979). Taipei: Wu
Nan Co., 1995.

Chen, Kung-lu. *Chung-kuo chin-tai shih* (Modern History of
China). Shanghai: Commercial Press, 1935.

Chen, Tung-teh. *Mao Tse Tung ho Nixon—chung-mei chien-chiao chia-mei* (Mao Tse Tung and Richard Nixon—The Secrets of Establishment of Diplomatic Relations between U.S. and PRC). Hong Kong: Kin Shih Press, 1989.

Chiang, Kai-shek. *Chung tsung-t'ung yen-lun hui-pien* (Collection of President Chiang's Speeches). Taipei: Cheng Chung Book Co., 1956.

Chiang, Kai-shek. *Chung-kuo chih ming-yun* (China's Destiny). Rev. ed. Taipei: Cheng Chung Book Co., 1944.

Fu, Ch'i-hsueh. *Chung-kuo wai-chiao shih* (Diplomatic History of China). Taipei: San Min Book Co. 1957.

Fu, Ch'i-hsueh. *San-sze-nien lai chung-mei chung-ou kuan-hsiti yuan-pei* (Sino-American Relations during the Past Three Decades). Taipei: Commercial Press, 1979.

Fung, Keh. *Ching-pai-nien mei-kuo tui-hwa wai-chiao cheng-tse* (Hundred Years United States Foreign Policy towards China). Taipei: Kao Tsang Book Co., 1957.

Hsiao, I-shan. *Ch'ing Shih* (History of the Ch'ing Dynasty). Taipei: *Chung Yang Wen-wu Kung-ying She*, 1955.

Hsiao, I-shan. *Chung-kuo chin-tai shih kai-yao* (Outline of Modern Chinese History). Taipei: San Min Book Co., 1963.

Hu, Shih. *Hu-Shih shou-kao* (The Hu Shih Papers). 10 vols. Taipei: Academia Sinica, Hu Shih Memorial Hall, Manuscript Section.

Huang Chia-mu. *Mei-kuo yu Tai-Wan* (The United States and Taiwan, 1784-1895). Taipei: Institute of Modern History, Academia Sinica, 1966.

Huang, Ta-shou. *Chung-kuo chin-tai shih* (History of Modern China.). Taipei: Ta Chung Kuo Book Co., 1953.

Huang, Tsen-ming. *Chung-kuo wai-chiao shih* (Diplomatic History of China). 4th ed. Taipei: Cheng Chung Book Co., 1967.

Huang, Tsen-ming, et. al. *Chung-kuo wai-chiao shih lun-chi* (Symposium on Chinese Diplomatic History). Taipei: *Chung Yang Wen-wu Kung-ying She*, 1957.

Kuo, Jung-chao. *Mei-kuo Ya-Er-Ta mih-yiao yu Chung-kuo* (A Critical Study of the Yalta Agreement and Sino-American Relations). Taipei: Buffalo Book Co., 1967.

Kao, Lon. *Chung Hua Min-kuo Wai-chiao Kuan-hsi tze Yuan-pei, 1972-1992* (The Development of the Foreign Policy of the Republic of China, 1972-1992). Taipei: Wu Nan Co., 1994.

Kuo, Ting-yee. *Chin-tai Chung-kuo shih* (Modern History of China). Taipei: Commercial Press, 1940.

Lee, Thomas Ben-ching. *Mei-kuo Wai-chiao Cheng-chai Nien-chiu* (Studies on U.S. Foreign Policy). Taipei: Cheng Chung Book Co., 1987.

Lee, Din-yi. *Chung-Mei wai-chiao shih* (History of Sino-American Relations, Vol. I, 1784-1860). Taipei: Li Hsung Book Co., 1960.

Lee, Jung-chiu. *Chen-Ch'u-kang shih-che tao Ya-Er-Ta hsieh-ting ch'i-chien ti Mei- kuo tui-Hwa kuan-hsi* (U.S. Relations with China from Pearl Harbor to Yalta Agreement). Ph.D. thesis, National Chengchi University, Taipei, 1970.

Lee, Po-hung, *Chung-Mei Wai-Chiao Kuan-Hsi* (Sino-American Diplomatic Relations). Rev. ed. Taipei: Commercial Press, 1972.

Li, Chieng-nung. *Tsui-chin san-shin nien Chung-kuo cheng-chi shih* (Chinese Political History of the Last Thirty Years). Shanghai: Commercial Press, 1932.

Li, Hung-chang. *Li Wen-Chung-kung ch'uan-shu: Chihtui* (Complete Works of Li Hung-chang: Letters). 2 vols. Reprint. Taipei: Wen Hai Press, 1963.

Ling, Hung-shun. *Chung-kuo t'ch-lu-chih* (A Comprehensive Survey of Railway Development in China). Taipei: World Book Co., 1963. Liu, Chiun-nan. *Chung-kuo chin-tai wai-chiao shih* (Diplomatic History of Modern China). Rev. ed. Taipei: Union Book Co., 1965.

Liu, Yen and Fong-se Lee. *Chung-kuo wai-chiao shih* (Diplomatic History of China.) Rev. ed. Taipei: San Min Book Co., 1962.

Ma, Ke-jen. *Chung-Mei Wei-Chiao Ping-Lun Liang-Pai-Pien* (Two Hundred Essays on ROC-US Relations). 2 vols. New York: The Chinese World Journal, 1984.

Pao, Tsun-peng, Din-yi Lee and Hsiang-hsiang Wu, eds. *Chung-kuo chin-tai shih lun-ts'ung* (A Collection of Writings on Modern Chinese History). Taipei: Cheng Chung Book Co., 1956.

Shaw, Yu-ming. *Chung-Mei Kuan-Hsi Neien-chuo Wen-Chi* (Studies in Sino-American Relations). Taipei: Bibliography Monthly Press, 1980.

Shen, Yun-lung. *Chung-kuo chin-tai shih ta-kang* (Outline of Modern Chinese History). 3rd ed. Taipei: Wen Hai Press, 1970.

Sun, Yat-sen. *Tsung-li-yi-chiao* (Treatise of Dr. Sun Yat-sen). Reprint. Taipei: Cheng Chung Book Co., 1962.

Sun, Yat-sen. *Kuo-fu chuan-chi* (Complete Works of Dr. Sun Yat-sen). 3 vols. Taipei: *Chung Yang Wen-wu Kung-ying She*, 1965.

Tsiang, Ting-fu. *Chung-kuo chin-tai-shi lung chi* (Treatise on Modern History of China). Taipei: Tai Si Yang Book Co., 1970.

Tsiang, Ting-fu. *Chung-kuo chin-tai shih ta-kang* (Outline of Modern Chinese History). Taipei: Chi Min Book Co., 1959.

Tso, Shun-sheng. *Chung-kuo chin-tai shih sze-chiang* (Treatise on Modern Chinese History). Taipei: San Min Book Co., 1962.

Tsou, Lu. *Chung-kuo Kuo-min-tang kai-shih* (A General History of the Kuomintang of China). Chungking: Cheng Chung Book Co., 1944.

Tu, Heng Chi. *Chung-Mei Hsin-Kuan-Hsi Yu Kuo-Chi-Fa* (New Sino- American Relations and International Law). 2nd ed. Taipei: Commercial Press, 1983.

Wang, C.C. *Ma-Sieh-Erh t'iao ch'u Kung shi-mo* (The Marshall Medication Mission to China). Taipei: Unpublished manuscript.

Wang, Ching Hung. *Chung-Mei Kuan hsi te Kuei-Chi* (The Path of ROC - US Relations). 2 vols. New York: The Chinese World Journal, 1987.

Yu, Chien. *Chung-Mei Wai-Chiao Kuan-Hsi sze Nein-Chuo* (Sino-American Diplomatic Relations). Taipei: Cheng Chung Book Co., 1973.

Yu, Num-moo. *Fei-chu pu-p'ing t'eng t'iao-yuch chih chin-ko* (The Abolition of Unequal Treaties in China). Taipei: Commercial Press, 1951.

Annuals, Journals, and Periodicals

Chung-kuo Li-shih Hsueh-hui (Chinese Historical Association). *Shih-hsueh-chi-k'an* (Bulletin of Chinese Historical Association). Taipei: *Chung-Kuo Li-shih Hsueh-hui*, 1969.

Chung-yang Yen-chiu Yuan (Academia Sinica). *Chin-tai shih yen-chiu so chi-k'an* (Bulletin of the Institute of Modern History). Taipei: Academia Sinica, 1969.

Tsing Hua Ta Hsueh (Tsing Hua University). *Tsing Hua Hsueh Pao* (Tsing Hua Journal of Chinese Studies). New Series. Taipei: Tsing Hua University, 1956.

Tu-li p'ing-lun she (The Independent Critic Inc.,). *Tu-li p'ing-lun* (The Independent Critic Weekly). Peiping: *Tu-li p'ing lun she*, 1932-1937.

Tung Fang Tsah Chih She (The Eastern Miscellany Inc.,). *Tung Fang Tash Chih* (The Eastern Miscellany Monthly). Shanghai, and later Taipei: Commercial Press, 1903.

Wai Chiao Pu (Ministry of Foreign Affairs). *Chung-kuo Wai-chiao nien-che* (Chinese Foreign Relations Yearbook). Nanking; Taipei: Cheng Chung Book Co., 1934-1940; 1988.

Wai-chiao P'ing-lun She (Review of Foreign Affairs, Inc.). *Wai-chiao P'ing-lun* (Review of Foreign Affairs). Nanking, and later Shanghai: Wai-chiao P'ing- lun She, 1932-1940.

II.   SOURCE MATERIALS IN ENGLISH

Bibliographical Guides And Research Aids

Bemis, Samuel Flagg, and Grace Gardner Griffin, eds. *Guide to the Diplomatic History of the United States*, 1775-1921. Washington, D.C.: Government Printing Office, 1935. Reprint. Gloucester, Mass.: Peter Smith, 1959.

Boorman, Howard L., and Richard C. Howard, eds. *Biographical Dictionary of Republican Chinese*. 3 vols. New York: Columbia University Press, 1970.

Chang, Chung-li and Stanley Spector. *Guide to the Memorials of Seven Leading Officials of Nineteenth Century China*. Seattle: University of Washington Press, 1958.

Chen, Pu-lai, and Cheng-chu Tang (eds.) *Chronology of President Chiang Kai- shek*. Translated into English by Sampson C. Shen. Taipei: China Cultural Service, 1954.

Cordier, Henri. *Bibliotheca Sinica*. 4 vols. Rev. ed. Paris: Guilmoto 1904-1908.

Fairbank, John King, and Kwang-ching Liu, eds. *Modern China: A Bibliographical Guide to Chinese Works, 1898-1937*. Cambridge Mass.: Harvard University Press, 1950.

Harkness, Peter A., and Buel W. Patch, eds. *China and U.S. Far East Policy, 1945-1967*. Washington, D.C.: Congressional Quarterly Inc., 1967.

Hucker, Charles O. *China, A CriticalBibliography*. Tucson: University of Arizona Press, 1962.

Hummel, Arthur William, ed. *Eminent Chinese of the Ch'ing Period, 1644-1912.* 2 vols. Washington D.C.: Library of Congress, 1943-1944.

Kaplan, Fredric M. and Julian M. Sobin. *Encyclopedia of China Today.* New York: Eurasia Press, 1979, 1980, 1982.

Kim, Hong N. *Scholar's Guide to East Asian Studies.* Washington, D.C.: Smithsonian Institution Press, 1979.

Kuo, Tai-Chin and R.H. Myers. *Understanding Communist China, Communist China Studies in the United States and the Republic of China, 1949-1978.* Stanford, CA: Hoover Institution Press, Stanford University, 1986.

Langer, William L. and Hamilton Fish Armstrong. *Foreign Affairs Bibliography: A Selected and Annotated List of Books on International Relations, 1919-1932.* New York: Harper Brothers, 1933.

Lee, Karen Sin-chu and Anna C.M. Tai. *An Annotated Bibliography of Selected Works about Republic of China.* Taipei: Kwang Hwa Publishing Co., 1981.

Liu, Kwang-ching. *Americans and Chinese, A Historical Essay and A Bibliography.* Cambridge: Harvard University Press, 1963.

Morehouse, M. and Edith Ehrman, eds. *American Institutions and Organizations Interested in Asia.* A Reference Directory. New York: Taplinger Company, 1961.

Teng, Ssu-yu, and Knight Biggerstaff. *An Annotated Bibliography of Selected Chinese Reference Works.* Rev. ed. Cambridge: Harvard University Press, 1950.

Thomson, James C. Jr. and Ernest R. May, eds. *American-East Asian Relations: A Survey.* Cambridge: Harvard University Press, 1971.

Woolbert, Robert Gale. *Foreign Affairs Bibliography: A Selected and Annotated List of Books on International Relations, 1932-1942.* New York: Harper Brothers, 1915.

Yuan, T'ung-li. *China in Western Literature.* New Haven: Yale University Press, 1958.

Primary Sources

Carnegie Endowment for International Peace. *Treaties and Agreements with and Concerning China, 1919-1929.* Washington, D.C.: Carnegie Endowment for International Peace, 1929.

Chinese Maritime Customs, ed. *Treaties, Conventions, etc. between China and Foreign States.* 2nd ed. 2 vols. Shanghai: The Inspectorate-General of the Chinese Maritime Customs, 1917.

Great Britain, Foreign Office. *China No. 1 (1928)-Papers Relating to the Settlement of the Nanking Incident of March 21, 1927.* Cmd. 3188. London: H.M. Stationery Office, 1928.

Koo, V.K. Wellington, ed. *Memoranda Presented to the Lytton Commission by China.* 2 vols. New York: The Chinese Cultural Society, 1932.

League of Nations. *Official Journal, Special Supplement, No. 177. Sino-Japanese Conflict.* Geneva: League of Nations, 1937.

MacMurray, John V. A., ed. *Treaties and Agreements with and Concerning China, 1894-1919. Vol. 1, Manchu Period, 1894-1911. Vol. 11, Republican Period, 1912-1919.* New York: Oxford University Press, 1921.

Mayers, William Frederick. *Treaties between the Empire of China and Foreign Powers. Shanghai: North China Herald, 1877.* Taipei: Cheng Wen Co., 1966.

Ministry of Foreign Affairs, Republic of China. *Statements and Answers to Press Queries by the Spokesman for the Ministry of Foreign Affairs.* Taipei: Ministry of Foreign Affairs, 1962.

Ministry of Foreign Affairs, Republic of China. *Statements and Communiques.* Taipei: Ministry of Foreign Affairs, Republic of China, 1962.

Ministry of Foreign Affairs, Republic of China. *Treaties between the Republic of China and Foreign States.* 6 vols. Taipei: Ministry of Foreign Affairs, 1982.

National Archives: Foreign Affairs Section. *Washington, D.C.: State Department Instructions to China Legation, Vols. 1-4.*

Tyau, Min-chien T.Z., ed. *The Special Conference on the Chinese Customs Tariff, October 1925-April 1962.* Peiping: Ministry of Foreign Affairs, 1928.

U.S. Congress, Senate. *Conference on the Limitation of Armaments. 67th Cong., 2nd Sess. Senate Document No. 126.* Washington, D.C.: Government Printing Office, 1922.

U.S. Congress, Senate. *Conditions in Manchuria. Senate Document No. 55. 72nd Cong., 1st Sess.* Washington, D.C.: Government Printing Office, 1932.

U.S. Congress. *Senate Report on the Investigation of the Pearl Harbor Attack. 79th Cong., 2nd Sess., Senate Document No. 244.* Washington, D.C.: Government Printing Office, 1946.

U.S. Congress. *Senate Committee on the Armed Forces and Foreign Relations. Military Situation in the Far East. Hearing, 82nd Cong., 1st Sess.* Washington, D.C.: Government Printing Office, 1951.

U.S. Congress, Senate. *Internal Security Sub-committee of the Committee on the Judiciary Document. The Amerasia Papers: A Clue to the Catastrophe of China. 91st Cong., 1st Sess.* Washington, D.C.: Government Printing Office, 1970.

U.S. Department of State. *1) A Decade of American Foreign Policy: Basic Documents, 1941-1949. 2) American Foreign Policy, 1950-1955: Basic Documents. 3) American Foreign Policy: Current Documents, 1956.* Washington, D.C.: Government Printing Office, 1959.

U.S. Department of State. *Bulletin. July 1, 1939. The Official Weekly Record of United States Foreign Policy.* Washington, D.C.: Government Printing Office, 1939.

U.S. Department of State. *The Conference of Brussels, November 3 - 24, 1937.* Washington, D.C.: Government Printing Office, 1947.

U.S. Department of State. *Conference at Cairo and Teheran, 1943. The Conference of Malta and Yalta, 1945.* Washington, D.C.: Government Printing Office, 1951, 1955.

U.S. Department of State. *1) Papers Relating to Foreign Affairs, 1862-1868. 2) Papers Relating to the Foreign Relations, 1870-1946. 3) Foreign Relations of the United States, Diplomatic Papers., 1947.* Washington, D.C.: Government Printing Office. Annual Volumes. The Far East. China.

U.S. Department of State. *Peace and War, United States Foreign Policy, 1931- 1941. In Quest of Peace and Security, Selected Documents on American Foreign Policy, 1941-1951.* Washington, D.C.: Government Printing Office, 1943- 1951.

U.S. Department of State. *Report of the Commission on Extraterritoriality in China, September 16, 1962.* Washington, D.C.: Government Printing Office, 1926.

U.S. Department of State. *United States Relations with China, With Special Reference to the Period 1944-1949.* Washington, D.C.: Government Printing Office, 1949.

Secondary Works

Books and Manuscripts

Acheson, Dean. *Present at the Creation, My Years in the State Department.* London: Hamish Hamilton, 1970.

Ahlers, John. *Japan Closing the "Open Door" in China.* Shanghai: Kelly and Walsh, 1940.

Almond, Gabriel A. *The American People and Foreign Policy.* New York: Harcourt, Brace & Co., 1950.

Anderson, George L., ed. *Issues and Conflicts, Studies in Twentieth Century American Diplomacy.* Lawrence: University of Kansas Press, 1959.

Armstrong, J. D. *Revolutionary Diplomacy, Chinese Foreign Policy and the United Front Doctrine.* Berkeley: University of California Press, 1977.

Bader, William B. and J. T. Bergner, eds. *The Taiwan Relations Act: A Decade of Implementation.* Indianapolis: Hudson Institute, 1989.

Ballantine, Joseph W. *Formosa, A Problem for United States Foreign Policy.* Washington, D.C.: The Brookings Institution, 1952.

Barber, Hollis W. *Foreign Policies of the United States.* New York: Dryden Press, 1953.

Barnett, A. Doak. *China and the Major Powers in Asia.* Washington, D.C.: Brookings Institution, 1977.

Barnett, A. Doak. *China Policy: Old Problems and New Challenges.* Washington, D.C.: Brookings Institution, 1977.

Barnett, A. Doak. *The Making of Foreign Policy in China, Structure and Process.* Boulder: Westview Press, 1985.

Bartlett, Ruhe J., ed. *The Record of American Diplomacy - Documents and Reading in the History of American Foreign Relations.* Rev. ed. New York: Alfred A. Knopf, 1964.

Bau, Ming-chien Joshua. *The Foreign Relations of China: A History and a Survey.* New York: Fleming H. Revell Co., 1922.

Beal, John Robinson. *John Foster Dulles: A Bibliography.* New York: Harper Brothers, 1957.

Bemis, Samuel Flagg. *A Diplomatic History of the United States.* 4th ed. New York: Henry Holt, 1957.

Bemis, Samuel Flagg. *A Short History of American Foreign Policy and Diplomacy.* New York: Henry Holt, 1959.

Bisson Thomas A. *America's Far Eastern Policy.* New York: MacMillan 1945.

Blum Robert. *The United States and China in World Affairs.* Edited by A. Doak Barnett. New York: McGraw Hill, 1966.

Board of Foreign Trade. *Reference Papers on Economic Development and Prospect of the Republic of China.* 2 vols. Taipei: Board of Foreign Trade, Ministry of Economic Affairs, ROC, 1991.

Borg, Dorothy. *American Policy and the Chinese Revolution, 1925-1928.* New York: MacMillan, 1947.

Brugger, Bill, ed. *China Since The "Gang of Four"* New York: St. Martin's Press, 1980.

Brezezinski, Zbigniew. *Power and Principle. Memories of the National Security Adviser, 1977-1981.* Rev. ed. New York: Farrer, Straus, Giroud, 1985.

Buchanan, A. Russell. *The United States and World War II.* 2 vols. New York: Harper and Row, 1964.

Buss, Claude A. *The Far East, A History of Recent and Contemporary International Relations in East Asia.* New York: MacMillan, 1955.

Cameron, Meribeth E., Thomas H. D. Mahoney, and George E. McReynolds. *China, Japan and the Powers.* New York: Ronald Press, 1952.

Chang, Carsun. *The Third Force in China.* New York: Bookman Associates, 1952.

Chang, Chi-yun. *Record of the Cairo Conference.* Taipei: China Culture Publishing Co., 1953.

Chang, Chi-yun. *The "Kuomintang" on the March*. Taipei: China Cultural Service, 1954.

Chang, Hsin-hai. *America and China, A New Approach to Asia*. New York: Simon and Schuster, 1965.

Chang, King-yuh. *A Framework for China's Unification*. 2nd ed. Taipei: Kwang Hua Publishing Co., 1987.

Chang, King-yuh, ed. *ROC - U.S. Relations Under the Taiwan Relations Act: Practice and Prospects*. Taipei: Institute of International Relations, National Changchi University, 1988.

Chang, Parris H. *Power and Policy in China*. 3rd ed. Dubuque, Iowa: Kendall-Hunt Publishing Co., 1990.

Chang, Shih-cheng. *The Legal and Political Status of Taiwan*. PH.D. Thesis, University of Santo Tomas, Manila, 1966.

Chao, Chin Yung. *Chinese Diplomatic Practices and Treaty Relations, 1842-1943*. Taipei: China Cultural Service, 1955.

Chao, Chin Yung. *Foreign Advisers and the Diplomacy of the Manchu Empire*. Taipei: China Cultural Publishing Co., 1954.

Cheng, Chu-yuan, ed. *Sun Yat-sen's Doctrine in the Modern World*. Boulder: Westview Press, 1989.

Chennault, Claire Lee. *Way of a Fighter: The Memoirs of Claire Lee Cheneault*. New York: Putnam, 1949.

Chesneaux, Jean. *China, The People's Republic, 1949-1976*. New York: Pantheon Books, 1979.

Chiang, Ching-kuo. *Perspectives—Selected Statements of President Chiang Ching-kuo, 1978-1983* Taipei: Government Information Office, 1984.

Chiang Kai-shek. *Soviet Russia in China, A Summing-up at Seventy.* Rev. ed. New York: Farrar, Straus and Giroux, 1965.

Chiang, Mon-lin. *Tides from the West.* Taipei: World Book Co., 1963.

Chien, Fredrick F. *Speaking as a Friend, Views of U.S.-ROC Relations growing out of 1974 and 1975 Visit to the United States.* 2nd ed. Taipei: Kwang Hwa Publishing Co. 1979.

Chien, Fredrick F. *More Views of a Friend, Views Expressed by Dr. Fredrick F. Chien during his 1975 Second Speaking Tour of the United States.* Taipei: Government Information Office, 1976.

Chien, Fredrick F. *Faith and Resilience, The Republic of China on Taiwan Forges Ahead.* Houston: Kwang Hwa Publishing (USA), Inc. 1988.

Chin, Hsiao-yu, ed. *Symposium on the History of the Republic of China.* 5 vols. Taipei: China and Cultural Service, 1981.

Chiu, Hung-dah and Karen Murphy, eds. *The Chinese Connection and Normalization.* Baltimore: University of Maryland School of Law, 1980.

Chiu, Hung-dah and Shao-chuan Leng, eds. *China: Seventy Years After the 1911 Hsin-hai Revolution.* Charlottesville: University Press of Virginia, 1984.

Chung, Henry. *The Oriental Policy of the United States.* New York: Fleming H. Revell Co., 1919.

Clough, Ralph N. *Island China*. Cambridge: Harvard University Press, 1978.

Clubb, O. Edmund. *Twentieth Century China*. New York: Columbia University Press, 1965.

Clyde, Paul H. and Burton F. Beers. *The Far East: A History of the Western Impact and the Eastern Response 1830-1965*. Englewood Cliffs: Prentice Hall, 1966.

Cohen, Paul A. *Discovering History in China, American Historical Writing on Recent Chinese Past*. New York: Columbia University Press, 1984.

Cohen, Warren I. *America's Response to China, A History of Sino-American Relations*, 3rd ed. New York: Columbia University Press, 1990.

Copper, John F. *Taiwan, Nation State of Province?* Boulder: Westview Press, 1990.

Crabb, Cecil V. Jr. and Kevin V. Mulcahy. *President and Foreign Policy Making, From FDR to Reagan*. Baton Rouge: Louisiana State University Press, 1986.

Crofts, Alfred and Percy Buchanan. *A History of the Far East*. New York: Longmans Green, 1958.

Current, Richard H., Frank Freidel and Harry T. William. *American History, A Survey*. New York: Alfred A. Knopf, 1965.

Curry, Roy Watson. *Woodrow Wilson and Far Eastern Policy, 1913-1921*. New York: Bookman Associates, 1957.

Curtis, Lionel. *The Capital Question of China*. New York: MacMillan, 1932.

Dai, Shen-yu., ed. *The Two Chinese Political Systems and Security in the Western Pacific*. Taipei: Asia and World Institute, 1984.

Daniels, Josephus. *The Wilson Era, Years of Peace—1910-1917*. Chapel Hill: University of North Carolina Press, 1946.

Daniels, Roger. *Asian America: Chinese and Japanese in the United States Since 1850*. Seattle: University of Washington Press, 1988.

De Conde, A. *A History of American Foreign Policy*. New York: Charles Scribner's, 1971.

Dennett, Tyler. *Americans in Eastern Asia, A Critical Study of the Policy of the United States with Reference to China, Japan, and Korea in 19th Century*. New York: MacMillan, 1922.

Donovan, R.J. *Eisenhower, The Inside Story*. New York: Harper Brothers, 1956.

Downen, Robert L. *The Taiwan Pawn in the China Game, Congress to the Rescue*. Washington D.C.: Center for Strategic and International Studies, Georgetown University, 1979.

Dreyer, June Teufel, ed. *Chinese Defense and Foreign Policy* New York: Paragon House, 1988.

Dulles, Foster Rhea. *American's Rise to World Power, 1898-1954*. New York: Harper Brothers, 1955.

Dulles, Foster Rhea. *China and America: The Story of Their Relations Since 1784*. Princeton: Princeton University Press, 1946.

Dulles, Foster Rhea. *Prelude to World Power, American Diplomatic History, 1860- 1900.* New York: MacMillan: 1955.

Dulles, Foster Rhea. *The United States Since 1865.* Ann Arbor: University of Michigan Press, 1959.

Dulles, John Foster. *War or Peace.* New York: MacMillan, 1957.

Edwards, Lee. *Missionary for Freedom: The Life and Times of Walter Judd.* New York: Paragon House, 1990.

Eisenhower, Dwight D. *Mandate for Change, 1953-1956.* New York: Doubleday, 1963.

Eisenhower, Dwight D. *Waging Peace, The White House Years, 1956-1961.* New York: Doubleday, 1963.

Fairbank, John King. *The United States and China.* 4th ed. Cambridge, Harvard University Press, 1983.

Fairbank, John King. *The Great Chinese Revolution, 1800-1985.* New York: Harper and Row, Publishers, 1986.

Fairbank, John King and Ssu-yu Teng, eds. *China's Response to the West: A Documentary Survey.* Cambridge: Harvard University Press, 1954.

Fairbank, John King. *Trade and Diplomacy on the China Coast.* 2 vols. Cambridge: Harvard University Press, 1953.

Feis, Herbert. *The China Tangle, the American Efforts in China from Pearl Harbor to the Marshall Mission.* Princeton: Princeton University Press, 1950.

Feis, Herbert. *The Road to Pearl Harbor: The Coming of War between the United States and Japan.* Princeton: Princeton University Press, 1950.

Feldman, Harvey and I.J. Kim, eds., *Taiwan in a Time of Transition.* New York: Paragon House, 1988.

Ferrel, Robert Hugh. . *American Diplomacy in Great The Depression.* New Haven: Yale University Press, 1957.

Fitch, Geraldine. *Formosa Beachead.* Chicago: Henry Regnery, 1953.

Fitzgerald, Charles Patrick. *China: A Short Cultural History.* 3rd rev. ed. New York: Praeger, 1961.

Freidel, F. *American in the 20th century.* New York: Alfred A. Knopf, 1970.

Friedman, Irving S. *British Relations with China, 1931-1939.* New York: Institute of Pacific Relations, 1940.

Gardner, J.W. *President John F. Kennedy: To Turn the Tide.* New York: Harper Brothers, 1962.

Gibert, Stephen P. and W. M. Carpenter. *American and Island China, A Documentary History.* New York: University Press of America 1989.

Goldstein, Steven M. and J. Mathews. *Sino-American Relations After Normalization, Toward the Second Decade.* New York: Foreign Policy Association, Inc. Headline Series, 1986.

Goldwater, Barry M. *With no Apologies.* New York: William Morrow Co. 1979.

Goebel, Dorothy Burne, ed. *American Foreign Policy: A Documentary Survey, 1776-1960*. New York: Holt, Rinehart and Winston, 1961.

Graebner, Norman A., ed. *Ideas and Diplomacy, Readings in the Intellectual Tradition of American Foreign Policy*. New York: Oxford University Press, 1964.

Grasso, M. June. *Truman's Two-China Policy*. New York: M.E. Sharpe Inc., 1987.

Greene, Fred. *The Far East*. New York: Rinehart, 1957.

Greene, Fred. *U.S. Policy and the Security of Asia*. New York: McGraw Hill, 1968.

Gregor, A. James and M. Hsia Chang. *The Republic of China and U.S. Policy, A Study in Human Rights*. Washington, D.C.: The Ethics and Public Policy Center, 1983.

Gregor, A. James. *The China Connection, U.S. Policy and the People's Republic of China*. Stanford: The Hoover Institution Press, Stanford University, 1986

Gregor, A. James. *Arming the Dragon, U.S. Security Ties with the People's Republic of China*. Washington, D.C.: Ethics and Public Policy Center, 1987.

Griswold, A. Whitney. *The Far Eastern Policy of the United States*. New Haven: Yale University Press, 1964.

Hahn, Emily. *China Only Yesterday: 1850-1950, A Century of Change*. Garden City: Doubleday, 1963.

Halpern, Abraham Meyer, ed. *Policies Toward China, Views From Six Continents*. New York: McGraw Hill, 1965.

Han, Lih-wu. *Taiwan Today.* Rev. ed. Taipei: Chang Chung Book Co., 1982.

Harding, Harry, ed. *China's Foreign Relations in the 1980's.* New Haven: Yale University Press, 1984.

Harding, Harry. *China and Northeast Asia, The Political Dimension.* Lanham, Md.: University Press of America, 1988.

Hinton, Harold C. *China's Turbulent Quest.* New York: MacMillan, 1970.

Hinton, Harold C. *Peking-Washington: Chinese Foreign Policy and the United States.* Beverly Hills, CA.: Sage Publications, 1977.

Holton, Richard H. and Wang Xi. *U.S.-China Economic Relations, Present and Future.* Berkeley: Institute of East Asia Studies, University of California, Berkeley, 1989.

Hornbeck, Stanley K. *The United States and the Far East: Certain Fundamentals of Policy.* Boston: World Peace Foundation, 1942.

Howard, Harry Paxton. *America's Role in Asia.* New York: Howerll Soskin Publishers, 1943.

Hsiao, Gene T., ed. *Sino-American Detente and Its Policy Implications.* New York: Praeger Publishers, 1974.

Hsieh, Chiao-chiao. *The Strategy of Foreign Aid.* Taipei: Government Information Office, 1985.

Hsu, Immanuel G.Y. *China's Entrance into the Family of Nations, The Diplomatic Phase, 1858-1880.* Cambridge: Harvard University Press, 1960.

Hsu, Shu-hsui. *The North China Problem.* Shanghai: Kelly and Walsh, 1937.

Hsu, Long-hsuen and Chang Ming-kai. *History of the Sino-Japanese War, 1937- 1945.* Translated into English by Wen Ha-hsiung. Taipei: Chung Wu Publishing Co., 1971.

Hu, Pu-yu. *A Brief History of the Chinese National Revolutionary Forces.* Translated into English by Wen Ha-shiung. Taipei: Chung Wu Publishing Co., 1972.

Ichihashi, Yamato. *The Washington Conference and After.* Palo Alto: Stanford University Press, 1928.

Iriye, Akira. *Across the Pacific, An Inner History of American-East Asian Relations.* New York: Harcourt, Brace and World, 1967.

Iriye, Akira, ed. *U.S. Policy Toward China.* Boston: Little Brown, 1968.

Jacobson, Harold Karan, ed. *America's Foreign Policy.* New York: Random House, 1960.

Jiang, Arnold Xiangze. *The United States and China.* Chicago: The University of Chicago Press, 1988.

Jacoby, Neil H. *U.S. Aid to Taiwan.* New York: Frederich A. Prager, 1966.

Jones, Maldwyn Allen. *American Immigration.* Chicago: University of Chicago Press, 1960.

Joseph, Philip. *Foreign Diplomacy in China, 1894-1900.* London: George Allen and Urwin, 1928.

Kane, Anthony J., ed. *China Briefing*. Boulder: Westview Press, 1989, 1990, 1991.

Keith, Ronald C. *The Diplomacy of Zhou Enlai*. New York: St. Martin's Press, 1989.

Kennan, George F. *American Diplomacy, 1900-1950*. Chicago: University of Chicago Press, 1951.

Kennan, George F. *Realities of American Foreign Policy*. Princeton: Princeton University Press, 1954.

Kim, Samuel S. *China and the World, New Directions in Chinese Foreign Relations*. 2nd ed. Boulder: Westview Press 1989.

King, Wunsz. *China and the League of Nations, the Sino-Japanese Controversy*. New York: St. John's University Press, 1965.

King, Wunsz. *China and the Washington Conference, 1921-1922*. New York: St. John's University Press, 1963.

Kintner, William and John F. Cooper. *A Matter of Two Chinas: The China-Taiwan Issue in U.S. Foreign Policy*. Philadelphia: Foreign Policy Research Institute, 1979.

Kissinger, Henry A. *Nuclear Weapon and Foreign Policy*. New York: W.W. Norton, 1969.

Kissinger, Henry A. *White House Years*. New York: Little, Brown, 1979.

Koen, Ross Y. *The China Lobby in American Politics*. New York: Harper and Row Publishers, Inc., 1974.

Lin, John Y., ed. *Red China's U.S. Policy, Secret Documents.* Taipei: Institute of Current China Studies, 1981.

Link, Arthur S. and William B. Catton. *American Epoch—A History of the United States Since the 1980's.* 3rd ed. New York: Alfred A. Knopf, 1963.

Liu, F.F. *A Military History of Modern China, 1921-1949.* Princeton: Princeton University Press, 1956.

Liu, Ta Jen. *A History of Sino-American Diplomatic Relations, 1840-1970.* Taipei: Chinese Culture University Press, 1978.

Lucas, J. G. *Agnew, Profile in Conflict.* New York: Charles Scribner's, 1970.

Lumley, F. A. *The Republic of China Under Chiang Kai-shek, Taiwan Today.* London: Barrie and Jerkins. 1976.

Lung, Milton M. T. *Foreign Affairs Administration.* Taipei: Youth Book, 1968.

Ma, Wen Hwa. *American Policy Towards China, as Revealed in the Debates of Congress.* Shanghai: Kelly and Walsh, 1934.

Maki, John M., ed. *Selected Documents: Far Eastern International Relations 1689-1951.* Seattle: University of Washington Press, 1957.

MacArthur, Douglas. *Reminiscences.* New York: Time Inc., 1964.

MacNair, Harley Farnsworth. *Modern Chinese History - Selected Reading.* 2 vols. 3rd. ed. Taipei: Commercial Press, 1966.

MacNair, Harley Farnsworth and Donald F. Lach. *Modern Far Eastern International Relations*. 2nd ed. New York: D. Van Nostrand, 1955.

McCormick, Thomas J. *China Market—America's Quest for Informal Empire, 1893- 1901*. Chicago: Quadrangle Books, 1967.

Maurer, Herrymon. *Collision of East and West*. Chicago: Henry Regenery, 1951.

Mazo, E. and S. Hess. *Nixon, A Political Portrait*. New York: Harper and Row, 1968.

Michael, Franz H. and George E. Taylor. *The Far East in the Modern World*. New York: Henry Holt, 1956.

Moorsteen, Richard, and Morton Abramowitz. *Remaking China Policy: U.S.-China Relations and Governmental Decision Making*. Cambridge: Harvard University Press, 1971.

Morse, Hosea Ballou. *The International Relations of the Chinese Empire*. 3 vols. London: Longman's Green, 1910-1918.

Morse, Hosea Ballou. *The Trade and Administrations of the Chinese Empire*. 3rd. ed. London: Longmans, Green, 1920.

Mosher, Steven W. *China Misperceived, American Illusions and Chinese Realty*. New York: Harper Collins Publishers, 1990.

Myers, Ramon H., ed. *A Unique Relationship—The United States and the Republic of China Under the Taiwan Relations Act*. Stanford: Hoover Institution Press, Stanford University, 1989.

Neils, Patricia, ed. *United States Attitudes and Policies toward China, the Impact of American Missionaries*. New York: M.E. Sharpe, 1990.

Nelsen, Harvey W. *Power and Insecurity, Beijing, Moscow & Washington, 1949- 1988*. Boulder: Lynnee Rienner Publishers, 1989.

Nevins, A., ed. *John F. Kennedy: The Strategy of Peace*. New York: Harper Brothers, 1960.

Nevins, A. and H. S. Commager. *A Short History of the United States*. New York: Random House, 1969.

Nixon, Richard M. *The Challenges We Face*. New York: McGraw Hill, 1960.

Nixon, Richard M. *In the Arena: A Memoir of Victory, Defeat and Renewal*. New York: Simon and Schuster, 1990.

Ogata, Sadako. *Normalization with China, A Comparative Study of U.S. and Japanese Processes*. Berkeley: Institute of East Asian Studies, University of California, 1988.

Osgood, R. E. *America and the World*. Baltimore: John Hopkins Press, 1970.

Peffer, Nathaniel. *The Far East*. Ann Arbor: University of Michigan Press, 1958.

Perkins, Dexter. *The Evolution of American Foreign Policy*. New York: Oxford University Press, 1948.

Pollard, Robert T. *China's Foreign Relations, 1917-1931*. New York: MacMillan, 1933.

Pratt, Julius W. *A History of United States Foreign* Policy Englewood, N.J.: Prentice Hall, 1965.

Pye, Lucian W. *Taiwan's Development and Its Implications for Beijing and Washington.* Taipei: Asia and World Institute, 1986.

Rankin, Karl L. *China Assignment, the Memoirs of Karl Lott Rankin.* Seattle: Washington University Press, 1964.

Reagan, Ronald. *An American Life, The Autobiography.* New York: Simon and Schuster, 1990.

Reinsch, Paul S. *An American Diplomat in China.* Garden City: Doubleday, 1922.

Remer, C.F. *A Study of Chinese Boycotts.* Reprint. Taipei: Cheng Wen, 1966.

Rostow, W. W. *An American Policy in Asia.* New York: John Wiley, 1955.

Rowe, David Nelson. *U.S. China Policy Today.* Washington, D.C.: University of Professors for Academic Order, 1979.

Rowe, David Nelson. *Ally Betrayed: The Republic of China.* Alexandria, Va.: Western Goals, 1982.

Rusk, Dean. *As I Saw It.* New York: W.W. Norton Co. 1990.

Schaller, Michael. *The U.S. Crusade in China, 1938-1945.* New York: Columbia University Press, 1979.

Schaller, Michael. *The United States and China in the Twentieth Century.* 2nd ed. New York: Oxford University Press, 1990.

Schlesinger, A. M. Jr. *A Thousand Days, John F. Kennedy in the White House.* Boston: Houghton Mifflin, 1965.

Schroth, T.N., et al. *China and U.S. Far East Policy, 1945-1967.* Washington, D.C.: Congressional Quarterly Series, 1967.

Senese, Donald J. and Diane D. Pickcunas. *Can the Two China Become One?* Washington, D.C.: The Council for Social and Economic Studies, 1989.

Shaw, Yu-ming. *A review of Sino-American Relations during the Past Century and Horoscope for the Future.* Taipei: Kwang Hwa Publishing Co. 1987.

Shaw, Yu-ming. *Beyond the Economic Miracle, Reflections on the Developmental Experience of the Republic of the China on Taiwan.* Taipei: Kwang Hwa Publishing Co., 1988.

Shen, James C.H. *The Review from Twin Oaks, A Collection of Selected Speeches, 1971-1974.* 2 vols. Washington, D.C.: James C.H. Shen, 1978.

Shen, James C.H. *The U.S. and Free China, How the U.S. Sold Out Its Ally.* Washington, D.C.: Acropolis Books, Ltd., 1983.

Shen, Tung-hsun and Morris W.H. Tien, eds. *ROC and U.S.A., 1911-1981.* Taipei: American Studies Association of the ROC, 1982.

Sheridan, James E. *China in Disintegration, The Republican Era in Chinese History, 1912-1949.* New York: The Free Press, 1977.

Snyder, Edwin K., A. James Gregor, and Maria Hsia Chang. *The Taiwan Relations Act and the Defense of the Republic of*

China. Berkeley: University of California, Institute of International Studies, 1980.

Solmon, Richard H., ed. *The China Factor, Sino-American Relations and the Global Scene.* Englewood Cliffs, N.J.: Prentice Hall, Inc. 1981.

Spanier, John W. *American Foreign Policy Since World War II.* Rev. ed. New York: Frederick A. Praeger, 1962.

Starr, John Bryan., ed. *The Future of U.S. - China Relations.* New York: New York University Press, 1984.

Steele, A.T. *The American People and China.* New York: MacGraw Hall, 1966.

Stilwell, Joseph Warren. *The Stilwell Papers.* New York: William Sloane, 1948.

Stimson, Henry L. *The Far Eastern Crisis: Recollections and Observations.* New York: Harper Brothers, 1936.

Stuart, John Leighton. *Fifty Years in China.* New York: Random House, 1954.

Sun, Yat-sen. *San Min Chu I. (The Three Principles of the People).* Translated into English by Frank W. Price. Taipei: China Publishing Co., 1973.

Sun, Yun-suan. *The Economic Development of Taiwan, Republic of China.* Taipei: Ministry of Economic Affairs, 1973.

Sutter, Robert G. *China Watch: Toward Sino-American Reconciliation.* Baltimore: John Hopkins University, 1978.

Sutter, Robert G. *Taiwan, Entering the 21st Century.* Lanham, Md.: University Press of America, 1988.

Tyan, Peter S. H. *Communist China Today: Domestic and Foreign Policies.* New York: Frederick A. Praeger, 1975.

Teng, Ssu-yu and John K. Fairbank. *China's Response to the West. A Documentary Survey, 1838-1923.* Cambridge: Harvard University Press, 1954.

Terrill, R. *800,000,000: The Real China.* Boston: Little, Brown, 1972.

Tong, Hollington K. *Chiang Kai-shek.* Rev. ed. Taipei: China Publishing Co., 1935.

Tong, Te Kong. *United States Diplomacy in China, 1844-60.* Seattle: University of Washington Press, 1964.

Truman, Harry S. *Memoirs. Vol. I. Year of Decisions: Vol. II. Years of Trial and Hope, 1946-1952.* 2 vols. Garden City: Doubleday, 1956.

Tsien, Tai. *China and the Nine Power Conference at Brussels in 1973.* New York: St. John's University Press, 1964.

Tsou, Tang. *America's Failure in China, 1941-1950.* Chicago: University of Chicago Press, 1963.

Tuchman, Barbara W. *Notes from China.* New York: Collier-MacMillan Co. 1972.

Tucker, Nancy Bernkopf. *Taiwan, Hong Kong, and the United States, 1945-1992.* New York: Twayne Publishers, 1994.

Tyau, Min-ch'ien T. Z. *The Legal Obligations Arising Out of Treaty Relations Between China and Other States.* Reprint. Taipei: Cheng Wen, 1966.

Tyau, Min-ch'ien T. Z., ed. *Two Years of Nationalist China*. Shanghai: Kelly and Walsh, 1930.

Van Alstyne, Richard W. *American Crisis Diplomacy, The Quest for Collective Security, 1918-1952*. Stanford: Stanford University Press, 1952.

Vinacke, Harold M. *A History of the Far East in Modern Times*. 6th ed. New York: Appleton-Century-Crofts, 1959.

Wanamaker, Temple. *American Foreign Policy Today*. New York: Bantam Books, 1964.

Wang, Yu San, ed. *Foreign Policy of the Republic of China on Taiwan, An Unorthodox Approach*. New York: Praeger Publishers, 1990.

Wedemeyer, Albert C. *Wedemeyer Reports*. New York: Henry Holt, 1958.

Wheeler, W. Reginald. *China and the World War*. New York: MacMillan, 1919.

Williams, Samuel Wells. *The Middle Kingdom*. 2 vols. Rev. ed. New York: Charles Scribner's, 1907.

Williams, William Appleman. *The Shaping of American Diplomacy - Readings and Documents in American Foreign Relations, 1750-1955*. Chicago: Rand McNally, 1956.

Willoughby, Westel W. *China and the Conference, A Report*. Baltimore: John Hopkins Press, 1922.

Willoughby, Westel W. *Foreign Rights and Interests in China*. 2 vols. Rev. ed. Baltimore: John Hopkins Press, 1927.

Wolff, Lester L. and D. L. Simon. *Legislative History of the Taiwan Relations Act, An Analytic Compilation with Documents on Subsequent Developments.* New York: The American Association for Chinese Studies. St. John's University, 1982.

Wright, Quincy, ed. *A Foreign Policy for the United States.* Chicago: University of Chicago Press, 1947.

Yin, Chin-yao. *A Review of the Washington-Peiping "Normalization" Question.* Taipei: Asian People's Anti-Communist League, ROC, 1978.

Young, Arthur N. *China and the Helping Hand, 1937-1945.* Cambridge: Harvard University Press, 1963.

Young, Kenneth T. *Negotiating with the Chinese Communists, the United States Experience, 1953-1967.* New York: McGraw Hill, 1968.

Young, Marilyn Blatt. *The Rhetoric of Empire: American China Policy 1895-1901.* Cambridge: Harvard University Press, 1968.

Young, Roland. *Congressional Politics in the Second World War.* New York: Columbia University Press, 1956.

Annuals, Journals, and Periodicals

American Historical Association. *Pacific Coast Branch, Pacific Historical Review* (Quarterly), Berkeley, 1932.

Association for Asian Studies. *Journal of Asian Studies* (Quarterly) Ann Arbor, 1957.

China Year Books

H. G. W. Woodhead, ed. *China Yearbook 1912-1929*, Tientsin.

H. G. W. Woodhead, ed. *China Yearbook 1930-1939*, Shanghai.

Chinese Council of International Affairs. *Chinese Yearbook 1935-1945.* Shanghai and later Chungking.

China Handbook Editorial Board. *China Handbook 1951-1956.* Taipei.

China Yearbook Editorial Board. *China Yearbook 1957-1980.* Taipei.

Hilit Publishing Editorial Board. *Republic of China: A Reference Book, 1983-1988.* Taipei.

Republic of China Yearbook Editorial Board. *Republic of China Yearbook, 1989.*

Carnegie Endowment for International Peace. *Foreign Policy.* (Quarterly), Washington, D.C.

China Academy, The Institute for Advanced Chinese Studies. *Chinese Culture.* (Quarterly), Taipei, 1957.

Chinese Social and Political Science Association. *The Chinese Social and Political Science Review.* Peiping, 1961-1937.

Council on Foreign Relations. *Foreign Affairs.* (Quarterly), New York, 1922.

Council on Foreign Relations. *The United States in World Affairs.* (Annually), New York, 1931. (Took over from World Peace Foundation in 1952)

Current History, Inc. *Current History.* (Monthly), 1914-
Philadelphia.

Far Eastern Association. *Far Eastern Quarterly, 1941-1956.*
Ann Arbor.

Institute of Pacific Relations. *Far Eastern Survey.* (Bi-weekly)
1932-1960, New York.

London University, School of Oriental and African Studies.
China Quarterly. (Quarterly) London.

North-China Daily News and Herald, Ltd. *North China Herald.*
(Weekly) 1850-1942, Shanghai.

ROC Government Information Office. *Free China Review.*
(Monthly) 1951, Taipei.

INDEX

H

I

Z